Reimagining Pensions

Reimagining Pensions

The Next 40 Years

EDITED BY

Olivia S. Mitchell and
Richard C. Shea

OXFORD
UNIVERSITY PRESS

OXFORD
UNIVERSITY PRESS

Great Clarendon Street, Oxford, OX2 6DP,
United Kingdom

Oxford University Press is a department of the University of Oxford. It furthers the University's objective of excellence in research, scholarship, and education by publishing worldwide. Oxford is a registered trade mark of Oxford University Press in the UK and in certain other countries

First Edition published 2016

Impression: 1

Published in the United States of America by Oxford University Press
198 Madison Avenue, New York, NY 10016, United States of America

British Library Cataloguing in Publication Data
Data available

Library of Congress Control Number: 2015943025

ISBN 978–0–19–875544–9

Printed in Great Britain by
Clays Ltd, St Ives plc

Preface

The US Congress passed the Employee Retirement Income Security Act (ERISA) to protect pension promises for millions of American workers and their families over 40 years ago. Yet decades after that bill became law, retirement security remains an elusive goal for the nation. Social Security and Medicare face financial strain. Large private sector employers have terminated or frozen their traditional defined benefit pensions, while public sector plans are beset by extraordinary funding problems. And the rise of defined contribution plans poses a new set of challenges to financially illiterate employees who must decide how much to save, how to invest, and how to manage their money in retirement.

Against this challenging backdrop, this newest volume in the Pension Research Council/Oxford University Press series provides new research explaining shortcomings of traditional pension risk management and offers new alternatives. Lessons from international experiences described here include insights from Singapore, Australia, Switzerland, and the Netherlands. The volume will interest employees and retirees, consumers and researchers, and employers seeking to design better retirement plan offerings. Additionally, investment managers seeking new ways to manage pension risk and regulators interested in alternative pension structures will also find much to learn from.

In the process of preparing this book, many people and institutions played key roles. Co-editor Richard C. Shea contributed numerous helpful suggestions as we designed and structured the analysis presented herein. We thank our Advisory Board and Members of the Pension Research Council, for intellectual and financial support. Additional support was received from the Pension Research Council, the Boettner Center for Pensions and Retirement Research, and the Ralph H. Blanchard Memorial Endowment at the Wharton School of the University of Pennsylvania. We also offer deep appreciation to Oxford University Press which publishes this series on global retirement security. The manuscript was expertly prepared and carefully edited by Donna St. Louis and Joseph Brucker.

Our work at the Pension Research Council and the Boettner Center for Pensions and Retirement Research of the Wharton School of the University of Pennsylvania has focused on aspects of pensions and retirement wellbeing for 60 years. This volume contributes to our mission, which is to generate research on and engage debate around policy for pensions and retirement security.

Olivia S. Mitchell
Executive Director, Pension Research Council
Director, Boettner Center for Pensions and Retirement Research
The Wharton School, University of Pennsylvania

Contents

List of Figures ix
List of Tables xiii
Notes on Contributors xv

1. Introduction: Changing Frameworks for Retirement Security 1
Olivia S. Mitchell

Part I. Assessing the Retirement System: Adequacy, Efficiency, and Stability

2. Are Retirees Falling Short? Reconciling the Conflicting Evidence 11
Alicia H. Munnell, Matthew S. Rutledge, and Anthony Webb

3. Retirement Plans and Prospects for Retirement Income Adequacy 37
Jack VanDerhei

4. The Changing Nature of Retirement 61
Julia Coronado

5. Entitlement Reform and the Future of Pensions 74
C. Eugene Steuerle, Benjamin H. Harris, and Pamela J. Perun

Part II. New Thinking about Retirement Risk Sharing

6. Risk Sharing Alternatives for Pension Plan Design: An Overview and Case Studies 95
Anna M. Rappaport and Andrew Peterson

7. United States Pension Benefit Plan Design Innovation: Labor Unions as Agents of Change 123
David S. Blitzstein

8. Back to the Future: Hybrid Co-operative Pensions and the TIAA-CREF System 139
Benjamin Goodman and David P. Richardson

9. Retirement Shares Plan: A New Model for Risk Sharing 161
Donald E. Fuerst

10. The Portfolio Pension Plan: An Alternative Model for Retirement Security 174
Richard C. Shea, Robert S. Newman, and Jonathan P. Goldberg

11. Cultivating Pension Plans 183
John M. Vine

Part III. Pension Reform: Lessons from Abroad

12. The Promise of Defined Ambition Plans: Lessons for the United States 215
A. Lans Bovenberg, Roel Mehlkopf, and Theo E. Nijman

13. Insights from Switzerland's Pension System 247
Monika Bütler

14. The Australian Retirement Income System: Comparisons with and Lessons for the United States 274
Rafal Chomik and John Piggott

15. Singapore's Social Security Savings System: A Review and Some Lessons for the United States 298
Benedict S. K. Koh

Endmatter 341
Index 345

List of Figures

2.1 Ratio of wealth to income by age from the Survey of Consumer Finances, 1983–2010 13

2.2 Percentage of all households falling short of target by age at retirement, base case, and with a reverse mortgage 17

2.3 Illustrative consumption by age, SSK, and NRRI as percent of income 20

2.4 Percentage of households aged 51–61 at risk, 2004 21

2.5 Illustrative consumption by age, SSK, and NRRI as percent of income, with children 22

2.6 Mean income and spending by income decile at time of retirement for Hurd-Rohwedder (2011) sample of households 24

2.7 Average actual and corresponding consumption-to-income ratio at time of retirement by income decile for Hurd-Rohwedder sample of households 25

3.1 Years in retirement before Boomers and Gen Xers run short of money, by pre-retirement income quartile: simulations with the 2014 version of the EBRI Retirement Security Projection Model® 50

3.2 Years in retirement before Boomers and Gen Xers run short of money, by relative longevity quartile: simulations with the 2014 version of the EBRI Retirement Security Projection Model® 51

3.3 Years in retirement before Boomers and Gen Xers run short of money, by quartile of stochastic health care cost: simulations with the 2014 version of the EBRI Retirement Security Projection Model® 52

4.1 More workers expect to work longer, but retirement ages are not yet following 63

4.2 Workers are retiring earlier than planned (%, 2 yr avg.) 64

4.3 Most workers expect to work for pay, but few retirees do 65

4.4 Real spending per capita by age of head of household. Older households have experienced the greatest increase in standard of living 66

4.5	Income from public and private pensions by age of head of household (% of total household income). Pension support is fading for older households	67
4.6	Income from work by age of head of household (% of total household income). More income support derives from work for older households	68
4.7	Households with a mortgage by age of head. Older households are taking on more leverage	69
4.8	Unemployment rates by age for men. Unemployment is still elevated among older men	70
4.9	Unemployment rates by age for women. Unemployment is still elevated among older women	71
4.10	Percentage of persons 55+ who left the labor force but want a job. Some discouragement remains among older workers	71
8.1	TIAA Average Crediting Rates versus Consumer Price Index: 1964–2013	144
8.2	Monthly returns to TIAA and Barclays aggregate: 1984–2013	146
8.3	TIAA monthly income per $100,000 for various cohorts	150
8.4	Real CREF stock annuity payments for various cohorts	155
8.5	Initial income choices by TIAA-CREF participants: 1988–2012	157
9.1	Diversified share vs. CPI 4 percent hurdle rate 1970–2013 logarithmic scale	171
9.2	Stable share vs. CPI 4 percent hurdle rate 1970–2013 logarithmic scale	172
12.1	Average total (employee plus employer) contributions to Dutch occupational pensions as percentage of gross wage income, 1980–2013	220
12.2	Average nominal funding rate of Dutch occupational pension funds, 1988–2013	221
12.3	Number of participants affected by cuts in Dutch occupational pensions in 2013	224
12.4	Risk profile of future real pension income in DA scheme	231
12.5	Horizon-dependent discount rate of a DA scheme	232
13.1	Interest rates for Swiss occupational pension plans	255
13.2	Labor force participation of elderly individuals in Switzerland	257
13.3	Divorce rates for couples between 55 and 75 and total Swiss divorce rates	260

13.4 Annuitization rates for six pension providers prior to the reform of the occupational pension law in 2005 (which triggered a number of changes). Stable parameters (exception: decrease in supermandatory conversion rate for Insurance I in 2004) 262

13.5 Percentage of capital annuitized as a function of accumulated second pillar wealth (upper curves). Percentage of individuals opting for a mixed payout (10% capital or more, plus 10% annuity or more) 265

14.1 Comparison of population, economy, and government budget 275

14.2 Comparison of population incomes 277

14.3 Comparison of demography 278

14.4 Comparison of pension system structure 279

14.5 Comparison of targeting and poverty 284

14.6 Comparison of income replacement 285

14.7 Comparison of alternate sources of income 286

14.8 Comparison of fiscal projections: central government expenditure on age-related pensions, 2002–2050 (% of GDP) 287

14.9 Comparison of coverage rates of private pensions 290

15.1 Central Provident Fund (CPF): overview 302

15.2 Comparative home ownership statistics 307

15.3 Cumulative use of Central Provident Funds. (Ordinary Account and Special Account combined) 308

15.4 Singapore property price indexes over time 309

15.5 CPF interest rate and Singapore's inflation rate over time 314

15.6 Portion invested and balance remaining in Singapore's CPF Ordinary (OA) and Special (SA) Accounts 323

List of Tables

2.1 Percentage of households 'at risk' at age 65 by age group over time 15
2.2 Percentage 'at risk' using the NRRI versus the 'optimal saving' approach: 1992 and 2004 18
2.3 Median respondent spending by retirement status for respondents aged 50 to 70 26
2.4 Median respondent spending by retirement status for respondents aged 50 to 70 27
2.A1 NRRI target replacement rates by household type and drawdown alternative 32
3.1 2014 Retirement Readiness Ratings™ with and without long-term care (LTC) and home health costs (HHC) 42
3.2 Probit estimates of the probability of running short of money in retirement 48
3.3 2014 retirement savings shortfalls (US$) by age cohort, marital status, and gender 53
3.4 2014 unconditional retirement savings shortfalls (US$), by years of future eligibility for participation in a defined contribution plan 54
4.1 Older households doing well 66
6.1 Major risks facing plan sponsors and participants in retirement plans 99
6.2 Strategies for managing and sharing risk 101
6.3 Risks assumed by various stakeholders under selected plan designs 103
6.4 Summary of methods for managing key selected risks 109
6.5 Principles for reformed New Brunswick pensions 114
8.1 TIAA-CREF asset classes, inception dates, and total assets under management for TIAA-CREF pension accounts and mutual funds, as of December 31, 2013 141
8.2 Average return performance of TIAA and the Barclays Aggregate 146
8.3 Weighted average of yearly accumulations and interest earnings by vintage 147
8.4 Current payout rate by vintage 148
8.5 Current payout rates by age 149

8.6	Asset class participation and proportion of contributions invested from 1993 to 2013	156
11.1	Number of plans	197
11.2	Number of active plan participants	197
11.3	Fortune 100 company offerings to new hires	198
11.4	Allocation of risks under DB and DC plans	201
11.A1	ERISA committee reports	206
12.1	Average indexation shortfall, 2008–14	224
12.2	Confidence in pension funds, the government, banks, and insurers (% of Dutch people that have some or a lot of confidence)	225
13.1	Features of the Swiss old age pension system	249
13.2	Size and structure of occupational pension plans	252
13.3	Demographic trends in Switzerland	256
13.4	Political support for a reduction in the conversion rate (annuity factor), individual data from telephone survey after the ballot	269
14.1	Choice in defined contribution schemes in OECD countries, 2013	292
15.1	Contributions and balances in the Singapore's CPF system	300
15.2	Singapore CPF contribution rates by employers and employees age 35 and under (% of monthly wage)	301
15.3	2014 contribution rates for various age groups (% of monthly wage)	302
15.4	Singapore CPF interest rates paid over time	303
15.5	Singapore CPF schemes	305
15.6	Dependent Protection Scheme (DPS) and MediShield Schemes under Singapore CPF over time	310
15.7	Contributions to MediSave Account by age groups (% of monthly wage)	311
15.8	CPF Minimum Sum Scheme (MSS)	313
15.9	Singapore CPF member average balances by age and sex	315
15.10	Performance statistics of Singapore CPFIS-included unit trusts	318
15.11	Summary data on costs associated with unit trust investment in Singapore	320
15.12	Simulation study showing the percentage of $1 investment eroded by expenses assuming zero investment return, by fund type and holding period (%)	320
15.13	Realized profits/losses for investments held under the Singapore CPF investment scheme Ordinary Account (CPFIS-OA): FY04–13	322

Notes on Contributors

David S. Blitzstein established Blitzstein Consultancy where he provides professional trustee services and strategic advice to labor unions and employee benefit trust funds. Previously he served as a collective bargaining expert on pension and health insurance for the United Food and Commercial Workers (UFCW) and the United Mine Workers of America, and he was the UFCW's Special Assistant for Multiemployer Plans. He is a Governor-appointed trustee of the Maryland State Retirement System and a Presidential appointee to the PBGC Advisory Committee. He received his undergraduate degree in History from the University of Pennsylvania and a Master of Science degree from the University of Massachusetts in Amherst.

A. Lans Bovenberg is a Professor of Economics at Tilburg University; he also serves as an independent member of the Social Economic Council in the Netherlands, the most important advisory body of the Dutch government on socio-economic matters. He also served on an important government committee advising the government on how to raise labor force participation in the Netherlands (the so-called 'committee Bakker'). Previously he worked as an economist at the International Monetary Fund and the Dutch Ministry of Economic Affairs in The Hague. He earned his Ph.D. from the University of California, Berkeley.

Monika Bütler is a Professor of Economics and Public Policy and the Managing Director at the Swiss Institute for Empirical Economic Research at the University of St. Gallen. She is a research coordinator for the international Network on Ageing and Pensions, Netspar, an affiliated researcher at CESifo, and an Associate Investigator at CEPAR. She has been a visiting professor at the University of New South Wales and a visiting scholar at the Universities of Virginia and Southern California and the Federal Reserve Bank of Richmond. She is a member of the Board of Management for the International Institute of Public Finance and an editor of the *Journal of Pension Economics and Finance.* She earned her degrees in Mathematics/Physics and Economics and her Ph.D. in Economics from the University of St. Gallen.

Rafal Chomik is an economist with experience in the public, private, and NGO sectors in the UK and France; he specializes in policy related research, tax-benefit modelling, and policy development across the fields of poverty, the labor market, and pensions. Currently he serves as Senior Research

Fellow at the ARC Centre of Excellence in Population Ageing Research, Australian School of Business at the University of New South Wales. He earned his Bachelor's degree from the University of Western Australia and his Master's from London Metropolitan University.

Julia Coronado is based in New York and is currently Chief Economist for Graham Capital Management. She has been Chief Economist, North America, for BNP Paribas since 2009. Prior to joining BNP Paribas, Julia was a Senior US Economist at Barclays Capital. She has also served as an Economist for the Federal Reserve Board of Governors in Washington, DC, in the Flow of Funds and Macroeconomic Analysis sections in the Division of Research and Statistics. Her current work focuses on forecasting the US economy, as well as monetary and fiscal policy. Her expertise and research interests lie in understanding the interactions between financial markets and the real economy. She currently serves on the Advisory Board of the Pension Research Council at the Wharton School and is a member of the Economic Advisory Panel of the Federal Reserve Bank of New York.

Donald E. Fuerst is the American Academy of Actuaries' Senior Pension Fellow; in this role he serves as the actuarial profession's chief policy liaison on pension, Social Security, and other retirement issues. His work promotes sound retirement policy by providing nonpartisan technical assistance to legislators and regulators. Previously he served as a member of the American Academy of Actuaries Committee on Accounting for Pension Costs, and the Society of Actuaries Education and Examination Committee. He earned his Bachelor of Science in Mathematics from Regis University in Denver and he is a Fellow of the Society of Actuaries, a Member of the American Academy of Actuaries, a Fellow of the Conference of Actuaries, and an Enrolled Actuary.

Jonathan P. Goldberg is a Project Attorney in the Employee Benefits and Executive Compensation practice group of Covington & Burling LLP, a multinational law firm headquartered in Washington, DC. Mr Goldberg is a 1994 *magna cum laude* graduate of Harvard University and a 2007 graduate of the University of Pennsylvania Law School, where he served as Senior Editor of the *University of Pennsylvania Law Review.* Prior to joining Covington & Burling, he worked as a litigator for six years in both the public and private sector, most notably as a Law Clerk in 2008–9 for Senior Judge Norma L. Shapiro of the United States District Court for the Eastern District of Pennsylvania.

Benjamin Goodman is a Director and Actuary at TIAA-CREF, where he has worked in a variety of positions, including Institutional Plan Pricing, Advice, Pension Plan Design, and Product Development. He graduated from Touro

College, and he is a Member of the American Academy of Actuaries and a Fellow of the Society of Actuaries.

Benjamin H. Harris is the Policy Director of the Hamilton Project; a Fellow in Economic Studies at Brookings; and Deputy Director of the Retirement Security Project at Brookings. Previously, he was a Senior Research Associate with the Urban Institute and the Urban-Brookings Tax Policy Center. Prior to joining the Urban Institute, he worked at the White House as a Senior Economist with the Council of Economic Advisers, where he specialized in fiscal policy and retirement security. He has also served as a Research Economist at the Brookings Institution and as a Senior Economist with the Budget Committee in the US House of Representatives. He earned his BA in economics at Tufts University, his Ph.D. in Economics from the George Washington University, his Master's degree in Economics from Cornell University, and another Master's degree in Quantitative Methods from Columbia University.

Benedict S. K. Koh is Professor of Finance and Associate Dean of the Lee Kong Chian School of Business at the Singapore Management University; he is also the Director of the Centre for Silver Security at the Sim Kee Boon Institute for Financial Economics. He has served on the board for the NUS Academic Staff Pension Fund and as associate editor of the *Asia Pacific Journal of Finance* and *Asia Pacific Journal of Management.* He is active in management consultancy as well as executive training for banks, companies, and government agencies. He earned his Ph.D. in Finance from the Wharton School of the University of Pennsylvania.

Roel Mehlkopf is a postdoctoral researcher at Tilburg University in the Netherlands and research fellow at Netspar. He is also affiliated with the Ministry of Social Affairs and Employment of the Netherlands, where he works as an economic advisor on the design of the new solvency framework for pension funds. Previously, he worked at the Netherlands Bureau for Economic Policy Analysis (CPB) where he was project leader of a value-based generational accounting analysis of the Dutch pension reform. He earned his Ph.D. degree in Finance from Tilburg University and he was a visiting scholar at the University of Pennsylvania. He also holds a Master of Science degree in Financial Econometrics from Tilburg University.

Olivia S. Mitchell is the International Foundation of Employee Benefit Plans Professor, as well as Professor of Insurance and Risk Management and Business Economics and Public Policy; Executive Director of the Pension Research Council; and Director of the Boettner Center for Pensions and Retirement Research, all at the Wharton School of the University of Pennsylvania. Concurrently she serves as a Research Associate at the NBER; Independent Director on the Wells Fargo Advantage Fund Trusts Board;

Co-Investigator for the Health and Retirement Study at the University of Michigan; Member of the Executive Board for the Michigan Retirement Research Center; and Senior Scholar of the Centre for Silver Security at the Sim Ki Boon Institute of Singapore Management University. She also advises the Centre for Pensions and Superannuation UNSW and serves on the Scientific Board for Netspar in the Netherlands; she is also Faculty Affiliate of the Wharton Public Policy Initiative. She currently is a Senior Editor of the *Journal of Pension Economics and Finance.* She received the MA and Ph.D. degrees in Economics from the University of Wisconsin-Madison, and the BA in Economics from Harvard University.

Alicia H. Munnell is the Peter F. Drucker Professor of Management Sciences at Boston College's Carroll School of Management. She also serves as the Director of the Center for Retirement Research at Boston College. Previously she was a Member of the President's Council of Economic Advisers and Assistant Secretary of the Treasury for Economic Policy. She also worked at the Federal Reserve Bank of Boston where she served as Senior Vice President and Director of Research. She earned her BA from Wellesley College, an MA from Boston University, and her Ph.D. from Harvard University.

Robert S. Newman is a partner in the Employee Benefits and Executive Compensation practice of Covington & Burling LLP, where he represents clients ranging from small employers to some of the nation's largest employers, including for-profit and tax-exempt entities. His practice includes designing, drafting, and amending a range of retirement plans (including 401(k) plans, ESOPs, and traditional and hybrid defined benefit plans) and welfare plans (including health, severance, and cafeteria plans). His research interests include pension plan policy, pension de-risking, and participant protections. He received a BA from Brown University and a JD from the New York University School of Law.

Theo E. Nijman is a Professor on Econometrics and Finance at Tilburg University in the Netherlands; he is also Scientific Director of Netspar, a Network for Studies on Pensions, Aging and Retirement, a consortium of ten universities and several insurance companies and pension funds. He is also Academic Coordinator of Inquire Europe, which brings together investment professionals interested in understanding and developing quantitative solutions to investment problems. Previously he served on the government-appointed Goudswaard committee on structural reforms in the Dutch second pillar pension provision to assure sustainability of the system, and he was a member of the Expert Committee of the Actuarial Society on 'Validity of the Actuarial Society's projected survival tables.' He is currently a member of the government committee on Valuation of Pension Liabilities (UFR Committee).

Pamela J. Perun is a psychologist and a lawyer who is self-employed as an employee benefits policy consultant. Previously she was an ERISA lawyer for large law firms in Boston and Washington, DC; currently she consults with the TIAA-CREF Institute in their thought leadership work on retirement policy, with the AARP Public Policy Institute in its work on state-based retirement plans for private sector workers, and with the Urban Institute, where she is participating in an analysis of tax preferences for retirement saving by low- and moderate-income Americans. She is also a Senior Fellow at WISER where she consults on improving the long-term financial security for women most at risk. She earned her BA from Wellesley College, a Ph.D. in Human Development (Adult Development and Aging) from the University of Chicago, and a JD from the University of California at Berkeley.

Andrew Peterson is Staff Fellow for Retirement Systems at the Society of Actuaries (SOA), where he serves as staff partner to the Pension Section of the SOA, directing volunteer activities. In addition, he provides retirement expertise to the SOA's education and research functions and provides a liaison between the SOA and other organizations in the retirement arena. He is a Fellow of the Society of Actuaries, an Enrolled Actuary, a Member of the American Academy of Actuaries, and a Fellow of the Conference of Consulting Actuaries. He is also a member of the National Academy of Social Insurance. He earned his BS degree in mathematics from Taylor University.

John Piggott is Director of the ARC Centre of Excellence in Population Ageing Research (CEPAR) at the University of New South Wales, where he is also Scientia Professor of Economics; he also holds an ARC Australian Professorial Fellowship. His Australian policy experience includes membership of both the Henry Tax Review Panel and the Ministerial Superannuation Advisory Committee. Internationally, he worked for nearly a decade with the Japanese government on pension and ageing issues, and he consulted with several other governments on pension issues, including Russia and Indonesia. He is a Visiting Professor at Zhejiang University, China, and previously was Visiting Scholar with the Department of Insurance and Risk Management, Wharton School of Business, University of Pennsylvania. He earned his Ph.D. and M.Sc. from the University of London and a BA from the University of Sydney.

Anna M. Rappaport is an actuary, consultant, author, and speaker, and a recognized expert on the impact of change on retirement systems and workforce issues, with Anna Rappaport Consulting. Previously she worked with Mercer Human Resource consulting. She serves on the Board of the

Women's Institute for a Secure Retirement (WISER), and the Advisory Board of the Pension Research Council; she is also a member of the GAO's Retirement Security Advisory Panel. She is a past-President of the Society of Actuaries and chairs its Committee on Post-Retirement Needs and Risks. She is a Fellow of the Society of Actuaries, a Member of the American Academy of Actuaries, and a member of the National Academy of Social Insurance. She earned her MBA from the University of Chicago Booth School of Business.

David P. Richardson is a Senior Economist at the TIAA-CREF Institute. Previously he held the New York Life Chair in Risk Management and Insurance at Georgia State University and served as Senior Economist for Public Finance at the White House Council of Economic Advisors. He also worked as a Financial Economist in the Office of Tax Policy at the US Treasury, and he taught at the Department of Economics at Davidson College. He earned an MA and a Ph.D. in economics from Boston College, and a BBA from the University of Georgia.

Matthew S. Rutledge is a research economist at the Center for Retirement Research at Boston College, where he conducts research on health insurance coverage, disability insurance application, the long-run effects of public disability receipt, unemployment insurance, Social Security claiming behavior, income volatility, and the effect of the macro economy on older workers. Previously he also worked for the Economic Research Initiative on the Uninsured and the Federal Reserve Bank of Boston. He earned his doctorate in economics from the University of Michigan in the fields of health economics, labor economics, and public finance.

Richard C. Shea is chair of Covington & Burling LLP's Employee Benefits and Executive Compensation practice, where he is widely regarded as a leading authority on cash balance, pension equity, and other complex benefit plan designs. Previously, he served as Associate Benefits Tax Counsel at the Treasury Department, where, together with his colleagues at the Treasury Department and the Internal Revenue Service, he was responsible for developing federal tax legislation and regulations governing employee benefits and executive compensation. He received his AB from Amherst College and his JD from the University of Virginia School of Law.

C. Eugene Steuerle is the Richard B. Fisher Chair at the Urban Institute. Previously, he served as Deputy Assistant Secretary of the Treasury for Tax Analysis, President of the National Tax Association, chair of the Technical Panel advising Social Security on methods, Vice-President of the Peter G. Peterson Foundation, and economic coordinator of the Treasury Department's efforts leading to the Tax Reform Act of 1986. He co-founded the Urban-Brookings Tax Policy Center, the Urban Institute Center on

Nonprofits and Philanthropy, and Act for Alexandria, a community foundation that he now also chairs. He earned his Ph.D. with distinction in public finance from the University of Wisconsin-Madison in 1975.

Jack VanDerhei is the Research Director of the Employee Benefit Research Institute (EBRI), a private, nonprofit, nonpartisan organization committed to original public policy research and education on economic security and employee benefits. He is also the director of both the EBRI Defined Contribution and Participant Behavior Research Program and the EBRI Retirement Security Research Program, and the co-director of the EBRI Center for Research on Retirement Income. He received his BBA and MBA from the University of Wisconsin-Madison and his MA and Ph.D. from the Wharton School of the University of Pennsylvania.

John M. Vine is the senior member and former head of the Employee Benefits Group at Covington & Burling LLP; his practice covers incentive compensation, deferred compensation, stock option, and fringe benefit programs, as well as pension, 401(k), employee stock ownership and stock purchase plans, severance programs, and health and welfare plans. He has also served as counsel to the ERISA Industry Committee (ERIC), an association of over 100 of the nation's largest employers. He has represented ERIC and corporate clients before the Treasury Department, the Internal Revenue Service, the Department of Labor, the Pension Benefit Guaranty Corporation, the Equal Employment Opportunity Commission, and the Congress on a wide variety of employee compensation and benefit issues. He received his AB degree from Amherst College and JD from Harvard Law School.

Anthony Webb is a Senior Research Economist at the Center for Retirement Research at Boston College. Previously, he was a senior research analyst at the International Longevity Center (ILC)-USA. His research focuses on the impact of pension type on the age of retirement and a number of studies of the role of annuities in managing retirement asset decumulation. He earned his doctorate in Economics from the University of California, San Diego, and his BA in Industrial Economics from the University of Nottingham and an MA in Economics from the University of Manchester.

Chapter 1

Introduction: Changing Frameworks for Retirement Security

Olivia S. Mitchell

The passage of the Employee Retirement Income Security Act (ERISA) of 1974 in the United States was spurred by the 1963 termination of the Studebaker Corporation's automaker's pension plan. That development wiped out or significantly reduced the pensions of thousands of Studebaker employees and retirees. In response, Congress undertook the crafting of this monumental and revolutionary legislation to address corporate pension underfunding and set new rules regarding defined benefit (DB) and other retirement plans. Additionally, ERISA established the Pension Benefit Guaranty Corporation (PBGC) as government-run insurer, to serve as a backdrop to US corporate pensions.

Despite the bill's far-ranging scope, in the years since its passage it has become evident that ERISA failed to achieve many of its intended objectives. The corporate pension scene today is in turmoil, and most private employers have terminated or frozen their traditional defined benefit plans. In their place, employers are increasingly substituting defined contribution (DC) retirement saving plans, which pose a new set of responsibilities on employees and their firms. In this volume we investigate how and why traditional approaches to pension risk management have failed, and we also explore new mechanisms that can help strengthen retirement security for the future.

Assessing the Retirement System: Adequacy, Efficiency, and Stability

There has been much energetic debate over the question of how well Americans prepare for retirement. In the first section of this volume, several authors offer their perspectives on the strengths and weaknesses of the current retirement system. One approach, by Alicia Munnell, Matthew Rutledge, and Anthony Webb, uses the National Retirement Risk Index

(NRRI). The authors apply this measure to a variety of datasets and conclude that more than half of working-age households in the US are at risk of failing to maintain their pre-retirement standard of living in retirement. Yet other analysts have arrived at less dire conclusions, and some even propose that the majority of older workers have accumulated an optimal level of retirement wealth. In order to evaluate what, if any, policies might be useful in strengthening retirement security, it is helpful to establish the sources of this dissonance.

Munnell and co-authors seek to reconcile the conflicting evidence by updating their NRRI projections and simulating how their results differ under different assumptions regarding preferences and drawdown strategies. For instance, they show that their findings are sensitive to assumed changes in household consumption before and after children leave home. On the one hand, adjusting their NRRI metric to allow for the presence and then the departure of children in the household yields results similar to those from the more sanguine analysts. On the other hand, there is some evidence that households do cut back spending as they age; further, households with insufficient resources also cut back their post-retirement consumption to a greater degree than households having sufficient retirement resources, by their computations.

Jack VanDerhei approaches the question of whether Baby Boomers and Gen Xers will have enough money saved for retirement from a different perspective. Here the author asks whether Americans will have enough assets to replicate 100 percent of their pre-retirement expenses, along with two lower thresholds. His Retirement Readiness Ratings show that 57–9 percent of older households will not fall short of money in retirement using the 100 percent criterion, taking into account both long-term care and home health costs. Additionally, people eligible to contribute to a DC pension are likely to be better off, compared to those ineligible.

In her work on a closely related topic, Julia Coronado examines the employment situation of the Baby Boom generation in the wake of the Great Recession of 2008–10. She notes that more than half of all workers retiring since the Great Recession reported that they retired earlier than planned, citing economic rather than health considerations. The younger end of that generation, and men in particular, were most likely to report disruptions in their work lives. Interestingly, while the Social Security 'full' retirement age is rising, peoples' actual behavior is going in the direction of earlier retirement. Coronado concludes that much of this is unintended retirement, and she suggests that this implies that future retirees will not be as well off as previous retirees.

To round out the assessment of America's retirement system, Gene Steuerle, Pamela Perun, and Benjamin Harris point out that the so-called 'entitlement' programs, Social Security and Medicare, face deep financial problems. The authors recommend that entitlement reforms take advantage of the additional resources provided by economic growth, along with growth in both the demand for and supply of older workers. To this end, they outline reforms aimed at three goals: better orientation of public sector retirement resources to needier and older populations; removal of obstacles to increased employment of older workers; and private-pension reform that provides the long-sought second tier of support in older ages. In particular, economic growth has provided households with significant increases in GDP per household, of $141,000 in 2014, projected to rise to $168,000 in 2024. Moreover, demand for older workers is likely to rise as population trends result in fewer younger workers, but they add that, right now, wealthier individuals actually account for the majority of the working elderly. Since Social Security benefits are progressive, they tend to be more valuable to the older, poorer population. As a result, the authors argue that changes in the benefit formulas will be necessary to keep from discouraging older people from working.

New Approaches to Retirement Risk Sharing

The middle section of this volume takes up alternative pension models, and these chapters do much to enlighten the discussion of reform proposals. In their chapter, Anna M. Rappaport and Andrew Peterson discuss the fact that pension plan designs have very different risk allocations depending on their design. Some models place virtually all risks on the plan sponsor, while others place the risk on covered workers and retirees. The writers suggest that policy changes will be needed to underpin new plan designs that do a better job of risk sharing. The most salient concerns are investment risk, interest rate risk, inflation risk, and longevity risk. Potential new models could involve moving to DC plans, paying retirees lump sums, indexing retirement ages, adjusting benefits for longer life spans, selecting assumptions for DB plan valuation that build in more mortality improvement, and using financial instruments to manage this risk. Even in DC plans, there can still be plan sponsor risk: for instance, there is fiduciary risk as well as workforce management risk that may arise if employees are unable to afford to retire.

An interesting case study of a private sector union is reviewed by David S. Blitzstein who demonstrates how labor unions can renegotiate the pension contract. In his chapter, he describes how one union responded proactively by developing a hybrid pension plan that sought to align stakeholders through equitable risk sharing. The new model was called a Variable Defined Benefit Plan (later referred to as the Adjustable Pension Plan or APP). It was structured like a DB plan, in that retirement and longevity risks were pooled, and all assets were pooled and managed professionally. But in contrast to a DB plan, the new model shares investment performance between the employer and plan participants. Specifically, the Variable Plan benefit is the greater of two benefits calculated each year: either a 'floor' defined benefit (a flat benefit accrual or salary-based career average formula), and a 'variable' benefit that fluctuates depending on actual investment performance. Moreover, the annual benefit accrual can never be lower than the floor benefit. Numerous other unions have expressed interest in this model as well.

Donald Fuerst also favors a variable annuity plan that will provide participants with lifetime income without exposing them to the risk of running out of money at advanced ages. In exchange for this income guarantee, participants accept the risk and rewards that actual investment returns provide. Moreover, a variable annuity plan offers the employer cost stability and predictability, similar to a DC plan, but the sponsor accepts longevity risk. His model, termed the Retirement Shares Plan, enhances the typical variable annuity plan by allowing participants to elect more stable benefits. That is, benefits are adjusted every year to reflect invest gains and losses, and the plan is relatively indifferent to discount rates. There is still debate about how aggressively to invest, between younger and older participants, which he argues can be dealt with using a limited set of portfolio alternatives.

A different approach to hybrid retirement plans would combine the best features of DB and DC plans according to the chapter by Benjamin Goodman and David P. Richardson. In their view, the TIAA-CREF system which began in 1918 and now covers millions of workers in the nonprofit sector, provides a useful example of how to incorporate features of hybrid cooperative design into a retirement plan. The Teachers Insurance and Annuity Association (TIAA) offers a contributory guaranteed fixed annuity plan, where participants have the right but not the obligation to annuitize assets, while the College Retirement Equity Fund (CREF) was the first commercially available variable annuity sold in the US. The plan is a co-operative structure, 'owned' by participants, and it features population and cohort risk pooling, while assets are fully portable within the system.

Echoing the theme that intelligent risk sharing between employers and individuals can greatly improve retirement outcomes Richard C. Shea, Robert S. Newman, and Jonathan P. Goldberg describe the Portfolio Pension Plan (PPP) model. This approach adapts a DB plan design to rebalance the allocation of risks to employers and individuals. In particular, it is modeled on a cash balance design in which the employee's account balance is adjusted based on investment returns and his portfolio is adjusted over time in line with his changing circumstances. Rather than credit a single rate for all participants, each individual's account balance in a PPP is adjusted based on the return to his individually tailored retirement investment portfolio. Several of the design features central to this plan have been incorporated into legislative proposals and regulations.

Turning to the regulatory environment in which new plans can be structured, John M. Vine believes that employers have migrated away from traditional DB plans because DC and some hybrid plans have proven more compatible with their own interests and those of their employees. Moreover, ERISA and other regulations have been intended to safeguard participants in existing plans, but they have failed to encourage the establishment of new plans covered under the regulation. Indeed, one result of ERISA's strictures is that states and the federal government are now proposing so-called 'Simple Choice' plans, which would avoid ERISA's regulatory framework by virtue of being entirely employee-financed.

Pension Reform: Lessons from Abroad

The final section of this volume offers a number of insights into new pension models being developed outside the US. The Netherlands has been a particularly fertile source of new ideas, including the 'Defined Ambition' (DA) plans proposed by Lans Bovenberg, Roel Mehlkopf, and Theo Nijman. Despite the fact that plan participants had believed that the old-style Dutch DB plans were safe, in fact 'guaranteed' promises could not be kept post-financial crisis. The authors favor DA plans as they allow firms to continue providing a distributional platform for pension saving, while reducing plan sponsor risk-bearing compared to the traditional DB environment. This, the authors contend, addresses behavioral and agency issues as well as imperfections of insurance and financial markets.

In a DA plan, pension entitlements would be stipulated as deferred annuities, and participants must share the capital market risk via a joint liability pool. The chapter focuses on workplace-based pension schemes that can provide lifetime income streams during retirement. All Dutch workers would be automatically enrolled in these plans, thereby reducing marketing and other transaction costs, and protecting individuals against myopia and other behavioral biases. The conversion of existing DB rights into DA rights will be complicated by the fact that, under traditional DB plans, individual property rights were not objectively valued. That is, these contracts were incomplete so it was unclear who bore which risks. Moreover, these risks were not well communicated to plan participants. The authors suggest that DC plans in the US could better manage risk for participants if investments could be more 'liability-driven'. In other words, retirement income needs would be identified as in the DA setting, and the target income streams would be used to construct investment portfolios.

In a discussion of Switzerland's pension system, Monika Bütler describes that country's three-pillar system and considers some of the challenges the system faces in the context of a rapidly aging society. A first pillar is a pay-as-you-go system that seeks to provide a subsistence level of income to all retired residents. A second pillar is an employer-based, fully funded occupational pension scheme, mandatory for all employees whose annual income exceeds a certain threshold. Means-tested supplemental benefits may be claimed if total income does not cover basic needs in old age. A voluntary third pillar, which is an individual tax-deductible savings account for retirement, completes the model. The first two pillars yield a gross replacement rate of about 60 percent, and a net replacement rate of 70–80 percent. Switzerland does have a high elderly labor force participation rate, but early retirement is permitted at ages 62 and 63, respectively, with a benefit reduction of 6.8 percent per year early. Future challenges for the Swiss retirement model include funding and long-term care financing, just as in the US.

In an interesting comparison of the Australian and US economies and demographics, Rafal Chomik and John Piggott evaluate how Australia's retirement income structure performs in terms of economic efficiency and efficacy in delivering old-age support. Australia's retirement income system is comprised by a flat-rate, non-contributory, affluence-tested age pension; this first pillar operates as a non-contributory transfer potentially available to all residents. A second pillar is a national mandatory defined contribution plan to which firms must contribute 9.25 percent (moving to 12 percent) of wages on behalf of their employees. Access to the second-pillar funds is available tax-free at age 60. There is also a third pillar made up of voluntary retirement saving. This structure has resulted in low poverty rates for people age 65+, and private pension coverage is also higher in Australia than in other developed nations. In addition, marginal tax rates are also higher. The authors suggest that more means-testing might be a path that the United States could pursue.

Singapore, like Australia, also has a national mandatory defined contribution retirement saving system. In his chapter, Benedict Koh describes how the Central Provident Fund (CPF) has functioned over the past half-century, along with its success in achieving nearly universal home ownership, health care coverage, and financial protection. Nevertheless, many people have inadequate retirement assets due to high transaction costs, lack of financial literacy, and inertia. Additionally, CPF participants may withdraw money to purchase homes, service mortgage payments, and finance premiums for insurance protection or children's tertiary education. People may also invest in a permitted list of financial products, but few have taken advantage of the large menu of investment instruments on offer to grow their retirement savings, instead leaving the monies in their CPF accounts where they earned a safe but low interest rate. Since 2013, it has also been mandatory for all CPF members to invest their RA savings in deferred life annuities that provide them with an income stream until their deaths.

Focusing on retirement saving adequacy, Koh explains that the CPF Board established the Minimum Sum Scheme with the goal of requiring members to retain a minimum level of savings for old age. From July 2013 onwards, members must set aside S$148,000 in their Retirement Account upon reaching age 55, which is believed sufficient to support a subsistence level of living. Nevertheless, many members lack sufficient cash savings, and currently fewer than half of those turning age 55 meet the Minimum Sum Scheme requirement. Some possible reforms could involve raising older persons' contribution rates, ways to help monetize peoples' homes, increasing investment returns, and extending retirement ages. Koh also discusses the positive effect of introducing new low-cost default portfolios such as target-date funds. In this sense, the Singaporean system has adopted elements of the US defined contribution model.

Conclusion

Forty years ago, many observers hailed ERISA and its amendments as absolutely instrumental for strengthening private sector employer pensions in America. And by some criteria, there is much to be proud of. In 1974, for instance, when ERISA was passed, the total assets of private pension plans amounted to $164 billion (Sirkin 1994). Now US private pension assets have grown to almost $25 trillion (ICI 2015), despite having passed through one of the toughest market downturns in history. Unfortunately, with hindsight, Steve Sass was prescient when he argued that 'ERISA neither solidified nor undermined the nation's private pension institution; it merely marked its high-water level' (1997: 229). Traditional DB pensions were the creation of big labor, big business, and big government. Today, employees and plan sponsors have a very different perspective on risk management, the workplace, and capital markets, compared to 40 years ago.

In the twenty-first century, we have a much clearer view of the common risks facing the world's retirement systems; these include rising but uncertain longevity, probably lower investment yields, and rising health care costs. This volume will generate discussion for years to come, on how to craft a pension system for workers, retirees, and plan sponsors of the future.

References

Blitzstein, D. (2015). 'Pension Benefit Design Innovation: Labor Unions as Agents of Change,' in O. S. Mitchell and R. Shea (eds), *Reimagining Pensions: The Next 40 Years.* Oxford: Oxford University Press, pp. 123–38.

Bovenberg, A. L., R. Mehlkopf, and T. E. Nijman (2015). 'The Promise of Defined Ambition Plans: Lessons for the United States,' in O. S. Mitchell and R. Shea (eds), *Reimagining Pensions: The Next 40 Years.* Oxford: Oxford University Press, pp. 215–46.

Bütler, M. (2015). 'Insights from Switzerland's Pension System,' in O. S. Mitchell and R. Shea (eds), *Reimagining Pensions: The Next 40 Years.* Oxford: Oxford University Press, pp. 247–73.

Coronado, J. (2015). 'The Changing Nature of Retirement,' in O. S. Mitchell and R. Shea (eds), *Reimagining Pensions: The Next 40 Years.* Oxford: Oxford University Press, pp. 61–73.

Fuerst, D. (2015). 'Retirement Shares Plan: A New Model of Risk Sharing,' in O. S. Mitchell and R. Shea (eds), *Reimagining Pensions: The Next 40 Years.* Oxford: Oxford University Press, pp. 161–73.

Goodman, B. and D. Richardson (2015). 'Back to the Future: Hybrid Co-op Pensions and the TIAA-CREF System,' in O. S. Mitchell and R. Shea (eds), *Reimagining Pensions: The Next 40 Years.* Oxford: Oxford University Press, pp. 139–60.

Investment Company Institute (ICI) (2015). 'Retirement Assets Total $24.7 Trillion in Fourth Quarter 2014.' Press Release. Washington, DC: ICI.

Koh, B. S. K. (2015). 'Singapore's Social Security Savings System: A Review and Some Observations for the United States,' in O. S. Mitchell and R. Shea (eds), *Reimagining Pensions: The Next 40 Years.* Oxford: Oxford University Press, pp. 298–339.

Munnell, A., M. Rutledge, and A. Webb (2015). 'Are Retirees Falling Short? Reconciling the Conflicting Evidence,' in O. S. Mitchell and R. Shea (eds), *Reimagining Pensions: The Next 40 Years.* Oxford: Oxford University Press, pp. 11–36.

Piggott, J. and R. Chomik (2015). 'The Australian Retirement Income System: Lessons for the United States,' in O. S. Mitchell and R. Shea (eds), *Reimagining Pensions: The Next 40 Years.* Oxford: Oxford University Press, pp. 274–97.

Rappaport, A. M. and A. Peterson (2015). 'Risk Sharing Alternatives for Pension Plan Design: An Overview and Case Studies,' in O. S. Mitchell and R. Shea (eds), *Reimagining Pensions: The Next 40 Years.* Oxford: Oxford University Press, pp. 95–122.

Sass, S. (1997). *The Promise of Private Pensions: The First Hundred Years.* Cambridge, MA: Harvard University Press.

Shea, R., R. S. Newman, and J. P. Goldberg (2015). 'The Portfolio Pension Plan, and Alternative Model for Retirement Security,' in O. S. Mitchell and R. Shea (eds), *Reimagining Pensions: The Next 40 Years.* Oxford: Oxford University Press, pp. 174–82.

Sirkin, M. S. (1994). 'The 20 Year History of ERISA.' *St. John's Law Review,* 68(2): 321–8. <http://scholarship.law.stjohns.edu/lawreview/vol68/iss2/3>.

Steuerle, C. E., P. Perun, and B. H. Harris (2015). 'Entitlement Reform and the Future of Pensions,' in O. S. Mitchell and R. Shea (eds), *Reimagining Pensions: The Next 40 Years.* Oxford: Oxford University Press, pp. 74–91.

VanDerhei, J. (2015). 'Retirement Plans and Prospects for Retirement Income Adequacy,' in O. S. Mitchell and R. Shea (eds), *Reimagining Pensions: The Next 40 Years.* Oxford: Oxford University Press, pp. 37–60.

Vine, J. (2015). 'Cultivating Pension Plans,' in O. S. Mitchell and R. Shea (eds), *Reimagining Pensions: The Next 40 Years.* Oxford: Oxford University Press, pp. 183–212.

Part I

Assessing the Retirement System: Adequacy, Efficiency, and Stability

Chapter 2

Are Retirees Falling Short? Reconciling the Conflicting Evidence

Alicia H. Munnell, Matthew S. Rutledge, and Anthony Webb

A fundamental question in the retirement arena is whether people will have adequate retirement income to maintain their pre-retirement standards of living. Existing studies offer conflicting assessments. On the one hand, the remarkable stability in the ratio of wealth to income by age from 10 Surveys of Consumer Finances indicates that current cohorts have substantially lower retirement assets relative to income in the United States than in the past. In the same vein, the National Retirement Risk Index shows that half of today's working households will not be able to maintain their pre-retirement living standards (Munnell et al. 2012). Another recent study using the Health and Retirement Study (HRS) and similar assumptions also concludes that about half of pre-retirees are not on track to maintain their pre-retirement consumption (Munnell et al. 2013). On the other hand, Scholz et al. (2006), using the HRS and a life cycle model of optimal wealth accumulation and decumulation, conclude that the majority of pre-retirees do have an optimal level of wealth. Separately, Hurd and Rohwedder (2013), using HRS consumption data, find that households who retired between 2001 and 2007 experienced only small declines in consumption, suggesting adequate resources.

This chapter attempts to explain why the different approaches yield such different answers. First, we present assumption-free evidence on wealth-to-income ratios from the last 10 Surveys of Consumer Finances. These ratios by age have remained virtually unchanged even though people are living longer, Social Security is less generous, 401(k) plans have replaced defined benefit (DB) plans, health care costs have increased dramatically, and interest rates have plummeted. The second section describes two studies that compare projected replacement rates with a consumption-smoothing target. We show that roughly half of US households are unlikely to maintain their pre-retirement standards of living. In a third section we argue that the optimal saving conclusion that emerges from the Scholz et al. model rests on two key assumptions: (1) households are content with declining levels of consumption in retirement; and (2) households reduce their consumption when children leave home. These assumptions make it much easier for older households to achieve target levels of wealth. To show the impact of these assumptions, we incorporate them in the National Retirement Risk Index. Our results show that these changes reduce the percent of households with inadequate savings produced by the optimal savings model. The fourth section turns to households' ability to maintain consumption after retirement. The questions here are whether the households studied by Hurd and Rohwedder possess sufficient resources to maintain their spending for the remainder of their lives, and whether they maintain their spending as they age.

Our conclusion is that an optimistic view of US retirement preparedness depends crucially on assumptions about behavior that may not reflect real-world activity or on consumption patterns that are unsustainable in the long run. Thus, our best assessment is that many retirees will fall increasingly short.

Wealth-to-Income Ratios Show Declining Preparedness over Time

While the *adequacy* of current US saving may be open to question, the *trend* in retirement saving relative to income is not. The Federal Reserve's triennial Survey of Consumer Finances (SCF) shows that the ratio of net wealth to income, a good indicator of the extent to which people can replace their earnings in retirement, has remained virtually unchanged at each age from 1983 through 2010.[1] In these ratios, wealth includes all financial assets, 401 (k) accumulations, and real estate less any outstanding debt; and income includes earnings and returns on financial assets. Importantly, wealth excludes the present expected value of income that the household will eventually receive from DB pension plans and Social Security.[2] As shown in Figure 2.1, the ratios at each age for each survey lie virtually on top of one another. The outlier is 2010, where the ratios are substantially below those in the other surveys at every age.

The stability of the ratio reveals a significant decline in retirement preparedness, particularly since five developments should have led to higher ratios of wealth to income. First, life expectancy has increased. Between 1983 and 2010, life expectancy at age 65 rose by 3.5 years for men and 1.8 years for women. As a result, for any given level of income, one would have expected workers to accumulate more wealth in order to support themselves over their longer retirement period. Second, Social Security replacement rates have declined as the Full Retirement Age has been rising from 65 to 67, and the actuarial reduction on benefits claimed early grows larger. Moreover, the growing prevalence of two-earner couples means that fewer

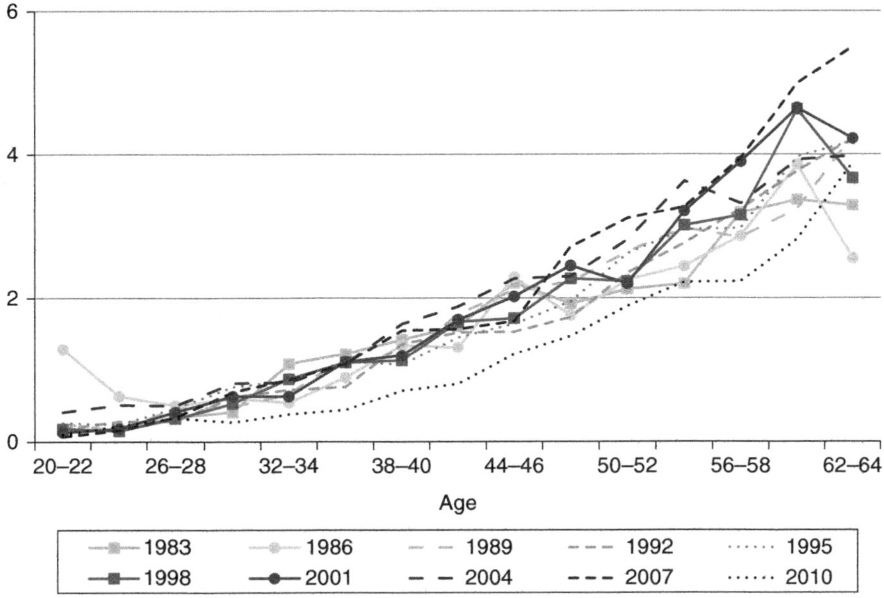

Figure 2.1 Ratio of wealth to income by age from the Survey of Consumer Finances, 1983–2010

Source: Authors' calculations based on US Board of Governors of the Federal Reserve System 2010.

households receive the spousal benefit. Third, US retirement plans have shifted over time from DB to defined contribution (DC). Whereas accruals of future benefits under DB plans are not included in SCF wealth, assets in 401(k) plans are included. The shift from unreported to reported retirement assets would have been expected to increase the wealth-to-income ratio. Fourth, health care costs have risen substantially and show signs of further increase. Out-of-pocket expenditures for premiums and copayments under Medicare Part B, the program that covers physician services, have risen from 6.8 percent of the average Social Security benefit in 1983 to 17.0 percent in 2010, and they are projected to climb further in the future.[3] The rising cost of health care should have led to higher wealth-to-income ratios today than in the past. Finally, real interest rates have fallen significantly since 1983, so any given level of wealth now produces less retirement income. If people were interested in generating a given stream of income, the significant decline in interest rates would have been expected to boost wealth accumulations.

Despite these developments, the stability of wealth-to-income ratios over the 10 SCF surveys between 1983 and 2010 indicates that people are less well prepared than in the past. If they had been over-prepared in the past, they might be fine in the future. But if people were not over-prepared in 1983, then retirees will fall short now.

Failure to Meet Replacement Rate Targets

Some analysts conclude that roughly half of today's working households will fall short in retirement. One approach uses the SCF to construct a National Retirement Risk Index (NRRI); another uses the HRS to calculate a baseline level of retirement income for people in their 50s against which one can measure the impact of alternative strategies such as changing asset allocations, working longer, taking out reverse mortgages, or controlling pre-retirement spending.

The National Retirement Risk Index

The NRRI compares projected replacement rates—retirement income as a percent of pre-retirement income—for today's working-age households to target rates that would allow them to maintain their living standards in retirement. It then calculates the percent at risk of falling short.[4] This calculation assumes that workers retire at 65 (a conservative assumption given that the average retirement age today is lower) and annuitize all their wealth (assumptions that maximize the income from any given amount of wealth).[5] The NRRI was initially constructed using the Federal Reserve's 2004 SCF, and it has been updated to incorporate the 2007 and 2010 surveys. The numbers presented here are based on an update for 2013.

Projecting household retirement replacement rates involves two calculations: estimating how much income households had before age 65 and estimating their post-retirement income. Retirement income is defined broadly to include income from financial assets in 401(k) plans and saved directly (net of non-mortgage debt), housing (net of mortgage debt), DB plans, and Social Security.[6] The approach uses the stable wealth-to-income patterns in the SCF to project where today's younger households are likely to be in terms of future financial and housing wealth. Instead of estimating total wealth directly, however, each component is projected separately. As noted, households are assumed to purchase an inflation-adjusted annuity with their financial wealth and with the proceeds of a reverse mortgage on their homes; retirement income includes imputed rent from the house.[7]

The items that comprise pre-retirement income include labor market earnings, the real return (assumed to be 4.6 percent) on 401(k) plans and other financial assets, and imputed rent from housing, minus mortgage and non-mortgage interest paid. Average pre-retirement lifetime income serves as the denominator for each household's replacement rate. With projections of pre- and post-retirement income, it is possible to calculate the projected replacement rate for each household when the head reaches 65.

Since the SCF does not include wealth from DB pensions and Social Security, the incomes from these two sources must be estimated separately. For DB pension income, our projections are based on income amounts reported in the SCF. For Social Security, benefits are calculated directly based on earnings histories constructed for all members of the household.

To determine the share of the retired population at risk, projected replacement rates are compared with pre-tax target replacement rates. The target permits the household to enjoy the same consumption in each period both before and after retirement. The calculation involves identifying an age-varying saving rate that results in an accumulation of wealth at age 65 sufficient to generate a level of post-retirement consumption that equals pre-retirement consumption. The calculations incorporate current federal and state income taxes, the Earned Income Tax Credit, Social Security taxes and benefits, house purchase, mortgage borrowing, and loan repayments. The target replacement rate is the ratio of post-retirement income to pre-retirement income associated with the optimal saving rate. The calculation of the level of retirement wealth sufficient to smooth consumption is sensitive to assumptions regarding investment returns, medical and nursing home costs, the scope for economizing in retirement, and the age of retirement. Nevertheless, Skinner (2007) shows that plausible alternatives to our approach yield higher ratios of required retirement wealth to pre-retirement income compared to ours.

The final step in creating the Index is to simply compare each household's projected replacement rate with its target. Those whose projected replacement rates fall more than 10 percent below the target are deemed to be at risk of having insufficient income to maintain their pre-retirement living standards. Thus, the Index is the fraction of *all* households that fall more than 10 percent short of that target. The percentages of households at risk for three age groups in 2007, 2010, and 2013 appear in Table 2.1. The percent at risk in 2013 declined only slightly from 2010, primarily because

TABLE 2.1 Percentage of households 'at risk' at age 65 by age group over time

Age group	2007	2010	2013
All	44	53	52
30–9	53	62	59
40–9	47	55	54
50–9	32	44	44

Source: Authors' calculations.

the strong performance of the stock market offset the tightening of the reverse mortgage provisions and the continued increase in Social Security's Full Retirement Age. Overall, the conclusions are clear: half of today's working-age households are at risk of not being able to maintain their standard of living in retirement.

Results from the HRS

A second analysis was designed to compare the effectiveness of asset allocation to other levers—controlling spending, working longer, and tapping home equity—in improving retirement security (Munnell et al. 2013). That study used data on working households aged 51–64 from the HRS, a nationally representative panel survey of older households conducted every two years since 1992.[8] Determining the retirement readiness of each household involved three steps.

The first identified a target replacement rate that allowed each household to maintain its pre-retirement standard of living. Target replacement rates that vary with marital status and income were drawn from Georgia State University's RETIRE Project (Palmer 2008). These rates were adjusted to reflect a projection that a significant proportion of the sample will have either repaid their mortgages by retirement, or be able to repay all or part of the balances by drawing on financial assets.[9]

The next step was to calculate the projected retirement replacement rate that each household would achieve if it continued on its present course, maintaining its current savings rate and asset allocation, and not taking a reverse mortgage. Total income at retirement in this baseline scenario consisted of Social Security, employer pensions, and income from financial assets. Social Security benefits were based on administrative data and income from current and deferred pensions on self-reports.[10] At retirement, the household was assumed to purchase a nominal joint- or single-life annuity with its financial assets, including 401(k) and IRA balances.

In a third step, the projected replacement rate was compared to the target rate for each household at each age from 60 to 70.[11] If the projected rate was below the target, the household was deemed to fall short in its retirement preparedness. The aggregate result for all households at a given age of retirement was the baseline measure for assessing the impact of the levers.

Figure 2.2 shows the percent of households falling short at each age under both the baseline assumption, and also assuming that the household took advantage of a reverse mortgage. The baseline results show substantially more households falling short at 65 than the NRRI, but once they take out a reverse mortgage (as do households in the NRRI) the share falling short at 65 drops to 48 percent—close to the NRRI in 2010 (53 percent).[12]

Figure 2.2 Percentage of all households falling short of target by age at retirement, base case, and with a reverse mortgage

Source: Munnell et al. (2013).

We conclude from these studies that a methodology which identifies a target replacement rate and compares that rate with projected retirement incomes finds almost half of American households are unable to maintain their pre-retirement incomes in retirement. Results from the SCF and the HRS are almost identical.

The Optimal Savings Alternative

In contrast to the target replacement rate approach, Scholz et al. (2006) concluded that most Americans were saving optimally, using HRS data. By this, they meant that households were saving more than enough to smooth lifetime marginal utility of consumption. They defined saving to include 401 (k) plan balances and housing equity as well as direct saving. These conclusions were based on a model of optimal wealth accumulation and decumulation over the life cycle that incorporated mortality, labor market, and health cost risk, and income from DB pensions and Social Security. The model was used to calculate the wealth that HRS households should have accumulated by their 50s, given assumed preference parameters along with the health and employment shocks experienced over their lifetimes. These optimal amounts were then compared with the amounts that HRS households actually accumulated. Those authors concluded that only 16 percent of households had less wealth than optimal.[13]

The question is why this optimal savings approach yields such comforting results. Two factors are at play: the cohort analyzed and model assumptions. The two assumptions that stand out are how households are assumed to consume their accumulated wealth in retirement, and how children affected replacement rate targets.[14]

Cohort analyzed

The optimal savings analysis found that only 16 percent of households saved less than optimally based on the original HRS cohort (age 51–61 in 1992). Interestingly, our NRRI measure for 1992 for those age 51–61 reported only 19 percent at risk. That is, focusing on the same age group in the same year, the two different methodologies yielded the same general conclusion: the vast majority of those households had saved enough to maintain pre-retirement living standards.

Between 1992 and 2004, however, the overall percent at risk increased substantially in the NRRI (see Table 2.2). The three main reasons are a decline in Social Security replacement rates because of a drop in one-earner couples and increases in the Full Retirement Age; a decline in real interest rates; and a shift from DB to DC pensions. The difference in households at risk between the NRRI and the optimization model in 2004 is substantial: the NRRI showed 35 percent of those age 50–58 to be at risk, while Scholz and Seshadri (2008) showed only 8 percent at risk.[15] To analyze this difference requires examining the implications of the underlying assumptions.

TABLE 2.2 Percentage 'at risk' using the NRRI versus the 'optimal saving' approach: 1992 and 2004

Age group	1992		2004	
	NRRI	Optimal savings	NRRI	Optimal savings
All groups	36	—	43	—
51–61	19	16	35	5

Note: The NRRI result for 2004 is for households aged 50–58. NRRI refers to the National Retirement Risk Index.

Source: Authors' calculations.

Assumptions underlying optimal saving

As noted, two key assumptions are how much households spend in retirement and how households spend once their children leave home. To evaluate how these affect results, we recalculate the percent at risk of being unable to maintain their living standards during retirement in the NRRI.

Retirement drawdown

The NRRI assumes that people will purchase an annuity when they retire so that they can spend a steady inflation-adjusted amount.[16] By contrast, the optimization model assumes that households undertake an optimal drawdown of unannuitized wealth, carefully trading off the risk of outliving their wealth against the cost of unnecessarily restricting their consumption. Given the preference parameters in Scholz et al. (2006), households optimally choose higher consumption in their 60s and significantly lower consumption by age 85. This declining consumption reflects the declining probability that the household will be alive.

Using numerical optimization techniques, and adopting Scholz et al.'s (2006) preference, mortality, and rate of return assumptions, we compute that a typical married couple undertaking a drawdown of unannuitized wealth will optimally consume 7.9 percent of wealth in the first year of retirement.[17] By contrast, the inflation-indexed annuity purchased by NRRI households provides an income amount of only 5.15 percent of wealth.[18] Thus to meet any target replacement rate, a typical household following the optimal drawdown strategy would only need to accumulate 66 percent (5.2/7.9) of the wealth needed by NRRI households. Of course consumption will decline during the course of retirement, but this is optimizing behavior given the assumed intertemporal elasticity of substitution.[19]

Integrating an optimal drawdown strategy into the NRRI requires two changes. First, as already discussed, wealth annuitization must be replaced by a declining drawdown rate. Second, because consumption falls in retirement, households can consume more during their working years. To equalize pre-and post-retirement consumption, the targets need to be raised (see Figure 2.3), partially offsetting the effect of the declining drawdown rate on the percent saving sub-optimally.

The speed of the decline in spending also depends on marital status (married couples have the greatest life expectancy and single men the shortest) and the percentage of wealth that is pre-annuitized through employer pensions and Social Security (the higher the percentage, the more rapid will be the decline). It also depends on the intertemporal elasticity of substitution,[20] which is assumed to equal 1/3, consistent with Scholz and Seshadri. Our procedure involves calculating, for each of 48

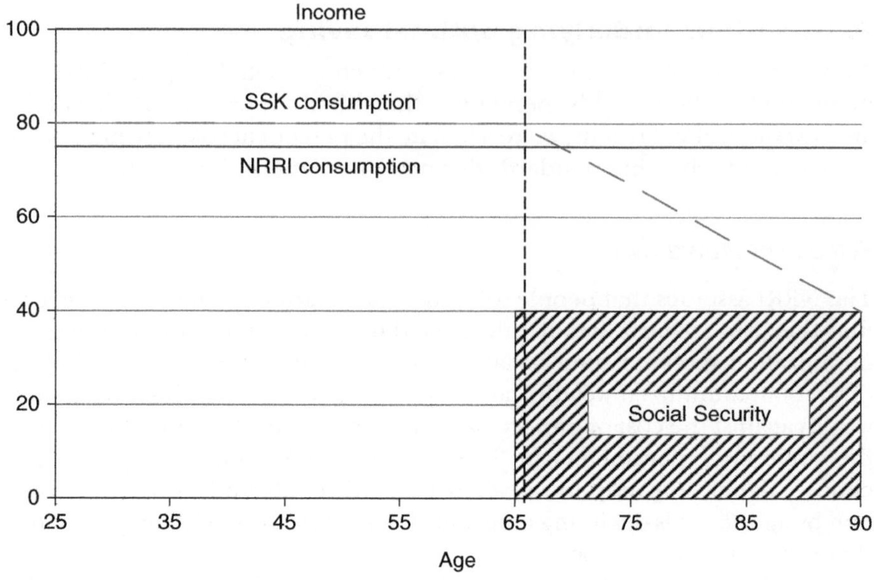

Figure 2.3 Illustrative consumption by age, SSK, and NRRI as percent of income

Notes: SSK refers to Scholz et al. (2006) computations, and NRRI refers to the National Retirement Risk Index.

Source: Authors' computations.

household types, a target replacement rate that will permit the household to enjoy the same level of consumption in each period prior to retirement and in the first year of retirement, and an optimally declining level of consumption in retirement. From these 48 household types, targets and drawdown rates are calculated for 12 types of households—low, medium, and high-earner single men, single women, one-earner couples, and two-earner couples—by taking weighted averages of renters and homeowners with and without DB pension coverage.

We find that imposing an assumption of an optimal drawdown boosts resulting replacement rate targets, but this increase is more than offset by a reduction in the amount of wealth required to finance each dollar of post-retirement consumption. As a result, the percent of those in their 50s at risk in 2004 declined from 35 percent under the original NRRI assumptions to 24 percent after the NRRI is adjusted to reflect optimal drawdown strategies (see Figure 2.4).

Children

A second important assumption is what happens to household consumption once the children leave home. Under the optimal savings approach, where

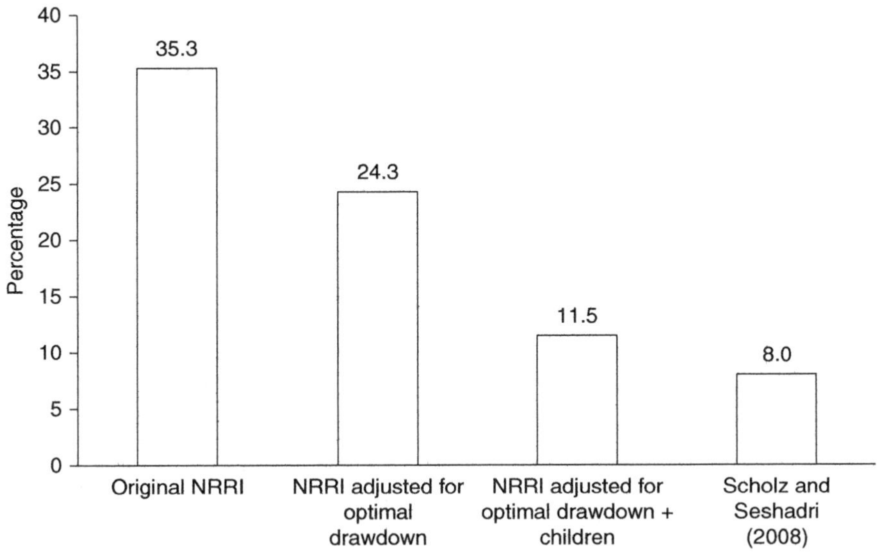

Figure 2.4 Percentage of households aged 51–61 at risk, 2004

Note: NRRI refers to the National Retirement Risk Index.

Source: Authors' computations.

the marginal utility of consumption varies with the size of the household, households optimally choose lower consumption once the children are gone. As a result, the households have lower replacement rate targets and need to save less for retirement than in cases where consumption remains steady.

Incorporating the impact of children on consumption into the NRRI model requires recalculating the NRRI targets for each of the 48 types of households and collapsing those groups into 12 household types. The new calculation retains the assumption that households reduce their consumption as they age. Adjustments to the targets are based on the equivalence scales from Scholz and Seshadri (2008), namely $(A_j + 0.7K_j)^{0.7}$ where A_j and K_j denote the number of adults and children in the household. The assumption is that children are born when the parents are age 27 and remain in the household for 18 years. Following Scholz and Seshadri (2007), the number of children varies with marital status and income tercile. Figure 2.5 shows the optimal consumption path for a typical household before and after adjustments for children. The new target replacement rate permits the household to enjoy the same level of consumption prior to the arrival of children, after they have left home, and in the first year of retirement, and a higher level of consumption while the children are at home.

The percentage at risk is then re-estimated using these new targets that reflect both the optimal drawdown and the assumption that consumption

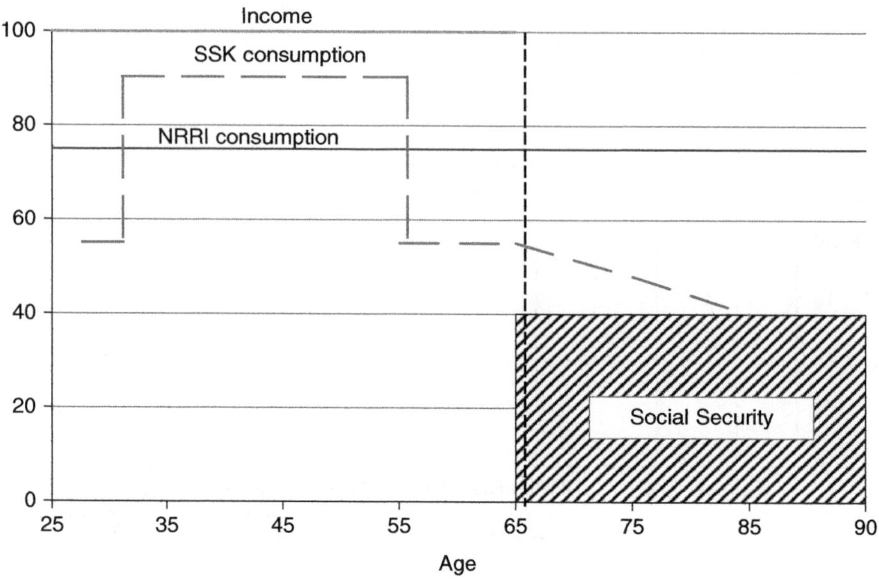

Figure 2.5 Illustrative consumption by age, SSK, and NRRI as percent of income, with children

Notes: SSK refers to Scholz et al. (2006) computations, and NRRI refers to the National Retirement Risk Index.

Source: Authors' computations.

varies with household size. The combined impact of the two adjustments reduces the percent at risk in 2004 from the original 35 percent to 11.5 percent, very close to the 8 percent reported by Scholz and Seshadri (2008).

The upshot of this discussion is that the standard economic assumptions embedded in the optimization model lead to low wealth accumulation targets and high initial incomes. The notion that households accept declining consumption in retirement implies that households will accumulate much less wealth to maintain their living standards. The assumption that parents reduce their consumption once children leave home means that households have lower saving targets and save more between the emptying of the nest and retirement, yielding few at risk. These two assumptions are the key factors that differentiate the conclusions from the two models.

Which assumptions are more plausible? Do people want steady real consumption in retirement (especially in view of rapidly rising health care costs and expensive long-term care) or will they accept declining payments? Do parents cut back on consumption when the children leave home, or do they spend the slack in their budgets? No one really knows the answer. While spending does decline as people age, the extent to which this pattern tracks declining income is unclear; people cannot spend what they do not have. On the side of steady consumption, financial planning tools invariably assume that households require level amounts. How households react when children leave home is also not well understood. One study found that household consumption did not decline, and per-capita consumption increased after children left (Coe and Webb 2010). Yet the sample size was small, so the effects of children remain an unresolved issue. Nevertheless, assumptions alter one's assessment of whether households are saving optimally, and one's view of the results depends on the plausibility of the underlying assumptions.

The Sustainability of Initial Retirement Consumption

Another argument in favor of the adequacy of current saving is that some researchers find only modest declines in total spending after retirement (Hurd and Rohwedder 2013). These data come from the HRS and a supplemental survey to the HRS, the Consumption and Activities Mail Survey (CAMS), conducted in 2001, 2003, 2005, and 2007 (and subsequently in 2009 and 2011). For most of their analysis, the authors use panel data from 439 households on actual spending before and after retirement, and on anticipated spending changes prior to retirement and recollections of spending changes after retirement. The authors find only small consumption declines (1–6 percent) post-retirement in total spending, non-durable spending, and food spending.[21] The authors surmised that these declines were consistent with the cessation of work-related expenses, more efficient shopping, or the loss of earnings due to early retirement as a result of a health shock.[22] Nevertheless, there was much heterogeneity. For instance, households in the lowest quartile showed large declines in consumption upon retirement—particularly when health was a reason for retirement and when they had a short planning horizon. Nevertheless, the overall message was that observed steady consumption profiles suggest that people are well prepared for retirement.

A possible explanation for the absence of any significant drop in consumption at retirement despite apparently inadequate resources is that retirees may initially consume too much, but then experience a reduction in consumption over time. We test this hypothesis in three ways. The first asks whether the Hurd-Rohwedder households possessed sufficient resources in their first year of retirement to maintain the same consumption levels for the remainder of their lives.[23] The second examines whether these households continued to maintain their immediate post-retirement consumption after six to 10 years of retirement. The third compares the trajectories of households having sufficient resources to maintain lifetime consumption with those of households having insufficient resources.

To calculate whether the 439 households possessed sufficient financial resources to maintain their first-year retirement spending later in life, we take account of financial resources (both inside and outside of retirement plans), Social Security, and employer pension income, net of federal income tax. We also assume that households take a reverse mortgage on their houses. All proceeds of the financial assets and reverse mortgage are then used to purchase an inflation-indexed annuity. Although few households actually do purchase inflation-indexed annuities, the income they could obtain approximates the amounts that households might consume out of their financial assets were they to follow conventional rule-of-thumb patterns (such as the 4 percent rule, Bengen 1994). We note that this income is substantially less than the amount they could enjoy in the first year, if they had decumulated those assets optimally.[24]

Results of this annuitization exercise appear in Figure 2.6. A household with average income and consumption in each of the bottom seven deciles of the income distribution will not have enough money to maintain its first year's consumption.

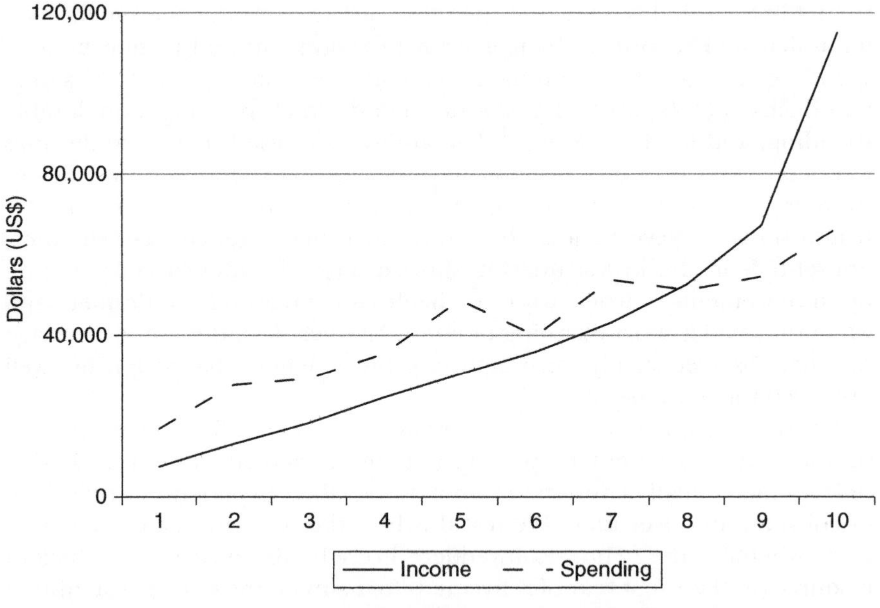

Figure 2.6 Mean income and spending by income decile at time of retirement for Hurd-Rohwedder (2011) sample of households

Source: Authors' calculations.

A possible concern with these results could be the potential impact of resources and consumption misreporting. Even if all households did save optimally, those who understated their income or overstated their consumption would be classified as under-resourced, while those who overstated their income or understated their consumption would appear to have excess resources. To address this concern, we minimize the assumed mismatch in reporting of income and consumption. This exercise involves sorting households by income and then by consumption, and calculating households' ability to fund the corresponding point of the distribution of spending, at each point of the income distribution. Results show that households in all but two deciles have a consumption-income ratio in excess of one, indicating their inability to maintain initial levels of consumption (see Figure 2.7).

A second approach is to see what happens to total spending of CAMS respondents in the years after their first observation in retirement. The treatment group is respondents who reported they were not retired at CAMS wave *t* (2001, 2003, or 2005), retired at CAMS wave *t+1*, and remain retired thereafter, a maximum of an additional four surveys. The control group is respondents who reported that they were not retired at wave *t* and *t+1* and remained not retired thereafter. For this exercise, we tighten the

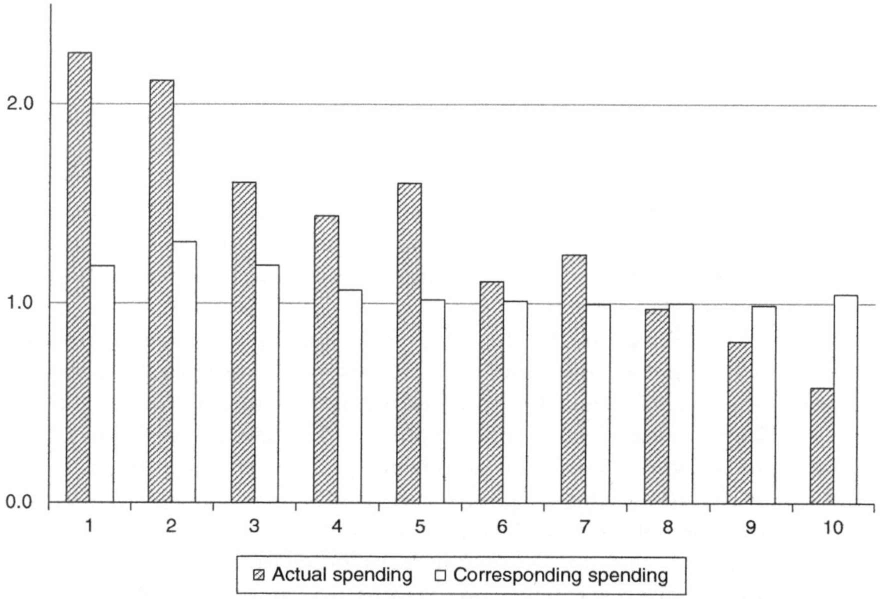

Figure 2.7 Average actual and corresponding consumption-to-income ratio at time of retirement by income decile for Hurd-Rohwedder sample of households

Source: Authors' calculations.

TABLE 2.3 Median respondent spending by retirement status for respondents aged 50 to 70

Observation period	Not retired at time *t*, retired at time *t+1* and thereafter		Not retired throughout	
	Consumption	Sample size	Consumption	Sample size
t	23,000	275	25,900	1,424
t+1	25,300	275	25,600	1,424
t+2	21,000	208	24,500	898
t+3	21,000	193	24,300	677
t+4	18,300	123	24,200	291
t+5	17,700	71	25,600	148
Percent change				
From *t* to *t+1*	9.5		−1.2	
From *t* to *t+5*	−23.4		−1.2	

Notes: Respondents are classified as retired if they reported that they were not working. Conversely, they are classified as not retired if they reported that they were working. The comparison is between individuals who were not retired at t and retired at *t+1* and those who were not retired at both waves. The consumption of respondents is reported at subsequent waves if their retirement status is the same as that at *t+1*, irrespective of their retirement status at other waves subsequent to *t+1*. The difference in the % change from *t* to *t+5* between the two groups is statistically significant at the 5% level.

Source: Authors' calculations.

definition of retirement from that used in the Hurd-Rohwedder analysis.[25] To be not retired in any wave, the respondent had to be both 'not retired' (the definition used by Hurd-Rohwedder) and 'working;' to be retired at any wave, the respondent had to be both 'retired' (the definition used by Hurd-Rohwedder) and not 'working.'[26] Our results show a sharp decline in total spending among those who retired (see Table 2.3). By the end of the period, median spending was 23 percent lower than when respondents were working. By contrast, median spending among those who did not retire remained relatively constant.

A possible explanation for the decline in consumption is that it could have been anticipated and hence reflects a high intertemporal elasticity of substitution. Nevertheless, the observed decline is much too large to be explained by optimal decumulation patterns. The average retirement age was 61, and households with the preference parameters assumed by Scholz et al. (2006) would optimally plan for consumption to decline by only 8 percent over the subsequent decade. Alternatively, for it to be optimal for consumption to decline by 23 percent, households would have to be almost risk neutral. Furthermore, the two groups are approximately the same average age at time *t* (59 for the retirees and 61 for those who continued to work). Absent implausibly large differences in mortality risk, if it were optimal for the consumption of retired households to decline by 23 percent,

TABLE 2.4 Median respondent spending by retirement status for respondents aged 50 to 70

Observation period	Not retired at time *t*, retired at *t+1* and thereafter			
	Insufficient	Sample size	Sufficient	Sample size
t	25,300	132	21,100	143
t+1	27,300	132	23,400	143
t+2	20,100	101	22,400	107
t+3	20,400	82	21,300	111
t+4	18,400	51	18,200	72
t+5	17,700	31	17,800	40
% change				
From *t* to *t+1*	7.9		10.9	
From *t* to *t+5*	−30.9		−15.6	

Note: See note for Table 2.3. The increase in the 'sufficient' sample size at *t+3* is the result of the inclusion of respondents who were retired at waves *t*, *t+1*, and *t+3*, but who were not retired at *t+2*.

Source: Authors' calculations.

it should also be optimal for the consumption of non-retired households to decline by about the same amount. In sum, it seems more likely that retiree households had to adjust consumption to fit within their lifetime budget constraints.

A third exercise compares the trajectories of households having sufficient resources to maintain their consumption for the remainder of their lives with those of households having insufficient resources. This exercise draws on the results of the first exercise and follows those with sufficient and insufficient resources over subsequent waves of the CAMS. We find that the spending for those with insufficient resources declined by 31 percent compared to 16 percent for those with sufficient resources (see Table 2.4). While the relative response is what one would have expected, the sample sizes are too small to be definitive.

Our best guess, overall, is that people tend to maintain their pre-retirement spending when they first retire, but then they cut back sharply thereafter. This reflects the fact that, except for those with very high incomes, HRS respondents in the Hurd-Rohwedder sample lacked adequate resources to maintain their initial levels of consumption throughout their retirement year.

Conclusion

Of all the studies, the evidence we find the most convincing about retirement preparedness is the simple calculation of wealth to income by age from the 10 Surveys of Consumer Finances. We show that these ratios remained unchanged over time, despite longer lives, declining Social Security replacement rates, the shift from DB to DC plans, rapidly rising health care costs, and low interest rates. In other words, people retiring in the future will be less prepared than those in the past, and we are not surprised that target replacement rate comparisons show that about half of households will be unable to maintain their standards of living in retirement.

In our view, studies showing that people are saving optimally hinge crucially on assumptions that imply they are willing to accept declining consumption as they age and sharply reduce their consumption when their children leave home. Applying these patterns to the National Retirement Risk Index reduces the percent at risk to levels very similar to the optimal savings studies. Yet the key question is whether these assumptions seem plausible. While bits and pieces of evidence exist on both sides of these assumptions, answers to this question are not yet conclusive. Moreover, the fact that consumption does not decline early in retirement ignores the fact that many people do not have the resources to continue consuming at that pace over their entire retired lives.

Technical Appendix

This appendix describes the methodology used to calculate three replacement rate targets: (1) the target used in the National Retirement Risk Index, which assumes that the marginal utility of consumption does not vary with household size and that the household purchases an annuity on retirement; (2) a revised target that retains the assumption that the marginal utility of consumption does not vary with household size, but that households undertake an optimal decumulation of unannuitized wealth in retirement; and (3) a further revised target that assumes that the marginal utility of consumption varies with household size, and that households undertake an optimal decumulation of unannuitized wealth in retirement.

The NRRI target

The NRRI target assumes that the household's goal is to accumulate sufficient wealth to generate a level of post-retirement consumption that equals consumption immediately before retirement. The household achieves this goal by choosing an age-varying savings rate. The target replacement rate is the ratio of post-retirement income to pre-retirement income associated with the optimal savings strategy. Pre-retirement income equals labor market earnings, imputed rent, and investment returns, minus mortgage and loan interest paid, all averaged over ages 20 to 65. Post-retirement income equals income from Social Security, employer pensions, and an inflation-indexed annuity, plus imputed rent. The household is assumed to purchase an inflation-indexed annuity with its financial assets plus the proceeds of a reverse mortgage. The calculations include federal, state (Massachusetts), and Social Security taxes based on 2006 law, including the Earned Income Tax Credit and the favorable tax treatment accorded to income from Social Security.

Targets are calculated for 48 types of households—those in the bottom, middle, and top tercile of the income distribution who are single men, single women, or one- or two-earner couples, with or without DB pensions, and who are homeowners or renters. Weighted averages are calculated to yield targets for three income terciles for single men, single women, and one- and two-earner couples.

The calculations assume that both housing and financial assets yield a historical real return. The secondary earner joins the household at age 25 with zero assets. Married couples, single men, and single women face annuity rates of 4.69, 5.22, and 4.90 percent, respectively, corresponding to the income payable on inflation-indexed annuities for members of the 1956 birth cohort at 2004 interest rates and expense loads. At age 30, homeowners purchase a house valued at twice their age-50 earnings with the aid of a 30-year mortgage at a real interest rate of 2.23 percent. At retirement, homeowners can borrow 53 percent of the value of the house on a reverse mortgage.

Low, middle, and high earners experience wage increases derived from Clingman and Nichols (2004). The calculations assume that young households are able to borrow if their desired consumption exceeds their net income. They also assume that, during their working lives, households optimally choose a level of consumption that increases at the rate of 1 percent a year.

Target adjustment for optimal accumulation

If the marginal utility of consumption does not vary with age or health status and if the rate of interest equals the rate of time preference, households that choose not to purchase an annuity will optimally choose declining consumption in retirement.[27] The rate of decline will be governed by mortality risk and the intertemporal elasticity of consumption. If the initial level of consumption, expressed as a percent of wealth at retirement, is higher than the income obtainable on an inflation-indexed annuity, households choosing an optimal decumulation of unannuitized wealth will need to accumulate less wealth than households purchasing an annuity. They will therefore be able to enjoy higher pre-retirement income and will face higher initial replacement rate targets. Assuming zero mortality before retirement, the optimal target is one associated with an age-varying savings rate that permits the household to enjoy the same consumption in the first period of retirement as it enjoyed during its working life, with an optimal decline in consumption thereafter.

The optimal savings rate and decumulation path is the one that maximizes:

$$\sum_{t=20}^{T}\sum_{m=1}^{m=3} B^{t-20}\rho_{m,t}U(C_{t,m}) \tag{1}$$

where m is marital status (married, surviving male, or surviving female), $\rho_{m,t}$ is the probability of being in marital status m at time t, and $C_{t,m}$ is consumption at time t in marital state m. Mortality is assumed to be zero prior to age 65, and households are assumed to have population mortality for the 1956 birth cohort after age 65. Following Scholz et al. (2006), the rates of interest and time preference are both assumed to equal four.

The household's utility function is of the following form:

$$U_m(C_t^m, C_t^f) = \frac{(C_t^m + \lambda C_t^f)^{1-\gamma}}{1-\gamma},\ U_f(C_t^f, C_t^m) = \frac{C_t^f + \lambda C_t^m)^{1-\gamma}}{1-\gamma} \tag{2}$$

where λ measures the jointness of consumption, C_t^m, C_t^f denote the consumption of the husband and wife at time t, and γ is the coefficient of risk aversion, assumed to be three, following Scholz et al. (2006). When λ equals one, all consumption is joint. When λ equals zero, none of the household's consumption is joint. We assume that λ equals 0.5.

Target adjustment for children

Scholz et al. (2006) assume that households attempt to smooth the marginal utility of per-adult equivalent consumption, calculated as follows:

$$\frac{(A_j + K_j)^{0.7}}{(A_j)^{0.7}} \tag{3}$$

where A_j and K_j are the number of adults and children in the house. In their model, the number of children and parental ages at which the children are born varies with income decile. Children are incorporated into the NRRI by assuming that households choose an age-varying savings rate and a replacement rate target that permits the household to enjoy constant per-adult equivalent consumption during its working life and an optimal decline in consumption in retirement. Children are assumed to arrive at age 27 and stay for 18 years. Bottom-tercile households are assumed to have the average number of children of households in the second income decile, middle-tercile households the average for the fifth decile, and top-tercile households the average for the ninth decile. The savings plan and target replacement rate are those that maximize equation (1), with the utility function modified as follows:

$$U_m(C_t^m, C_t^f) = \frac{(\delta C_t^m + \delta\lambda C_t^f)^{1-\gamma}}{1-\gamma}\frac{(\delta C_t^f + \delta\lambda C_t^{fm})^{1-\gamma}}{1-\gamma} \tag{4}$$

where δ is $\frac{(A_j)^{0.7}}{(A_j+K_j)0.7}$

If the optimal strategy is to save zero financial assets, the target is set at the level that the household will achieve if it saves nothing, but arrives at retirement debt-free.

Appendix Table 2.A1 reports weighted average targets for low-, middle-, and high-tercile single men, single women, one-earner couples, and two-earner couples calculated under the assumption that households: (1) annuitize; (2) undertake an optimal drawdown of unannuitized wealth; and (3) choose higher consumption when the children are at home.

APPENDIX TABLE 2.A1 NRRI target replacement rates by household type and drawdown alternative

	Low income			Middle income			High income		
	Annuitization	Optimal drawdown	Optimal drawdown w/children	Annuitization	Optimal drawdown	Optimal drawdown w/children	Annuitization	Optimal drawdown	Optimal drawdown w/children
One-earner couple	77	90	71	69	78	65	66	74	55
Two-earner couple	70	82	65	65	76	60	65	74	55
Single male	69	79	63	65	73	58	63	69	50
Single female	74	85	65	65	74	58	64	69	50

Note: The target replacement rates are weighted averages. NRRI refers to the National Retirement Risk Index.

Source: Authors' calculations.

End notes

1. For a selection of research papers using the SCF, see <http://www.federalreserve.gov/econresdata/scf/scfindex.htm>.
2. The exact definition of income in the SCF includes wages, investment income, interest and dividend income, capital gains or losses, unemployment payments, alimony, welfare, pension income, and some other less common income; it is essentially all pre-tax income that comes into a household in a given year.
3. This information comes from unpublished data from the Centers for Medicare and Medicaid Services, Office of the Actuary.
4. For a fuller discussion of the National Retirement Risk Index, see Munnell et al. (2006).
5. Under a reverse mortgage, a homeowner borrows against the equity in his house and receives money from a lender. Unlike a home equity loan, no loan payments or interest are due until the individual dies, moves out, or sells the house. When one of these events occurs, the borrower or the estate is responsible for repaying the loan in full.
6. The NRRI does not include income from work, since the goal of the Index is to assess the retirement security of households once they make a complete exit from the labor force.
7. For couples, the annuity provides the surviving spouse two-thirds of the base amount. While inflation-indexed annuities are not popular with US consumers, they provide a convenient tool for converting a lump sum of wealth into a stream of income. And while inflation-indexed annuities provide a smaller initial benefit than nominal annuities, over time they protect a household's purchasing power against the erosive effects of inflation.
8. For an overview of the HRS, see Juster and Suzman (1995).
9. The target replacement rates used in the HRS study differ from those in the NRRI. These differences reflect not only the treatment of mortgage debt, but also differences in the denominator. The denominator in the NRRI replacement rate target includes imputed rent and investment returns minus interest paid and is averaged over the household's working life. The denominator in the HRS study is labor market earnings averaged over the previous 10 years.
10. Social Security benefits are calculated from actual or imputed earnings records when self-reported data are missing.
11. For more details on the methodology, see Munnell et al. (2013).
12. This exercise assumes a nominal annuity, whereas the NRRI assumes the purchase of an inflation-indexed annuity. Nominal annuities provide a higher initial income than inflation-indexed annuities, increasing the likelihood that households will achieve their targets, albeit at the risk of falling below their targets later in retirement.
13. An updated version of the analysis for 2004 showed even lower levels of households at risk (Scholz and Seshadri 2007).

14. Two issues not considered here are the treatment of the house and the need for precautionary saving. The authors assume that housing wealth is available to fund consumption, so the household is in the same situation as a renter. To avoid implausibly rapid declines in non-housing consumption, households would have to move to a smaller and smaller house. Clearly people do not do this in the real world (Venti and Wise 2002), so the assumed decline in total consumption produces severe pressure on non-housing consumption. If housing represented one third of total consumption, non-housing consumption would decline by 45 percent from age 61 to 85. The other issue is the assumption that households invest in a risk-free asset yielding a real 4 percent return. It has not been possible to earn a risk-free 4 percent return since around the year 2000, so to earn a 4 percent return households would need to assume investment risk. Under CRRA utility, households optimally respond to investment risk by undertaking precautionary saving and, averaged over draws of investment returns, optimally accumulate more than they would have accumulated in the absence of investment risk. The assumption of a 4 percent risk-free investment return leads to an overstatement of the percentage of households who have saved at least optimally.
15. The 8 percent is a weighted average of the 5.2 percent for households born from 1942 to 1947 and the 10.2 percent for those born from 1948 to 1953.
16. Although households can also purchase nominal annuities that provide a declining real income, at plausible preference parameters and prevailing annuity prices, they will prefer the level consumption obtainable from a real annuity. 'Mortality credits,' the reallocation of resources from those who die to those who survive, enable annuities to pay higher returns than equivalent unannuitized investments, particularly at older ages. This additional return makes annuity purchasers more willing than non-purchasers to forego consumption at younger ages in return for additional consumption at older ages.
17. This calculation ignores medical costs and assumes that one half of the household's wealth is pre-annuitized Social Security wealth. Scholz et al. (2006) assume a real return of 4 percent, a coefficient of risk aversion of three, and a rate of time preference of 3 percent. The calculation is based on population average mortality for the 1936 birth cohort when calculating the optimal drawdown rate for the Scholz et al. (2006) sample, who were mostly born from 1931 to 1941. Subsequent birth cohorts would consume somewhat smaller percentages, reflecting their greater life expectancy.
18. The NRRI calculations assume market expense loads, mortality improvements based on Social Security Administration projections, and that interest rates revert to levels prevailing in 2004. The 5.15 percent annuity rate is for households born before 1952. Subsequent birth cohorts are projected to face lower annuity rates.
19. The assumed intertemporal elasticity of substitution, under the assumption of constant relative risk aversion, equals the inverse of the coefficient of risk

aversion. If the assumed intertemporal elasticities of consumption were lower, post-retirement wealth paths would be flatter, requiring the household to accumulate more wealth to generate a given amount of first year retirement income. If, at the extreme, the households had an intertemporal elasticity of substitution of zero, they would optimally spend only the interest of 4 percent and would require 29 percent more wealth at retirement than the NRRI households.

20. The intertemporal elasticity of substitution measures how responsive consumption growth is to the real interest rate.
21. The finding of only a small drop contradicts earlier studies that identified a retirement-consumption puzzle (Hurst 2008; Bernheim et al. 2001; Banks et al. 1998). It was considered a puzzle because the mechanism underlying the drop was not well understood.
22. The authors also contend that the decline is consistent with the optimal decline in consumption implied by the traditional life cycle model, which they assert should equal the mortality rate, assuming the rate of time preference equals the interest rate. In fact, the prediction of the life cycle model for households exhibiting constant relative risk aversion is that the optimal decline equals the mortality rate divided by the coefficient of risk aversion. This calculation implies that for a typical 61-year-old married couple with a coefficient of risk aversion of three, the decline in consumption over a two-year period would be 1 percent.
23. Consumption includes both property taxes and purchases of automobiles and other durables, including automobile finance charges.
24. On the other hand, it is more than the amount that they would consume were they to undertake an 'optimal' decumulation as in Hurd and Rohwedder (2011), who find that most newly retired households possess sufficient amounts.
25. Hurd and Rohwedder (2013) impose the additional restriction that the respondent remained retired in the following wave if observed in that following wave.
26. This adjustment was necessary because many of those retired were working and some of those working characterized themselves as retired. Respondents are also categorized as working if they report they are in part-time/less than part-time employment.
27. This also sets aside the utility of leisure.

References

Banks, J., R. Blundell, and S. Tanner (1998). 'Is there a Retirement-Savings Puzzle?' *American Economic Review*, 88(4): 769–88.

Bengen, W. P. (1994). 'Determining Withdrawal Rates Using Historical Data.' *Journal of Financial Planning*, 7(4): 171–80.

Bernheim, B. D., J. Skinner, and S. Weinberg (2001). 'What Accounts for the Variation in Retirement Wealth among US Households?' *American Economic Review*, 91(4): 832–57.

Coe, N. B. and A. Webb (2010). *Children and Household Utility: Evidence from Kids Flying the Coop*, Working Paper, 2010–16. Chestnut Hill, MA: Center for Retirement Research at Boston College.

Clingman, M. and O. Nichols (2004). *Scaled Factors for Hypothetical Earnings Examples under the 2004 Trustees Report Assumptions*, Actuarial Note, 2004.3. Washington, DC: US Social Security Administration.

Hurd, M. D. and S. Rohwedder (2011). *Economic Preparation for Retirement*, NBER Working Paper, 17203. Cambridge, MA: National Bureau of Economic Research.

Hurd, M. D. and S. Rohwedder (2013). 'Heterogeneity in Spending Change at Retirement.' *Journal of the Economics of Ageing*, 1(2): 60–71.

Hurst, E. (2008). *The Retirement of a Consumption Puzzle*, NBER Working Paper, 13789. Cambridge, MA: National Bureau of Economic Research.

Juster, F. T. and R. M. Suzman. (1995). 'An Overview of the Health and Retirement Study.' *Journal of Human Resources*, 30 (suppl.): S7–S56.

Munnell, A. H., N. Orlova, and A. Webb. (2013). 'How Important is Asset Allocation to Financial Security in Retirement?' in O. S. Mitchell and K. Smetters (eds), *The Market for Retirement Financial Advice.* Oxford: Oxford University Press, 89–106.

Munnell, A. H., A. Webb, and L. Delorme. (2006). *A New National Retirement Risk Index*, Issue in Brief, 48. Chestnut Hill, MA: Center for Retirement Research at Boston College.

Munnell, A. H., A. Webb, and F. Golub-Sass. (2012). *The National Retirement Risk Index: An Update*, Issue in Brief, 12-20. Chestnut Hill, MA: Center for Retirement Research at Boston College.

Palmer, B. A. (2008). *2008 GSU/Aon RETIRE Project Report*, Research Report Series, 08-1. Atlanta, GA: J Mack Robinson College of Business, Georgia State University.

Scholz, J. K. and A. Seshadri (2007). *Children and Household Wealth*, Working Paper, 2007-158. Ann Arbor, MI: University of Michigan Retirement Research Center.

Scholz, J. K. and A. Seshadri (2008). 'Are All Americans Saving "Optimally" for Retirement?' Presented at the 10th Annual Joint Conference of the Retirement Research Consortium in Washington, DC, Aug. 7–8.

Scholz, J. K., A. Seshadri, and S. Khitatrakun (2006). 'Are Americans Saving "Optimally" for Retirement?' *Journal of Political Economy*, 114(4): 607–43.

Skinner, J. (2007). 'Are you Sure you're Saving Enough for Retirement?' *Journal of Economic Perspectives*, 21(3): 59–80.

US Board of Governors of the Federal Reserve System (2010). *Survey of Consumer Finances, 1983–2010.* Washington, DC: US Board of Governors of the Federal Reserve System.

Venti, S. F. and D. A. Wise (2002). 'Aging and Housing Equity,' in O. S. Mitchell, Z. Bodie, P. B. Hammond, and S. Zeldes (eds), *Innovations in Retirement Financing*. Philadelphia: University of Pennsylvania Press, 254–81.

Chapter 3

Retirement Plans and Prospects for Retirement Income Adequacy

Jack VanDerhei

Policymakers, regulators, academics, and individual workers alike have long been focused on quantifying retirement security through the prism of retirement income adequacy, and for good reason. Beginning in the late 1990s, the Employee Benefit Research Institute (EBRI) launched a major project to provide this type of measurement on behalf of several states concerned about the potential cost(s) to social insurance programs should their residents lack sufficient income when they reached retirement age. After conducting studies for Oregon, Kansas, and Massachusetts, we developed a national model for this purpose in 2003—the EBRI Retirement Security Projection Model® (RSPM). It was updated in 2010 to incorporate several significant shifts in plan design and the financial markets, notably the impacts of defined benefit (DB) plan freezes, automatic enrollment provisions for 401(k) plans, and the crises in the financial and housing markets.[1] Since that time we have continued to update RSPM on an annual basis to incorporate the impact of changes in financial and real estate market conditions, as well as for underlying demographic trends and modifications in 401(k) participant behavior (based on a database of the actual account activity of some 24 million 401(k) participants).

The aggregate federal deficit number, taking into account current social security retirement benefit levels and the assumption that net housing equity is utilized 'as needed,' is currently estimated to be $4.1 trillion for all Baby Boomers and Gen Xers.[2] Yet while trillion-dollar deficits are useful in focusing attention on this problem, they do little to help policymakers understand exactly *where* these deficits are coming from—an appreciation that is key to evaluating and implementing effective remedies.

This chapter begins with a brief background on and an overview of the model. Results are then reviewed for the impact retirement plans have on prospects for retirement income adequacy. Baseline results for the probability of *not* running short of money in retirement (measured by the EBRI Retirement Readiness Ratings® (RRRs)) are presented, in combination with a sensitivity analysis to illustrate the impact of changing assumptions with respect to a series of variables, including rate of return, utilization of housing for financing retirement, and potential modifications to future social security retirement benefits. The next section focuses on how RRR varies with respect to longevity risks and the impact of potential long-term health care costs in retirement (e.g. nursing home costs). This is followed by an analysis of the years until households are projected to run short of money in retirement, and the size of the present value of accumulated deficits in retirement (measured by the Retirement Savings Shortfalls (RSS)). A final section offers a brief summary and conclusions.

Quantifying Retirement Income Adequacy

There are several ways to quantify retirement income adequacy. Most models either (1) account only for the accumulation side of the equation and then rely on some type of replacement rate measure as a threshold for success, or (2) make use of a life cycle model that attempts to smooth/spread some type of consumption-based utility over the decision-maker's lifetime.

The EBRI Retirement Security Projection Model® takes a different perspective. Our goal was to determine what percentage of future retirement cohorts would run short of money in retirement and when. Accordingly, the RSPM did not rely on a replacement rate target as a measure of success, because very few households annuitize all (or even most) of their individual accounts in retirement. In other words, a replacement rate focus would overlook the potential longevity risk. Moreover, while an annuity purchase price used in a replacement rate target does rely on an implicit assumption with respect to (at least some) future market returns, it does not typically account for the potential investment risk associated with 'risky' asset allocations. And finally, an obstacle in terms of maintaining retirement income adequacy for households who might otherwise have sufficient financial resources at retirement age is the risk of long-term care costs for a prolonged period. Few retirees have long-term care insurance policies that would cover the potentially catastrophic financial impact of this exposure. Consequently, any attempt to incorporate this into a simple replacement rate threshold needs to be carefully assessed against actual implications.

A life cycle smoothing model was also rejected for the development of RSPM given the extraordinary low levels of 'optimal' savings for low-income individuals at retirement. While there is little doubt that some households may benefit from means-tested programs in retirement (including early eligibility for Medicaid), from a policy perspective, we were interested in setting a threshold that would allow households to afford average expenditures throughout their retirement, while at the same time accounting for uninsured medical costs in retirement (including long-term care costs).

The EBRI Retirement Security Projection Model®

One objective of RSPM is to simulate the percentage of the population at risk of not having income adequate to cover average expenses and uninsured health care costs (including long-term care costs) throughout retirement, by income and age groups. RSPM also provides information on the distribution of the likely number of years before those at risk run short of money, as well as the percentage of preretirement compensation they would need as additional savings in order to have a 50, 75, or 90 percent probability of attaining retirement income adequacy.

VanDerhei and Copeland (2010) describe how households are tracked through retirement age and how their retirement income/wealth is simulated for the following components: social security, defined contribution (DC) balances, individual retirement account (IRA) balances, DB annuities and/or lump-sum distributions, and net housing equity.

A household is considered to run short of money in this model if aggregate resources in retirement are insufficient to meet average retirement expenditures. The latter are defined as a combination of deterministic expenses from the Consumer Expenditure Survey (as a function of age and income) and some health insurance and out-of-pocket, health-related expenses, plus stochastic expenses from nursing home and home health care (at least until the point such expenses are covered by Medicaid).[3]

The baseline version of our model assumes all workers retire at age 65,[4] that they immediately begin drawing benefits from social security and DB plans (if any), and, to the extent that the sum of their expenses and uninsured medical expenses exceed the projected, after-tax annual income from those sources, immediately begin to withdraw money from their individual accounts (DC and cash balance plans, as well as IRAs). If there is sufficient money to pay expenses without tapping into the tax-qualified individual accounts, those balances are assumed to be invested in a non-tax-advantaged account where the investment income is taxed as ordinary income. Individual accounts are tracked until they are depleted. At that point, any net housing equity is assumed to be added to retirement savings in the form of a lump-sum distribution (rather than a reverse annuity mortgage, or RAM). When all retirement savings are exhausted and if the social security and DB payments are insufficient to pay expenses, the individual is designated as having run short of money.

One of the model's primary outputs is the production of RRRs for various subgroups of the population. The RRR is defined as the percentage of simulated life-paths that do *not* run short of money in retirement.

Results

Our model focuses on four output metrics for retirement income adequacy:[5] Retirement Readiness Ratings; years until the household runs short of money in retirement; Retirement Savings Shortfalls; and the percentage of additional compensation that must be saved annually until retirement for a 50, 75, or 90 percent chance of covering simulated expenses. These metrics have been used to analyze the impact of retirement plans on prospects for retirement income adequacy under several scenarios, including those that follow.

Annuitizing DC and IRA balances at retirement age

VanDerhei and Copeland (2004) analyzed the impact of annuitizing DC and IRA balances at retirement age and therefore needed to simulate a significant number of future life-paths to capture the longevity risk experienced by retirees. The output metric used was the median percentage of additional compensation that must be saved annually until retirement for a 75 percent chance of covering simulated expenses. Assuming that all DB participants took lump-sum distributions at retirement, the average annual increase in additional savings needed was 14.9 percent, whereas assuming that all individual accounts were annuitized at retirement had an impact twice as large—but in the opposite direction (a 30.0 percent decrease in additional annual savings needed).

Impact of deferring retirement age

VanDerhei and Copeland (2011) added a new feature that allowed households to defer retirement age past age 65, to determine whether retirement age deferral is indeed sufficiently valuable to mitigate retirement income adequacy problems for most households.[6] The answer, unfortunately, is not always 'yes,' even if retirement age were deferred into the 80s. RSPM baseline results indicate that the lowest pre-retirement income quartile would need to defer retirement age to 84, before 90 percent of the households would have a 50 percent probability of success. Although a significant portion of the improvement takes place in the first four years after age 65, it tends to level off in the early 70s before picking up in the late 70s and early 80s. Households in higher pre-retirement income quartiles start at a much higher level, and therefore gain less from deferring retirement. If the success rate is moved to a threshold of 70 percent, only two out of five households in the lowest-income quartile would attain retirement income adequacy even if they deferred retirement age to 84. Increasing the threshold to 80 percent reduces the number of lowest pre-retirement income quartile households satisfying this standard at a retirement age of 84 to approximately one out of seven. A factor that makes a major difference in the percentage of households satisfying the retirement income adequacy thresholds at any retirement age is whether the worker is still participating in a DC plan after age 65. Doing so results in at least a 10 percentage point difference in the majority of the retirement age/income combinations investigated.[7]

Impact of the low interest rate environment

VanDerhei (2013b) also used RSPM to show that 25–7 percent of Baby Boomers and Gen Xers who would have had adequate retirement income (under historical average return assumptions) were simulated to end up running short of money in retirement, if the historically low interest rates at the time were assumed to be permanent.

Retirement Readiness Ratings

A notable finding of our modelling was the significant importance of stochastic health care costs on overall retirement income adequacy (VanDerhei 2012a). This term is meant to include health care costs in retirement that are not likely to occur every year (in fact they may never occur for many households), but when they do, they may have a catastrophic financial impact due to their daily cost and/or duration. Unlike many other retirement projection models,[8] RSPM has explicitly included the costs of nursing home and home health care costs in its decumulation model to account for these contingencies. We show the potential impact of ignoring these costs on measurements of retirement income adequacy.

Baseline results

Our baseline scenario labels households with sufficient resources to cover 100 percent of simulated retirement expenses as those who do *not* run short of money in retirement. Yet some retirement planners suggest that many households can successfully cut expenditures when financially constrained. Therefore, we also recompute results for thresholds of two other simulated expense levels.

Panel A of Table 3.1 provides the ratings by age cohort computed at three different income adequacy thresholds: 100, 90, and 80 percent of simulated retirement expenses. It also provides RRR values for two different scenarios: one where stochastic health care costs (i.e. long-term care and home health

TABLE 3.1 2014 Retirement Readiness Ratings™ with and without long-term care (LTC) and home health costs (HHC)

	% of simulated retirement expenses		
	100	90	80
Panel A: by age cohort			
Early Boomers			
With LTC and HHC	56.7	67.4	82
Without LTC and HHC	71.94	79.43	88.27
Late Boomers			
With LTC and HHC	57.7	67.4	81
Without LTC and HHC	75.61	81.42	88.94
Gen Xers			
With LTC and HHC	58.5	69.8	83.7
Without LTC and HHC	79.03	87.17	95.87
Panel B: by pre-retirement income quartile			
Lowest income quartile			
With LTC and HHC	16.8	30	54.6
Without LTC and HHC	29.97	44.25	69.66
Second			
With LTC and HHC	52.6	65.7	0.827
Without LTC and HHC	79.93	90.54	0.9663
Third			
With LTC and HHC	71.7	81.9	92.7
Without LTC and HHC	93.64	97.52	99.23
Highest income quartile			
With LTC and HHC	86.4	92.9	97.9
Without LTC and HHC	98.73	99.58	99.87
Panel C: by future years of eligibility for a defined contribution plan			
None			
With LTC and HHC	39.67	50.58	69.09
Without LTC and HHC	62.16	70.84	84.31
1–9			
With LTC and HHC	60.63	70.93	83.96
Without LTC and HHC	86.33	91.64	96.78
10–19			
With LTC and HHC	73.15	81.74	91.32
Without LTC and HHC	92.04	95.58	98.4
20+			
With LTC and HHC	85.48	91.56	96.83
Without LTC and HHC	97.91	98.94	99.64

Notes: Percentage of simulated life paths that will not run short of money in retirement at various thresholds. Early Boomers refer to those born 1948–54. Late Boomers refer to those born 1955–64. Gen Xers refer to those born 1965–74.

Source: Author's computations.

costs) are included, and those in which they are excluded. More than half of the Early Boomers (56.7 percent) are projected to have sufficient retirement resources to cover 100 percent of their simulated expenses in retirement (including long-term care and home health costs). This value increases to more than two-thirds (67.4 percent) if only 90 percent of the simulated expenses need to be covered, and to 82.0 percent if the threshold is decreased to 80 percent of simulated expenses. By contrast, when the Early Boomers' life-paths are simulated assuming no long-term care and home health costs, the RRRs increase substantially (this is the implicit assumption of models that do not take these expenses into account). Now 71.9 percent will not run short of money at a threshold of 100 percent of simulated expenses, rising to 79.4 percent at a 90 percent of simulated expense threshold, and 88.3 percent at an 80 percent expense threshold.

Looking across cohorts, readiness rates for Late Boomer and Gen Xers are very similar to those for Early Boomers when long-term care and home health costs are included.[9] For the younger cohorts, when these costs are omitted, the RRR values show a definite upward trend in the fraction projected to have sufficient financial resources.

Panel B in Table 3.1 provides readiness rates by pre-retirement wage quartiles at the three different thresholds, for both health care cost scenarios.[10] Unlike Panel A, Panel B indicates large disparities between the various categories analyzed. At a 100-percent simulated expense threshold for the scenario that includes long-term care and home health costs, only 16.8 percent of the simulated life-paths for those in the lowest-income quartile have retirement resources sufficient to prevent them from running short of money in retirement. More than three times as many (52.6 percent) of those in the second-income quartile are projected to have sufficient resources, compared to 71.7 percent for those in the third-income quartile. The maximum value is of 86.4 percent for the highest-income quartile. Some of this disparity declines if the thresholds are relaxed. At an 80 percent of simulated expense threshold, more than half (54.6 percent) of the lowest income quartile are now projected to not run short of money in retirement. This value increases to 82.7 percent for the second quartile, 92.7 percent for the third quartile, and 97.9 percent for the highest income quartile.

Panel C of Table 3.1 shows the positive impact of *future* years of eligibility for a DC plan (regardless of whether the employee chooses to participate) for Gen Xers by pre-retirement wage quartile.[11] Again, all three thresholds are shown for both scenarios with respect to long-term care and home health costs. For Gen Xers with no future eligibility for a DC plan, the RRR value is only 39.7 percent, suggesting that more than 60 percent would run short of resources in retirement. This value increases more than 20 percentage points to 60.6 percent projected to not run short for those with 1–9 future years of eligibility in a DC plan, and to 73.2 percent of those in this category with 10–19 future years of eligibility in a DC plan. For those with 20 or more future years of eligibility in a DC plan, 85.5 percent are projected to not run short.

Similar results are found for Gen Xers at the other expense thresholds. For example, at an 80 percent of simulated expense threshold, the RRR values range from 69.1 percent for those with no future years of eligibility to 96.8 percent for those with 20 or more years.

Sensitivity analysis

A model as complex as RSPM relies on a large number of assumptions to simulate the financial circumstances of households over their life cycles, to determine if and when they will ultimately run short in retirement. Some of the most important include rates of return in the financial market; how net housing equity is used to finance retirement; and future benefit streams from social security. This section summarizes the impacts of these three assumptions (VanDerhei 2014). In each case, the sensitivity analysis assumes a threshold of 100 percent of simulated expenses, and long-term care and home health costs are included.

Rate of return assumptions

The baseline rate of return used in the 2014 RSPM was generated from stochastic annual returns with a log-normal distribution and an arithmetic mean of 8.6 percent real return for stocks and 2.6 percent real return for bonds (Finke et al. 2013). Net returns were computed by subtracting 78 basis points from gross returns.[12] Although these parameters were based on historical evidence from 1926–2011 (the most recent results available the last time the baseline return assumptions were reset), some may question whether they are too optimistic for today's Baby Boomers and Gen Xers. Therefore, various ad-hoc reductions (10, 25, and 50 percent) in real returns for both stocks and bonds are also applied, to measure their impact on RRR outcomes.

The RRR for the baseline return assumptions for Early Boomers is 56.7 percent, indicating that just over half of the cohort is projected to have sufficient funds in retirement to cover the expenses outlined. If real returns are decreased by 10 percent (0.86 percent for stocks and 0.26 percent for bonds), the RRR value falls by 1.5 percentage points to 55.2 percent. Decreasing projected real returns by 25 percent results in a reduction to 53.3 percent, while decreasing real returns by 50 percent results in a 6.6 percentage point reduction from the baseline assumptions to 50.1 percent. Similar results obtain for the Late Boomers and Gen Xers, though given their somewhat longer average investment horizons, one would expect somewhat larger impacts on their RRRs. Indeed, the difference between the baseline RRR results and those with the 50 percent lower returns increases from 6.6 percentage points for the Early Boomers to 6.8 percentage points for the Late Boomers and 7.8 percentage points for the Gen Xers.

When we explore the impact of return assumptions on the lowest preretirement wage quartile, we find a minimal impact, which is to be expected given their relatively low DC and IRA balances. The difference between the baseline RRR results and those with the 50 percent real return reduction for this group is only 0.2 percentage points. This range increases to 5.0 percentage points for the second-income quartile and 6.5 percentage points for the third-income quartile before falling to 4.6 percentage points for the highest-income quartile.[13]

Housing utilization assumptions

In our baseline model, net housing equity is assumed to be accessible as a lump sum when needed. This produces an RRR value of 56.7 percent for Early Boomers. If net housing equity is instead assumed to be annuitized at retirement, the percent of individuals projected to have sufficient financial resources in retirement decreases to 52.6 percent. If net housing equity is not used at all for retirement, the RRR drops to 50.4 percent. Similar results obtain for Late Boomers and Gen Xers.

Modifications in social security retirement benefits

Our baseline RSPM runs assume that future social security retirement benefits under current law will not be modified. Nevertheless, the current Social Security Trustee's Report projects that the funds for Old-Age, Survivors, and Disability Insurance (OASDI) will be exhausted by 2033 (US SSA 2013). This may require benefit reductions for at least some cohorts of retirees. To assess the potential impact of such a change, pro-rata reductions are applied to social security retirement benefits for the sensitivity analysis, and aggregate shortfalls are converted into a pro-rata reduction for all retirees on an annual basis. This would result in a reduction in social security retirement benefits of 21.9 percent in 2033 and would eventually reach a level of 27.0 percent in 2090.[14]

Our simulations show this would have only a minimal impact on the Early Boomers, decreasing RRR from 56.7 percent to 56.0 percent. But those in the Late Boomer cohort would be more affected, reducing the RRR by 2.2 percentage points (from 58.5 to 56.3 percent). The reductions would affect the Gen Xers for a larger portion of their retirement years, and consequently their RRR would decrease by 6.8 percentage points (from 57.5 to 50.9 percent).

Given the progressive nature of the social security benefit formula, the lowest-income quartile would experience the largest impact, with an RRR reduction of 10.6 percentage points; the value drops by more than half, from 20.9 to 10.3 percent. The impact is smaller for their higher-paid counterparts, for whom social security benefits generally comprise a smaller proportion of post-retirement income. The second-income quartile experiences an RRR reduction of 8.0 percentage points, compared with 5.8 percentage points for the third-income quartile and only 3.5 percentage points for the highest-income quartile.

What drives Retirement Readiness Ratings?

We have also analyzed the replacement-rate levels required to provide retirees with a 50, 75, and 90 percent probability of having 'sufficient' retirement income (VanDerhei 2006, 2014). A 'building block' approach was adopted where the risks of investment, longevity, and stochastic long-term health care costs were added in incremental layers.[15] In each case, the analysis was conducted assuming a threshold of 100 percent of simulated expenses and that long-term care and home health costs were included.

Longevity

To assess the impact of longevity on retirement income adequacy, we compute longevity quartiles by family status, gender, and age cohort. We find that the RRR (75.8 percent) for the Early Boomers simulated to die in the earliest relative quartile is 19.1 percentage points above the overall average for this age cohort, suggesting that those who die earliest have a better likelihood of not running short. The RRR decreases to 63.1 percent in the second-longevity quartile and 44.9 percent in the third-longevity quartile. For the Early Boomer cohort with the longest relative longevity, the RRR falls all the way to 37.9 percent. Similar patterns are found for younger age cohorts, but there is a noticeable increase in the RRR range between the earliest and latest longevity quartile: 37.9 percentage points for Early Boomers, 41.3 percentage points for Late Boomers, and 49.2 percentage points for Gen Xers.

Stochastic long-term health care costs

To analyze healthcare costs, we arrange our simulated paths into four groups from lowest to highest (based on the present value at age 65 per capita stochastic health care costs in 2014 dollars). Early Boomers in the bottom quartile of the health care cost distribution have a RRR of 73.4 percent (meaning that nearly three-quarters of this group will have sufficient funds), while the RRR for those in the top cost quartile—those with highest projected health care costs—drops to 22.9 percent (for a difference of 50.5 percentage points). The younger age cohorts experience similar results, with a somewhat larger range (52.4 percentage points for the Late Boomers and 58.7 percentage points for the Gen Xers).

The probability of not running short of money in retirement is virtually zero for the lowest-income quartile with the highest health care costs.[16] Those in the lowest-income quartile with the lowest health care costs have a much higher probability of having enough money, with an RRR value of 30.0 percent. The second-income quartile has the largest range in RRR values between the lowest and highest quartile of stochastic health care costs (77.1 percentage points), followed by the third-income quartile (66.9 percentage points). The range for the highest-income quartile (40 percentage points) is somewhat larger than the lowest-income quartile (29.9 percentage points); however, the range for both is truncated by the definitional limits of the RRR calculation.

Regression results for retirement readiness ratings

The previous sections analyzed one by one the important ways that Boomer and Gen Xer households are projected to run short of money in retirement. Next we analyze these factors as a group using multivariate regression. Table 3.2 provides six different sets of probit estimates of the probability of running short of money in retirement: using three thresholds each for single and married households. In each case, the scenario includes the costs of long-term care and home health costs.

The top panel in Table 3.2 uses a dependent variable equal to zero if the household does not run short of money in retirement at a 100 percent of simulated expense threshold, or equal to one if it does. The second panel uses a similar definition at a 90 percent threshold, while the third panel uses an 80 percent threshold.

The variables used in this analysis are defined as follows:

- The INCOME variables are dummy variables placing each household into age-specific income quartiles based on indexed career earnings similar to those used in the Average Indexed Monthly Earnings (AIME) calculations (without truncation at the upper end). INCOME2 designates the second income quartile, INCOME3 the third income quartile and INCOME4 the highest income quartile (INCOME1 designating the lowest income quartile is the omitted reference category).
- SINGLEMALE = 1 for males and 0 for females.

TABLE 3.2 Probit estimates of the probability of running short of money in retirement

Single males and single females				Married households			
Parameter	Estimate	St. Error		Parameter	Estimate	St. Error	
Intercept	−2.251	0.002	***	Intercept	−1.062	0.006	***
AGE	18.201	0.021	***	AGE	11.429	0.055	***
INCOME2	−1.248	0.000	***	INCOME2	−1.050	0.002	***
INCOME3	−1.989	0.000	***	INCOME3	−1.849	0.002	***
INCOME4	−2.663	0.001	***	INCOME4	−2.821	0.002	***
SINGLEMALE	−0.408	0.000	***	ELIGIBLE	−0.017	0.000	***
ELIGIBLE	−0.348	0.000	***	DEATHAGE	12.857	0.067	***
DEATHAGE	26.354	0.024	***	LTC	3.959	0.003	***
LTC	3.440	0.001	***				
Parameter	Estimate	St. Error		Parameter	Estimate	St. Error	
Intercept	−1.503	0.002	***	Intercept	−0.649	0.007	***
AGE	16.310	0.021	***	AGE	8.369	0.063	***
INCOME2	−1.115	0.000	***	INCOME2	−0.941	0.002	***
INCOME3	−1.840	0.000	***	INCOME3	−1.644	0.001	***
INCOME4	−2.513	0.001	***	INCOME4	−2.592	0.001	***
SINGLEMALE	−0.460	0.000	***	ELIGIBLE	−0.028	0.000	***
ELIGIBLE	−0.362	0.000	***	DEATHAGE	2.020	0.078	***
DEATHAGE	11.111	0.024	***	LTC	3.751	0.003	***
LTC	3.604	0.001	***				
Parameter	Estimate	St. Error		Parameter	Estimate	St. Error	
Intercept	0.054	0.002	***	Intercept	0.605	0.010	***
AGE	14.055	0.022	***	AGE	9.826	0.091	***
INCOME2	−0.912	0.000	***	INCOME2	−0.997	0.002	***
INCOME3	−1.566	0.001	***	INCOME3	−1.527	0.002	***
INCOME4	−2.237	0.001	***	INCOME4	−2.371	0.002	***
SINGLEMALE	−0.431	0.000	***	ELIGIBLE	−0.012	0.001	***
ELIGIBLE	−0.357	0.000	***	DEATHAGE	−24.771	0.116	***
DEATHAGE	−17.087	0.027	***	LTC	3.656	0.004	***
LTC	3.513	0.001	***				

* significant at 10% level; ** significant at 5% level; *** significant at 1%. See text for variable definitions.

Sources: Author's computations.

- The ELIGIBLE variable denotes the percentage of future years of work with an employer offering a DC plan.
- DEATHAGE = the age of death (second death in the case of families).
- LTC = the present value of long-term care and home health care costs (in thousands of 2014 dollars).
- The AGE variable is the current age of the individual (older of the two individuals for married).

In each of the six regressions, the AGE variable has a positive effect, suggesting that older cohorts will actually have a higher probability of running short of money in retirement. The INCOME variables designate the probability of running short of money in retirement relative to the lowest income quartile. In each of the six regressions, the coefficients are monotonically decreasing, which indicates that the higher the relative income level, the lower the probability of running short of money in retirement.

The ELIGIBLE variable is negative in each of the six regressions, suggesting that, all else equal, the more future years a household is eligible for participation in a DC plan (relative to the number of future years they work prior to retirement), the smaller their probability of running short. The LTC variable is positive in all six regressions, which suggests that the larger the present value of long-term care and home health costs (in constant dollars), the higher the probability of running short.

The SINGLEMALE variable is negative in each of the three regressions it was used. This suggests that, compared to single females, men have a smaller probability of running short of money in retirement after controlling for the other factors.

The DEATHAGE variable (designating the age of simulated death) is the only variable whose sign changes as the thresholds vary. For the 100 and 90 percent thresholds, the coefficient is always positive, suggesting that the longer a household lives, the larger the probability that it will run short of money in retirement. By contrast, when the threshold of simulated expenses is lowered to the 80 percent level, the sign changes, indicating an opposite result.[17]

Years Until the Households Run Short of Money in Retirement

We are also interested in when shortfalls might occur, if they do. Figures 3.1 through 3.3 provide this type of information for the Boomer and Gen Xer demographics. The analysis is more complicated than a simple computation of when individuals or families run short of *retirement income* (which in most cases will be never, due to lifetime social security benefits). As noted above, an individual or family is considered to 'run short of money' here if the household's aggregate retirement resources are insufficient to meet its aggregate average retirement expenditures goal. This is defined as a combination of deterministic expenses from the Consumer Expenditure Survey (as a function of income) and some health insurance and out-of-pocket health-related expenses, plus stochastic expenses from nursing home and home health care expenses (at least until the point they are picked up by

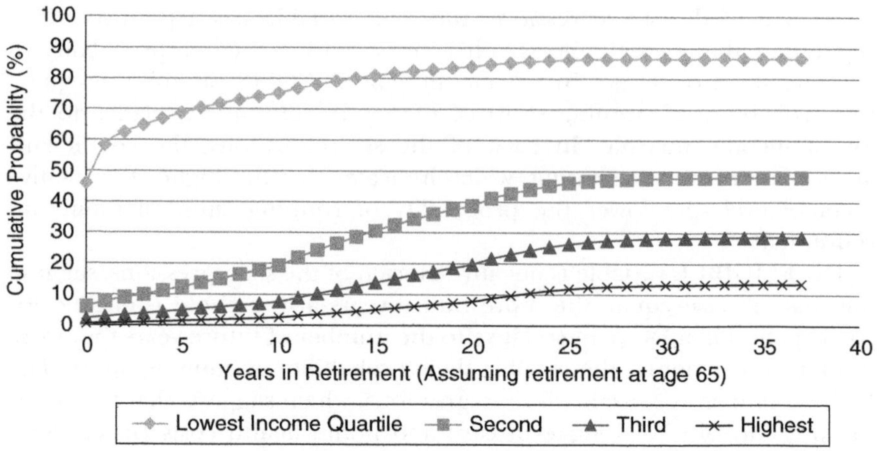

Figure 3.1 Years in retirement before Boomers and Gen Xers run short of money, by pre-retirement income quartile: simulations with the 2014 version of the EBRI Retirement Security Projection Model®

Note: An individual or family is considered to run short of money in this version of the model if their aggregate resources in retirement are not sufficient to meet aggregate minimum retirement expenditures defined as a combination of deterministic expenses from the Consumer Expenditure Survey (as a function of income) and some health insurance and out-of-pocket health-related expenses, plus stochastic expenses from nursing home and home health care expenses (at least until the point they are picked up by Medicaid). The resources in retirement will consist of Social Security, account balances from defined contribution plans, IRAs and/or cash balance plans, annuities from defined benefit plans (unless the lump-sum distribution scenario is chosen), and (in some cases) net housing equity (in the form of a lump-sum distribution).

Source: Author's computations.

Medicaid). In each case, the analysis is conducted assuming a threshold of 100 percent of simulated expenses, and long-term care and home health costs are included.

Figure 3.1 shows the distribution of how long retirement money will last for Baby Boomers and Gen Xers (assuming retirement at age 65), by pre-retirement income quartile. For example, after 10 years of retirement, three-quarters of those in the lowest income quartile are projected to have run short of money, 19 percent in the second income quartile, 8 percent in the third income quartile, and 2 percent in the highest income quartile. After 20 years of retirement, 84 percent of those in the lowest income quartile are projected to have run short of money, 39 percent in the second income quartile, 20 percent in the third income quartile, and 8 percent in the highest income quartile. A total of 87 percent of those in the lowest income quartile who retire at age 65 are projected to eventually run short of

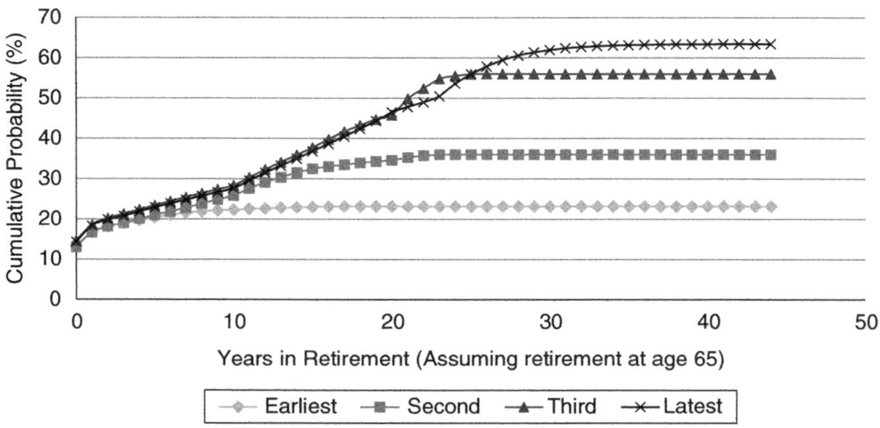

Figure 3.2 Years in retirement before Boomers and Gen Xers run short of money, by relative longevity quartile: simulations with the 2014 version of the EBRI Retirement Security Projection Model®

Note: An individual or family is considered to run short of money in this version of the model if their aggregate resources in retirement are not sufficient to meet aggregate minimum retirement expenditures defined as a combination of deterministic expenses from the Consumer Expenditure Survey (as a function of income) and some health insurance and out-of-pocket health-related expenses, plus stochastic expenses from nursing home and home health care expenses (at least until the point they are picked up by Medicaid). The resources in retirement will consist of Social Security, account balances from defined contribution plans, IRAs and/or cash balance plans, annuities from defined benefit plans (unless the lump-sum distribution scenario is chosen), and (in some cases) net housing equity (in the form of a lump-sum distribution).

Source: Author's computations.

money while they are still alive. This value decreases to 48 percent for those in the second income quartile, 29 percent for those in the third income quartile, and 14 percent for those in the highest income quartile.

Figure 3.2 shows the distribution of how long retirement money will last for Baby Boomers and Gen Xers (assuming retirement at age 65) by relative longevity quartile. For example, after 10 years of retirement, 22 percent of those in the earliest longevity quartile class are projected to run short of money compared to 28 percent of those in the latest longevity quartile. After 20 years of retirement, 23 percent of those in the earliest longevity quartile class are projected to have run short of money compared to 46 percent of those in the latest longevity quartile. A total of 23 percent of those in the earliest longevity quartile class who retire at age 65 are projected to eventually run short of money while they are still alive. This value increases to 63 percent for those in the oldest longevity quartile.

Figure 3.3 shows the distribution of how long retirement money is projected to last for Baby Boomers and Gen Xers (assuming retirement at age

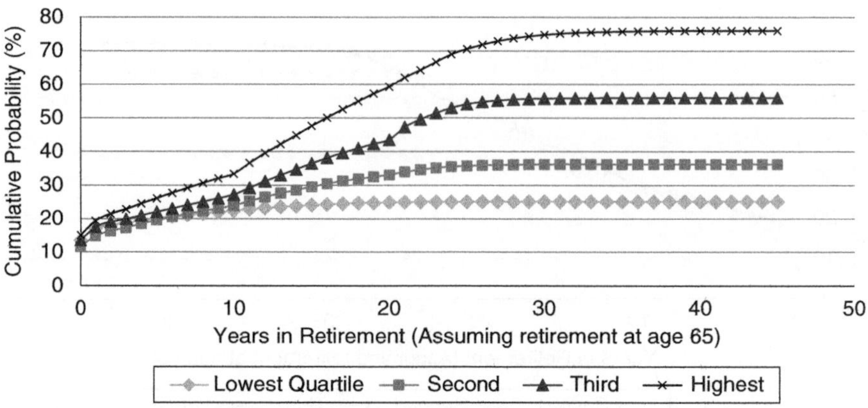

Figure 3.3 Years in retirement before Boomers and Gen Xers run short of money, by quartile of stochastic health care cost: simulations with the 2014 version of the EBRI Retirement Security Projection Model®

Note: An individual or family is considered to run short of money in this version of the model if their aggregate resources in retirement are not sufficient to meet aggregate minimum retirement expenditures defined as a combination of deterministic expenses from the Consumer Expenditure Survey (as a function of income) and some health insurance and out-of-pocket health-related expenses, plus stochastic expenses from nursing home and home health care expenses (at least until the point they are picked up by Medicaid). The resources in retirement will consist of Social Security, account balances from defined contribution plans, IRAs and/or cash balance plans, annuities from defined benefit plans (unless the lump-sum distribution scenario is chosen), and (in some cases) net housing equity (in the form of a lump-sum distribution).

Source: Author's computations.

65) by quartile of health care cost. For example: after 10 years of retirement, 22 percent of those in the lowest health care cost quartile are projected to run short of money compared to 33 percent of those in the highest health care cost quartile. After 20 years of retirement, 25 percent of those in the lowest health care cost quartile are projected to have run short of money compared to 59 percent of those in the highest health care cost quartile. A total of 25 percent of those in the lowest health care cost quartile who retire at age 65 are projected to eventually run short of money while they are still alive. This value increases to 76 percent for those in the highest health care cost quartile.

Retirement Savings Shortfalls

It is also useful to model just how large the accumulated deficits are likely to be, conditional on a shortfall. We analyze this assuming a threshold of

TABLE 3.3 2014 retirement savings shortfalls (US$) by age cohort, marital status, and gender

	Single Male	Single Female	Married
Panel A: includes those with no shortfall			
Early Boomers	33,778	62,734	19,304
Late Boomers	31,342	65,277	19,566
Gen Xers	38,065	74,256	21,379
Panel B:conditional upon having a positive shortfall			
Early Boomers	93,576	104,821	71,299
Late Boomers	102,287	112,651	76,222
Gen Xers	129,861	133,790	82,083

Note: The Retirement Savings Shortfalls (RSS) are determined as a present value of retirement deficits at age 65.

Source: Author's computations.

100 percent of simulated expenses, and including long-term care and home health costs.

Panel A of Table 3.3 shows the shortfalls by cohort, marital status, and sex, for both Baby Boomers and Gen Xers. We provide information on average individual retirement income deficits as present values at age 65, and we represent how much extra would have to be saved by age 65, to eliminate expected retirement deficits (which, depending on the simulated life-path, could be a relatively short period or could last decades). The additional savings required for those on the verge of retirement (Early Boomers) vary from $19,304 (per individual) for married households, increasing to $33,778 for single males and $62,733 for single females. Even though the present values are defined in constant dollars, the RSS for both genders increase for younger cohorts, mainly due to the assumption that health care-related costs will increase faster than the general inflation rate.

While the RSS values in Panel A of Table 3.3 may appear to be relatively small, considering they represent the sum of present values that may include decades of deficits, it is important to remember that less than half of the simulated life-paths modeled were considered to be 'at risk.' In other words, the average RSS values represented in Panel A of Table 3.3 are reduced by the inclusion of simulated retirement life-paths that will not run short of money. Looking only at those situations where shortfalls are projected, Panel B of Table 3.3 shows that the values for Early Boomers vary from $71,299 (per individual) for married households, $93,576 for single males, and $104,821 for single females. In sum, the average shortfall is large if we focus only on households with a projected shortfall.

As noted above, eligibility for participation in a DC plan can have a significantly positive impact on reducing projected savings shortfalls.

TABLE 3.4 2014 unconditional retirement savings shortfalls (US$), by years of future eligibility for participation in a defined contribution plan

	Income Quartiles				
Years of Future Eligibility	Lowest	Second	Third	Highest	Total
0	107,519	74,901	57,179	32,466	78,297
1–9	100,326	73,550	44,821	24,058	52,113
10–19	85,647	49,132	22,201	8,380	32,937
20+	88,857	34,539	13,310	4,751	16,782

Note: The Retirement Savings Shortfalls (RSS) are determined as a present value of retirement deficits at age 65.

Source: Author's computations.

Table 3.4 provides information on the average individual retirement income deficits by the number of future years eligible for coverage in a DC retirement plan for Gen Xers. The deficit values for those assumed to have no future years of eligibility (simulated to never be employed in the future by an organization that provides access to those plans) is $78,297 per individual. That shortfall decreases substantially for those with 1–9 years of future eligibility, to $52,113, and even further to $32,937 for those with 10–19 years of future eligibility. Gen Xers fortunate enough to have at least 20 years of future eligibility in those programs could find their average shortfall at retirement reduced to only $16,782.

Table 3.4 also provides similar information about the impact of future eligibility for DC plans for Gen Xers, although this time the analysis also controls for relative levels of pre-retirement income. For those in the lowest-income quartile, the average deficit declines from $107,519 for those with no years of future eligibility to $88,857 for those with 20 or more years. A similar reduction is found for the higher-income quartiles.

Conclusion

Will Americans have enough to live on in retirement? We address this question using a variety of 'success' thresholds and circumstances for the Baby Boomer and Gen Xer generations, most of whom have not yet retired, and for whom changes in behavior and/or policy might still positively influence outcomes.

As outlined, the results are sensitive to assumptions, thresholds, and definitions. If one assumes that 100 percent of simulated expenses in retirement is an adequate income goal, then in aggregate, between 57 and 59 percent of the simulated retirement paths for households in those age cohorts will not run short of money in retirement. Choosing a less restrictive threshold increases the percentage of households found to have adequate retirement income: at 90 percent of simulated retirement expenses, between 67 and 70 percent of the households will not run short of money in retirement, and at 80 percent of simulated expenses level, the values increase to 81–84 percent. If one chooses (explicitly, or as many models do today, implicitly) to ignore nursing home and home health costs in retirement, the percentages of households deemed to have adequate retirement income increases even further.

Sensitivity analysis shows that the RRR values are relatively robust with respect to return assumptions. Even with a 50 percent reduction in historical real returns, RRR values only decrease 6.6–7.8 percentage points on average, depending on the age cohort, suggesting a relatively modest impact on retirement readiness by market returns. Assumptions on how housing values are used to finance retirement are more important; yet, on average, the difference between utilizing the net housing equity as a lump sum once other retirement resources are depleted versus not utilizing it at all changes the RRR values by only 4.4–6.3 percentage points, depending on the age cohort.

While it is widely accepted that employment-based retirement plans have played a significant role in providing retirement income to American workers, this chapter also quantifies the impact these programs have in the determination of retirement income adequacy.[18] Analyzing the importance of eligibility for and participation in DC plans is difficult, in view of the various employee behaviors that must be modeled to account for participation, contribution, and asset allocation choices, as well as cash-out versus rollover activity at job change. It is also critically important to accurately portray the variation in plan design among DC plans. This chapter shows that one of the most important factors in determining whether Gen Xers (those with the longest remaining time in the workforce) will have sufficient retirement income is eligibility for participation in an employment-based DC plan. RRR values double for Gen Xers in the lowest-income quartile, when comparing those with 20 or more years of future eligibility to those with no years of future eligibility, while those in the second- and third-income quartiles experience increases in RRR values by 27–30.3 percentage points. Unfortunately not all households are covered by retirement plans for a substantial portion of their working careers.[19] As a result, many households, especially those in the lower income quartiles, appear to be in danger of running short of money in retirement.

For those projected to run short of money in retirement, how rapidly will the shortfall occur? We show that 26 percent of Boomer and Gen Xer households are simulated to run short of money within 10 years of retirement under our baseline assumptions (and at a 100 percent of simulated expense threshold). This increases to 37 percent after 20 years. The timing also depends on income; for the lowest income quartile, 75 percent are found to run short of money within 10 years of retirement, and 84 percent within 20 years.

Another way to quantify the shortfalls for those simulated to run short of money in retirement is to compute the present value of all future deficits as of retirement age. In essence, this is the additional amount of money each household would need to have (on an after-tax basis) to avoid running short of money in retirement. Looking only at cases where shortfalls are projected, the values for Early Boomers vary from $71,299 (per individual) for married households, increasing to $93,576 for single males and $104,821 for single females. These values are larger for younger cohorts. For Gen Xers, the values vary from $82,083 (per individual) for married households, increasing to $129,861 for single males, and $133,790 for single females.[20]

Finally, we have shown that a great deal of the readiness variability can be reduced by risk-management techniques at or near retirement. For example, annuitizing a portion of DC and IRA balances could increase the probability of not running short of money in retirement (VanDerhei 2006; Park 2011). Moreover, affordable long-term care insurance would appear to provide an extremely useful technique to help control the threat of health care cost risk, especially for those in the second- and third-income quartiles.

End notes

1. A brief chronology of RSPM is provided in Appendix A of VanDerhei (2014).
2. This is a decrease from the 2012 number of $4.3 trillion (VanDerhei 2012*b*). The 2012 number is somewhat smaller than the $4.6 trillion reported in VanDerhei (2010); however, the baseline assumptions used in the 2010 analysis did not provide for the utilization of net housing equity to ensure retirement income adequacy. When the 2012 analysis is repeated with the same assumptions as used in 2010, the aggregate deficit actually increased to $4.8 trillion.
3. The stochastic component of health expenditures is the result of simulated health events that would require long-term care in a nursing home or home-based setting for the elderly. Neither of these simulated types of care would be reimbursed by Medicare, because they would be for custodial (rather than rehabilitative) care. To determine whether an individual has these expenses, the following process is undertaken. Each individual reaching the social security normal retirement age has a probability of being in one of four possible assumed 'health' statuses: (1) not receiving either home health or nursing home care; (2) home health care patient; (3) nursing home care patient; (4) dead. The individual is randomly assigned to one of these four categories with a likelihood based upon the estimated probabilities of each event. If the individual does not need long-term care, no stochastic expenses are incurred. Each year, the individual again

faces these probabilities (the probabilities of being in the different statuses changes as the individual becomes older after reaching age 75, then again at age 85). This continues until death or the need for long-term care. For those who have a resulting status of home health care or nursing home care, their duration of care is simulated based upon the distribution of the durations of care. After a nursing home stay or episode of home health care, each individual has a probability of being discharged to one of the other three states based upon the discharge estimates. The stochastic expenses incurred are then determined by the length of the stay/number of days of care times the per diem charge estimated for the nursing home care and home health care, respectively. For any person without the need for long-term care, this process repeats annually. The process repeats for individuals receiving home health care or nursing home care at the end of their duration of stay/care and subsequently, if not receiving the specialized care again on their next birthdays. Those simulated to die, of course, are not further simulated. As with the basic health care expenses, the qualification of Medicaid by income and asset levels is considered to see how much of the stochastic expenses must be covered by the individual to determine his final expenditures for the care. Only those expenditures attributable to the individual—not the Medicaid program—are considered as expenses to the individual and included the 'deficit' calculations.

4. See VanDerhei and Copeland (2011) and VanDerhei (2012*a*) for an analysis of the impact of increasing retirement ages beyond 65.
5. EBRI's use of RSPM typically is confined to analysis of the current retirement system. However, it has periodically been used to evaluate potential changes to the system, primarily from proposed legislative changes. VanDerhei (2011*d*), RSPM was used to provide preliminary evidence of the impact of the '20/20 caps' on projected retirement accumulations proposed by the National Commission on Fiscal Responsibility and Reform. Later that year, it was used to support testimony before the Senate Finance Committee (VanDerhei 2011*b*) in analyzing the potential impact of various types of tax-reform options on retirement income. This was expanded in VanDerhei (2011*a*). VanDerhei (2012*c*) used new survey results to update the analysis of the potential impact of various types of tax-reform options on retirement income, and VanDerhei (2013*a*) used RSPM to analyze the Obama administration's fiscal year (FY) 2014 budget proposal to include a cap on tax-deferred retirement savings that would limit the amounts accumulated in specified retirement accounts to that necessary to provide the maximum annuity permitted for a tax-qualified defined benefit plan under current law.
6. This assumes that the worker is physically able to keep working and that there continues to be a suitable demand for his or her skills.
7. VanDerhei (2012*a*) provided additional evidence on whether deferring retirement to age 70 would provide retirement income adequacy for the vast majority of Baby Boomers and Gen Xers.

8. Many other models either ignore these costs or use deterministic adjustments to replacement rates. However, Bajtelsmit et al. (2013) also use Monte Carlo simulation to simultaneously model stochastic financial, health, long-term care, and life risks.
9. For purposes of this analysis the age cohorts are defined as:
   - Early Boomers (born 1948–54);
   - Late Boomers (born 1955–64);
   - Gen Xers (born 1965–74).
10. Pre-retirement income in RSPM is determined in a manner similar to the average-indexed-monthly-earnings computation for social security with three modifications. All earned income is included up to the age of retirement (i.e. there is no maximum taxable wage base constraint, and the calculation terminates at retirement age); instead of indexing for changes in average national wages, the model indexes based on assumed, after-tax rate of return based on asset allocations that are a function of the individual's age in each year; and percentile distributions are then established based on population statistics for each five-year age cohort.
11. Only Gen Xers are shown in this portion of the analysis, given their longer future working careers until age 65. The analysis focuses on eligibility instead of participation to highlight the public policy issues behind plan sponsorship. Moreover, the gradual evolution from voluntary enrollment type 401(k) plans to automatic enrollment makes the interpretation of the impact of participation problematic.
12. Deloitte Consulting and ICI (2011) found that the median participant-weighted fee for 401(k) plans—including administrative, record-keeping, investment, and other expenses—was 78 basis points.
13. The lack of a monotonically increasing range may seem counterintuitive at first. However, many of those in the highest-income quartile have financial resources considerably above the threshold needed to cover 100 percent of simulated expenses and are more immunized from the impact of a rate-of-return reduction than those in the second- and third-income quartiles.
14. Alternative modifications would result in the same aggregate financial situation for the social security trust fund but would have different distributional consequences. For instance, one could add a new bend point in the Primary Insurance Amount (PIA) formula that would result in a larger reduction for those with a larger Average Indexed Monthly Earnings value.
15. EBRI is currently working on a separate study to model sequence of return risk that will need to be completed before investment risk in the decumulation period can be appropriately analyzed in RSPM.
16. Note that, even though Medicaid eligibility is factored into RSPM, an extended stay in a nursing home is still likely to leave those alive at the end of the nursing home stay (or the surviving spouse) in a financially depleted condition.

17. Future research will analyze this in more detail.
18. VanDerhei (2011*c*) has used RSPM to show the tremendous importance of DB plans in achieving retirement income adequacy for Baby Boomers and Gen Xers. Overall, the presence of a DB accrual at age 65 reduces the 'at-risk' percentage by 11.6 percentage points. The DB plan advantage (as measured by the gap between the two at-risk percentages) is particularly valuable for the lowest-income quartile, but also has a strong impact on the middle class (the reduction in the at-risk percentage for the second and third income quartiles combined is 9.7 percentage points).
19. See Copeland (2013), Dushi et al. (2011), and Anguelow et al. (2012) for discussion of retirement plan participation levels.
20. Another way to analyze this is to compute the *additional* percentage of compensation that needs to be saved for a 50, 75, or 90 percent chance of 'success.' See VanDerhei and Copeland (2010) for more detail.

References

Anguelow, C. E., H. M. Iams, and P. J. Purcell (2012). 'Shifting Income Sources of the Aged.' *Social Security Bulletin*, 72(3): 59–68.

Bajtelsmit, V., L. O. Foster, and A. Rappaport (2013). 'Strategies for Mitigating the Risk of Outliving Retirement Wealth.' *Financial Services Review*, 22(4): 311–30.

Copeland, C. (2013). *Employment-Based Retirement Plan Participation: Geographic Differences and Trends, 2012*, EBRI Issue Brief, 392. Washington, DC: Employee Benefit Research Institute.

Deloitte Consulting and Investment Company Institute (2011). *Defined Contribution/401(k) Fee Study: Inside the Structure of Defined Contribution/401(k) Plan Fees: A Study Assessing the Mechanics of the 'All-In' Fee.* New York: Deloitte and ICI.

Dushi, I., H. M. Iams, and J. Lichtenstein (2011). 'Assessment of Retirement Plan Coverage by Firm Size, Using W-2 Tax Records.' *Social Security Bulletin*, 71(2): 53–65.

Finke, M., W. D. Pfau, and D. M. Blanchett (2013). 'The 4 Percent Rule is Not Safe in a Low-Yield World.' *Journal of Financial Planning*, 26(6): 46–55.

Park, Y. (2011). *Retirement Income Adequacy with Immediate and Longevity Annuities*, EBRI Issue Brief, 357. Washington, DC: Employee Benefit Research Institute.

United States Social Security Administration, Board of Trustees (2013). *The 2013 Annual Report of the Board of Trustees of the Federal Old-Age and Survivors Insurance and Federal Disability Insurance Trust Funds.* Washington, DC: Social Security Administration. <http://www.ssa.gov/oact/tr/2013/tr2013.pdf>.

VanDerhei, J. (2006). *Measuring Retirement Income Adequacy: Calculating Realistic Income Replacement Rates*, EBRI Issue Brief, 297. Washington, DC: Employee Benefit Research Institute.

VanDerhei, J. (2010). Testimony before the US Senate Health, Education, Labor and Pensions Committee. *The Wobbly Stool: Retirement (In)security in America* (T-166), Oct. 7.

VanDerhei, J. (2011*a*). *Tax Reform Options: Promoting Retirement Security,* EBRI Issue Brief, 364. Washington, DC: Employee Benefit Research Institute.

VanDerhei, J. (2011*b*). Testimony before the US Senate Finance Committee. *Tax Reform Options: Promoting Retirement Security* (T-170), Sept. 15.

VanDerhei, J. (2011*c*). 'The Importance of Defined Benefit Plans for Retirement Income Adequacy.' *EBRI Notes,* 8: 7–16. Washington, DC: Employee Benefit Research Institute.

VanDerhei, J. (2011*d*). 'Capping Tax-Preferred Retirement Contributions: Preliminary Evidence of the Impact of the National Commission on Fiscal Responsibility and Reform Recommendations.' *EBRI Notes,* 7: 2–6. Washington, DC: Employee Benefit Research Institute.

VanDerhei, J. (2012*a*). 'Is Working to Age 70 Really the Answer for Retirement Income Adequacy?' *EBRI Notes,* 8: 10–21. Washington, DC: Employee Benefit Research Institute.

VanDerhei, J. (2012*b*). 'Retirement Income Adequacy for Boomers and Gen Xers: Evidence from the 2012 EBRI Retirement Security Projection Model®.' *EBRI Notes,* 5: 2–14. Washington, DC: Employee Benefit Research Institute.

VanDerhei, J. (2012*c*). 'Modifying the Federal Tax Treatment of 401(k) Plan Contributions: Projected Impact on Participant Account Balances.' *EBRI Notes,* 3: 2–18. Washington, DC: Employee Benefit Research Institute.

VanDerhei, J. (2013*a*). *The Impact of a Retirement Savings Account Cap,* EBRI Issue Brief, 389. Washington, DC: Employee Benefit Research Institute.

VanDerhei, J. (2013*b*). 'What a Sustained Low-yield Rate Environment Means for Retirement Income Adequacy: Results From the 2013 EBRI Retirement Security Projection Model®.' *EBRI Notes,* 3: 2–12. Washington, DC: Employee Benefit Research Institute.

VanDerhei, J. (2014). *What Causes EBRI Retirement Readiness Ratings™ to Vary: Results from the 2014 Retirement Security Projection Model®,* EBRI Issue Brief, 396. Washington, DC: Employee Benefit Research Institute.

VanDerhei, J. and C. Copeland (2004). *ERISA at 30: The Decline of Private-Sector Defined Benefit Promises and Annuity Payments: What Will it Mean?* EBRI Issue Brief, 269. Washington, DC: Employee Benefit Research Institute.

VanDerhei, J. and C. Copeland (2010). *The EBRI Retirement Readiness Rating™: Retirement Income Preparation and Future Prospects,* EBRI Issue Brief, 344. Washington, DC: Employee Benefit Research Institute.

VanDerhei, J. and C. Copeland (2011). *The Impact of Deferring Retirement Age on Retirement Income Adequacy,* EBRI Issue Brief, 358. Washington, DC: Employee Benefit Research Institute.

Chapter 4

The Changing Nature of Retirement

Julia Coronado

Change is the only constant when it comes to retirement planning and income provision over the 40 years since the 1974 passage of the US Employee Retirement Income Security Act (ERISA). In 1979, most private sector workers (82 percent) who were covered by a pension plan had a defined benefit (DB) plan. By 2011, a minority (31 percent) had DB plans, while defined contribution (DC) plans, which did not exist in their current form when ERISA was signed, became the only retirement coverage for 69 percent of private sector workers (EBRI 2014*a*). Changes in benefit provision can only be partially linked to the passage of ERISA, since the public sector, not covered by ERISA, has also seen changes in the structure of retirement benefit provision, albeit more gradual ones.

Many of these changes in the retirement landscape were driven by demography. In 1970, an average man reaching the age of 65 could expect to live to 78.1 years of age, while a woman could expect to live to age 82. Forty years later, a 65-year-old man could expect to live to 82.7 and a woman to 85.3, an increase of 15–35 percent in the number of retirement years that needed to be financed, assuming retirement ages don't change (CDC 2014). But times have changed. Long-running surveys of people's retirement plans and experiences suggest a steady and substantial increase in their expected retirement ages as well as changing plans to work for pay in retirement. Yet these same surveys reveal a conundrum: large fractions of retirees, the majority in recent years, report retiring earlier than planned, and the fraction working in retirement is substantially below people's plans. Either individuals are so cautious that they oversave and find themselves in a surplus position at older ages (a view refuted by a large body of data and research), or there is something else afoot.

This chapter argues that older workers have had a difficult time executing their plans, owing to persistently weak labor market conditions for older employees. Many older workers have been forced into earlier retirement than planned due to job loss, and many who seek work are unable to find employment or can only find part-time jobs. While labor market conditions have been difficult for workers of all ages, older workers have a harder time finding another position once separated from a job. We conclude that people should be factoring uncertainty about labor market outcomes into their retirement planning decisions in addition to increased uncertainty from exposure to risky investments.

In what follows, we first describe key findings from the Retirement Confidence Survey, the longest-running annual survey of retirement attitudes, plans, and experiences. Next we corroborate these findings with evidence on older households from the Consumer Expenditure Survey. Results highlight the different experiences and future prospects of different generations. A third section looks at labor force outcomes and decisions using the Current Population Survey. Involuntary unemployment and underemployment are not unique to older workers, but these come at a vulnerable time in life. We conclude with some thoughts regarding implications for policy and research.

Watch What I Say, Then What I Do

Since 1993, the Employee Benefit Research Institute has surveyed a representative sample of US current workers and retirees about attitudes and self-reported decisions related to retirement in the Retirement Confidence Survey (RCS).[1] It poses a core set of questions to cohorts over time to reveal shifting trends in attitudes and decisions that can then be cross-checked with other data sources (EBRI 2014*b*). For this reason, the RCS captures the recent decline and partial rebound in Americans' confidence in their ability to afford a comfortable retirement. Indeed, confidence in retirement security has fallen in recent years: the share of current workers either very or somewhat confident in having the resources needed to live comfortably in retirement hovered around 70 percent in the 1990s through 2007; then it dropped sharply to just above 50 percent, before recovering to 55 percent in 2014. Among retirees, the high water mark was also in 2007 when 79 percent were very or somewhat confident they had enough money to live comfortably throughout their retirement years. This fell below 50 percent in the crisis, hitting a trough at 47 percent in 2013 before rising somewhat to 57 percent in 2014.

It is striking that today's retirees do not have much higher levels of confidence than do workers and that nearly half of them think their resources will not last throughout retirement. Arguably, the potentially depressive effect of the secular decline in DB pension coverage on retirement confidence was offset by rising equity and home values in recent decades. Even though the equity market has more than fully recovered losses registered during the financial crisis, and home values in most parts of the United States have also recovered well overall, the recent financial market volatility has tangibly revealed to workers and retirees alike the risks inherent in DC retirement vehicles.

The RCS captures a steady increase in the expected age of retirement among current workers. Figure 4.1 indicates that the fraction of workers expecting to retire after age 65 has risen steadily, from just over 10 percent in 1991, to roughly one-third of respondents in recent years. The rising trend has not been a function of business cycles or the financial crisis; rather, it likely reflects longer life expectancies, better physical health, and a more service-oriented economy, as well as the declining prevalence of DB pension plans with their strong incentives for earlier retirement. Nevertheless, Figure 4.1 also shows that plans for later retirement are not evident in the share of people retiring post-65 (about 15 percent).

Some reasons for the gap between retirement plans and retirement experience are provided in Figure 4.2. A fairly large proportion of retirees exits the labor force earlier than planned, and this share has risen notably in recent years, such that nearly half of all retirees report early exit from the labor force. The survey also queries respondents on their reasons for early exits, and many reasons cited in the 2014 survey suggest adverse consequences for standards of living. For example, 61 percent cited health problems or disability, 22 percent noted work-related reasons including firm

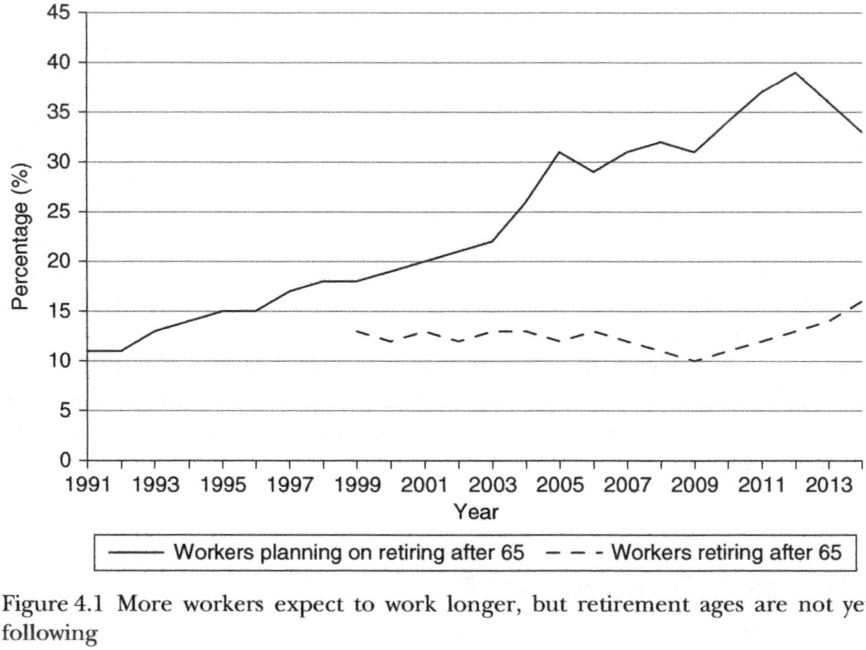

Figure 4.1 More workers expect to work longer, but retirement ages are not yet following

Source: EBRI (2014*b*).

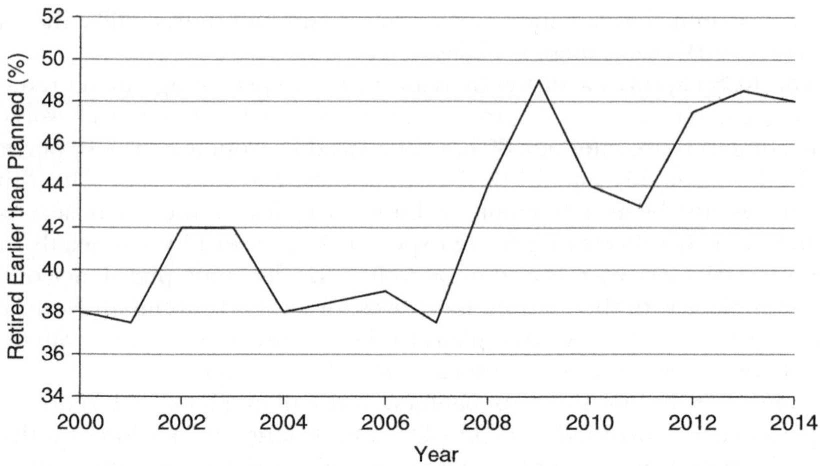

Figure 4.2 Workers are retiring earlier than planned (%, 2 yr avg.)
Source: EBRI (2014*b*).

downsizing and closure, and 18 percent cited having to care for a family member. In other words, many people do a poor job planning for the many contingencies that end up affecting their ability to continue working at older ages.

This poor planning manifests itself in an even larger gap between the share of workers reporting that they intend to continue working for pay in retirement and the share that actually does so. Figure 4.3 shows that roughly two-thirds of people currently working expect to continue working for pay in retirement, up from 55 percent in 1998. Yet the share of retirees that actually does work for pay has been relatively steady over time, at close to 25 percent. Reasons people cite for planning on working for pay post-retirement relate to their enjoyment of working, their desire to stay active, and their wanting extra spending money. Some people may find they simply do not need to work, or alternatively that poor health or care needs for a loved one can outweigh the benefits of working or make it infeasible. In any event, there appears to be a decline in the value of investments, as some cite the need for more money to make ends meet as a reason they plan to continue working.

Changing Generational Experience

Another explanation for the large gap between the share of people saying they will retire later and the share actually doing so is that the retirement

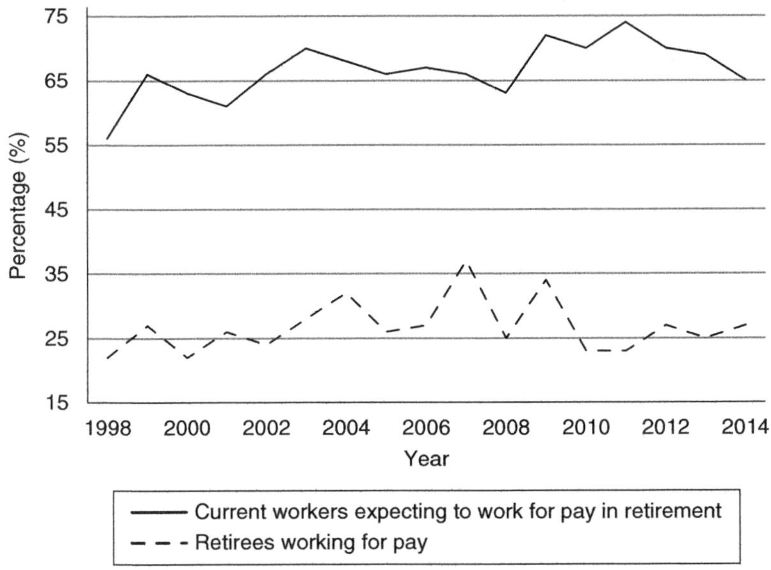

Figure 4.3 Most workers expect to work for pay, but few retirees do
Source: EBRI (2014*b*).

experience may be evolving rapidly across cohorts. Changes in pension coverage, asset returns, and labor market conditions may imply past retirees will be more financially comfortable and secure than future retirees, which is reflected in the plans of current workers. Ultimately, people save to smooth their consumption over their lifetimes, so data from the Consumer Expenditure Survey (CES) on per capita household spending across age groups can shed light on the well-being of current and future retirees (BLS 2014).

The CES confirms that there are important generational disparities, with older households realizing larger gains in their standards of living in recent decades compared to younger households, particularly in the aftermath of the Great Recession. Table 4.1 and Figure 4.4 show the evolution of average real per capita household consumption spending by age of the head of household between 1984 and 2012. All households saw an increase in average real levels of spending since 1984, but the largest gain (by a notable margin) was among households age 75+, who saw a 66 percent gain in real spending since 1984 versus a 6 percent gain for households age 35–44. In 1984, the level of per capita spending had a hump-shaped life cycle pattern rising between the ages of 25 and 64, then falling back as households aged and presumably engaged in more household production in place of out-of-pocket spending. This may also reflect gaps in consumption insurance

TABLE 4.1 Older households doing well

Real per capita spending				
Age of head of household	2012 vs. 1984 (% change)	2012 vs. 2007 (% change)	1984 level ($ 2009)	2012 level ($ 2009)
25–34	15	−4	14,550	16,691
35–44	6	−15	15,164	16,111
45–54	28	−2	16,916	21,697
55–64	46	−5	17,105	24,992
65–74	58	0	15,237	24,090
75+	66	1	12,703	21,086

Source: BLS (2014).

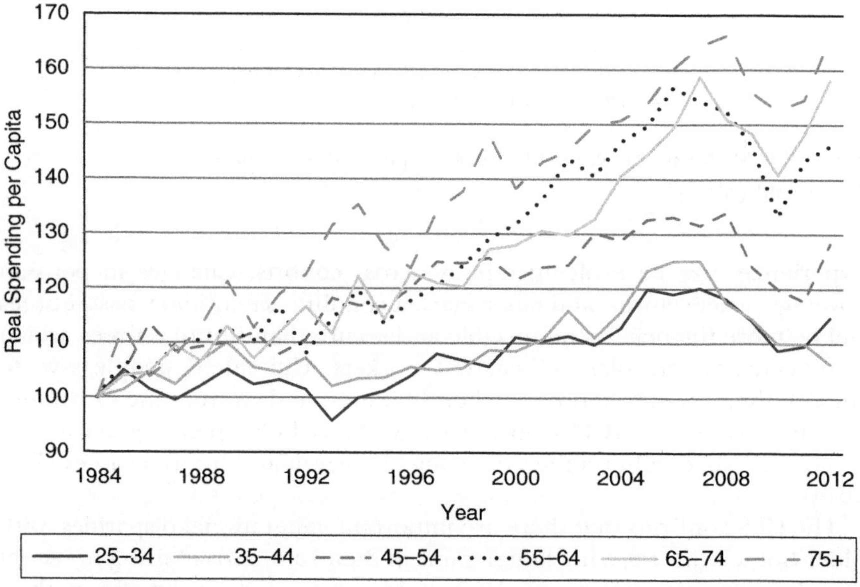

Figure 4.4 Real spending per capita by age of head of household. Older households have experienced the greatest increase in standard of living

Note: 1984 is 100.

Source: BLS (2014).

among the elderly. By contrast, in 2012, average per capita spending rose in a nearly linear fashion with age, falling back moderately for households age 75+. Disparities across age groups have also grown: in 1984, households spending the most were the 55–64 group who spent 17.5 percent more than the lowest spending cohort (age 25–34). In 2012, the biggest spenders

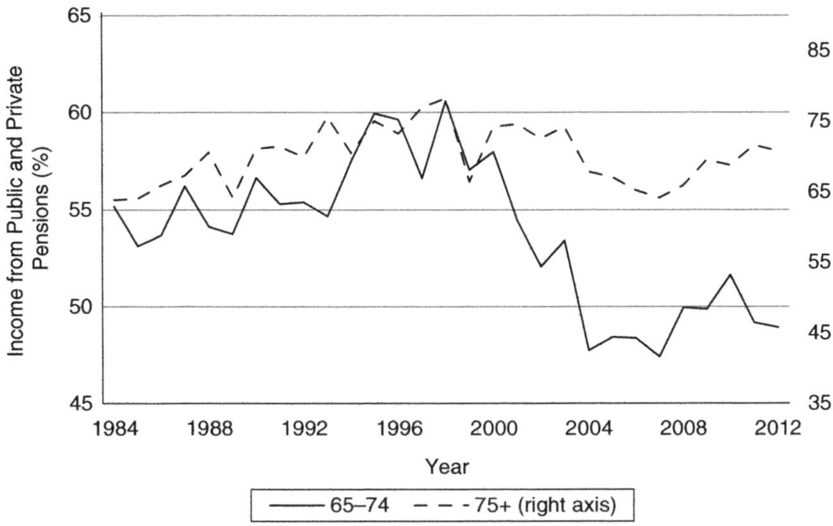

Figure 4.5 Income from public and private pensions by age of head of household (% of total household income). Pension support is fading for older households

Source: BLS (2014).

were still those age 55–64, but they spent 55.1 percent more than the lowest spenders (now age 35–44). Whereas the 1984 data suggest good but not perfect consumption smoothing across generations, the 2012 data are more suggestive of outright generational inequalities in living standards.

When it comes to financing consumption, CES data offer a different picture from some of the trends depicted by the RCS. Figure 4.5 shows the erosion of support from public and private pensions, even within already-retired cohorts. Households where the head is age 75+ continue to rely on pensions for two-thirds of their income on average; by contrast, households age 65–74 have seen that share decline from the late 1990s level of 60 percent in recent years. Given trends in pension coverage and the tendency of DB pensions to implement reforms that made the largest cuts to the youngest participants, the share of household income from traditional pensions is likely to continue to fall for future retirees. In contrast to the RCS, however, the CES shows a marked increase in the share of household income coming from work for pay among households age 65–74, from about 30 percent in the 1980s to almost 45 percent in recent years (see Figure 4.6). This could reflect later retirements among the younger tail of the age group, an increase in work for pay after retirement, or both. Thus the CES presents less of a tension between reported trends in worker expectations for retirement and the recent behavior of retirees.

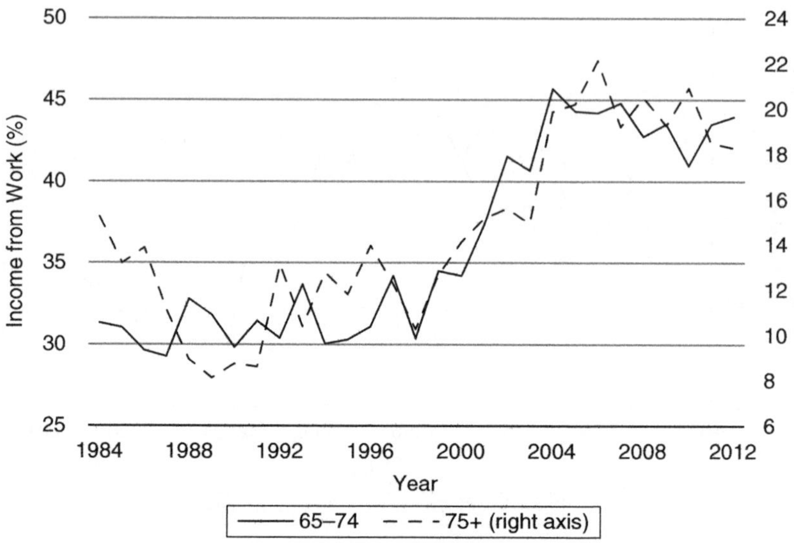

Figure 4.6 Income from work by age of head of household (% of total household income). More income support derives from work for older households
Source: BLS (2014).

Older households were not immune to the leveraging that brought the US economy to the brink of disaster in 2008–09. Traditionally, one of the simplest retirement plans had been for homeowners to pay off their mortgages prior to retirement, thereby lowering their income needs without changing their standards of living. Figure 4.7 shows that the share of households approaching or entering retirement age with mortgages was small and fairly stable through the late 1990s, but it jumped in the 2000s. For older workers, fixed mortgage obligations against falling home values likely impacted their ability to retire and downsize, and this implied more hardship and replanning for those who experienced job loss. Most recently, the CES showed a decline in the share of households age 55–64 with mortgages, likely reflecting a renewed emphasis on paying off fixed obligations. The fall in the share of households holding mortgages was also mirrored in the younger age groups, as both foreclosure and falling homeownership rates contributed to a decline in household leverage. In other words, retirement replanning seems to be underway, as households adjust to riskier economic realities than presumed prior to the Great Recession.

On balance, the CES results agree with the changing retirement landscape captured in the RCS. Additionally, they reflect that changes are already underway with a combination of later retirement and/or work for pay taking the place of declining pensions among the younger half of older households.

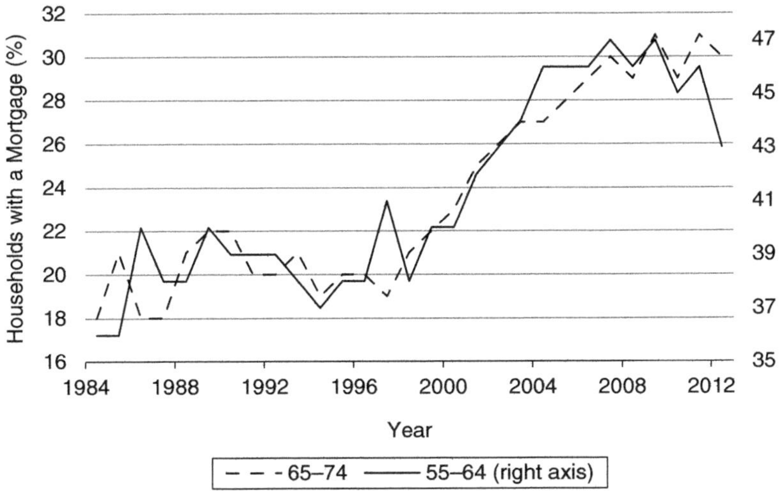

Figure 4.7 Households with a mortgage by age of head. Older households are taking on more leverage

Source: BLS (2014).

Shocking Experiences

Evidence from the RCS and CES also confirms that more people will want to continue working at their career jobs longer and work for pay in some capacity, even after they consider themselves to be retired from a 'main' job. Yet the RCS also highlights that people do not always have a choice about executing their plans and may be forced into early retirement. Another data source, the Current Population Survey (CPS), confirms that older workers have experienced considerable unemployment and underemployment in recent years. For instance, older workers who lose their jobs face greater difficulty finding employment than comparably qualified, or even less-qualified, younger workers. The implication is that workers must factor considerable uncertainty about their ability to work later in life into their planning process, rather than assume they can work as long as they want.

Also, older workers are not insulated from the business cycle. Figure 4.8 shows the unemployment rate for older men, which rises and falls with the rest of the economy. Indeed, in some respects, older workers arguably fared worse than others during the most recent downturn. The unemployment rate for all workers peaked at 10 percent in October 2009 at the height of the Great Recession, falling short of its prior peak in 1982 of 10.8 percent. However the unemployment rate for men age 55–64 set an all-time high of 8.0 percent in 2010, easily surpassing its prior peak of 6.2 percent in 1983.

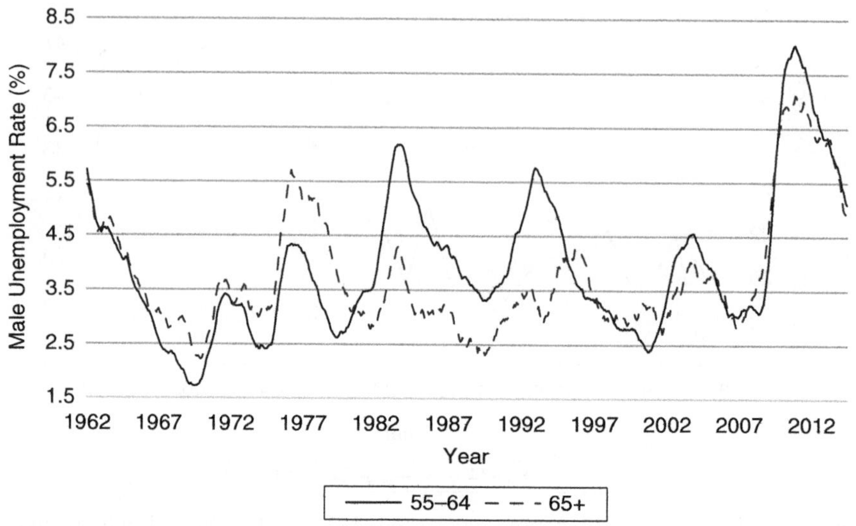

Figure 4.8 Unemployment rates by age for men. Unemployment is still elevated among older men

Source: BLS (2014).

The experience of men age 65+ relative to prior cycles was even worse; their unemployment rate peaked at 7.1 percent in 2012, nearly 3 percentage points above their 1983 peak of 4.3 percent. While the unemployment rate was consistently lower for older male workers than the population average, older worker groups had the worst unemployment experience during the Great Recession in post-WWII history. It is therefore unlikely that even the most prudent planners among this age group could have anticipated the likelihood of experiencing an unemployment shock. The story is much the same for older women (Figure 4.9); although their unemployment rates were lower than men's on an absolute basis, they experienced by far the worst degree of unemployment in the post-WWII period.

Fortunately, unemployment rates have been coming down rapidly in recent years, but for some groups, they remain at or above prior recessionary peaks. The persistence of unemployment among older workers highlights the difficulty older workers tend to experience in finding work once unemployed. Moreover, the unemployment rate understates the severity of underemployment among older workers. Figure 4.10 shows the degree of discouragement among persons age 55+: this is defined as the percent of the population that has given up looking for work and hence is not counted as unemployed, but wants a job and would work if one were available.

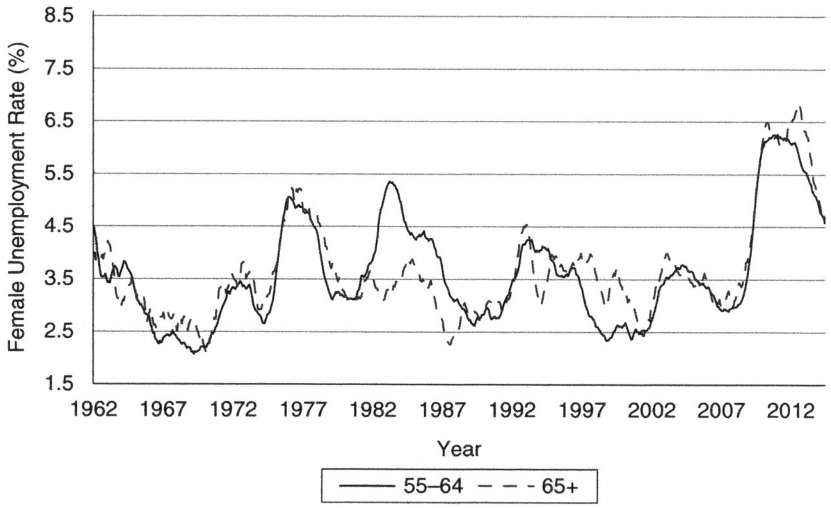

Figure 4.9 Unemployment rates by age for women. Unemployment is still elevated among older women

Source: BLS (2014).

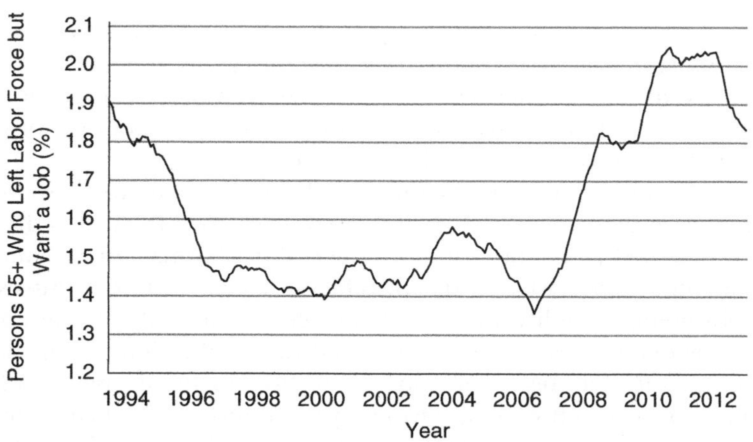

Figure 4.10 Percentage of persons 55+ who left the labor force but want a job. Some discouragement remains among older workers

Source: BLS (2014).

Discouragement rates rose rapidly during the Great Recession and, like the unemployment rate, made progress but remain quite elevated.

Another group of under-employed individuals are people employed in part-time positions who would prefer full-time work. This 'shadow' labor force has been frequently cited by Federal Reserve Board Chairs as a headwind to the recovery and a reason the unemployment rate understates the degree of labor market slack. Workers of all ages have experienced large amounts of under-employment by this metric, and in fact older workers have fared relatively better in a cyclical sense as the share of involuntary part-time employment remains below prior recessionary peaks. Nonetheless, given that unemployment rates remain above the norms of prior expansions, the 0.5 percent of discouraged workers, and about 1 percentage point of involuntary part-time workers, suggests that a nontrivial minority of older households continues to experience reductions in consumption. Of course, younger workers too experienced shocks that will have long-term impacts on expectations and retirement plans. The good news is that households have developed prudence and are remaining less inclined to take on debt as the recovery has proceeded. The bad news is that this is a somewhat self-limiting process that has slowed down the recovery.

Conclusion

The retirement reality is changing rapidly because those close to retirement will enjoy less support from pensions and face greater investment and labor market risk to finance their consumption needs at older ages. As a result, current workers report plans to retire later and continue working for pay in retirement, and recent data confirm their plans.

More effective retirement planning will require that workers prepare better, rather than try and turn the clock back to a level of retirement support that the US economy can no longer afford. Saving and consumption decisions must acknowledge the possibility of economic downturns and unemployment, volatility in investment returns, and the vulnerabilities implied by entering retirement with fixed debt obligations. Some simple rules of thumb may be helpful in this regard, including paying off the mortgage prior to retirement, having a year of disposable income in cash to navigate unanticipated unemployment, and defining a certain multiple of household income that should be saved to finance consumption spending, depending on one's planned retirement age. US workers have shown an ability to adapt through the Great Recession, so we anticipate that retirement preparedness is not an impossible goal.

Endnote

1. For more detail on the Retirement Confidence Survey, see the Employee Benefit Research Institute's website: <http://ebri.org/surveys/rcs>.

References

Bureau of Labor Statistics (BLS) (2014). *Consumer Expenditure Survey.* Washington, DC: BLS. <http://www.bls.gov/cex>.

Center for Disease Control (CDC) (2014). *Life Expectancy at Birth, 65 and 75 Years of Age by Sex, Race and Hispanic Origin.* Atlanta, GA: CDC. <http://www.cdc.gov/nchs/data/hus/2011/022.pdf>.

Employee Benefit Research Institute (EBRI) (2014*a*). *FAQs about Benefits—Retirement Issues.* Washington, DC: EBRI. <http://www.ebri.org/publications/benfaq/?fa=retfaq>.

Employee Benefit Research Institute (EBRI) (2014*b*). *Retirement Confidence Survey.* Washington, DC: EBRI. <http://www.ebri.org/surveys/rcs>.

Chapter 5

Entitlement Reform and the Future of Pensions

C. Eugene Steuerle, Benjamin H. Harris, and Pamela J. Perun

The United States retirement system is in a state of flux. Large public health programs, notably Medicare and Medicaid, have been a cornerstone of American retirement, but unfortunately these programs are on an unsustainable path due to the aging of the population and prolonged growth in costs for both the federal government and retirees themselves. Social Security's future solvency, while less of a budgetary challenge than the major health programs, is also in doubt, with adjustments to either revenue or benefits required to bring the program into long-term balance. At the same time, the decades-long transformation of the private, employer-based retirement system is nearly complete, with most private savers working to accumulate liquid assets for retirement rather than credit towards a lifetime pension.

All three systems affecting the elderly—health, Social Security, and employer-based retirement plans—have not been reformed substantially in decades. Indeed, in our view, they have adapted too slowly to fundamental changes in the broader demographic and fiscal landscape. Close to one-third of all adults are scheduled to be on Social Security for one-third of their adult lives, and only a modest percentage of households has private assets at time of retirement near the value of their government health and retirement benefits. As a result, all of the growth in government spending over the next two decades is slated to go for Social Security, Medicare, Medicaid, and interest on the debt.

To be clear, we believe there are viable and feasible reform options, but agreeing on them requires shifts in both policy priorities and federal law. To this end, we offer a series of policy alternatives which could result in an environment that would better protect the most vulnerable retirees and minimize adverse effects on the middle class and the economy as a whole.

Budget Pressures and Entitlement Reform

The federal budget continues to be plagued by long-term pressures. The combination of growing and unprecedented spending on major entitlement programs, porous income and corporate tax codes riddled with tax subsidies, the absence of interest in any new major source of revenues (such as an energy tax or a national value-added tax), rising expected interest payments, the long, slow recovery from the Great Recession, and limited ability to further cut non-entitlement spending all point to a situation that requires entitlement reform, as at least part of any long-term solution.

One metric of budget pressures is the federal debt as a share of the gross domestic product (GDP). Federal debt has risen from 28 percent of GDP in 1970 to 72 percent of GDP today, with a steep rise between 2007 and 2012, when the tax base shrank and federal expenditures rose in an effort to reverse the economic recession.[1] Looking forward, the outlook is bleak without a reversal in policy: the Congressional Budget Office (CBO) predicts that federal debt to GDP will steadily rise to 100 percent by 2038 (CBO 2013c).

Economists have been unable to identify a precise threshold at which the debt-to-GDP ratio begins to cause severe economic harm, but evidence suggests that the United States will not be able to maintain the level predicted by CBO without suffering some adverse economic consequences. Reinhart and Rogoff (2010) note that nations can expect significant economic harm once their debt-to-GDP ratios exceed 90 percent. Other work suggests that Reinhart and Rogoff's calculations were mistaken (Herndon et al. 2013), and that sluggish economic growth causes high debt, not the other way around (Dube 2013). Nevertheless, while the exact empirical relationship between growth and debt is not well established, several studies have noted other adverse economic effects from debt such as higher interest rates, interest costs even if rates remain steady, and reduced private saving (Elmendorf and Mankiw 1999; Gale and Orszag 2004).

The squeeze on other government functions is among the reasons that health and retirement programs are at the forefront of long-term deficit reduction focus. Major health programs and Social Security increasingly dominate the federal budget and national spending, with their spending as a share of GDP rising to 8 percent and 6 percent by 2038, respectively, leaving little room for other initiatives such as transportation, education, and infrastructure investment. Even defense spending, which received a massive share of the federal budget for the first decades after World War II, is expected to comprise just 12 percent of federal spending in 2024. Meanwhile, interest spending, perhaps the one 'non-negotiable' aspect of the federal budget, is expected to skyrocket from 6 percent of federal spending in 2012 to 15 percent in 2024.

Recent legislation has modestly improved the short-run budget outlook but achieved deficit reduction largely through increased tax rates on upper-income taxpayers and steep cuts to discretionary spending. The Budget

Control Act of 2011 (BCA) instituted $2.2 trillion in deficit reduction between 2012 and 2021, mostly by means of caps on discretionary spending and automatic cuts in spending (mainly discretionary) through 'sequestration.'[2] A little over a year later, Congress passed the American Taxpayer Relief Act (ATRA), which forestalled the bulk of a very large scheduled increase in taxes during recovery from the recession by extending most expiring tax cuts for all but the highest-income taxpayers, although it also removed $620 billion from the deficit when measured relative to ongoing policy.[3] The end result of these two bills was a modest improvement in the short-run budget outlook achieved through higher taxes on upper-income taxpayers and cuts in discretionary spending. The low-hanging fruit has now been plucked, but the long-term pressures remain.

Asking the middle class for higher tax burdens or cuts in entitlements has proved to be a tough sell by Congress to the American public; there seems to be mixed public appetite, at best, for either strategy. On taxes, an American Enterprise Institute 2010 survey conducted prior to the increased tax rates on upper-income taxpayers found that Americans were split on whether it was more important to reduce the deficit (47 percent) or cut taxes (46 percent) (Bowman and Rugg 2012). A *Washington Post* survey from around the same time was less ambiguous, reporting that 60 percent of Americans supported higher taxes on households with more than $250,000 in income as a deficit-reduction strategy (Teixeira 2012).

Americans appear more unified in their distaste for cuts to Social Security and Medicare. For example, one study found that only 13 percent of Americans favored cutting Social Security as a way to reduce the federal deficit, and 72 percent strongly opposed Social Security cuts as a deficit-reduction strategy (AARP 2010); another study found that 75 percent of Americans indicated that 'we should consider increasing Social Security benefits' (Tucker et al. 2013). Lastly, it is unclear whether the American public is convinced that deficit reduction is even a top priority, with 69 percent of respondents to a 2013 Pew Research poll answering that maintaining Social Security and Medicare benefits trumped deficit reduction as a national priority (Pew Research Center 2013). Of course, for many of those polled, cuts in Medicare and Social Security might affect them or their family, whereas tax increases on higher-income taxpayers would be borne by someone else.

The Inevitability of Entitlement Reform

In spite of polls indicating limited public support for any cost-bearing by the middle class, solutions to the long-term fiscal imbalance will almost certainly include reform to the entitlement programs from which they benefit. Other solutions are generally insufficient to fix the problem in isolation. For example, Urban-Brookings Tax Policy Center researchers estimated that in order to reduce annual fiscal deficits to 2 percent of GDP through upper-income tax increases alone would require raising the top two statutory tax rates to over 50 percent (Altshuler et al. 2010). Cuts to non-entitlement programs have already been a major part of short-term deficit reduction, with sequestration-led cuts and supposed lack of any new major appropriation driving down discretionary spending to just 5 percent of GDP by 2024. Lastly, while the growth in economy-wide health costs is an important contributor to the rising debt-to-GDP ratio, the debt is still projected to rise to 112 percent of GDP if excess cost growth—the growth rate of per-capita health spending in excess of GDP growth—falls to zero (Auerbach et al. 2014). In short, while taxes, non-entitlement spending, and health costs play an important role in projected deficits, reaching long-term fiscal balance is a nearly impossible goal without also addressing entitlement spending.

Part of the challenge with cutting entitlement spending is that these programs are tied closely to the aging of the population. The United States is expected to undergo an unprecedented surge in old-age citizens over the next four decades: by 2050 one-fifth of Americans will be age 65 or older, compared to just 12 percent in 1950 (CBO 2013c). In addition, the share of Americans age 85 or older will rise to 4 percent by 2050—a ten-fold increase since 1950 (CBO 2013b). Population aging is the largest factor in explaining the growth in Social Security, Medicare, and Medicaid, accounting for over half (54 percent) of the growth in these programs between 2013 and 2038 (CBO 2013c).

Indeed, the United States has already seen a pronounced increase in health spending: inflation-adjusted health spending increased by nearly 400 percent between 1980 and 2011—from roughly $400 billion in 1980 (in $2011) to $2.7 trillion in 2011 (Council of Economic Advisors 2013). Most of this increase can be attributed to factors other than aging of the population and population growth. This rise in health spending, projected to continue into the future, has translated into rapidly rising public health expenditures. Excess cost growth accounts for 28 percent of the growth and the expansion of Medicaid and the exchange subsidies—subsidies for low- and middle-income households who purchase health insurance through health care exchanges—accounts for 19 percent of the growth. While recent data have provided some cause for optimism, Steuerle (2013) shows that a slow-down in cost growth in excess of the rate of growth of GDP does not necessarily mean a slow-down in the percent of the growth in income being absorbed by health care alone.[4] For example, if health care grew to 30 percent of GDP and then stabilized at that level, there would be no 'excess cost growth' but health care would still absorb 30 percent of all income growth.

We caution against the notion, however, that slowing the rate of entitlement spending growth is the only mechanism for achieving fiscal balance. While we have little hope that discretionary spending cuts can meet their currently scheduled target for decline, reform could also include adjustments to tax revenue, by either raising tax rates or limiting tax expenditures.[5] CBO projections show federal revenues as a share of GDP at 18.4 percent, well below the levels experienced in the late 1990s and just a notch above the average level from 1950 to today.

Structural Transformation of the Private Retirement System and its Consequences

The private pension system, which is also a key pillar in the American retirement system, similarly faces an uncertain future. In 2013, retirement assets totaled $21.9 trillion—amounting to more than one-third of all household financial assets (ICI 2013). That includes $2.9 trillion held in private sector defined benefit (DB) plans, $5.6 trillion held in defined contribution (DC) plans, and $6.2 trillion held in Individual Retirement Accounts (IRAs). In 2000, when total assets held for retirement equaled only $11.6 trillion, comparable figures were $2.0 trillion in DB plans, $2.9 trillion in DC plans, and $2.6 trillion in IRAs.

This phenomenal growth in assets held in DC plans and IRAs (which largely represent assets rolled over from DC plans) reflects a fundamental shift in the private pension system. Beginning roughly in the mid-1980s, private sector employers began terminating their DB plans. From a high point of over 175,000 plans in 1983, only some 45,000 plans remained by 2011 (US Dept of Labor 2013). Over 80 percent of those plans were small plans, covering fewer than 100 participants. Large plans with more than 1,000 participants, however, account for most private sector DB plan participants. The Pension Benefit Guaranty Corporation (PBGC), which insures most but not all private sector DB plans, reported that in 2011 there were over 33 million insured participants (representing 90 percent of all participants), but fewer than 40 percent of those were active workers in 2010. The remaining 60 percent of workers had either retired or changed jobs. The PBGC reported that the percentage of private sector wage and salary workers covered by insured DB plans fell from a high of over 30 percent in 1980 to a current low of 14 percent in 2010 (PBGC 2012).

Beginning in 1992, 401(k)-type plans became the engine driving the growth in retirement plan assets. By 2011, the number of these plans more than tripled to over 500,000, and the number of participants eligible to contribute also tripled to 66 million workers (US Dept of Labor 2013).[6] These plans are more attractive to employers than DB plans due to their limited long-term financial commitment, reduced regulatory and fiduciary burden, and lower costs of plan sponsorship. The net benefits to employees are less clear cut, with employees taking on significant saving and near-total investment responsibility in exchange for greater control over their accounts.

The 401(k)-type plan system is still maturing, although it is some 30 years old. The ability of some participants, especially those who save consistently, to accumulate significant retirement savings indicates that the 401(k) system has the potential to evolve into a robust second tier in the American retirement system. To date, however, benefits of 401(k) plans have accrued primarily to older, longer-tenured, higher-paid employees at large companies. Recent policy changes to the DC model, such as offering automatic enrollment, automatic escalation in contributions, less complex investment menus, less expensive investment options, and more financial education may make the 401(k) plan a more efficient engine of retirement savings over time. Nevertheless, this will mainly help those employees who have a plan at work, save, invest well, and do not withdraw early.

Critics of the current system point to its all too evident present inadequacies, notably its failure to provide all employees with a plan and failure to generate for many employees adequate savings for retirement (Munnell et al. 2012). They also point out that the current tax treatment of retirement accounts, the second largest tax expenditure after health care, is expensive and inequitable. (Tax expenditures operate like government spending for designated purposes but through targeted tax breaks.) In 2013, the tax expenditure for pension contributions and earnings was $137 billion, representing 0.9 percent of GDP. Moreover, 66 percent of the benefits of this exclusion accrued to the top 20 percent in income, while only 2 percent and 5 percent, respectively, accrue to those in the 10–20 percent and 20–40 percent income groups (CBO 2013a). The saver's credit, in contrast, is designed to assist low- and middle-income savers but it is small compared to other incentives, costing just $1.2 billion in 2014 (Office of Management and Budget 2014).

Retirement assets represent a significant financial asset of most households. Retirement accounts represented 38 percent of assets, the single largest financial asset held by households in 2010, up from 29 percent in 2001. But only a slight majority of households owns such an asset, and the share fell in the wake of the Great Recession. Between 2007 and 2010, ownership of such accounts decreased, with steeper declines for middle-income, middle-aged households; by contrast, balances for upper-income households increased (Bricker et al. 2012).

The dispersion in retirement account balances is reflected in the sources of income for retirement-age Americans. Today, Social Security is the dominant income source for elderly Americans in the bottom half of the income distribution. In 2013, for Americans 65 and older, Social Security payments comprised 85 percent of income for those in the bottom income quartile and 83.5 percent of income for those in the second income quartile. Other income sources were relatively insignificant. Those in the bottom income quartile received 6.6 percent of income from SSI and public assistance, while those in the second income quartile received 6.2 percent of income from pensions (Poterba 2014). Income from earnings and assets were very low for each of these income groups.

In sharp contrast, elderly Americans in the top half of the income distribution received substantial income from accumulated saving. The third income quartile still depended on Social Security payments—making up 56.5 percent of income—but also received nearly 30 percent of income from pension and asset income. Those in the top income quartile depended even more on income from accumulated saving, with 35.6 percent of income coming from pension and asset income (Poterba 2014). On average, those in the top half of the income distribution depend on income from saving—both within and outside of retirement accounts—for retirement security, while those in the bottom half of the income distribution do not.

Trends in Labor Force Participation

When it comes to discussions of reform of either private or public retirement systems, there is a tendency among the mathematically trained—economists, actuaries, and accountants, along with pension, finance, and business professionals—to stress the financial side of the issue. Yet many of the problems that affect both systems relate largely to labor market trends. Today, workers enjoy retirement for close to one-third of their adult lives, Social Security benefits are received on average 11 years longer than when benefits were first paid in 1940, and private retirement assets must similarly last much longer. Meanwhile, the combination of additional years in retirement and the decline in the birth rate means that close to one-third of adults are expected to be on Social Security soon. A related concern is that the employment rate among all adults has been declining recently (even independent of the Great Recession), and it is scheduled to continue to decline with the aging of Baby Boomers.

Retiring so many people for so long is simply not viable, which is a problem plaguing developed countries around the world. This labor market issue is not going to be solved by financial manipulations. To provide income in retirement at the same relative level as before retirement, roughly speaking, people would need to save around one-third of their incomes each year. Alternatively, it would require a Social Security tax rate of about 33 percent if government were required by itself to provide that level of income support.[7]

On the positive side, labor force participation trends suggest that longer work lives are becoming more common in the United States, so some adjustment is already starting to occur. For most of the second half of the twentieth century, the average age at retirement among men declined substantially. In 1950, about 70 percent of men age 55 and older were in the labor force, but only about 40 percent were still working by the mid-1990s. Labor force participation by women exhibited very different patterns during the same period as they expanded their presence in the labor force. The participation rate of women age 24–54 essentially doubled between 1950 and 2000, while that of similarly aged men declined slightly. For both older men and women, however, the mid-1990s began a period of pronounced uptick in labor force participation. Increases for men largely occurred among men in their 60s, while women of all age groups increased their labor force participation (National Academy of Sciences 2012).

Projections of labor force participation through 2050 anticipate that the role of older workers will increase substantially, as the supply of young (16–24 years) and prime age (25–54 years) declines. Older workers are expected to offset some of this decline, and one projection shows their labor force participation increasing from about 12 percent in 1990 to 24 percent around 2020 and then continuing to grow to more than 27 percent by 2050 (National Academy of Sciences 2012). Steuerle and Quakenbush (2012) have argued that this figure may be low, drawing on historical Social Security projections that have consistently underestimated future labor force participation among older workers. The projection error derives from ignoring labor demand for older workers in the face of a reduced opportunity for employers to hire younger workers.

Demand, however, can play an uneven role. Age discrimination in employment is one key variable. The Age Discrimination in Employment Act, enacted almost 50 years ago, is designed to protect workers over age 40 from workplace discrimination, but subsequent court decisions have made it difficult for plaintiffs to pursue litigation successfully. The United States Equal Employment Opportunity Commission reports an increasing case load of age discrimination claims, yet some two-thirds of claims are denied at the agency level (EEOC 2013).

The jobless rate for workers age 55 and over reached record highs in the Great Recession. Unemployment seems to be a larger issue here than continuation of employment. Although the rate of unemployment for older workers is below that of younger workers, older workers who became unemployed spent more time looking for work. Almost half remained jobless for 27 weeks or longer, compared to close to 30 percent of workers age 16–24, and over 40 percent of workers between 25 and 54 (US Dept of Labor 2010).

One focus of research on the labor demand side has been on the service industry, which comprises about one-third of the United States employment base. Between 1980 and 2010, employment among workers age 65–74 increased by 40 percent, with 30 percentage points of that growth attributable to the service industry alone (Maestas et al. 2013). Specifically, a 1-percentage point gain in labor demand in the service industry in this age group led to a 1 percent increase in staying on the job, about a 7 percent increase in returning to the labor force, and a 3 percent decrease in retirement. There is also evidence of a 4 percent increase in wages for workers staying on the job and an 11 percent increase for those returning to the labor force, along with reduction in claiming Social Security benefits of 14 percent at age 62, 7 percent at age 63, and 11 percent at age 64. In other words, employer demand for older workers in an industry that offers less physically demanding work, flexible hours, and greater interaction with people leads to increased work and longer labor force participation.

In terms of older workers' labor supply, recent research indicates that education and health status are key variables. While older workers at all educational levels increased their labor force participation between 2000 and 2010, workers with at least a college education were much more likely to continue to work. Less-educated workers responded less, perhaps because their jobs lacked appeal, perhaps because of a higher Social Security replacement rate, and perhaps because of a higher probability of chronic health issues or more physically taxing work (Johnson 2013).

Psychological as well as economic factors seem to have been influential in promoting longer work. Discussions about what is or should be the 'full retirement age' in the media and in communications from the Social Security Administration have raised the profile of this issue. The public is becoming increasingly aware of the advantages of working longer and delaying receipt of Social Security benefits for greater financial security in retirement (Butrica et al. 2006; Song and Manchester 2007; Steuerle and Cushing-Daniels 2010).

Steps to a More Secure Retirement

Fortunately, the United States confronts its future in a relatively strong position. The nation remains rich, with a GDP of more than $140,000 per household, and government spending and tax subsidies (at all levels) of $55,000 per household (Steuerle 2014). Those numbers are expected to continue to grow over time, doubling perhaps in three or four decades, even assuming a below-average rate of growth. To take better advantage of our options, we can therefore exploit the additional resources made possible by economic growth, and the increased demand for older workers. Three major types of policy changes deserve serious consideration. First, the growth in public old-age benefits over time can be targeted to the most vulnerable elderly, particularly those in the bottom third or half of the lifetime income distribution. Second, public pension reforms can encourage longer work lives and orientation of benefits to the oldest ages. Third, private pension reform can also recognize increased longevity and demand for older workers while simultaneously making workplace saving more automatic and accessible for workers, particularly at small- and medium-sized firms.

Increasing Social Security's progressivity and limiting the rate of benefit growth for those with greater means

Social Security's progressive rate schedule reveals that it is intended to provide more to those in greater need. Yet some research has shown that benefits are not as progressive as one might think; indeed, excluding disability insurance, it is not clear that the system as a whole is progressive at all, given that annuitization favors those in better health, and other regressive factors, such as the design of spousal and survivor insurance (Steuerle et al. 2004; Brown et al. 2006; Steuerle et al. 2013). Nevertheless, it would be quite easy to design a minimum benefit or similar feature that could insure that those with lower lifetime incomes, say, the bottom two quintiles, would receive a higher level of lifetime and annual benefits than they receive now.[8] This can be achieved in a Social Security system with benefits either larger or smaller than the ones currently scheduled. The key reform would orient some of the future growth in Social Security benefits towards those with lower lifetime incomes.

Whatever benefit cuts or tax increases are enacted to restore some long-term actuarial balance, almost inevitably they will be paid for by those with the most means. Without recommending any particular proposal, it is worth noting that such reductions in benefits (or increases in taxes) have side effects that need to be taken into account. For instance, if a slower rate of benefit growth were extended downward to those near the middle of the income distribution, and minimum benefit changes did not extend upward to them, then private pension reform becomes even more imperative. Also, if lifetime benefit growth rates are slowed through annual benefit cuts in all ages (e.g. an increase in what is called the 'normal retirement age' in Social Security), the incentives for work likely will be lower than such changes as an increase in the early retirement age or the reallocation of lifetime benefits more toward later years. Put another way, that share of benefit cuts in very old age may do little for labor force participation.

Encouraging longer work and shorter retirement

Employment patterns are significantly influenced by aging, but aging itself is a bit of a misnomer, since it is composed of two very different forces. Living longer does not by itself put additional pressure on government programs or private retirement; typically it only does so if those additional years of life, largely due to better health, are accompanied by an increase in years of government-supported retirement and no corresponding increase in labor. A decline in the birth rate, however, does mean an increase in the percentage of the population eventually moving into more dependent older years. Its influence on current employment rates remained hidden until Baby Boomers started attaining their 60s.

Government (and private pension) policy oriented toward need would tackle the increase in the percentage of the population who will be in, say, the last 10 years of life when ability to work decreases and health limitations rise. That does not mean that such policy needs to keep extending benefits for more and more years as people live longer. Indeed, if old age is defined by something like being in the last 10 years of life on an expected basis, then Social Security has moved over the years to being more and more a middle-age retirement system, one that provides ever smaller shares of benefits over time to true old age.

Given trends outlined in this chapter, three changes in the design of public retirement programs deserve strong consideration. First, the earliest retirement age could increase, while years of support on average could be capped at current levels or even decreased. It is possible to protect vulnerable populations with minimum benefits and disability programs, without providing so many years of support to middle- and upper-income and healthy families. The perverse nature of today's unreformed system becomes apparent when upper-income people receive, for example, five more years of additional Social Security support at $30,000 a year (or the actuarial equivalent if they work longer) to provide five or fewer years of additional support at $10,000 to those with low incomes.

To the extent these changes lead to higher labor output, the economic benefits extend far beyond Social Security: higher GDP, higher personal income, and higher tax revenues. It is the one reform that allows for both higher benefits and lower tax rates, all other things being the same. For example, an increase in the early retirement age generally increases Social Security taxes and benefits in tandem because of the actuarial adjustments, but it simultaneously increases personal income, along with income and Medicare taxes.

Yet another way to increase labor output is to backload benefits in Social Security, providing a lower up-front benefit for most in exchange for higher benefits payable at older ages. For instance, a lower benefit could be provided until average years of remaining life expectancy approach about 10, and then the benefit could rise thereafter. This could be done without reducing benefits, on average, for those in lower income classes, through higher minimum benefits and similar adjustments already discussed. In addition to beneficial effects on personal income and non-Social Security taxes, back loading also converts Social Security into a system that provides most protection when needed, in the later years of life, not late middle age.

Signals from public benefit plans also matter for private behavior, even when there are few or no changes in net economic incentives. Here, we have referred to the early 60s as late middle age, at least as measured by average life expectancy. Evidence is mounting that Social Security communications telling people they are 'old' and entitled to support at age 62, or that 'normal' retirement is at age 66 today, have a significant influence on retirement decisions beyond any change in net economic incentives (Steuerle and Cushing-Daniels 2010). Refining those signals can have enormous influence on behavior, not just on near-retirees but on financial planners and employers who often follow those signals in designing, offering, and planning private retirement options.

Expanding the private pension system

Assuming, as is likely, that the 401(k)-type plan will continue to be the dominant plan type for the foreseeable future, its expansion calls for three elements: (1) access to a plan at work for more workers; (2) an improved rate of contributions and return on investments; and (3) mechanisms to secure income in retirement years. Few would argue with the merits of such changes, but it is important to recognize that their success would entail substantial revenue cost to the government. While such costs are unlikely in the current environment of deficit cutting, we believe they can easily be accommodated in the broader context of Social Security reform because at that point the government is already going to be reallocating trillions of dollars of benefits and taxes for very long periods of time. Traditionally, Social Security reform tries to achieve balance for at least 75 years.

Access to a retirement plan at work has long been recognized as the single most important element in improving the private pension system, yet many workers, particularly those who need retirement savings the most, remain outside the system. Legal reforms now offer employers tax credits for sponsoring a plan, special plans with little or no discrimination tests like the auto-enrollment safe harbor 401(k) plan, and reduced fiduciary liability through participant investment discretion and the use of Qualified Default Investment Alternatives as investment options. Yet there has been no appreciable increase in the percentage of employers, particularly small to mid-size employers, willing to offer plans. Small- and medium-size employer reluctance to do so is understandable because of the costs associated with complexity (partly due to all the choices available), dealings with accountants and planners, and potential fiduciary responsibilities.

One clear obstacle to expanding pension coverage is the voluntary nature of the United States pension system. Imposing a mandate on employers to sponsor a plan, proposed on and off for the last 50 years or so, may not be a realistic policy option in today's political climate. Imposing a soft mandate in the form of a 'play or pay' requirement in the spirit of the Affordable Care Act's employer mandate also seems politically infeasible. But it may be feasible to attract small and mid-size employers to a simple plan that expands participation by lower-paid workers. For example, in exchange for a range of benefits, the proposed 'Super Simple' 401(k) plan requires participating employers to provide a minimum contribution and include all employees through auto-enrollment at a moderate contribution rate. With an additional saver's credit contribution from the government, lower-paid employees could receive total annual contributions of, say, 8 percent of income, a healthy start to accumulating significant assets. In exchange, the Super Simple would have minimal rules, higher allowed levels of salary deferral contributions, and little or no fiduciary liability for employers (Perun and Steuerle 2008).

Creative possibilities also exist if we reconceptualize the role of the employer as plan sponsor in the 401(k) plan system. In the old DB plan system, it was necessary to have an employer-centric system where plan sponsorship entailed significant legal obligations to ensure that employers made good on their pension promises. In a DC plan system where the majority of the risks and responsibilities for saving fall on workers, where independent financial services companies provide investments, and where professional administrators manage the plan, it is self-defeating to continue to insist that employers as plan sponsors remain the ultimate guarantors of the plan and all its functions.

There is increasing recognition that the next bold move in the evolution of the 401(k) plan system could be to transform employers into facilitators of their employees' saving. This merely requires activating an employer's payroll system to transfer employee contributions to a saving plan run by an external entity. Such a system has been in place for decades in the 403(b) plan universe where employers typically make supplemental savings plans available to their employees. In such plans, employers are not fiduciaries, and their primary responsibility is to transfer elective contributions, limited in amount as in the 401(k) world, to the plan chosen by the employee.

The MyRA plan, recently announced by the Obama administration, represents a small step towards such a transformation of the role of the employer in the for-profit world. Granted, the MyRA account would not have all the bells and whistles of a full-fledged saving plan, but it could provide a badly needed 'starter' account for small savers. A more substantial proposal which revitalizes the old payroll deduction IRA that has been in the code for decades is the 'Auto-IRA' proposal endorsed by the Obama administration. Utilizing an auto-enrollment, payroll-deduction model, the Auto-IRA would also release employers from the obligations of a plan sponsor or fiduciary.

A related proposal for USA Retirement Funds would create a new retirement plan system for uncovered workers, in which the role of the employer would be limited to enrolling workers and facilitating payroll deduction contributions. USA Funds would be administered by a board of trustees who would act as fiduciaries, and also engage professional money managers and plan administrators. Finally, several states have decided to enter the pension arena on behalf of private sector workers lacking a plan at work. California has adopted the Secure Choice Retirement Savings Trust statute to build such a system if research and design results indicate that implementation is feasible.

The chief drawback of most of these proposals is that they all lack employer contributions, since under current law employers who contribute to a plan become fiduciaries. Yet without employer contributions, it will be difficult for these plans to generate assets sufficient for a secure retirement through employee savings alone. Assuming that these new plans have robust regulatory structures, changing pension law to accommodate employer contributions without attaching imposing fiduciary duties could be considered.

In summary, the private pension system has morphed from a DB to a DC system without much thought or pre-planning. With so many proposals for change to today's system to make it more inclusive and productive, there is now an opportunity for serious pension reform as well. A key consideration should be a revised role for the employer in today's employee-centric saving system, focusing on facilitating employee savings supplemented by employer contributions.

Conclusion

Long-term pressures on the broader economy almost inevitably affect considerations of retirement system reform, whether public or private. Today, those pressures include a continuing decline in the adult employment rate and the corresponding rise in demand for older employees as other sources of labor become more scarce; public retirement and health entitlement programs so out of balance that they are starting to crowd out education and other spending; the tendency to provide more years of retirement support simply as people live longer; the growth in the percentage of the population that is truly old because of a drop in birth rates; and private retirement plans that are inadequate for most, along with the gradual evolution of defined contribution plans to employee-centric models.

We have noted ways that entitlement reform can accommodate those forces while allowing private pension system reform to come along hand-in-hand and fill other gaps in the future needs of households. Regardless of particular approach, the ultimate measures of success include improved financial security for those retiring with near or below poverty incomes, an increase in the percentage of the middle- and lower-income population with significant private financial assets in retirement, and an enabling of greater labor force participation to increase both individual incomes and government revenues to help achieve these goals.

Endnotes

1. The debt-to-GDP ratio doubled between the end of 2007 and the end of 2012, rising from 36.3 percent in 2007 to 72.6 percent in 2012.
2. Kogan (2012) provides a discussion of the mechanics of BCA.
3. ATRA avoided steep increases in tax payments by permanently extending several ongoing tax cuts that had been scheduled to expire, many of which had been extended annually, sometimes retroactively. Major components include a permanent extension in the alternative minimum tax patch; extension of income tax cuts originally enacted during the Bush administration for taxpayers with incomes below $450,000 if married and $400,000 if single; and a 40 percent estate tax rate coupled with a $5 million exemption indexed to inflation. See Harris et al. (2013) for further details.
4. The growth in Medicare, Medicaid, and out-of-pocket medical spending declined precipitously in the five years spanning 2006 to 2011 relative to the prior five years (National Academy of Sciences 2012; Holahan and McMorrow 2013).
5. 'Tax expenditures' refer to deductions, credits, exclusions from income, and special tax rates on other forms of income that reduce tax liabilities for some households.
6. By 2012, the share of employers who sponsored a 401(k)-type plan had risen to 60 percent, up from 51 percent in 2009 (Copeland 2013). Overall, participation by employees offering such a plan was 43 percent in 2012, up from roughly 35 percent in 2009.
7. Some calculations indicate that a lower level of income in retirement is feasible because some costs, such as transportation, are lower, but these calculations usually fail to include health care, where average costs under current practices

rise dramatically in older age and either government or the individuals themselves must cover those costs (Skinner 2007).

8. It turns out that many of those with limited lifetime incomes, particularly women, have only a scattered work history, so such a minimum benefit needs to be designed both around low lifetime earnings subject to tax (the base for the current rate formula), as well as some other accommodations such as some minimum credit for some years of child rearing.

References

AARP (2010). *Social Security 75th Anniversary Survey Report: Public Opinion Trends.* Washington, DC: AARP. <http://www.aarp.org/work/social-security/info-08-2010/social_security_75th.html>.

Altshuler, R., K. Lim, and R. Williams (2010). 'Desperately Seeking Revenue.' *National Tax Journal,* 63(2): 331–52.

Auerbach, A., W. G. Gale, and B. H. Harris (2014). *Federal Health Spending and the Budget Outlook: Some Alternative Scenarios,* Engelberg Center for Health Care Reform Working Paper. Washington, DC: Brookings Institution.

Bowman, K. and A. Rugg (2012). 'What Did the Public Think about Taxes in 2011?' On the Margin, *Tax Notes.* May 14: <https://www.aei.org/publication/what-did-the-public-think-about-taxes-in-2011>.

Bricker, J., A. B. Kennickell, K. B. Moore, and J. Sabelhaus (2012). 'Changes in U.S. Family Finances from 2007 to 2010: Evidence from the Survey of Consumer Finances.' *Federal Reserve Bulletin,* 98(2). Washington, DC: Board of Governors of the Federal Reserve System.

Brown, J. R., J. L. Coronado, and D. Fullerton (2006). *The Progressivity of Social Security,* NBER Working Paper, 7520. Cambridge, MA: National Bureau of Economic Research.

Butrica, B. A., K. E. Smith, and C. E. Steuerle (2006). *Working for a Good Retirement,* Retirement Project Working Paper, 06–03. Washington, DC: Urban Institute.

Congressional Budget Office (CBO) (2013a). *The Distribution of Major Tax Expenditures in the Individual Income Tax System.* Pub. No. 4308. Washington, DC: CBO.

Congressional Budget Office (CBO) (2013b). *Rising Demand for Long-Term Services and Supports for Elderly People.* Pub. No. 4240. Washington, DC: CBO.

Congressional Budget Office (CBO) (2013*c*). *The 2013 Long-Term Budget Outlook.* Pub. No. 4713. Washington, DC: CBO.

Copeland, C. (2013). *Retirement Plan Participation: Survey of Income and Program Participation (SIPP) Data, 2012,* Notes, 34(8). Washington, DC: Employee Benefit Research Institute.

Council of Economic Advisors (2013). *Economic Report of the President.* Washington, DC: GPO.

Dube, A. (2013). *A Note on Debt, Growth and Causality,* Working Paper. <http://arindube.com/working-papers>.

Elmendorf, D. W. and N. G. Mankiw (1999). 'Government Debt,' in J. B. Taylor and M. Woodford (eds), *Handbook of Macroeconomics.* Amsterdam: Elsevier, 1(3): 1615–69.

Gale, W. G. and P. Orszag (2004). 'Budgets, Deficits, National Saving, and Interest Rates.' *Brookings Papers on Economic Activity,* 2004(2): 101–210.

Harris, B. H., C. E. Steuerle, and C. Quakenbush (2013). *Today's Unsustainable Budget Policy: A Recount,* Urban Institute and Brookings Institution Working Paper. Washington, DC: Urban-Brookings Tax Policy Center.

Herndon, T., M. Ash, and R. Pollin (2013). *Does High Public Debt Consistently Stifle Economic Growth? A Critique of Reinhart and Rogoff,* PERI Working Paper, 322. Amherst, MA: Political Economy Research Institute.

Holahan, J. and S. McMorrow (2013). 'Medicare and Medicaid Spending Trends and the Deficit Debate.' *New England Journal of Medicine,* 367(5): 393–5.

Investment Company Institute (ICI) (2013). *2013 Fact Book.* Washington, DC: The Investment Company Institute. <http://www.ici.org/research/stats/retirement/ret_13_q3>.

Johnson, R. W. (2013). 'Why Don't Less-Educated Older Adults Work Longer?' Paper presented at the symposium Towards a Policy Agenda for an Aging America, sponsored by the TIAA-CREF Institute and the Alfred P. Sloan Foundation, Washington, DC, Nov. 19.

Kogan, R. (2012). *How the Across-the-Board Cuts in the Budget Control Act Will Work.* Washington, DC: Center on Budget and Policy Priorities. <http://www.cbpp.org/files/12-2-11bud2.pdf>.

Maestas, N., K. J. Mullen, and D. Powell (2013). *The Effect of Local Labor Demand Conditions on the Labor Supply Outcomes of Older Americans,* Working Paper, WR-1019. Santa Monica, CA: Rand Corporation.

Munnell, A. H., R. C. Fraenkel, and J. Hurwitz (2012). *The Pension Coverage Problem in the Private Sector,* CRR Brief 12–16. Chestnut Hill, MA Center for Research at Boston College.

National Academy of Sciences, National Research Council (2012). *Aging and the Macro Economy: Long-Term Implications of an Aging Population.* Washington, DC: National Academies Press.

Office of Management and Budget (OMB) (2014). *Budget of the United States Government: Analytical Perspectives.* Washington, DC: GPO.

Pension Benefit Guaranty Corporation (PBGC) (2012). *PBGC Pension Data at a Glance (1975–2011).* Tables S-31 and S-32. <http://www.pbgc.gov/documents/pension-insurance-data-tables-2011.pdf>.

Perun, P. and C. E. Steuerle (2008). *Why Not a 'Super Simple' Saving Plan for the United States?* Opportunity and Ownership Project Report, 3. Washington, DC: Urban Institute.

Pew Research Center (2013). *Obama Job Approval Slips as Economic Pessimism Rises.* Washington, DC: Pew Research Center. <http://www.people-press.org/2013/03/21/obama-job-approval-slips-as-economic-pessimism-rises>.

Poterba, J. M. (2014). *Retirement Security in an Aging Society,* NBER Working Paper, 19930. Cambridge, MA: National Bureau of Economic Research.

Reinhart, C. M. and K. S. Rogoff (2010). 'Growth in a Time of Debt.' *American Economic Review,* 100(2): 573–8.

Skinner, J. (2007). 'Are you Sure you're Saving Enough for Retirement?' *Journal of Economic Perspectives,* 21(3): 59–80.

Song, J. and J. Manchester (2007). 'Have People Delayed Claiming Retirement Benefits? Responses to Changes in Social Security Rules.' *Social Security Bulletin,* 67(2): 1–23.

Steuerle, C. E. (2013). 'A New Basis for Forecasting Long-Term Health Spending: Federal Budget Implications,' in *Sustainable U.S. Health Spending: Public Sector Imperative, Private Sector Urgency.* Washington, DC: Altarum Institute, 29–34.

Steuerle, C. E. (2014). *Dead Men Ruling: How to Restore Fiscal Freedom and Rescue our Future.* New York: Century Foundation.

Steuerle, C. E., A. Carasso, and L. Cohen (2004). *How Progressive is Social Security and Why?* Straight Talk on Social Security and Retirement Policy, 37. Washington, DC: Urban Institute.

Steuerle, C. E. and B. Cushing-Daniels (2010). *Retirement and Social Security: A Time Series Approach Based on Remaining Life Expectancy,* Working Paper. Washington, DC: Urban Institute.

Steuerle, C. E. and C. Quakenbush (2012). *Correcting Labor Supply Projections for Older Workers Could Help Social Security and Economic Reform,* Program on Retirement Policy Brief, 35. Washington, DC: Urban Institute.

Steuerle, C. E., K. E. Smith, and C. Quakenbush (2013). *Has Social Security Redistributed to White from People of Color?* Program on Retirement Policy Brief, 38. Washington, DC: Urban Institute.

Teixeira, R. (2012). *Public Opinion Snap Shot: 2 Things the Public Wants Policymakers to Remember.* Washington, DC: Center for American Progress. <https://www.americanprogress.org/issues/public-opinion/news/2012/12/03/46489/public-opinion-snapshot-2-things-the-public-wants-policymakers-to-remember>.

Tucker, J. V., V. P. Reno, and T. N. Bethell (2013). *Strengthening Social Security: What Do Americans Want?* Washington, DC: National Academy of Social Insurance. <http://www.nasi.org/sites/default/files/research/What_Do_Americans_Want.pdf>.

United States Department of Labor (2010). *Record Unemployment among Older Workers Does Not Keep them Out of the Job Market,* Issues in Labor Statistics. Summary 10–04. Mar. Washington, DC: US Department of Labor, Bureau of Labor Statistics.

United States Department of Labor, Employee Benefit Security Administration (2013). Private Pension Plan Bulletin Historical Tables and Graphs. Washington, DC: US Department of Labor, Bureau of Labor Statistics.

United States Equal Employment Opportunity Commission (EEOC) (2013). *Charge Statistics FY 1997 to FY 2013.* Washington, DC: Equal Employment Opportunity Commission.

Part II

New Thinking about Retirement Risk Sharing

Chapter 6

Risk Sharing Alternatives for Pension Plan Design: An Overview and Case Studies

Anna M. Rappaport and Andrew Peterson

Pension plan designs range from those that place virtually all of the risk on the plan (and plan sponsor) to those that place nearly all of the risk on the individuals covered by the plan. Traditional defined benefit (DB) plans may be found at one end of this spectrum, while defined contribution (DC) plans are at the other. Neither is ideal, so new alternatives are needed to provide better retirement security on a sustainable and affordable basis. Fortunately, there is increasing attention being given to new plan types that increase risk sharing and thus fit more in the middle on the risk sharing spectrum (Fuerst 2015; Blitzstein 2015). This chapter identifies the various risks and discusses methods of sharing them, both in traditional DB plans and in hybrid plan designs. Next we discuss different methods of risk sharing and provide considerations when adopting them. Two case studies identify recent developments.

Our focus is on the perspectives of various stakeholder groups, primarily the plan sponsor (who is often the employer), and the benefit plan participant or retiree. Other stakeholders include financial services companies and the public at large, who also have an interest in this topic, but these broader considerations are beyond the scope of the chapter.

Context and Background

The United States retirement system is made up of a combination of Social Security, employer-sponsored pension plans, personal savings, and (increasingly) continued work during retirement. Employer support for pensions has shifted over time, from DB plans to DC plan arrangements. The current system has a number of problems, including the fact that traditional DB plan costs are perceived to be too volatile. Also, many organizations are either closing traditional DB plans to new entrants or freezing benefit accruals for all with the intention of terminating the plan when it is financially viable to do so. These actions indicate that such plans are often viewed as unsustainable. Some DB plans are in financial trouble and may not be able to pay the full promised benefits. In addition, some well-funded DB plans have moved into a state of financial trouble because they granted too many benefit increases and subsidies at early retirement.

Many individuals do not have the motivation, knowledge, or skill to provide a satisfactory retirement income on their own. Many DC plan participants will not have adequate benefits at retirement because of contributing too little, using the money too early, or not earning enough investment income due to overly conservative or poorly timed decisions. While lifetime income is the most secure way to deliver benefits during retirement, few DC plan benefits are paid as lifetime income, and many plans do not offer such an option.

There has been a major shift to DC plans underway for a number of years. The structure of DC plans has been changing to improve the benefits that they are delivering and to make them less reliant on individual decisions. At the same time, experts discussing the pension system have pointed out that risk pooling is very desirable, and that other options may better serve the societal need for a well-designed and functional retirement system.

Research Findings

Several recent projects have explored principles for better plan design along with new approaches to evaluate pension systems. The American Academy of Actuaries AGES report (2014) looks at four factors necessary for an effective and strong future pension system. These include alignment, governance, efficiency, and sustainability. While the report does not directly propose specific plan designs, several of the issues it raises are linked to plan design. Alignment speaks to linking plan management to the capabilities and needs of each of the stakeholder groups, so as to have the plan work well for both plan sponsors and participants. It also implies a plan design that works for participants with long service with a single employer as well as for those with a series of jobs or with periods in and out of the labor force. Governance refers to a plan structure that has direction and controls as part of the overall design. If adjustments are built into expectations for the plan, the combination of both design and governance is needed to make it work well. Efficiency speaks to grouping smaller plans into larger multiple-entity arrangements, providing opportunities for retirement asset accumulation through a working career, minimizing leakage during the payout and accumulation phases, encouraging pooling of risks and appropriate risk sharing, keeping expenses low, and assisting in narrowing the variability of benefits by fostering hedging of risks to support guarantees. Efficiency lowers costs and allows more contributions to be used for benefits rather than covering plan expenses. Sustainability speaks to intergenerational equity, appropriate cost allocation among stakeholders, weathering market shocks, and achieving an appropriate balance between these results while providing adequate benefits. In addition, self-adjusting systems are proposed as a method of achieving sustainability.

The Society of Actuaries Retirement 20/20 project served as a precursor to and background for the Retirement for the AGES project. It brought together a variety of stakeholders in several forums and collected papers to identify some of the best ideas internationally for building a pension system absent current regulatory constraints. Alignment of stakeholder interests, self-adjusting systems, and risk sharing were among the ideas explored. Six themes identified in that project are: (1) systems should consider new norms for work and retirement and the role of the normative retirement age; (2) systems should align stakeholders' roles with their skills; (3) systems should be designed to self-adjust; (4) systems should be better aligned with financial markets; (5) systems should clarify the role of the employer; and (6) retirement systems will not succeed without improvements in the health and long-term care systems (Society of Actuaries 2007). The discussions in the Retirement 20/20 project point to several ideas that enter the discussion on risk sharing and plan design: the importance of appropriate retirement ages, using self-adjusting features, recognizing workplace realities, and understanding the roles of various stakeholders.

The Melbourne Mercer Global Pension Index reviews the operation of the overall pension system in 20 countries and grades the systems on overall categories of adequacy, sustainability, and integrity (Mercer 2013). The ratings include both public benefits (social insurance) and the private system. The scores are based on responses to questions in each category. The degree of variation in the responses by country is much greater for some questions than for others. An individual country may be rated highly on some questions and poorly on others. Several issues raised in the index study are important to plan design and risk sharing. The areas for improvement frequently refer to retirement ages and how people retire, including raising the minimum age for retirement benefits, raising state pension ages, and improving labor force participation at older ages. There is a wide variation in ratings, and Denmark is currently the only country rated with an A grade.

Both the Melbourne Mercer index and the Society of Actuaries Retirement 20/20 project recognize the importance of retirement ages in the long-term future of retirement systems. The former study asked about time of retirement in terms of the gap between retirement ages and life expectancy today and in 2035. The low scores for average period of pension payment today are 7.3 in India and 12.4 in Mexico. The high scores are 19.7 in France and 21.4 in Korea (Mercer 2013). The 2013 index report also included a new question to explore phased retirement. In response to questions about whether employees could receive private plan benefits, continue working part-time, and continue accruing benefits or contributing to their plans, six of the twenty countries received a maximum score, six received a score of zero, and eight were given something in between (Mercer 2013). Additional demographic questions focused on fertility rates and expected old age dependency rates in 2035. Another major area of focus is the method used to pay benefits during retirement, with a focus on the extent to which lifetime income is used. The discussion of private plans is heavily focused on DC plans. Noteworthy for this chapter are the wide variations in systems by country, the importance of sustainability, the importance of lifetime income payouts, and the recommendation for adjusting retirement ages and options with demographic changes.

Considerations Affecting Plan Design in the Future

When designing a retirement plan, a wide range of risks should be considered, both pre- and post-retirement. While investment, inflation, and longevity risk are always important, several additional risks are worth noting: these include employment risk, business risk, and the risk of poor choices. Some, such as the risk of family change, do not directly impact plan design and will not be discussed. In Table 6.1, we summarize the list, along with factors facing plan sponsors and participants in retirement and when they generally apply—whether in the pre- or post-retirement phase. Failure to focus on the range of risks when considering alternatives may result in incorrect conclusions.

In the debate about the future of the United States pension system, questions arise as to whether these plans should be voluntary or mandatory and universal. Moreover, a system can be mandatory at the employer level, but still optional for individual employees. Another area of disagreement is whether lifetime income should be mandated, or instead strongly encouraged for all or some part of retirement assets.

Sustainability, the ability of a retirement system to last through economic cycles and demographic changes, is critical to the long-term success of the retirement system (American Academy of Actuaries 2014). What is needed to maintain sustainability varies with the regulatory climate and method of accounting used by plan sponsors. The move to more transparency and use of market values has increased the focus on short-term results. While this move has not changed the underlying economics of retirement plans, it has made it more important that there be safety valves enabling pension plan sponsors to deal with extreme economic conditions. Self-adjusting systems, to be discussed here, offer examples of safety valves.

TABLE 6.1 Major risks facing plan sponsors and participants in retirement plans

Risk	Definition	Pre- or post-retirement risk
Investment	Risk that returns on invested assets are different from what is expected	Both
Interest rate risk	Risk of unexpected changes in interest rates leading to changes in value of defined plan liabilities, changes in annuity prices, and to changes in the interest earnings on fixed dollar investments and bank accounts	Both and also at time of retirement
Inflation risk	Risk resulting from loss of purchasing power due to unexpected increases in price levels.	Both
Longevity risk	Risk resulting from differences in the level of population mortality and/or the risk that any particular individual will live longer (or shorter) than expected	Primarily post-retirement
Employment risk	Risk that individual will lose job prior to retirement or leave and lose future benefit accruals; also includes risk of being pushed into retirement earlier than planned	Pre-retirement
Business risk	Risk that business sponsoring plan will do poorly, impacting jobs, that employer will decide to change plans, or be acquired leading to plan change	Primarily pre-retirement, but also post-retirement if benefits being paid from plan are not fully funded
Risk of poor choices	Risk that participant will not make good choices leading to insufficient savings and/or a poor plan for using funds post-retirement	Both and at time of retirement
Fiduciary risk	Risk that plan sponsors and service providers don't meet fiduciary requirements; sponsor may be subject to penalties if they fail to meet them	As long as funds remain in the plan
Solvency risk	Risk that any entity providing benefits will become insolvent, or unable to pay benefits and that there will be a default on all or part of benefit payments	Both
Public policy risk	Risk that policy will change or be enforced in a way that creates adverse impact	Both

Source: Authors' analysis.

The effectiveness of a retirement system for participants depends on accumulating enough resources for retirement and on using them effectively in retirement. Lump sums are generally an inefficient way of using resources in retirement, because these eliminate the efficiency of risk pooling and place longevity risk on participants. In addition, they provide more funds to those who die earlier rather than to those who live long. This is an issue in both DB and DC plans (Mercer 2013; Society of Actuaries 2007). A discussion of designs for the future and methods of risk sharing needs to include the post-retirement period. Table 6.1 includes information on when risks apply and identifies which risks are applicable to the post-retirement period.

Different Ways to Share Risk

By risk sharing, we mean the distribution of risk between various plan or system stakeholders. The Society of Actuaries Retirement 20/20 report identified four primary stakeholders: society, employers, participants, and markets (2007). In the present context we slightly expand these categories to identify stakeholders as employer plan sponsors, participants, financial service companies, policymakers, guarantee organizations, and the public at large. Risk can also be shared by different groups of plan participants, between participants and employers, between participants and financial service companies, etc. As laid out in Table 6.2, risk can be shared in different ways, through plan design or benefit structure, financing structures, self-adjusting systems, pooling, multiple entity arrangements, third party guarantees, and backup guarantee funds. Next we offer a discussion of how risk sharing approaches can be used in pension systems, either one at a time or in combination.

Using plan design to define risk sharing and allocation

Methods of defining risk sharing and allocation through plan design include allocating risk directly in the method of determining benefits, adjusting benefits based on funding level or some other defined trigger (self-adjusting system), and/or including contingent benefits in the plan.

DB and DC plans allocate risk directly as part of plan design. Traditional DC plans with lump sum payouts place essentially all risk on plan participants (although some plans do pool investment risk in the pre-retirement phase). Variable annuity policies may include a floor guarantee on investment returns or on income to be paid out, thereby sharing risk between an insurance company and the policyholder. These plans put most risk on the individual but do place some risk on the insurance company. A charge is

TABLE 6.2 Strategies for managing and sharing risk

Strategy	Description	Type of sharing	Comments
Plan design	Defines benefit and obligations of parties	Between plan sponsor and participant	Different types of plan structures share risk differently; variations can moderate risk sharing
Financial structure	Defines who pays for benefits and how cost shared, and allocated over time	In contributory plans, risk shared between plan sponsor and participant, risk may also be shared with third party	In noncontributory plans, no sharing of financial risk
Self-adjusting systems	Provisions in plans that adjust arrangements based on circumstances	Used to moderate risk sharing	Can apply to plan design or financial structure
Risk pooling	Spreads risk over a group of participants and defines pool	Spreads between individual participants, or entities within same risk pool	Some risks pool well, for some anti-selection is a potential problem, and some do not pool at all
Multi-entity arrangements	Uses a single plan to provide benefits to participants from multiple entities	May share risks between entities depending on type of arrangement	
Third party guarantees	If benefits are insured, then a third party, usually an insurance company, offers a guarantee	Involves sharing risk with third party in exchange for a market price	
Backup guarantee funds	Governmentally or industry sponsored arrangements to provide backup guarantees; provide protection for solvency risk	Shares risk across pension plans, banks or insurance companies; provides protection to individuals	US examples are the Pension Benefit Guaranty Corporation, the FDIC, and state insurance guarantee funds. Other countries have generally similar programs.

Source: Authors' analysis.

levied for each guarantee purchased. If the variable annuity policies are used to fund an employer-sponsored plan, the employer may share some of this risk.

Traditional non-contributory final average pay DB plans which do not offer indexing of benefits after retirement place most risk on the plan sponsor, but the post-retirement inflation risk is held by the participant. The participant is also at risk in the event of plan sponsor bankruptcy or failure to provide needed funds to the plan.[1] In addition, the participant is at risk with respect to future benefit accruals.[2] This is an important issue since the benefit accrual pattern in these plans provides for much higher accruals as the participant nears retirement. These plans involve risk pooling, so that mortality and investment risk are shared within the risk pool. The plan sponsors bear all risks assigned to these risk pools. In a single employer plan, one employer bears the risk, whereas in a multiple entity arrangement, the risks may be shared between entities depending on the structure of the arrangement. Traditional career average pay pension plans allocate investment and longevity risk to the plan sponsor, and inflation risk, both pre- and post-retirement, to the participant. The custom for many organizations that sponsored such plans was to provide for periodic ad hoc updates to the career average benefit, shifting some of the inflation risk to the plan sponsor. Increases were at the discretion of the plan sponsor, providing for a different method of risk allocation.

Table 6.3 provides more detail by contrasting how plan sponsors and participants face risks in the most common types of retirement plans. Table 6.3 also shows that both groups bear some risk, even in traditional DB and DC plans. Traditionally, larger employers balanced the risk borne by the individual and the employer by offering both DB and DC plans. Such combinations could be tailored to the needs of the organization and also provide some balancing between employees of different ages. Traditional final average pay DB plans provided relatively small benefits for those who left the firm early in their careers, and much better benefit accruals later, particularly at the point of approaching unreduced retirement benefits. By contrast, DC plans provided significantly greater retirement benefits for early career participants, due to investment income expected to accumulate over the many years during which the account balances were invested prior to retirement.

Many employers have adopted hybrid plans, and innovative ideas for new designs are emerging. A recent study on hybrid pension plans identified a wide range of hybrid arrangements and a broad range of risks (Turner 2014). The study included both actual arrangements in existence and proposed new ideas, including types of hybrid plan designs that divide risks between those that apply to the pre-retirement period versus after retirement. It also split plans between those that shift risk to participants in pre-retirement, to participants at retirement, to participants post-retirement, and to participants both pre- and post-retirement. Hybrids can be structured to start from a DB design and shift some of the risks to participants, or to start from a DC design and shift some of the risks to a third party or plan sponsor. That study also created a pension risk index and rated several plans with respect to both participant and employer risk.

Risk sharing adjustments built into plan designs may include provisions such as cost-of-living increases that are temporarily discontinued if funding levels drop below a threshold; alternatively, cost-of-living additions can be

TABLE 6.3 Risks assumed by various stakeholders under selected plan designs

Plan type	Plan sponsor risks	Participant risks	Comments
Final average pay defined benefit	In non-contributory plans, full risk that costs exceed expected. Risks include longevity, investment, interest rate risk, and pre-retirement inflation risk.	In most plans, post-retirement inflation risk. Risk that plan will be modified or terminated, or early employment termination. In contributory plans, participants may share risks usually borne by plan sponsor.	Costs reflect benefits already earned and expected future benefits. Benefits already earned are protected on plan termination. Risks can be moderated by adding provisions to adjust benefits based on funding levels.
Career average pay defined benefit	In non-contributory plans, full risk that costs exceed expected. Risks include longevity, investment, and interest rate risk.	Inflation risk. Risk that plan will be modified or terminated. In contributory plans, participants may share risks usually borne by plan sponsor.	It is customary in some plans to provide ad-hoc updates, covering some part of the impact of inflation. Risks can be moderated as mentioned above.
Cash balance	In non-contributory plan, full risk that costs exceed expected. Risks include investment, interest rate risk and some longevity risk (depending on participant choices).	Inflation and most longevity risk. Risk that plan will be modified or terminated. In contributory plans, participants may share risks usually borne by plan sponsor.	Cash balance plans use different return indices subjecting sponsor and participants to varying levels of investment risk. Prevalence of lump sum decisions impacts longevity risk.
Defined contribution	Fiduciary risk if plan not managed properly. Risk that employees will be unable to afford to retire and create workforce management challenges.	Longevity, investment, and inflation risk.	Investments generally not pooled. Risks can be reduced by guaranteeing a floor investment return, but this comes with a price. Such provisions offered in variable annuity contracts.
Collective defined contribution	Fiduciary risk if plan not managed properly. Risk that employees will be unable to afford to retire and there will be difficult human resource issues.	Longevity, investment and inflation risk. Longevity risk may be pooled depending on how benefits are paid. Investment risk may be shared depending on plan structure.	This is a defined contribution plan with pooled investments. Some such plans require annuity payouts.

Note: Some risks discussed in text such as solvency and business risk, and the risk of poor decisions not included in this analysis.

Source: Authors' analysis.

discretionary or contingent on some funding level. This combines benefit design and financing to achieve risk sharing. Other benefit adjustments—permanent or temporary—can be used when funding levels cross certain barriers. Some newer designs, such as plans offered in the Netherlands (Bovenberg et al. 2015) and New Brunswick (Leech and McNish 2013) offer this type of risk adjustment. If funding levels return to the threshold levels, benefit adjustments may be temporary.

The participating group annuity plans used from the 1930s to the 1960s provided that insurance companies could assume most of the risk, while still sharing some with policyholders. The purchase price included a margin for adverse experience, and this amount was returned to the policyholder in the event of good experience. In this way, these plans shared risk between the insurer and the plan sponsor policyholder. They could also increase benefits in the event of good experience, and in that situation, the participant also became part of the risk sharing arrangement.

Using plan financing structure to share risk

Plans that include both employee and employer contributions can share risk through financing adjustments, when the plan's financial status influences contributions to the plan, benefits levels, or both. This is a form of sharing risk across stakeholders. If contributions are set as a level percentage of pay, risk is also shared among the current group of participants, with younger employees paying more than their current share of the cost in DB plan arrangements.

Benefits can also be adjusted up or down based on built-in adjustment rules and/or funded status. Adjusting benefits based on share values or investment returns, or indexing retirement ages with changes in life expectancy, are examples of such adjustments. Benefits may also be adjusted based on funded status thresholds. These adjustments share risk across stakeholder groups and may also share risk within stakeholder groups.

Using self-adjusting systems to manage risk

The studies discussed so far emphasize self-adjusting systems. Self-adjusting systems refer to programs that include built-in features that respond to specified conditions (usually adverse experience) without direct involvement of the plan sponsor. These adjustments can link to both design and funding and can be embedded in a variety of risk management strategies, which can be important when there are shifts in demographic, economic, or business conditions. For example, participating insurance contracts were an early form of self-adjusting system. Cost-of-living increases that are contingent on the funded status of the plan, and provisions that reduce benefits or increase contributions based on funded status, are also forms of self-adjustment.

To date, many retirement systems have not responded effectively to demographic changes (Rappaport 2014). Retirement age increases are needed to enhance the system sustainability in many countries (Mercer 2013), which can also be an adjustment mechanism, if retirement ages automatically increase with life expectancy. It will be very helpful to focus on expanding opportunities for older persons to continue to work and opportunities to phase into retirement (Mercer 2013).

Using risk pooling

Risks that are most readily poolable are those which members do not control and cannot predict (such as life expectancy). When members of a risk pool can control or predict the occurrence of the event being protected, there is the potential for anti-selection.

In a mandatory system such as Social Security, mortality risks are pooled across all beneficiaries, and benefits are paid for life. Those who live longer receive benefits longer, while those who die early receive less in lifetime benefits. The mortality experience reflects the entire population. By contrast, the employer-sponsored DB plan with only an income option pools risk over the employee population that qualifies for benefits. The mortality experience reflects the types of workers in the plan sponsor organization. For example, a coal mining company will have very different mortality from a law firm. The immediate annuity business of an insurance company pools the mortality risk of its policyholders. Since healthier people tend to buy annuities, the insurer's mortality experience must recognize that this group lives longer than Social Security beneficiaries or all employees. It is possible to set up multiple risk classifications and risk pools for annuities to reflect these differences in risk levels. For annuities, this approach is used in both the United Kingdom and in the United States, though it is more common in the former.

The challenges of setting up a risk sharing arrangement using a risk pool include achieving a reasonable spread of risk and being able to charge a reasonable price for the arrangement. When life insurance is sold to individuals, it is priced according to the age and health status of the purchaser. Through a process known as underwriting, the risk is evaluated, and people in poor health may be refused personal life insurance or charged an extra premium. When life insurance is provided to an employer group, it is priced according to the demographic and industry characteristics of the group. The group, rather than the individual, is underwritten.

In a given population at a point in time, a fraction of the pool will be expected to die within the next year. Because life expectancies are changing over time, the number of people expected to die in a similar population a few years later will usually be different. When life expectancies are increasing, the number of deaths expected at each age will decrease over time. The terms 'systemic risk' and 'idiosyncratic risk' are used to understand risk related to changing mortality rates within the population. Idiosyncratic risk is the risk that a particular participant will live longer than expected. Systemic risk is the risk that life expectancy improves by more than expected for the entire cohort. Systemic risk is not poolable, whereas idiosyncratic risk is poolable. Pension and annuity plans that offer lifetime guarantees of income are subject to both types of longevity risk: idiosyncratic longevity risk is managed by pooling, but systemic risk is generally held to be unhedgeable, since few if any assets are widely available to hedge it (Turner 2014).

Establishing multiple entity arrangements

Multiple entity arrangements offer a means to share risk across groups of participants and a way to create larger pools by combining smaller entities. Employers range in size from single individuals and small employers with fewer than ten employees, to major organizations with hundreds of thousands or even millions of employees. Large entities are able to achieve economies of scale, have resources to use strong professional help, and if they pool risk, create large risk pools. Small entities are able to access a greater variety of retirement plan options on a much more economical basis if they can join with a larger entity, provided it fits their needs. Multiple entity arrangements can offer DC and DB plans, or versions of newer hybrid plans. The legal structure of the jurisdiction in which they operate governs the options available to establish such plans. These plans differ in how they operate and in their resulting success. New types of multiple entity plans may be needed in the future, particularly if smaller employers are to have access to retirement plans.

Many United States and Canadian public pensions are multiple entity plans, covering several different entities. For example, the Illinois Municipal Retirement Fund (IMRF) covers 175,000 members linked to 2,900 employers within the state. The system administers a retirement, death, and disability plan in Illinois, and it is a DB plan, with contributions shared by employers and employees. Benefits are guaranteed by the Illinois Constitution, and municipalities and counties outside of the City of Chicago are required to participate in the plan. Many other local government entities can join the plan by choice (IMRF 2012). With this type of plan, a public plan administrator deals with many different entities and offers a variety of services. It may offer a single benefit program or multiple programs from which to choose. The public plans have choices about how they set up their operations and which risks they share and how.[3] They normally would have one set of pooled investments for DB plans and one risk pool for purposes of mortality risk. They also would normally reflect entity demographics in setting contributions. Such public plan systems may be viewed as offering many of the same services as an insurance company, though they are not licensed as insurance companies. Public plans can be made mandatory for the eligible government units by action of the appropriate legislative body.

The pension operations of many religious denominations are also like multiple entity plans, again generally without being formally classified as insurance companies. They can be similar to some of the public pension entities, and if the plans are established as church plans in the United States, they are not subject to the same regulation as private plans. Two examples are the programs sponsored by the Episcopal and the United Methodist Churches (Church Pension Group 2014; General Board of Pensions of the United Methodist Church 2014).

Industry plans are used in the Netherlands (Bovenberg et al. 2015), unlike in the United States. Some US observers view TIAA-CREF as similar to an industry plan for higher education (American Academy of Actuaries 2014; Goodman and Richardson 2015). Multi-employer plans within the United States serve as industry plans within the unionized portion of industries including trucking and iron work.

US multi-employer plans offer pension benefits to unionized employees, and they are jointly managed by employees and representatives of the company (or companies).[4] These plans negotiate contributions and provide benefits defined through a DB formula. Risk is shared across all participating entities, without any adjustment for differences in demographics or when the entity entered the plan. When an employer leaves the plan, it is assessed a withdrawal liability, with the basis of that liability set by law. Some of these plans have seen a major downward spiral as employment patterns have changed and particular occupations and/or industries represented by covered employees declined. For instance, milk deliverers and milliners are examples of occupations that have virtually disappeared today. Some of these plans did not work well, because they were not structured to manage the risk well, particularly in light of demographic and industry challenges.

Third party guarantees and guarantee funds

Risk can also be shifted to third parties through the purchase of financial instruments such as insurance, with a market price set for the risk transfer. Risk can also be partly transferred to a backup guarantee fund. State insurance pools provide guarantees to back up some insurance contracts. The US Pension Benefit Guaranty Corporation (PBGC) provides guarantees for private sector pension benefits. Bank deposits in the United States up to certain limits are guaranteed by the Federal Deposit Insurance Corporation. In addition, there are various examples of guarantee funds in other countries, such as the UK's Pension Protection Fund. Each government-sponsored guarantee fund has its own method of financing. The existence of such funds changes the risk profile of specific benefits. It can also create moral hazard if companies take excessive risks, knowing they are protected.

Risk Sharing as Applied to Different Types of Risks

This chapter has defined the risks, general methods of sharing them, and their allocation to plan sponsors and participants. Table 6.4 offers a more detailed look by identifying specific methods of managing investment risk, interest rate risk, inflation risk, and longevity risk. Here we compare risk management methods available to plan sponsors with those available to participants, expanding on the ideas presented in Tables 6.2 and 6.3 by offering a range of methods for risk sharing.

Investment risk

DC plans in the US allocate investment risk to participants who can select their own investment mix from a menu of choices. The plan administrator is responsible for structuring the choices and usually there is a default investment option viewed as suitable for participants who do not make investment elections. Target date funds that vary the investment allocation according to the time to retirement are now a common default option in the United States. This is quite different from individual retirement accounts (IRAs) where individuals can choose any investment available in the market, and people can work with a variety of different service providers in establishing a plan.

Traditional DB plans allocate investment risk and choice to the plan sponsor. Liability driven investments offer one route to managing investment risk,[5] but this may result in a higher long-term cost, due to giving up higher expected equity returns. However, under some economic scenarios, this strategy could result in lower long-term costs.

There are variations in plan design that allocate the risk differently. For example, cash balance plans with crediting rates based on an economic

TABLE 6.4 Summary of methods for managing key selected risks

Risk	Plan sponsor risk management	Participant risk management
Investment	Move from defined benefit to defined contribution plan Use liability-driven investments Manage investment mix, diversification, use of investment managers, choice of investment vehicles Transfer to insurance company	Transfer to financial institution Manage investment mix and Investments Use advice Note: When lump sum paid at retirement, totally up to participant after that
Interest rate risk	Use liability-driven investment strategy Offer gradual purchase of annuity income over time Move to defined contribution plans Pay out lump sums Use account based defined benefit plan that credits interest to accounts based on an index	If purchasing annuity, do so gradually over time Consider risk in choice of investments
Inflation risk	Use plan design to allocate risk between plan sponsor and employee Invest in assets that help manage this risk Note: Benefits can be indexed or partly indexed: indexation changes the amount of risk management needed	Save more Use inflation indexed bonds Purchase annuity including inflation indexing
Longevity risk	Move to defined contribution plans Pay out lump sums Index retirement ages Adjust benefits for longer life spans Choose assumptions for defined benefit plan valuation that build in enough mortality improvement Use financial instruments to manage this risk	Use of lifetime income payout Spend only investment income Select withdrawal rate that is hoped to be safe—only partially manages risk Retire later Set long planning horizon

Source: Authors' analysis.

index allocate investment choice and most of the investment risk to the employer, but they then share investment risk somewhat with plan participants depending on the index used for crediting investment returns and the method of linking actual fund investments to the interest credited to participant accounts. Variable annuity contracts with floor guarantees share risk between policyholders and financial institutions. The policyholder may be able to choose between funds but cannot choose individual investments. Collective DC plans such as those used in the Netherlands have a common investment fund and share investment risk across the group of plan participants.

Interest rate risk

Interest rate risk leads to changes in the value of defined plan liabilities, as well as changes in annuity prices. Current interest rates are also a major factor in immediate annuity prices as well as for returns on fixed dollar investments which may be an important component of retirement plan investments. Interest rates have been very low for the last several years; some argue they are artificially low due to government intervention. This has made immediate annuities and bonds more expensive and resulted in increasing DB obligations.

Inflation risk

Inflation risk includes both pre- and post-retirement inflation risk. Inflation is a very important risk in funded retirement arrangements, whether DB, DC, or hybrid. Plans that use a final average earnings formula implicitly provide some coverage for pre-retirement inflation and place that risk on the plan sponsor; the latter have declined in prominence.

Most public employee plans, UK pensions, and the US Social Security system offer benefits indexed for inflation during the payout period. Private US plans rarely include such provisions, so inflation erodes the value of benefits. When benefits are indexed, all or part of the inflation risk rests with the plan sponsor. Inflation is often a consideration in setting investment mix. Other than inflation-indexed bonds, however, no investments offer a direct hedge against inflation.

Longevity risk

Plan sponsors can manage idiosyncratic mortality risk through pooling. Systemic risk is addressed in DB plans through the choice of actuarial valuation assumptions. The issue is resolved when mortality improvements adequate to match experience are built into the valuation. Longevity risk can also be addressed by adjusting benefits or retirement ages if longevity changes more or less than expected. The Swedish notional DC plan adjusts benefits for changes in life expectancy as of age 65 (Turner 2014).

One way to address systemic longevity would be to increase retirement ages on an indexed basis. In the United States and Canada, there has been a gradual increase in retirement ages in the last few years, but lifespans have increased far more. An expert commission in Quebec summarized the impact of changes in work life and life expectancy (Rappaport 2014). In 1970, expected work life was 46 years, and expected retirement was 13 years. By 2009, expected work life was 39 years, and expected periods of retirement were 23 years. The ten-year increase in periods of retirement is the result of a five-year increase in life expectancy and a five-year decrease in expected retirement ages (Rappaport 2014). The situation is further complicated because longevity and longevity improvement vary by economic status, occupation, and education. Long periods of retirement are creating a major challenge with regard to the sustainability of employee benefit and social benefit programs. The differences in longevity by economic status and occupation create equity concerns when there are discussions of raising or indexing retirement ages.

Business and employment risk

As noted above, final average pay plans concentrate much of the benefit accrual in the later years of employment. Accordingly, employees who leave their jobs early give up larger benefit accruals. There is also the concern that their employer may freeze or terminate the plan, or change the plan structure. In either case, the participant loses out on future benefit accruals. Employees are also subject to employment risk in the event of job loss, or business risk in the event the business does poorly, impacting employment prospects, salary increases, and maybe the future of the pension plan.

When the benefits are provided through DC plans, there is much less business risk to the employee. DC plans usually vest quickly, and most often, accruals earned in early years of employment are high relative to what is earned later. However, if accounts are invested in company stock, this poses a potentially significant business risk for participants. There is also business risk for the employer in that employees may not have adequate funds to retire. This can be troublesome to the business for workforce management reasons.

Risk of poor choices

DC plans typically allow for more individual choices than do DB plans. Non-contributory private sector DB plans may not require any choices until benefits are paid. By contrast, DC plans require choices about how much to save and how to invest those funds. At the point of retirement, these plans require choices about how benefits will be paid, and some of these choices may be irrevocable. Increasingly, many US plans use default options such as auto-enrollment and auto-escalation to minimize the impact of poor choices, including using one's assets too early or taking them as a lump sum distribution and using a portion for immediate consumption. Interestingly, there is a recent challenge with regard to participant choice: some plan sponsors have offered pensioners a lump sum buyout as part of a corporate derisking strategy. This creates a challenging financial decision that some older participants may not be well equipped to make.

Fiduciary and litigation risk

Plan sponsors in the US are subject to fiduciary requirements designed to protect participants against mismanagement, conflicts of interest, and fraud. Fiduciary risk refers to the risk that a sponsor fails to fulfill his requirements and can then be held responsible. For instance, the DC plan sponsor takes on fiduciary responsibility for choosing the investment options offered in private DC plans. The best defense is a demonstration that a prudent process was used to select and monitor the investment options in the fund. This responsibility helps explain plan sponsor reluctance to include annuity income payouts in their plans.

Solvency risk

Solvency risk refers to the risk that an entity providing benefits will become insolvent or unable to pay benefits, resulting in a default on benefit payments. In DB plans, the employer or plan sponsor is responsible for plan funding. Private pensions in the United States have benefits insured by the PBGC up to specified limits in the event of bankruptcy, but participants bear risk when promised benefits exceed the PBGC limits. Participants also bear the risk of insolvency in situations where there are no backup guarantee funds, as in the public sector. There is also some risk that a backup guarantee fund could have solvency problems.

Public pension plans have traditionally been seen as not subject to solvency risk, since public entities usually do not go bankrupt. Moreover, public plan benefits are often protected by state constitutions. This view has recently been called into question by the bankruptcy of the city of Detroit, Michigan. A federal judge recently held that Detroit's obligations to pay pensions were not protected in a federal Chapter 9 bankruptcy, even though they were expressly protected by the Michigan Constitution (Davey et al. 2013). The December 2013 Detroit ruling is expected to be further challenged in the courts, but it opens up the question of whether and in what circumstances pension benefit protection provided by state constitutions will prevail.

In DC plans, individual participants bear most of the solvency risk if the financial institution or particular investment funds become insolvent. Various kinds of financial institutions have some funds guaranteed by a backup fund. For example, United States insurance companies and banks are part of guarantee arrangements, but these are subject to limits. Moreover, these guarantee funds do not protect against poor investment results, but rather the bankruptcy of the institution offering the financial product. US employers or plan sponsors have fiduciary responsibility for determining the investment options in private plans.

Case Study: Pension Reform in New Brunswick

In 2012, the Canadian province of New Brunswick adopted a new plan framework called the Shared Risk Pension Plan. The framework included: (1) a new design that split benefits between a base benefit and ancillary benefits; (2) protocols to keep the plan's operation on track; and (3) a new risk management regulatory framework to ensure compliance with the program (Munnell and Sass 2013). This new design is available to public and private pensions, and it may be used for conversion of existing pension plans or establishment of new plans (Financial and Consumer Services Commission 2012). The program was developed by a government appointed Task Force who recommended that each public sector plan in New Brunswick be converted to the new plan (Government of New Brunswick 2013). At the time it was announced, it was supported by a number of public and private sector pension plans and by unions representing more than one-third of provincial government bargaining employees.[6] As of late 2012, the City of Saint John and Co-op Atlantic filed for approval of shared risk plans (Government of New Brunswick 2013), and in 2014, the Shared Risk Plan model was either adopted or announced for adoption by several Canadian DB pension plans.[7]

The principles for reforming New Brunswick pensions were set forth by the Task Force designing the reform (Government of New Brunswick 2013). As shown in Table 6.5, these seek to balance sustainability and risk pooling. They speak to plan design, transparency, financing, results measurement, and governance.[8]

The New Brunswick model weaves together plan design and plan financing. Funding levels can trigger benefit adjustments, either up or down. The traditional method used for DB pension funding uses best estimate assumptions, implying a 50 percent probability that contributions will not need to be increased. The risk sharing model provides for more stringent funding along with a specific method of adjusting benefits. If the funding level drops too low, benefits can be reduced or put on hold. If the funding increases beyond a certain point, benefits put on hold can be restored. 'Base' benefits are strongly supported, using a standard of success of at least 97.5 percent likelihood that adequate funding will be maintained without adjustment of benefits over a twenty-year modeling horizon. 'Extra' benefits, such as cost-of-living increases or early retirement provisions, are considered ancillary

TABLE 6.5 Principles for reformed New Brunswick pensions

	Principle
1.	Pension plans must be subject to robust risk management, including annual review and stress tests to ensure compliance.
2.	Pension plan must provide benefit security, which includes risk management targets focused on a high level of benefit security and governance by an independent trustee.
3.	Plan must be able to demonstrate sustainability.
4.	Plan must be affordable, which means that contributions must be stable and affordable for both employer and employees.
5.	Plan must be equitability designed—no single age cohort should unduly subsidize another, and no one should be able to 'game' the system.
6.	The plan must be transparent. Who shares in the risks and rewards and by how much must be clear and pre-established.
7.	Benefit changes as a result of conversion will apply only in the future; everyone keeps the pension amount that has already been credited.
8.	There should be no sudden shocks to members and retirees' retirement plans.
9.	All groups of employees should be treated consistently including part-time employees.
10.	At inception, the actuarial assumptions must be closely related to market benchmarks such as International Accounting Standard #19.

Notes: Language simplified and adapted. Item 10 was not included in legislation as ultimately adopted. It has been observed that Item 7 led to some participant confusion, and that there may also be some confusion about what benefit has already been earned and what benefit will be earned in the future.

Source: Government of New Brunswick (2013): 8, 9.

benefits, and these are also supported using a target contribution sufficient to fund 75 percent of these benefits on average over a twenty-year time horizon (Government of New Brunswick 2013). In rare and unforeseen circumstances, base benefits might need to be reduced; in such a case, the reduction will be borne by all plan beneficiaries including active employees, deferred vested employees, and retirees. This differs from the traditional DB approach where benefits were protected first for retirees and deferred vested participants, and where reductions generally applied first to future accruals, and then to those who had not reached retirement age.

In the Shared Risk model, the plan sponsor can offer a plan that pools risk for plan sponsors and taxpayers. In the conversions seen to date, this plan design has replaced prior final average pay DB plan benefits with career average pay benefits (although the legislation does not require use of a career average formula). Also, cost-of-living indexing has been replaced by contingent indexing, meaning indexing is contingent on funding levels. Final average pay accruals are frozen at the time of conversion. Contributions are shared and increased as needed based on financial results (Government of New Brunswick 2013). The legislation enabling these plans limits contribution changes to 2 percent of payroll and to 25 percent of the initial contribution level, intended to keep the plans affordable and sustainable. It is expected that the shared risk structure will encourage employees to work longer, leading to retirement at older ages. One report indicates that the targeted retirement year will rise three to four years for early career employees (Government of New Brunswick 2013).

It is worth noting that the legal structure governing these plans differs from US pension requirements.[9] Specifically, the Canadian plan must be operated by independent trustees operating at arm's length from the employer. Trustees are required to have an annual actuarial valuation, a risk management structure, and an investment policy. The plan framework sets requirements for a funding policy and measurement of plan liabilities, and actuarial liabilities are to be 'prudently valued.'[10] Funding policy must be established so that, in normal times, the plan's financial position is adequate to grant indexing and other ancillary benefits. For plans with contingent indexing, the funding policy must explain when contingent indexing starts and stops, and at what levels contingent payments are to be made. The funding policy also must include an explicit deficit recovery plan. Provincial legislation allows for the Superintendent of Pensions to establish guidance with regard to a minimum standard to address underfunding (Government of New Brunswick 2013). In conversions to date, it has been common to use a funding methodology that includes an open group funded ratio of 110 to 120 percent to be achieved over 15 years. However, a plan can start at a different point if it passes risk management tests in the statute.[11]

The Canadian Shared Risk Pension Plan was possible because former Premier David Alward established an expert Task Force in 2010 (Government of New Brunswick 2013). Also, provincial demographics made pension reform quite urgent: its population is older than the rest of Canada, with nearly 20 percent of residents over age 65 (Leech and McNish 2013). In the last decade, private sector companies in New Brunswick, including the St Anne-Nackawic Pulp Company and Fraser Paper, had gone bankrupt with inadequate funds in their DB pension plans, leading to benefit losses by both active workers and retirees (Leech and McNish 2013). At the time of the St Anne-Nackawic Pulp Company bankruptcy, the law provided that assets must be used first to cover retirees, terminated employees, and employees age 55 and over. In 2005, the law was amended so that benefit losses were shared between retirees and active employees. Both participant groups lost benefits in multiple bankruptcies, driving the interest in reform (Leech and McNish 2013).

The government task force found major problems in the funding levels of both private and public sector plans. Of the existing DB plans registered in New Brunswick, only a few were fully funded (Leech and McNish 2013). The City of Saint John faced a pension deficit of C$130 million, an amount nearly equal to its 2011 revenue of C$138 million. These problems had arisen due to a history of inadequate funding, poor economic conditions, demographics, and extra benefits to induce early retirement (Leech and McNish 2013).

A climate for change resulted from the expert Task Force, as well as a great deal of communication and a high level of commitment from various stakeholders. Paul McCrossan, the actuary on the Task Force, stressed that solutions could be found provided that all parties made sacrifices. The Task Force negotiated with several key labor leaders, so that when the Premier introduced the proposed pension reforms and the Task Force report to the public, key labor leaders were at his side and part of the presentation (Leech and McNish 2013). Many of the ideas used in reform in New Brunswick had also been used in the Netherlands (Bovenberg et al. 2015).

Case Study: A Different Type of Defined Contribution Plan

An alternative new model for corporate pensions is the Savings InSight™ plan offered by Buck Consultants and implemented in 2014 (Buck Consultants 2014). This plan is a DC plan designed to meet the needs of different groups of participants: those who prefer to have the plan sponsor do it for them, those who want guidance and shared responsibility, and those who wish to do it themselves. It includes auto-enrollment and auto-increases, and a modeling tool to enable participants to modify their decisions and customize them.

The plan design enables the employers to structure benefits so they fit into the firm's human resources needs. A plan sponsor participates in setting plan parameters for the target retirement age, payout period, definition of 'living standards,' investments, and salary increases. These parameters influence participants' recommended contributions and increase the potential for an adequate retirement income payable at the selected target retirement age. They also communicate an expected retirement age to the individual participant. These plan features also offer an attractive workforce management tool, compared to traditional DC plans.

Recommended contributions vary by individual, but they are usually much higher than default contribution rates typically used for auto-enrollment in DC plans (Xerox 2013; Buck Consultants 2014).[12] Contributions are tailored to each individual based on his own data.[13] Unlike many retirement calculators, this plan uses actual participant records to produce an automated calculation customized to personal situations and account balances. It has been structured to produce an 'adequate' retirement benefit for those participants who do not take action. In this way, the plan is similar to a conventional target benefit approach.[14]

The recommended contribution is a 'nudge' or suggestion. In addition to this recommendation, the modeling tool also 'nudges' participants who use it by showing how different decisions can alter retirement income streams. This structure goes beyond DB plans, in that it gives those participants who seek choices the chance to make their own decisions. Contribution percentages are also recalculated annually, and if there is a recommended increase, an automatic contribution increase is implemented. A participant can always opt out or modify the amounts. The modeling tool can also be used to evaluate alternatives. If the initial contribution or the recommended increase is too large, the tool can offer a transition program. In this plan, the default auto-investment is a target date fund, the Qualified Default Investment Alternative (QDIA). The plan uses the assumed rate of return for the QDIA, but the participant may select whatever investments he wishes. If a participant invests in funds that do not perform as well as the QDIA assumptions, his contribution rate is then recalculated to make up for the lost earnings.[15]

The benefit default is an installment payout for the number of years selected by the plan sponsor, with automatic adjustments as may be needed to maintain the targeted payout. The individual assumes his longevity and investment risk, but the payments are structured to reduce the chance that his fund will run out of money. The payment is calculated so that there is a notional side fund or buffer, to help cover market fluctuations. Good investment performance increases the side fund, and poor performance reduces it. The program sends monthly retiree benefit checks, and adjustments are made, as needed, to increase the probability that the payments will continue over the target payout period. Retirees retain full access to their funds, and they may withdraw more than the retiree check (but not less). This is reflected in the year-end gain/loss. Additional adjustments would likely be required to meet US regulatory requirements.

Examples of Recent Developments

New Brunswick offers an example of a new DB structure integrating design, funding, and plan management, while the Savings InSight™ plan is a DC plan modified to produce many of the benefit delivery and human resources aspects of DB plans (although it lacks an income guarantee). Numerous other plan sponsors have also made changes to modify risk sharing. In the US, for instance, some employers have frozen or terminated DB plans and moved into DC plans. This has primarily resulted in risk shifting rather than risk sharing. A smaller number of private sector employers has moved to cash balance plans.

The US public sector has also made many changes to modify risk sharing and improve DB plan sustainability. For instance, the National Association of State Retirement Administrators (NASRA 2014) documents recent changes to restore or improve sustainability in 56 statewide public plans. These changes have included increases in employee contributions and the method of determining them, changes in cost-of-living increases, increases in retirement ages, and changes in primary benefit formulas. Some provisions explicitly link to the plan's funded status. For example, in 2010, the Minnesota Teachers suspended their cost-of-living increase for existing retirees for two years, and they then reduced the cost-of-living increase from 2.5 percent per year to 2.0 percent per year until the plan funding ratio rose to 90 percent. The Montana Public Employees Retirement Association (PERA) in 2013 reduced its cost-of-living adjustment to 1.5 percent for all current and future retirees, as long as the system was less than 90 percent funded. The cost-of-living adjustment will be reduced 0.1 percent for each 2 percent below a 90 percent funding level (NASRA 2014). NASRA (2013) also reports a new focus on hybrid plans in the public sector, since some employers have found that closing their traditional pension plans to future employees does not meet important retirement security, human resource, and fiscal objectives.

Findings

To make future retirement plans more effective for risk protection, it will be useful to develop new arrangements which pool some risk and provide for different risk sharing. The two case studies described here offer some insights. Other approaches include modifications of traditional plans, generally called hybrids, which assign various risks to either the plan sponsor or participants in the plan design. The new DC-based hybrid, already described, does include ongoing adjustments to both contributions and benefit payments as part of the default options built into the plan.

Conclusion

In sum, we show that it is feasible to offer a retirement plan that pools risk and is efficient, but which also limits the sponsor's downside in adverse conditions. A relatively easy way to do this is to use a plan design that shares risk and offers some self-adjusting features. The risk sharing mechanisms discussed here could also, in theory, be added to most DB plan designs. For instance, the de-risking effort could move final average pay DB plans to a career average pay design with self-adjusting features and added benefits contingent on financial results. The de-risking could include recognition of increasing longevity through self-adjusting increases in retirement ages or self-adjusting reductions in benefit levels. DB plans could be structured to respond to future increases in longevity. It is likewise feasible to enhance DC plans so they include self-adjusting features and offer much better retirement security. Designs can be flexible to meet individual needs while also reflecting diverse organizational needs. A key item on the future retirement policy agendas is to pursue policy changes that will support desirable plan designs including optimal risk sharing.

Acknowledgements

The authors wish to thank colleagues who reviewed drafts and offered suggestions. Particular thanks are due to Paul Lai Fatt, who assisted us with the New Brunswick Case Study, and to Ted Goldman and Jerry Levy from Buck Consultants who assisted us with the Savings InSight™ Case Study.

Endnotes

1. This risk is reduced to the extent plans are insured by a guarantee fund. For example, benefits provided by private sector plans in the US are insured up to specified limits by the Pension Benefit Guaranty Corporation. Such funds also exist in other locations such as Ontario, Great Britain, Japan, etc.
2. This statement about future accruals applies to private sector plans in the US. The situation is much more mixed with respect to public sector plans. Some have future accruals protected and others do not.
3. Public pension plans are normally set up by local or state legislation. The choices open to the plans depend on the legislation. The regulation is very different from private sector plans in the US.
4. In the US, a 'multi-employer' plan is a specific type of plan authorized under federal law. These plans have joint union-management governance, and are subject to different requirements with regard to plan termination and Pension Benefit Guaranty Corporation premiums. They are a subset of the broader class of multiple entity arrangements.
5. Liability-driven investments are investments structured so that the term of the investments matches or is closely linked to the duration of the expected payments from the plan. Liability-driven investments reduce investment risk considerably.
6. Unions supporting the plan when it was announced included the New Brunswick Nurses Union, the New Brunswick Union, the Canadian Union of Public Employees (CUPE) Local 1212 (New Brunswick Council of Hospital Unions), and New Brunswick Pipe Trades, and it had been announced that these unions would be adopting the new model for specific plans (Government of New Brunswick 2013).

7. Information on the New Brunswick plan is taken from government reports as indicated in the references and supplemented by an interview with Paul Lai Fatt from Morneau Sobeco, an actuary who is actively involved in working with plans in New Brunswick.
8. The principles as shown in Table 6.5 are from the reference cited. The authors have learned from discussion with an actuary working in New Brunswick that Principle 10 was not included in the legislation as finally passed, and that Principle 7 has proved to be difficult in operation. Plan members have found it difficult to understand what is guaranteed and what is not. It was also pointed out that while accrued benefits are preserved on conversion, there are some improbable circumstances where they would be reduced.
9. Private pension plans in the US are subject to the Employee Retirement Income Security Act (ERISA) which sets forth detailed requirements for funding and plan governance. There is no similar requirement applicable to public plans in the US, and there is wide variation in practice and requirements by state. The New Brunswick model authorized by legislation effective July 1, 2012 uses very different requirements. Regulations were issued in Aug. 2012 effective July 1, 2012 (Financial and Consumer Services Commission 2012). The prompt issuance of regulations is also very different from the US.
10. The Task Force report on the design indicated a discount rate close to 4.5 percent based on market conditions in mid-2013 when the report was issued, as well as mortality tables that include current best estimates of mortality improvement (Government of New Brunswick 2013).
11. Actuarial valuations can use either a closed group or an open group. Funding valuations for most plans are closed group, whereas open group valuations are commonly used to plan benefit and other changes. The closed group approach focuses on the currently covered population group for a pension plan, including active participants and participants currently receiving a benefit or due to receive a benefit in the future. A *closed group* projection requires *demographic assumptions* about how current participants are expected to withdraw, retire, become disabled and die. The open group approach includes not only the currently covered population group for a pension plan (as defined in *closed group*), but also including future anticipated new entrants (i.e. new employees) to a system. In addition to the *demographic assumptions* required for a *closed group* projection, an *open group* projection requires assumptions about the age, service, and salary profile of new entrants and whether an employee population is expected to grow, stay in a steady state, or decline. The open group funded ratio is the assets plus the present value of the next 15 years of excess contributions (employee contributions plus employer contributions less normal cost), all divided by the liability of the base benefit.
12. The information on the Savings Insight™ program was provided partly from literature from the firm as indicated in the references and supplemented by an interview with Ted Goldman, National Retirement Leader at Buck Consultants.

13. Adequate is defined by each company adopting the plan, and the plan sponsor has choices in that regard.
14. A target benefit plan is a DC plan that uses an underlying formula to define a specified retirement benefit. It then calculates a recommended contribution to the plan that is expected to accumulate sufficient funds, using an assumed rate of investment earnings, to provide the targeted benefit at retirement. In such a plan a different contribution rate is calculated for each employee reflecting that employee's demographics, salary, and current account balance.
15. QDIA is Qualified Default Investment Alternative. Under US federal regulations, these investment alternatives are permitted for default options in defined contribution plans governed by ERISA.

References

American Academy of Actuaries (2014). *Retirement for the Ages*. Washington, DC: American Academy of Actuaries. <http://www.actuary.org/Retirement-for-the-AGES>.

Blitzstein, D. (2015). 'Pension Benefit Design Innovation: Labor Unions as Agents of Change,' in R. Shea and O. S. Mitchell (eds), *Reimagining Pensions: The Next 40 Years*. Oxford: Oxford University Press, 123–38.

Buck Consultants (2014). 'Savings Insight™,' (updated 2014) <https://www.buckconsultants.com/Services/Retirement/savingsinsight.aspx>.

Church Pension Group (2014). 'CPG: About Church Pension Group,' (updated 2014) <https://www.cpg.org/global/about-us/overview>.

Davey, M., B. Vlasic, and M. W. Walsh (2013). 'Detroit Ruling on Bankruptcy Lifts Pension Protections,' *New York Times*. Dec. 3. <http://www.nytimes.com/2013/12/04/us/detroit-bankruptcy-ruling.html>.

Financial and Consumer Services Commission (2012). New Brunswick Regulation 2012–75 under the Pension Benefits Act (O.C.2012-251), New Brunswick, Canada.

Fuerst, D. (2015). 'Retirement Shares Plan: A New Model of Risk Sharing,' in O. S. Mitchell and R. Shea (eds), *Reimagining Pensions: The Next 40 Years*. Oxford: Oxford University Press, 161–73.

General Board of Pensions of the United Methodist Church (2014). <http://www.gbophb.org>.

Goodman, B. and D. Richardson (2015). 'Back to the Future: Hybrid Co-op Pensions and the TIAA-CREF System,' in O. S. Mitchell and R. Shea (eds), *Reimagining Pensions: The Next 40 Years*. Oxford: Oxford University Press, 139–60.

Government of New Brunswick (2013). *Rebuilding New Brunswick: The Case for Pension Reform*. New Brunswick, Canada: Government of New Brunswick.

IMRF (Illinois Municipal Retirement Fund) (2012). 'Information for units of government considering participation in IMRF' (updated June 2012) <http://www.imrf.org/employers/prospective-employers.htm>.

Mercer (2013). *Melbourne Mercer Global Pension Index, October, 2013*. Melbourne: Australian Centre for Financial Studies.

Munnell, A. H. and S. A. Sass (2013). *New Brunswick's New Shared Risk Pension Plan,* State and Local Pension Plans, 13. Boston, MA: Center for Retirement Research at Boston College.

Leech, J. and J. McNish (2013). *The Third Rail.* Toronto, ON: McClelland & Stewart.

NASRA (2013). 'State Hybrid Retirement Plans.' *NASRA Issue Brief,* Sept. 2013. Washington, DC: NASRA.

NASRA (2014). *Selected Approved Changes to State Public Pensions to Restore or Preserve Plan Sustainability.* Washington, DC: NASRA.

Rappaport, A. M. (2014). 'How Well Have Retirement Systems Adapted to Longer Life?' in *Living to 100 Monograph.* Schaumburg, IL: Society of Actuaries.

Society of Actuaries (2007). *Building the Foundations for New Retirement Systems: Retirement 20/20 Conference Report.* Schaumburg, IL: Society of Actuaries.

Turner, J. A. (2014). 'Hybrid Pensions: Risk Sharing Arrangements for Pension Plan Sponsors and Participants.' Society of Actuaries Research Paper. Schaumburg, IL: Society of Actuaries.

Xerox (2013). 'Buck Consultants Addresses Retirement Readiness with Savings InSight, an Automated Workplace Savings Solution' (updated Sept. 2013) <http://news.xerox.com/news/Buck-Consultants-Savings-InSight-automated-workplace-retirement-savings-program>.

Chapter 7

United States Pension Benefit Plan Design Innovation: Labor Unions as Agents of Change

David S. Blitzstein

> Above all, strong but independent employee representation is required on the governing boards of the pension funds. Both the present job and the future pension are employee interests. Both require guardianship for the employee through his representatives... and as a good many American labor leaders learned from New York City, the integrity of the employee's pension fund assets (increasingly the employee's main asset, and his main resource next to his job) needs to be protected. (Drucker 1976: 146)

> In the present crisis, unions continue to shoulder their traditional responsibilities of being spokesmen for employees in demanding that economic and political leaders take steps to propel the economy forward. The new question is whether the unions should also accept part of the responsibility of defining the policies, the directions, programs and projects for these ends, so as to help their following attain the desired level of high economic activity, and the rising economic and social well-being to which unions are committed. What steps should they take to discharge these responsibilities competently? (Barkin 1983: 425)

The study of retirement and pension benefit design for the past 30 years has traditionally concentrated on the economics and behavioral features of defined benefit (DB) and defined contribution (DC) delivery systems. Little has been written about the institutions that sponsor and drive the direction of pension benefit design in our society. One institution that has shaped the United States retirement system in the post-World War II era is the labor movement. In fact, labor unions played a key role in establishing DB pensions for millions of workers in the late 1940s. The stage was set by the success and ingenuity of larger-than-life union leaders including Sidney Hillman and John L. Lewis, who established industry-wide multiemployer pension plans in the clothing and coal industries. Their early efforts in achieving collectively bargained pension plans set the pattern for other major industries like steel and auto. By 1950, the United Steel Workers and the United Auto Workers negotiated company pension plans with the major industry employers (Sass 1997).

The US DB pension system was not created in the corridors of Congress. Instead, it emerged from a messy process of labor–management negotiations involving industrial strife, contentious litigation, and threats of government intervention. Peter Drucker (1976) and Solomon Barkin (1983), whose statements introduce this chapter, were prescient observers and commentators on the role of corporations and unions in the twentieth century. Both experts looked beyond pure market economics, to focus instead on the role of institutions to better understand social, economic, and political events and trends. They especially identified with and studied the role of labor unions as economic decision-makers. This chapter focuses on the role that unions have played, and can play in the future, in redesigning the US pension system.

Today, the DB system is in the throes of an existential crisis. Pension plans that organized labor helped create in the mid-twentieth century went into decline after 1980 and were displaced by DC plans. The decline of the DB plan system over this period correlates closely with the decline of organized labor in the US. Moreover, two financial shocks during the first decade of the twenty-first century deeply challenged DB plans' very existence. But if change and Schumpeterian 'creative destruction' are natural outcomes of capitalism, then the questions of how social and economic change is managed and what replaces moribund institutions become worthy of thought and study.

In the next 20 years, the US will experience a transformation of the occupational pension system. How this transition is managed and the form it takes will determine retirement outcomes for much of the American workforce. Even though the US labor movement has been weakened, it is still strategically positioned in a number of high-profile private sector industries and firms. Moreover, unions still play a dominant role in the public sector. This puts labor unions in a unique role to renegotiate the pension social contract in key parts of the American economy.

In this chapter, we relate through a case study how one labor union, the United Food and Commercial Workers International Union (UFCW), sought to manage an ongoing crisis among its collectively bargained multiemployer pension plans by introducing a hybrid plan to replace its traditional DB pension plans. In what follows, we describe the development of that hybrid plan and how it gained influence beyond the UFCW and the industries it represents.

Multiple Financial Crises in the 2000s Destabilize the UFCW's Traditional Defined Benefit Plans

The UFCW is a North American labor union with 1.3 million members in the US and Canada. Its membership predominately works in retail food and food manufacturing, and upwards of 90 percent of its membership is covered by collectively bargained pension plans. Two-thirds of the UFCW membership, mostly in the retail food supermarket industry, participate in DB multiemployer pensions administered by joint boards of trustees equally represented by labor and management. The UFCW and thousands of signatory employers together sponsor 60 multiemployer plans with $25 billion in assets covering a total of 1.4 million active workers, inactive workers who have earned a non-forfeitable benefit, and retirees. The current ratio of active to inactive participants is about 1:1. UFCW members work in low to moderate wage industries characterized by high turnover and part-time work. The average DB pension benefit is only $500–$600 per month, at present. Some long-service career members do receive pensions that are multiples of three to five times the stated pension.

As they entered the twenty-first century, most UFCW multiemployer pension plans were strongly funded using expected return assumptions averaging 7.5 percent. Illusory funding surpluses that emerged during the frothy capital markets of the 1990s were used for benefit improvements including expensive early retirement subsidies. Funding policy discipline waned as bargaining parties agreed to multi-year contribution holidays. Perverse federal tax policy that capped the tax deductibility of employer contributions for fully funded pension plans promoted bad behavior by stakeholders. A herd mentality also drove sponsors to invest aggressively in high volatility growth assets, and 60–70 percent allocations to stock were the norm.

When the Tech Bubble in stocks burst beginning in 2000, DB pensions were unprepared for a 'perfect storm' of asset drawdowns and declining interest rates. Funding ratios dropped by over 30 percentage points, on average, as markets slid for three consecutive years, something not experienced since the market crash in 1973–4. The UFCW's response to these new, gaping funding deficits was multi-faceted. At the fund level, trustees started assessing investment risk more seriously by diversifying portfolios away from public equity. At the bargaining table, labor and management crafted new pension funding agreements that increased employer contributions and reduced future service benefit accruals. A number of these funding agreements had automatic trigger mechanisms that required changes in contributions and benefits based on certain projected actuarial events.

The plans began improving their funding position after 2003, but it became apparent that funding recovery would be slow and that some plans had been badly damaged. Many were projected to trigger the dire regulatory status called 'minimum funding deficiency' under the Employee Retirement Income Security Act (ERISA), which would impose onerous lump-sum contributions and surtaxes on employers. These events stimulated a movement to reform the federal pension funding rules, culminating in Congress passing the Pension Protection Act (PPA) in 2006. This was the first major reform of pension funding rules since ERISA became law in 1974 and the Multiemployer Pension Plan Amendments Act (MPPAA) was passed in 1980. The UFCW took an active role in lobbying for PPA, joining the retail food industry employers and the National Coordinating Committee for Multiemployer Plans (NCCMP), the multiemployer community lobbying arm, in an effective labor–management coalition.

The PPA created a range of funding zone certifications for multiemployer plans from 'safe' (green zone) to 'endangered' (yellow zone) to 'critical' (red zone). Plans are required to annually certify their zone status to the Internal Revenue Service (IRS). If a plan certifies yellow zone (<80 percent funded), the plan trustees have 270 days to implement a Funding Improvement Plan (FIP) that returns the plan to financial health within 10–13 years. If the plan certifies red zone (<65 percent funded), the trustees must promulgate a Rehabilitation Plan (RP) that returns the plan to financial health within 10–13 years. Both FIP and RP plans provide direction and funding discipline to the collective bargaining parties. Red zone plans had the ability for the first time under ERISA to reduce or eliminate accrued early retirement and disability benefits for all plan participants except retirees (PBGC 2013).

Pension plans had not yet recovered from the asset drawdowns of the Tech Bubble when they were struck by the devastating shock of the Great Financial Crisis of 2008–09. Many plans lost the equivalent of 30 percentage points of funding in one year, and 70 percent of multiemployer plans certified yellow or red zone in 2009. The funding damage was so dramatic that in 2008 Congress passed an amendment to PPA titled the Worker, Retiree, and Employer Recovery Act (WRERA), which allowed plans to defer actions required under PPA for one year. A second phase of Congressional action in 2010 with the Pension Relief Act (PRA) allowed multiemployer plans to amortize investment losses incurred in 2008–09 over 29 years, in contrast to the fifteen-year period legislated by PPA.

The UFCW Assesses the Damage of the Twenty-First-Century Pension Crisis

The UFCW reacted aggressively to these financial threats by conducting an internal review and critique of its pension plans unconstrained by prior beliefs or union politics. The union's response was somewhat unique due to two institutional advantages. First, it had created an internal staff capability and expertise to advise the leadership on all matters related to pensions and health insurance. Secondly, the union leadership, to its credit, had the confidence to objectively evaluate bad news and consider unconventional solutions that would resolve serious problems undermining the benefit security of its membership.

In early 2006, in anticipation of PPA legislation, the union conducted a funding analysis of its plans by applying a number of Pension Benefit Guaranty Corporation (PBGC) funding and solvency screens to measure plan sustainability. The results were sobering. Two-thirds of the UFCW's plans triggered two or more of the PBGC's screens, and more than a third of the UFCW's plans were less than 70 percent funded. Just as troubling, a number of UFCW funds that had been fully funded in 2006 were now projected to have minimum funding deficiency problems in 10 years or fewer, and they could be expected to trigger yellow or red zone status in four to five years based on draft PPA legislation.

At the same time that the UFCW was conducting its internal pension study, a number of accounting, financial, and regulatory pressures were being felt. The Financial Accounting Standard Board (FASB) proposed new rules that would have required multiemployer plan corporate sponsors to report unfunded liabilities on their income and balance sheets at market value using risk-free rates, instead of the plan's discount rate. In addition, credit rating agencies like Moody's and Standard & Poor began to research multiemployer plan sponsors and industries, highlighting the growth in off-balance sheet pension debt by firm and industry (Moody's 2006). Concurrently, Congress tripled multiemployer plan premiums to the PBGC, which was itself experiencing growing deficits, and required plans to report a current liability funding ratio based on annuity rates that suggested even weaker funding ratios for plans.

This confluence of events served as the background to the internal UFCW pension study presented to the union's leadership in spring 2006. The report raised for the first time a series of difficult policy questions for the UFCW's leadership. One was whether UFCW multiemployer plans were financially sustainable, and what the cost of plan sustainability might be. Another focused on whether signatory employers could afford this cost given the competitive environment. Additionally, the report asked what the ramifications of the pension crisis for the stability of the UFCW's collective bargaining system might be, focusing on the economic trade-offs for the union and its members. Reviewing the options in light of the pension crisis, and assuming pension benefits could be frozen for a generation, raised questions about the economic consequences for members' retirement incomes. And crucially, if a union deemed its current plans to be unsustainable, the question arose as to what alternative plan designs might be considered.

These policy questions raised a series of political dilemmas for the UFCW, which also became the subject of discussion. Questions arose about how the membership and local union leaders might respond to the pension crisis, and whether the membership might internalize its fear and anger against the union leaders. Additionally, leaders worried that the UFCW and its sponsored plans might be subject to litigation. Naturally, questions were raised about whether the membership would support a strategy by the union to reform and redesign its plans. Of course, any reform would raise the issue of how the union would manage intergenerational equity issues as pension benefits became more differentiated between demographic groups based on when they began working in the industry. And finally, there were concerns that pension plan failures might inhibit the UFCW's ability to organize and attract new members.

After assessing the political risks, the UFCW leadership opted for a proactive, solution-based approach to the pension crisis, deciding that the status quo was more dangerous than renegotiating a new pension contract.

The Question of DB Plan Sustainability

The pension crisis that started in the first decade of the twenty-first century coincided with a number of emerging structural trends synonymous with the maturing life cycle of these plans, many of which were 50–60 years old. Plan demographics had changed dramatically due to stagnant union growth and the impact of technological change. The absolute number and growth of retirees each year exceeded additions to the active worker population, which was the basis for employer contributions. Active pension participants were now supporting one to two inactive participants, a reversal from earlier decades when the plans were new and growing (Kocken 2011).

These demographic trends generated net negative cash flows to the DB plans, with annual benefit and administrative payments exceeding annual employer contributions. Not surprisingly, this created a drag on asset growth and an additional burden on expected investment returns. Additionally, negative cash flows were projected to nearly double over the next decade, in a number of UFCW plans.

Another characteristic of mature DB pensions is that they become quite dependent on investment income, making the plans particularly sensitive to investment return volatility. Investment income in mature pension plans accounts for 70–80 percent of total annual income. And as many DB plans discovered in the last decade, investment volatility can dramatically affect the plan's funding balance. As the assets of mature pension plans grow, they become even more vulnerable to the rule of large numbers. A 10 percent drawdown on $1 billion is 10 times that on a $100 million asset base. Larger pension plans are also highly leveraged, with assets equal to multiples of 30–50 times contributions. This makes it nearly impossible to recover from large asset drawdowns by increasing employer contributions.

Modern portfolio theory failed the DB pension system during the first decade of the twenty-first century. Pension portfolios that were assumed to be highly diversified, turned out to actually be highly correlated with public equity risk and therefore vulnerable to major asset declines. The secular decline in interest rates compounded the perfect financial storm facing pension plans. In reaction to the threat of depression, extraordinary monetary policy exercised by the Federal Reserve sent interest rates even lower, adding to the investment pressures on pension plans. DB pensions with long liability durations faced challenging asset liability mismatches, when long bond rates were below 4 percent. At the same time, the situation created perverse incentives for plans to take more investment risk than they could manage, in an effort to earn expected returns of 7–8 percent. The mature DB pension model became hypersensitive to capital market volatility: a few years of negative returns destroyed a decade of asset growth and defunded once-healthy DB plans, driving many into a death spiral.

Inspirations for Benefit Design and Governance Innovation

This structural analysis of traditional DB plans convinced the UFCW that the sustainability of their pension system was at risk, requiring it to search for alternatives. This was in keeping with its history of innovating in the pension arena. In 1984, the UFCW National Pension Fund took advantage of high interest rates and eliminated its unfunded liabilities by purchasing an annuity from MetLife for the plan's past-service liability at highly favorable prices. That transaction allowed the plan to restart the fund as a future-service-only plan. Groups differentiated by area and industry were experience-rated separately based on their individual demographics, but they continued to share investment and administrative experience. The new future service plan was conservatively funded through a regimented process where the plan recalculated the actuarial cost of benefits every two to three years and required the collective bargaining parties to reset contributions given the updated costs. This structure gave the plans a DC-type quality, where labor and management determined the contribution/benefit formulas that fit their special market conditions. This unique funding/benefit system, with its self-adjusting mechanisms, was a major reason why the UFCW National

Pension Fund remained fully funded and retained a PPA green zone status throughout the crisis.

Another example of UFCW design/governance creativity was seen with a plan sponsored by UFCW Local 1518 in British Columbia, Canada. The trustees of that multiemployer plan foresaw the secular decline in interest rates in the 1990s, and they made a politically courageous decision to move away from a model that measured liabilities based on expected returns to one that targeted liabilities to certain market interest rates. Instead of spending transitory surpluses on benefit improvements during the mid-1990s, the Local 1518 Plan adjusted its benefit liabilities to market interest rates and adopted a highly effective liability driven investment program that maintained a fully funded status despite the storms of the first decade of the twenty-first century. The experience of the UFCW Local 1518 Plan suggested a viable investment risk management model worth emulating.

An important influence on UFCW staff was its consultations with Keith Ambachtsheer, an internationally recognized pension strategist and big-picture thinker. Ambachtsheer conceived of DB plans as complex risk sharing arrangements, and he devised rules of the 'pension deal' based on a contractual model where terms must be clear and transparent (Ambachtsheer 2007). His view that risk sharing must be fair and symmetrical provided a theoretical framework for the UFCW to benchmark its ideas for building a hybrid plan. The Ambachtsheer principles of a clearly stated targeted pension benefit, a clearly stated expected cost of delivering the target benefit, a clearly stated risk-bearing deal between the various stakeholder groups, and a clear statement about how risk would be managed within the pension plan, formed the philosophical building blocks for the UFCW benefit design. In addition, Ambachtsheer's work with leaders in two of the world's most successful retirement systems, the Canadian and Dutch, offered best practice insights into achieving optimum governance and benefit design.

The UFCW was also influenced by the 2006 introduction of a 'Retirement Shares Plan' (RSP) conceived by Don Fuerst and Mercer Consulting (see Fuerst 2015). The RSP was a form of Variable Benefit Plan established by IRS Revenue Rulings in the 1950s, which allowed accrued benefits to vary based on plan investment performance. Variable Benefit Plans fell out of favor after the 1973–4 market crash, when these plans had no choice but to enforce severe cuts in retiree benefits. One important Variable Benefit Plan that did survive is the Pension Plan of the Major League Baseball Players. RSP is similar to a DB career accumulation pension: a percentage of each year's pay is used to buy retirement shares at the year-end purchase price of the shares. The benefit earned each year then varies with investment performance. The employee can change the investment mix each year and adjust his individual risk. At the normal retirement age, the employee receives an annual retirement income based on the number of retirement shares accumulated over his working life. During retirement, annual income also varies with investment performance (Fuerst 2006). The RSP risk sharing approach became a model for the UFCW benefit design project.

Deciding on Pension Design Priorities: The UFCW Evaluation Process

The UFCW constituted a team of pension experts, including legal experts, actuaries, and pension investment consultants, to research and develop a new hybrid design from late 2006 through 2009. In early deliberations, the UFCW pension task force (the Committee) began formulating its goals and objectives. A substantial part of this discussion focused on pension legacy issues and how to transition to a new pension system. While these legacy and transition issues are critically important, they are not the subject of this chapter (see Blitzstein 2013).

The Committee began its work by rejecting the traditional DB and DC models. The UFCW's concerns about the recurring structural flaws in the traditional DB plan were as already described. The financial crisis had effectively exposed the myth that all investment risk in DB plans could be absorbed by employers, since participants' experience with multiple rounds of pension benefit reductions suggested otherwise. At the same time, the UFCW recognized the various risks facing corporate plan sponsors. Changes in pension accounting rules, the opinions of credit rating agencies, and the ability of firms to withstand the balance sheet volatility of DB pension liabilities had to be recognized by the UFCW in its new plan design exercise. Avoiding the risk of generating new unfunded pension liabilities became a priority in the UFCW design exercise.

The Committee considered adopting 401(k) plans, but these were rejected because their design imposed unacceptable risks on workers and retirees. These plans' direct shifting of investment, mortality, and retirement risk to participants ruled them out. The Committee was also suspicious of the behavioral economics foibles relevant to DC plans, regarding participant contribution and investment decisions. In addition, the low-to-moderate wage levels in the industries represented by the UFCW raised questions about whether DC plans could generate affordable and adequate retirement benefits. A further consideration was DC plans' inability to provide early retirement options, disability benefits, and lifetime annuities.

Similarly, the Committee also rejected cash balance plans as these did not offer an equitable alignment of risk between employees and employers. In particular, employees gained no upside investment opportunity, and employers were still at risk for investment downturns. The fact that annual floor accruals decrease with age also presented the UFCW with concerns about intergenerational conflicts among its membership. Another problem was that cash balance plan forfeitures from turnover automatically reduced employer costs, instead of remaining in the plan asset pool. A final negative regarding cash balance design was these plans' emphasis on lump sum payment at retirement instead of lifetime annuities.

This exercise of evaluating existing plan designs was valuable because it focused the UFCW's efforts to build its own customized retirement model. While the Mercer Retirement Shares Plan did offer some useful aspects, it did have some features that were contrary to UFCW's goals and principles. For example, the UFCW rejected the concept of employee investment choice within the risk-sharing structure of RSP, and so it did not adopt the RSP benefit variability feature for retiree benefits.

The internal discussion produced a new plan set of design goals, which included the following:

- Benefits should be fairly priced using interest rates more representative of long-term historic interest rates.
- The new plan design had to be structured in a way that aggressively managed investment risk.
- The new plan design had to support stable employer contributions, along with a high probability of plan full funding.
- The stakeholders should expect the plan design to meet regulatory standards and scrutiny.
- The new plan design had to be matched with an effective and disciplined governance model.
- Pension benefit payments would be paid in the form of lifetime guaranteed annuities.
- The new plan design had to deliver on the contractual pension promise.

The Mechanics of the UFCW Variable Defined Benefit Plan Take Shape

The UFCW hybrid plan design had taken on form and structure by the end of 2007. The Committee referred to its creation as the Variable Defined Benefit Plan (Variable Plan); it later became known as the Adjustable Pension Plan (APP). This plan was structured like a DB in that retirement and longevity risks were pooled, and all assets were pooled and managed professionally. But in contrast to a DB plan, the Variable Plan shared positive and negative investment performance between the employer and plan participants. The Variable Plan benefit is defined as the greater of two benefits calculated separately each year: a 'floor' defined benefit (that can be either a flat benefit accrual or salary-based career average formula), and a 'variable' benefit that fluctuates depending on actual investment performance. Each year's benefit accrual can never be lower than the floor benefit.

The floor benefit is priced using a 'floor interest rate' plus plan demographics. An initial floor benefit was modeled to be $600 per year (the equivalent of $50 per month per year of service). The floor accrual does not change due to plan investment experience. However, the Variable Plan design anticipated that the floor benefit accrual could be sensitive to changing plan demographics and would have to be recalibrated periodically. The floor interest rate is also the performance benchmark for the variable benefit. The Variable Plan design envisioned setting the floor interest rate at 4.5–5 percent, a rate 30–40 percent lower than the expected return rates used by multiemployer private and public plans. The basis for the floor interest rate was long-term corporate interest rates (of 20–30-year maturity). The median corporate interest rate over the period 1919–2007 was 5.25 percent and the 25th percentile was 3.75 percent. In 2007, the average corporate long term rate was priced at 4.7 percent.

The variable benefit accrues in units (similar to RSP shares). Start-up unit values are set at an arbitrary level (e.g. $10.00 per unit). Unit values are adjusted each year based on actual investment returns compared to the floor interest rate benchmark. Every year, the units earned equal the floor accrual divided by unit value at the beginning of the year (e.g. units earned = $600 divided by $10 = 60 units). The variable benefit is then equal to the number of units times the unit value. This structure is important because, in combination with the floor benefit, it complies with the definitely determinable benefit accrual rules of ERISA, and it also allows for variable benefit changes year to year. In effect, participants are accruing units rather than benefit dollars.

With regard to the variable benefit, the Committee created two rules for surplus management, for the purpose of safeguarding plan funding. These were as follows:

- Any surplus return in excess of a designated percent (e.g. 7–10 percent) would be capped ('Surplus Cap') and not applied to the variable benefit. These excess returns would become a reserve or margin that would be available as a contingency against future negative investment performance.
- Excess returns earned below the Surplus Cap would be applied to the variable benefit by increasing unit values or units held (not by increasing the floor accrual rate). This approach does not increase the member's ultimate benefit, and as a result does not increase the employer's risk for unfunded liabilities. Issuing additional units provides the greatest flexibility for allocating excess returns through the variable benefit.

The Committee also applied the lessons of asset/liability leverage in maturing plans discussed earlier, to the payment of retiree benefits. A Variable Plan would establish a policy that required the plan to annuitize or immunize all retiree payments when they became effective. The goal was to insure the retiree liability as best as possible, and to ensure that large asset/liability mismatches would not occur; additionally, the intent was to preclude retiree liabilities from dominating the plan's balance sheet over time.

The Committee devoted much of its limited budget to testing the financial robustness of the Variable Plan. Two Canadian consulting firms with insurance liability modeling capabilities were asked to recommend the most efficient investment strategy to deploy in order to meet the Variable Plan objectives. The Committee had two objectives: to achieve a minimum return of 5 percent each year with a risk parameter that anticipates a low standard deviation of 5 percent; and to seek an excess return above 5 percent without impairing the first objective. After running a number of optimal asset allocation strategies, the Committee selected a beta-test asset allocation scenario that consisted of 5 percent cash, 36 percent investment grade bonds, 8 percent below-investment grade bonds, 15 percent inflation-linked bonds, 25 percent hedge funds, 10 percent real estate, and 1 percent commodities. When back-tested within the limitations of historic financial information and capital market assumptions, this asset allocation portfolio generated a 6.83 percent return with a standard deviation of 3.54 percent. Using the most recent highly volatile period 1998–2009, the portfolio returned on average 6.64 percent, including −5.96 percent in 2008, but with all other years returning above 5 percent. The Committee enhanced this strategy by adding a cash-matching Liability Driven Investment (LDI) strategy that matched the plan's projected liability cash flows each year for the next 20 years of liabilities. Stochastic modeling results suggested that this combined strategy would generate plan surpluses consistently, allowing a variable benefit upside.

The Committee was satisfied that it had created the appropriate policies and funding safeguards for the Variable Plan that fulfilled the original objectives and principles for introducing a hybrid plan to its affiliate local union officers. This DB floor was priced conservatively, with upside benefit potential controlled by a surplus return cap, and with funding risk managed by a flexible unit value benefit system and complimented by a low volatility investment strategy anchored by LDI cash matching liabilities.

The Committee also discussed what could possibly go wrong with the model, and it determined that the one uncontrollable factor in the future of the Variable Plan pertained to governance and policy discipline. The ultimate question was whether pension boards of trustees could break with the conventional pension investment and governance practices of the past, so as to instead adopt and enforce policies unique to the Variable

Plan. The Committee was convinced that it could not legally bind boards of trustees to the original policy rules of the Variable Plan. Only continued trustee education and institutional memory could secure the future.

The UFCW Takes the Variable Plan Public

In January of 2009, the UFCW presented the Variable Plan for the first time to the employer members of the Joint Labor Management Committee of the Retail Food Industry (JLMC). Established in 1974 by the organized supermarket companies along with the UFCW and the International Brotherhood of Teamsters (IBT), the JLMC provides a forum for union and company officers to discuss strategic public policy and collective bargaining issues. In a presentation about the pension crisis, the UFCW introduced the Variable Plan concept as a potential solution for the industry. The employers were impressed with the union's directness and the proactive nature of the presentation. After the meeting, the Kroger Company, the largest employer of UFCW members, invited the UFCW to present its analysis of the pension crisis and the Variable Plan to its February 2009 conference of Kroger trustees.

At the same time, the UFCW leadership mobilized an internal education campaign to address solutions to the pension crisis. Presentations were made to the UFCW's two most important governing bodies, the UFCW Executive Board consisting of 50 vice presidents, and the Local Union Advisory Committee which accounted for about 80 local unions and councils not already represented on the Executive Board. The UFCW local union leadership was receptive to the Variable Plan idea and appreciative that the UFCW leadership and staff were taking the initiative by actively seeking practical responses to the pension crisis. In May of 2009, the UFCW held a one-day 'Pension Summit' for union trustees, at which the Variable Plan was showcased and described in detail. Keith Ambachtsheer, Director of the Rotman International Center for Pension Management at the University of Toronto, was a guest speaker and offered expert guidance and support to the UFCW's efforts to renegotiate its pension contracts and establish the new, more sustainable pension design model. During the conference, UFCW trustees responded positively to the Variable Plan. Consensus support developed in favor of advancing the Variable Plan idea and beginning a dialogue with employers.

Throughout 2009–10, the UFCW met with its largest employers to present the Variable Plan. In 2011, Kroger and the UFCW began a serious discussion about restructuring four multiemployer plans covering 180,000 participants, where Kroger was the dominant contributing employer (Blitzstein 2013). All four plans were underfunded and certified red zone plans. Kroger was receptive to the UFCW strategy of issuing public debt to accelerate funding of the legacy pension deficits, with a cost of bringing these merged plans to full funding of nearly $1 billion. The UFCW pressed for the adoption of the Variable Plan, but Kroger rejected the hybrid plan because of the uncertainty of the Variable Plan's regulatory status and the cost of replicating current benefits using lower interest rates required by the Variable Plan. Ultimately, the UFCW and Kroger reached an historic pension deal effective January 1, 2012, with a new pension contract creating the UFCW Consolidated Fund. This would be 10 years in duration, merge the four plans, prohibit benefit reductions during the contract term, establish a new salary-based future service plan that targeted an agreed-to replacement income, and commit Kroger to fully funding the plan and keeping it green zone under PPA through 2022.

While the first attempt to introduce the Variable Plan failed, the effort served a purpose by giving the UFCW a level of bargaining leverage and credibility with Kroger and other employers, supporting the union's goals in stabilizing four underfunded plans. Under the new pension deal with the UFCW, the union conceded its fiduciary authority over the Consolidated Fund's investment policy. In contrast to the beliefs of the UFCW and many pension experts, Kroger argued that it could manage the investment risk of a traditional DB; the firm was also confident that its strong cash flow and balance sheet could absorb the investment risk of the Consolidated Fund. The ten-year UFCW/Kroger pension contract will test Kroger's theory and resolve.

The Variable Plan Model Gains Acceptance outside the UFCW

The Variable Plan has continued to gain attention in pension policy circles and with the labor movement. It was presented to conferences sponsored by the Pension Rights Center, as well as the Pension 20/20 Research Initiative led by the Society of Actuaries (SOA). Several unions made inquiries about the Variable Plan and a number of collectively bargained plans outside the UFCW have adopted the Variable Plan. For instance, Variable Plans were established by Hotel & Restaurant Local 26 in Boston, Massachusetts; the Masters, Mates, and Pilots in Baltimore, Maryland; the Newspaper Guild (an affiliate of the Communications Workers of America) with both the New York Times and the Consumers Union; and the Sheet Metal Workers' National Fund. In addition, the Maine Public Employees Retirement System enacted legislation to adopt the Variable Plan for new hires from 2015.

The Variable Plan has also gained attention in other circles. The National Coordinating Committee for Multiemployer Plans (NCCMP), the lobbying arm of the multiemployer community, presented Congress with a set of proposals to reform the multiemployer pension system in 2013. These proposals were based on the work of the Retirement Security Review Commission which recently published its findings (see DeFrehn and Shapiro 2013). The section of the Commission study that promoted 'innovation' proposed that the Variable Plan be formally added to the IRS code. Additionally, in Congressional hearings, the Variable Plan has gained a number of endorsements from Congressional leaders and staff.

Conclusion

The US occupational pension system has experienced a painful and disruptive decade. The retirement paradigm that emerged after World War II is disappearing in the private sector, and it faces political and financial challenges in the public sector. Recent Boeing/IAM negotiations in Seattle as well as the Detroit bankruptcy provide further evidence of the unraveling of the pension deal. The transition from the old to a new pension order has been underway since 1980, accelerated recently due to major economic and financial crises. The future retirement security of tens of millions of American workers and retirees is in the balance.

While conventional economic theory often ignores or minimizes the institutional role of unions and other pension stakeholders in the private and public pension system, this case study of how unions approached the retirement challenge will help determine the course of history for much of the aging workforce. Constructing a fair and equitable pension deal can be successful, as illustrated here. Jim Leech, the CEO of the Ontario Teachers' Pension Plan, has recently highlighted the role that labor unions have played in transforming pension plans in New Brunswick, Canada, and the Netherlands (Leech and McNish 2013). The US labor movement, along with other pension stakeholders, has an historic opportunity to revive the pension contract in America.

References

Ambachtsheer, K. P. (2007). *Pension Revolution.* Hoboken, NJ: John Wiley & Sons, Inc.

Barkin, S. (1983). *Worker Militancy and its Consequences.* New York: Praeger Publishers.

Blitzstein, D. S. (2013). 'Restructuring Occupational Pension Plans in Crisis: A U.S. Labor Management Case Study.' *Rotman International Journal of Pension Management,* 6(1): 12–19.

DeFrehn, R. G. and J. Shapiro (2013). *Solutions Not Bailouts: A Comprehensive Plan from Business and Labor to Safeguard Multiemployer Retirement Security, Protect Taxpayers and Spur Economic Growth: A Report on the Proceedings, Findings and Recommendations of the Retirement*

Security Review Commission of the NCCMP. Washington, DC: NCCMP. <http://www.nccmp.org/forEmails/SolutionsNotBailouts.pdf>.

Drucker, P. F. (1976). *The Unseen Revolution.* New York: Harper & Row Publishers.

Fuerst, D. E. (2006). 'Risk Allocation in Retirement Plans: A Better Solution.' *Journal of Applied Corporate Finance,* 18(1): 95–103.

Fuerst, D. E. (2015). 'Retirement Shares Plan: A New Model of Risk Sharing,' in O. S. Mitchell and R. C. Shea (eds), *Reimagining Pensions: The Next 40 Years.* Oxford: Oxford University Press, 161–73.

Kocken, T. (2011). 'Why the Design of Maturing Defined Benefit Plans Needs Rethinking.' *Rotman International Journal of Pension Management,* 4(1): 44–50.

Leech, J. and J. McNish (2013). *The Third Rail.* Toronto: McClelland & Stewart.

Moody's Investor Service, Global Credit Research (2006). *Multiemployer Pension Plans: Moody's Analytical Approach—Rating Methodology.* New York: Moody's.

Pension Benefit Guaranty Corporation (PBGC) (2013). *Multiemployer Pension Plans, Report to Congress Required by the Pension Protection Act of 2006.* Washington, DC: PBGC. <http://www.pbgc.gov/documents/pbgc-report-multiemployer-pension-plans.pdf>.

Sass, S. A. (1997). *The Promise of Private Pensions.* Cambridge, MA: Harvard University Press.

Chapter 8

Back to the Future: Hybrid Co-operative Pensions and the TIAA-CREF System

Benjamin Goodman and David P. Richardson

Over the past 30 years, defined contribution (DC) plans have emerged as the primary employment-based retirement program for millions of US workers.[1] DC plans provide covered workers with substantial latitude in determining whether to participate, how much salary to contribute, how to invest assets, and how to take distributions from the plans. As participation in DC plans has grown, more households bear increased responsibility for managing the various risks to their retirement savings. A growing body of research finds that many DC plan participants have difficulty making decisions that maximize their chances of achieving retirement security. For example, workers may make poor retirement plan decisions because they are prone to behavioral biases or have low financial literacy.[2] Policymakers recently began enacting changes to the DC plan system with the goal of reducing the chances of participants making systematic mistakes. Major changes enacted as part of the Pension Protection Act of 2006 included new rules for qualified plan default provisions that were designed to increase worker participation, achieve a minimum rate of retirement contributions, and provide automatic investment diversification. These changes focused on helping households manage risk during the accumulation phase, but they provided no guidance for the distribution phase of these retirement plans.

As the US population ages, there is a need to ensure that retirement programs can carry individuals not just to, but also through, retirement. This has resulted in renewed interest in plan designs that include guaranteed income options to help households manage various retirement income risks. Among the ideas being considered, policymakers are requiring default (or mandatory) annuity features and encouraging the expanded use of hybrid plan designs.

This chapter provides an overview of how TIAA-CREF, a Fortune 100 financial services company providing retirement services to the non-profit and public sectors, incorporates features of a co-operative hybrid pension into retirement plan design. We define a co-operative pension as a retirement plan that distributes all assets (net of operating costs) to system participants over time. A hybrid pension combines elements of both a defined contribution (DC) plan and a defined benefit (DB) plan. The TIAA-CREF system combines a DC structure during the accumulation phase, with workers allocating contributions to investment choices that include mutual funds and deferred fixed and variable annuities; a DB structure during retirement by providing the option to annuitize part (or all) of retirement assets; and a co-operative structure for individuals who participate in the fixed annuity component over their working and retired lives.

In what follows, we first provide a brief overview of the TIAA-CREF system. Next we discuss how TIAA Traditional, a guaranteed fixed annuity, and the CREF variable annuity work, and we discuss past performance. We then review some recent data on participant experience. A final section concludes.

The Basics of TIAA-CREF

Teachers Insurance and Annuity Association—College Retirement Equities Fund (TIAA–CREF) is multi-faceted financial services organization offering a range of pension, IRA, life insurance, brokerage, financial guidance and advice, wealth management, banking, endowment, and planned giving services. Here we focus on the structure of core pension business which serves over 3.9 million individuals and more than 15,000 institutional clients.[3] Many institutions offer at least two plans—a primary plan (which may accept only employer contributions), and a supplemental plan (which typically accepts only employee contributions). Because TIAA-CREF serves the non-profit and public sector markets, some institutions are subject to the Employee Retirement Income Security Act (ERISA) while others are not. Numerous sources provide information on corporate structure, governance, and risk management aspects of TIAA-CREF.[4] Our focus in this chapter is how the system impacts participant outcomes.

Participants in the TIAA-CREF system choose from a menu of investments when building their retirement portfolios. Table 8.1 provides information on the asset classes and investment choices available to participants as of December 31, 2013; it also documents the rapid growth in the investment choice set over the past 20 years. Participants can also invest in one guaranteed asset, the TIAA Traditional annuity. This asset class was the genesis of TIAA in 1918; it provides a guarantee of principal, a guaranteed interest rate, and additional declared dividends in excess of the guaranteed rate.[5] In 1952, CREF became the first organization to offer a variable annuity when it introduced the CREF stock account. This account allowed participants to directly purchase (and bear the associated investment risks of) an equity asset class within their retirement plans. In 1988, CREF began offering a fixed income asset class with the introduction of the CREF Money Market account. A fourth asset class—balanced—was added in 1990 with the introduction of the CREF Social Choice fund.[6] The TIAA Real Estate fund in 1995 introduced a fifth asset class—real estate. As shown in Table 8.1, a number of additional equity, fixed income, real estate, and balanced asset class fund options have been added to the investment menu thereafter.

TABLE 8.1 TIAA-CREF asset classes, inception dates, and total assets under management for TIAA-CREF pension accounts and mutual funds, as of December 31, 2013

Asset Class and Investment Account	Date of Inception	Assets ($ mil.)	% of Total
Guaranteed			
TIAA Traditional	April 23, 1918	259,504	43.8
Equity			
CREF Stock	July 1, 1952	126,458	39.4
CREF Global Equities	March 1, 1990	19,128	
CREF Growth	April 29, 1994	19,409	
CREF Equity Index	April 29, 1994	15,858	
TIAA-CREF Equity Mutual Funds (21)	October 1, 2002	52,478	
Fixed Income			
CREF Money Market	April 1, 1988	11,979	8.2
CREF Bond Market	March 1, 1990	13,078	
CREF Inflation Linked Bond	May 1, 1997	7,644	
TIAA-CREF Fixed Income Mutual Funds (9)	March 31, 2006	16,006	
Real Estate			
TIAA Real Estate	October 2, 1995	16,908	3.1
TIAA-CREF Real Estate Securities Mutual Fund	October 1, 2002	1,286	
Multi-Asset			
CREF Social Choice	March 1, 1990	13,341	5.5
Lifecycle funds (10)	October 15, 2004	18,203	
Lifestyle funds (5)	December 9, 2011	243	
TIAA-CREF Managed Allocation Mutual Fund	March 31, 2006	710	

Notes:

a) All variable products reported on the SEC (net) assets reporting basis.

b) The data sources for this table includes all pension, retirement class, and institutional class mutual fund assets and the totals are different from the following information which summarizes data for premium-paying TIAA-CREF participants in primary plans only.

Source: Authors' calculations.

Notable among these were the introduction of the CREF inflation-linked bond fund (1997), retirement class mutual funds (2002), and the target-date series of life cycle mutual funds in 2004. In 2013, TIAA-CREF offered a total of 57 investment options across five different asset classes, divided about 39 percent in equity and 61 percent in non-equity asset classes.

At retirement, participants have a menu of distribution options available for converting assets into retirement income. For instance, they have access to a full menu of annuity options including fixed and variable, single and joint, standard and graded, various length guaranteed (or certainty) periods, transfer payout, and interest-only payments. Participants may also take systematic withdrawals, lump-sum payments, or required minimum distributions. The flexibility of the distribution menu allows participants to customize their retirement incomes to suit their consumption and estate planning needs.

Prior to 1988, however, the TIAA-CREF system could be characterized as a co-operative hybrid retirement plan. The hybrid component was facilitated through a plan design that required defined contributions to be allocated to units of deferred annuities; at retirement, participants converted these assets into a lifetime income benefit stream. The co-operative component was associated with a system design that distributed all assets (net of operating costs) to participants over time. Though the firm no longer requires the conversion of assets into lifetime annuities, the co-operative arrangement remains in place for participants choosing to utilize annuities. In what follows, we describe how TIAA and CREF work and show how the two products remain an integral part of many participants' retirement income plans.

TIAA Traditional

The TIAA Traditional annuity is a guaranteed fixed annuity product that can be purchased while working or in retirement by investing in deferred TIAA annuity units through an employment-based retirement plan. The overall concept of 'investing' in TIAA is quite simple during a participant's working life. Contributions are made by a participant (or on behalf of the participant by his/her employer).[7] Each contribution has a guaranteed lifetime minimum rate of return based on the month and year in which the contribution is made. For most of our participants, this guaranteed minimum rate is 3 percent.[8] All TIAA participants are thus guaranteed (subject to TIAA meeting its claim-paying ability) to have an account balance that continually grows at the stated minimum rate. In addition, in any year the TIAA Trustees declare that 'additional amounts' will be credited to participant accounts, this in effect provides an interest rate greater than the guaranteed minimum rate.

A participant (or surviving spouse, partner, or beneficiary) has the right but not the obligation to turn the accumulated units of TIAA into a stream of lifetime income. The decision to contractually convert into lifetime income typically happens upon retirement, although it can occur at later ages. Similar to the accumulation phase, the TIAA annuity contract has a guaranteed minimum payout rate; the TIAA trustees can declare additional amounts to increase the total payment beyond this minimum guarantee on an annual basis. A full menu of annuity choices is available and includes options for single or joint life, standard or graded, and certainty periods of various lengths.[9] If a participant chooses not to take a lifetime annuity, other income options are available, such as receiving interest-only payments, taking the Required Minimum Distribution (RMD) amounts, or opting for an annuity certain. The accumulated balance can also be transferred out of TIAA in roughly equal-sized periodic payments using a Transfer Payout Annuity (TPA), with the transferred amounts moved into other TIAA-CREF investments or taken out of the system, though the latter may depend on employer-specific plan rules.[10]

While the concepts behind TIAA are simple, features of the system make including a TIAA deferred annuity in an investment portfolio somewhat complex. First, every year for the last half century, the TIAA trustees have declared additional amounts for both the accumulation and the payout rates. For this reason, participants and advisers who considered only the minimum guarantee would have underweighted the expected return contribution on the product. Second, TIAA has a unique 'vintage' system that applies different crediting rates to marginal accumulations based on the time of original contribution. Thus, the total return earned on total contributions is unique to each individual's history of contributions. Third, there is typically limited liquidity and cashability for TIAA accumulations held in employer-sponsored retirement plans, which limits the ability to rebalance one's portfolio. Each of these features is addressed in what follows.

TIAA crediting rates during the accumulation phase

Participants can purchase TIAA deferred annuity units through their retirement plan by allocating part of their contributions to them, or by transferring other retirement assets into the product. Accumulated TIAA units earn a lifetime guaranteed minimum rate of return that is determined by the type of retirement plan contract. For many participants, this guaranteed minimum is 3 percent, though more recent plan contracts have adopted a

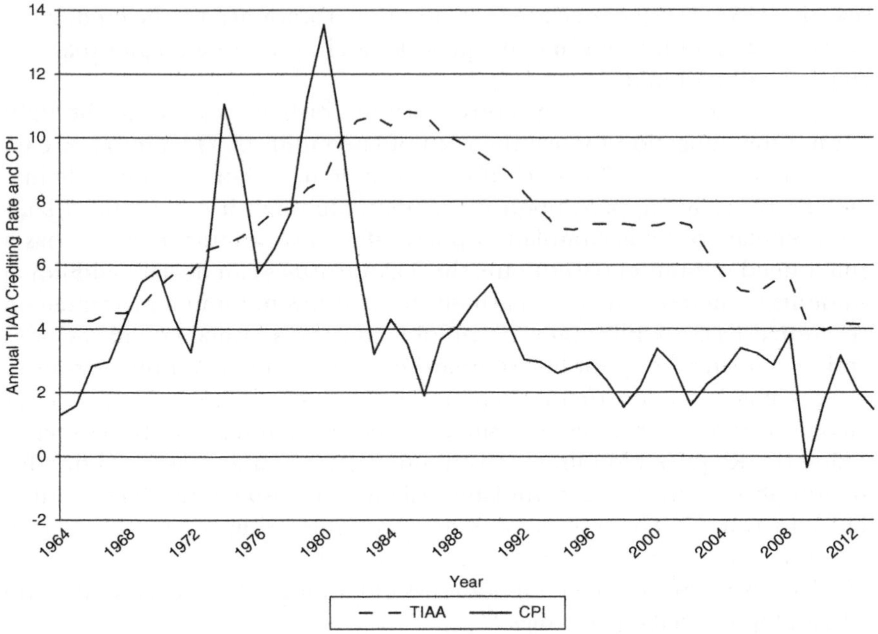

Figure 8.1 TIAA Average Crediting Rates versus Consumer Price Index: 1964–2013
Source: Authors' calculations.

year-to-year floating guaranteed rate of at least 1 percent and at most 3 percent.[11] For the past few decades, actual credit rates have been much higher than the guaranteed minimums specified in plan contracts. Figure 8.1 shows the average crediting rate earned by units in illiquid employer-based contracts over the past 50 years.

Figure 8.1 shows that the average crediting rate has been generally positively correlated with long-term nominal interest rates, but not with inflation. The crediting rate increased as interest rates rose from the 1960s through the 1970s, and the reverse has occurred over the past three decades. Note also that the TIAA crediting rates have exceeded 3 percent for over 40 years, sometimes substantially, and the TIAA crediting rate has also exceeded the rate of inflation for decades.[12] This pattern of crediting rates is due to the long term nature of the underlying portfolio investments, the insurer's ability to buy and hold investments (especially government bonds), the size of the general account (which helps facilitate investment in alternative assets), and low expenses.

When a participant is credited with earnings on his existing TIAA assets, his new accumulation receives the same guaranteed minimum rate. As a simple example, suppose a participant makes a one-time allocation of $100 to TIAA and has a plan contract with a guaranteed minimum rate of 3 percent. After 10 years, the minimum accumulation would be $134.39. If instead, during the first year, the actual crediting rate was 5 percent, then after 10 years the guaranteed minimum accumulation would be $137.[13] The additional 2 percent earned in the first year is guaranteed once it has been earned.

As an illustration using historical returns, assume a participant made a one-time allocation to TIAA of $100 on January 1, 1984 and had a plan contract with a guaranteed minimum crediting rate of 3 percent. A thirty-year projection of his guaranteed minimum accumulation as of January 1, 2014 would have been $242.73. But when we apply the actual crediting rates to this participant's TIAA accumulations, the actual amount accumulated was $846.61, an amount nearly 3.5 times larger than the guaranteed minimum. Of course, past performance is no guarantee of future results, so if today's low interest rate environment persists into the foreseeable future, there is a strong likelihood that a 2044 actual accumulation from a one-time $100 contribution in 2014 will result in a smaller total return. Nevertheless, it is important to understand that considering only the guaranteed minimum accumulation rate of 3 percent likely understates the potential value of investing in a TIAA account.

Another important aspect of investing in TIAA is the lack of downside volatility in the participant's total return. When market interest rates rise or fall, bond holders can experience portfolio gains or losses to their total returns because of the interaction between interest rates and bond prices. By contrast, TIAA participants always earn a positive return because the interest rate risk is managed within the TIAA general account. This lack of participant downside investment risk compares favorably to other 'safe' fixed income investments—namely bond funds—that are required to distribute capital gains and losses to participants. Figure 8.2 compares the past 30 years of monthly returns in TIAA with the Barclays Aggregate Bond Fund returns.[14] The bond funds had negative monthly returns about 30 percent of the time over the sample period. The likelihood of short-term negative bond returns is a particularly important consideration for older workers nearing retirement who seek to rebalance their portfolios away from equities and toward fixed income products. Using this strategy in a rising interest rate environment may have near-retirees bearing excessive interest rate risk relative to an alternative strategy of holding TIAA. This is because the latter pools the risk within a general account which is not required to distribute capital losses to participants.

Table 8.2 provides additional evidence of the advantages of pooling investment risk across participants within the TIAA general account. The average return performance of TIAA and the Barclays aggregate give the appearance of similar performance across various time periods. Taking

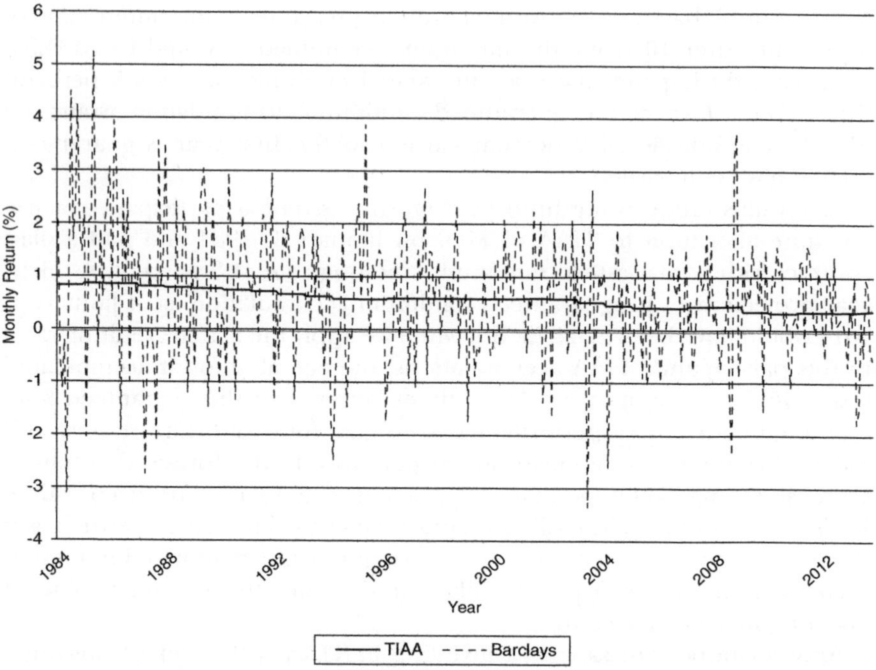

Figure 8.2 Monthly returns to TIAA and Barclays aggregate: 1984–2013
Source: Authors' calculations.

TABLE 8.2 Average return performance of TIAA and the Barclays Aggregate

	5 years	10 years	20 years	30 years
TIAA Traditional				
Average return (%)	4.5	4.3	5.9	7.4
# of negative months	0	0	0	0
Sharpe ratio				2.0
Barclays Aggregate Bond				
Average return (%)	4.3	4.4	5.6	7.5
# of negative months	17	38	77	106
Sharpe ratio				0.3

Source: Authors' calculations.

into account the funds' volatility (as shown in Figure 8.2), however, indicates that participants bear substantially more risk in the bond funds compared to TIAA. The Barclays aggregate had negative returns in about 30 percent of the months, compared to zero negative months for TIAA. The difference in Sharpe ratios highlights the additional risk to participants within the bond fund, as compared to the accumulations held in the TIAA general account.

Contributions and the TIAA vintage system

An unusual feature of the TIAA Traditional annuity is its vintage system for crediting returns that participants earn on their contributions. Generally speaking, the vintage system exists because TIAA is structured as a non-profit 'co-operative' annuity with a long-term investment horizon. When a participant contributes to TIAA Traditional, assets are purchased to back the total lifetime expected impact of that contribution. Contributions made at different points in time (called 'vintages') can therefore earn different crediting rates, because assets backing the various vintages of contributions will tend to have different rates of return.

This vintage system can make it difficult for some to understand their total TIAA returns, because most participants contribute to the fund over their working lives and not as a simple lump-sum at a point in time. As a result, most TIAA participants tend to have accumulations in many different vintages, so their overall average return is a blend of the returns to the various vintages.[15] The vintage system is akin to a co-operative pension, in that all the participants of a particular vintage 'own' the underlying vintage assets and share in their returns.

Table 8.3 provides a hypothetical example of how the vintage system contributes to a participant's TIAA returns. The total average return in the table is calculated as the weighted average of the accumulations attributable to each of the various vintages. For most contracts, interest earnings

TABLE 8.3 Weighted average of yearly accumulations and interest earnings by vintage

Vintage	Accumulation	Interest rate (%)
2000–2007	15,555	4.25
2008	10,234	5.00
2009	9,479	4.50
2010–2013	12,905	3.75
Total	48,173	4.32

Source: Authors' calculations.

TABLE 8.4 Current payout rate by vintage

Vintage	Payout Rate at Age 65 (%)
Pre-1992	9.73
1992–1997	7.72
1998–2008	7.19
2009–2013	6.33–7.01
New Money	6.50
Average Policyholder	7.60

Source: Authors' calculations.

above the 3 percent guarantee are placed in the new vintage, so the average interest earned on total accumulations can thus change on a daily basis.

The TIAA vintage system was created to treat participants fairly relative to their tenure within the system. The alternative of using a single total portfolio rate might drive down returns for existing participants when interest rates fall, and by necessity it would require reduced new money rates when interest rates rise. The vintage system reduces exposure to this type of interest rate risk.

The 'co-operative' characteristics of the vintage system extend through the accumulation phase into retirement, so they can also affect the annuity settlement crediting rate.[16] This is because the settlement rate will reflect the various vintages of investment experience, as well as an additional amount from the return of unneeded contingency reserves.[17] Given TIAA's non-profit co-operative annuity structure, when the contingency reserves are no longer needed, the firm distributes them to the participants who helped generate them. Absent unusual circumstances, the longer a participant has assets in TIAA, the higher the payout rate, because the older vintages have larger contingency reserves. Table 8.4 illuminates this concept by showing current payout rates by vintage.

Two important features of the TIAA system are worth emphasizing. First, the comparison of vintages to 'new money' rates shows the difference in payout rates that a long-term participant in TIAA receives, compared to someone who converts other retirement assets into a TIAA annuity on the contract settlement date. For example, a long-term participant annuitizing assets with vintages from 1990 to 2008 would have a payout rate of between 7.19 percent and 9.73 percent, depending on the timing of his contributions. By contrast, a person converting retirement assets into a TIAA annuity today would receive the 'new money' rate of 6.5 percent. Second, participants cannot pick and choose which vintages they want to sell or annuitize—all decisions are pro-rata across various vintages to deter participants from gaming the system when interest rates change. Continuing the previous example, if a long-term participant annuitizes half his TIAA assets, then the crediting rate is weighted pro-rata across his various vintages.

TIAA annuity payout rates

Participants choose if, when, how, and how much they annuitize from their holdings of TIAA assets. A participant may decide he does not need to annuitize any retirement wealth and so can continue holding TIAA assets through retirement. Alternatively, he can take interest-only payments, allow Required Minimum Distribution (RMD) rules to generate payments, or convert those assets using a Transfer Payout Annuity (TPA).[18] For those choosing annuitization, a full range of choices is available including options for single versus joint life, standard versus graded, and a range of guarantee options. Once a participant decides when, how, and how much to annuitize, his TIAA assets are converted into an annuity payment stream using the current applicable annuity payout rate. Given the vintage system described above, this rate is likely to be unique to each participant.

TIAA provides a guaranteed minimum payout defined in terms of expected lifetime income. Expressing the payout as income per $1,000 of TIAA accumulation, most contracts currently have an age 65 minimum guarantee of $4.11 of monthly lifetime income, or over $49 per year. TIAA has also historically credited additional amounts to the payout rate. For example, as of January 1, 2014, the initial income per $1,000 on 'new money' at age 65 was $5.54 a month, or over $66 per year. All of these payments are stated as rates, with the guaranteed minimum payout rate equal to 4.93 percent and the 'new money' payout rate equal to 6.6 percent.

As is well known, annuity payout rates vary depending on several factors, including an annuitant's age, annuity option elected, and the current interest rate. Table 8.5 provides examples of current payout rates. Participants annuitizing at younger ages, those choosing two-life annuities, and/or those electing a certainty or guarantee period (e.g. a life annuity that also includes a guaranteed minimum number of payments) will receive a lower payout rate compared to older annuitants and those opting for a single life annuity

TABLE 8.5 Current payout rates by age

	Single				Joint and 100%
	No guarantee			20 year guarantee	No guarantee
	Age 55	Age 65	Age 75	Age 65	Ages 65
Payout rate	5.50	6.60	8.90	6.00	5.70
Guaranteed Minimum rate	4.10	4.90	6.40	4.70	4.30

Source: Authors' calculations.

with no guarantee period. While the payout rate will differ based on these factors, the expected total lifetime benefit will be roughly equal across ages and options. By contrast, differences in the current interest environment at the time of retirement can result in different payout rates and different expected lifetime benefits. For example, while the current new money payout rate for an age 65 annuitant is 6.5 percent, many years ago it was quite a bit higher, hitting a peak of about 14 percent in the early 1980s.

One challenge in explaining the annuitization decision process is that, unlike with mutual fund investments, there is no single 'price' for annuities. That is, the guaranteed minimum interest rate is known, but the participant's actual payout rate depends on age, option, and interest, plus the additional impact on the rate from the vintage system and additional credited amounts. Because these additional amounts are not guaranteed, a prospective annuitant retiree will not know his/her actual income per $1,000 accumulation until very close to the settlement date. Furthermore, the additional amounts can change, even for those who have already turned their accumulations into lifetime income. Figure 8.3 shows that TIAA has declared numerous increases to post-annuitization payout rates to annuitants in different cohorts. As Figure 8.3 shows, initial income per $100,000

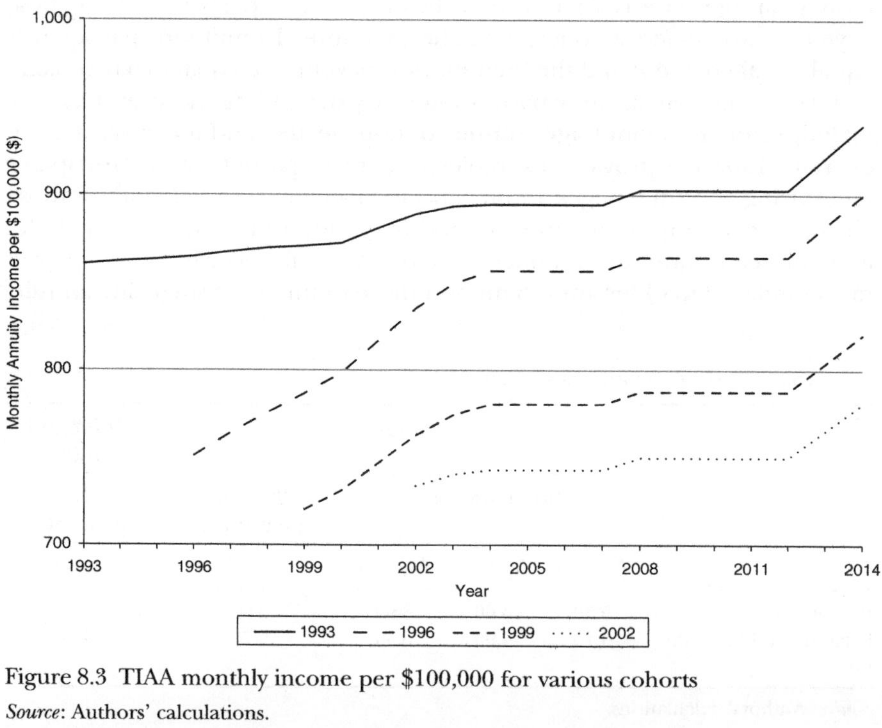

Figure 8.3 TIAA monthly income per $100,000 for various cohorts
Source: Authors' calculations.

has varied over the past 20 years.[19] Notably, there were no reductions since 1993, even though this period included the 2001 recession and the 2008 financial crisis.

Combining accumulation and payout features: A hybrid co-op pension product

We have characterized TIAA as a co-op hybrid pension product based on its features and structure. TIAA has a DC component because participants allocate retirement contributions to TIAA over their working lives and accumulate units of a deferred guaranteed fixed annuity. The vintage system has features of a co-operative pension because of TIAA's non-profit annuity structure—meaning that the risk pooling, returns, and board decisions on the distribution of underlying no-longer-needed contingency reserves is proportional to the accumulated shares owned by each vintage cohort. Likewise, the guaranteed minimum crediting and payout rates during the accumulation and payout phases, respectively, provide a co-operative structure for distributing returns and income from system assets while effectively pooling market risk. At retirement, the features of the participating annuity options provide a minimum level defined benefit pension with a high likelihood of receiving additional amounts.

Design complexity is an issue for this type of product within a retirement plan investment menu. A growing body of research indicates that individuals face both behavioral and financial literacy hurdles when making retirement decisions, and complexity can be a major driver of poor decision-making.[20] Research also indicates that low annuitization rates can be partially explained by behavioral biases.[21] For example, prospect theory indicates that, after working a lifetime and accumulating retirement wealth, retirees may have a difficult time writing a big check from their accounts to receive a series of small checks in the form of annuity income. Including hybrid pension products in the investment menu (in the form of deferred fixed annuities) can help participants overcome this behavioral bias, by encouraging them to allocate contributions to the deferred annuity over time to receive a series of larger checks in retirement. Guaranteed minimums can also help with loss aversion, because every contribution is guaranteed to grow at a minimum rate and produce income for lifetime retirement income at that minimum rate. Other features, such as the vintage system and allocation of additional amounts, should increase demand for these products, yet they also add complexity. So while research in behavioral finance and financial literacy has improved plan design during the accumulation phase, much work remains to be done with respect to the distribution phase.

A simple example highlights the challenges. No precise projection of future lifetime benefits from TIAA is available, but a rough estimate can be calculated using today's crediting and payout rates. For example, at age 35, a one-time $100 contribution is guaranteed to increase to $243 by age 65. With a guaranteed minimum payout rate of 4.9 percent, this one-time contribution will generate at least $12 in annual income as a single life annuity. A more realistic example estimates the guaranteed income benefit received starting at age 65, assuming level contributions of $100 monthly over 30 years. Applying the current guaranteed minimum guaranteed rates results in about $2,842, while applying average current rates would imply about $4,347 in annual income.

This simple example shows that including this type of hybrid product in a retirement plan could nudge participants to focus on retirement outcomes, rather than simply wealth accumulation. Advice engines can provide different outcome metrics under a variety of other assumptions. For example, by assuming a contribution equal to a fixed percentage of salary, one can describe the final benefit as a replacement rate (projected benefit divided by final salary), using either the minimum guaranteed interest and payout rates, or current rates (or even historical average TIAA rates).

Another advantage of this type of hybrid product is that the guaranteed minimum income floor allows participants to customize their retirement investment portfolios to seek higher returns (and more risk), or to reduce total risk exposure by allocating more assets to a higher income floor. The flexibility of distributions in retirement is also a feature. Participants have the right but not the obligation to convert their accumulations into lifetime income. Participants are free to use their accumulations in any way they choose, subject to contractual limits. For example, a participant in poor health might not want to annuitize, might choose a joint life annuity to provide for a spouse or partner, or might choose a single life annuity with a guarantee period to ensure assets revert to the estate in case of an early death.

The CREF Variable Annuity

CREF became the first commercially offered variable annuity product in the US in 1952, with an intuitive and simple design concept.[22] During the accumulation phase, CREF investments appear to perform similar to mutual fund investments. Participants who allocate contributions to CREF purchase fractional shares (units) of a basket of underlying assets. The daily share value changes, based on the performance of the assets held in the fund. But there is a key difference between CREF and mutual funds: while mutual funds have capital gain distributions and/or pay dividends, the declared amount is used to add to the participant's number of shares owned. In CREF, the units are valued daily and any gains or dividends are added to the unit value.

As shown in Table 8.1, there are currently eight different CREF accounts. The first was the CREF Stock account, which provides a broadly diversified basket of equities with foreign and domestic stocks (large and small cap), and combines both active and passive management. Other accounts include an Index fund, Growth account, Global account, Bond fund, Inflation-Linked Bond fund, Social Choice fund, and a Money Market account. Participants are free to choose any allocation to these accounts, as well as TIAA Traditional, TIAA Real Estate, or any other mutual funds included in the plan sponsor's menu.

Another difference between CREF and a mutual fund is that, in the payout phase, the CREF participant has the right but not the obligation to convert his accumulations into a stream of lifetime income. Similar to TIAA, participants choose if, when, how, and how much of their CREF accumulations to annuitize. Participants may take non-annuity distributions similar to mutual funds or lump-sum or systematic withdrawals (there may be limits based on plan rules), or instead they can simply draw down their accumulations based on the Required Minimum Distribution (RMD) rules.

A unique feature of the CREF payout annuity is that it offers post-settlement asset allocation choices. Conversion from one CREF annuity to another CREF annuity and/or to a TIAA annuity is permitted. Thus if an annuitant wants to 'lock in' gains after a good year, or simply wants to reduce or increase the risk of his annuity payment stream, he can transfer some or all of his assets across accounts. Accordingly, the participant can collect payments for life.

One consequence of purchasing a variable annuity is that the retiree does not know from payment to payment how much income he will receive from the annuity. This uncertainty must be balanced against the possibility of achieving greater investment returns than those promised by a fixed annuity. In essence, CREF (or any variable annuity) provides an instrument for those who seek the security of lifetime income and also wish to participate in the equity and/or bond markets.

The size of life annuity payment per $1,000 of assets converted will depend, among other factors, on the annuitant's age at settlement, how long he is expected to live from that age (single or joint mortality), and an assumed investment return (AIR). In the case of a fixed annuity like TIAA, the insurer has a high degree of confidence in what the underlying investments are expected to earn, so the payment calculation is straightforward. By contrast, expectations are less certain regarding what assets will earn in a CREF variable annuity. This is because the equity market may be bullish or bearish, and interest rates may rise or fall. CREF uses a 4 percent AIR to calculate the initial annuity payment and then each year (or month for those who choose to revalue their payments monthly), the payment is adjusted by comparing the 4 percent AIR with the actual return earned. If the CREF funds earn more than 4 percent, the payment is increased; if the fund earn less than 4 percent, the payment decreases. CREF may also adjust the annuity payment based on changes in system expenses, group mortality, or other factors (these have been very minor over time).

Some might ask why CREF uses a 4 percent AIR, and the answer is not simple. Part of the explanation is that the firm seeks to reduce potential volatility of participant outcomes based on past market experience. If CREF used a lower AIR, it would result in a lower initial payment, but participants would be more likely to receive increases and those increases would tend to be larger. Using a higher AIR would result in high initial payments, but it would also bring a greater likelihood of subsequent decreases in payments.

Consider a 65 year-old participant with a contract for a CREF single life annuity with a ten-year guaranteed period. Using the standard 4 percent AIR results in an initial annual payment of about $6,680 per $100,000 in assets converted. If instead, we use a 0 percent AIR, the initial payment would be $4,181; using a 6 percent AIR generates an initial payment of $8,076. Suppose in the following year, the actual return of the CREF fund were 6 percent. Then the annuities with 0 percent, 4 percent, and 6 percent AIR would get a 6 percent, 2 percent, and 0 percent increase, respectively. Given its experience, CREF uses the 4 percent AIR to accomplish the overall goals of sufficient initial income with some potential for increases that can help keep pace with inflation.

How effective has the 4 percent AIR been in achieving these goals? The answer depends on the date of annuity settlement. Figure 8.4 shows the evolution of payments per initial $1,000 income from a variable annuity using the CREF stock account. We show paths for cohorts with settlement dates in ten-year intervals from 1955 to 1985, noting that the horizontal axis shows years from settlement and not standardized years. For example, the twentieth year payment for the 1965 cohort is equivalent to the initial year payment for 1985 cohort. The $1,000 line represents a perfectly inflation-hedged annuity. For most cohorts, a variable annuity using the CREF stock account has done well in keeping pace with inflation, on average. This was particularly true for cohorts with settlement dates after 1980.

Recent Participant Experience in the TIAA-CREF System

The TIAA-CREF system has undergone substantial change over the past 25 years. Prior to 1989, TIAA-CREF could be considered a pure co-operative

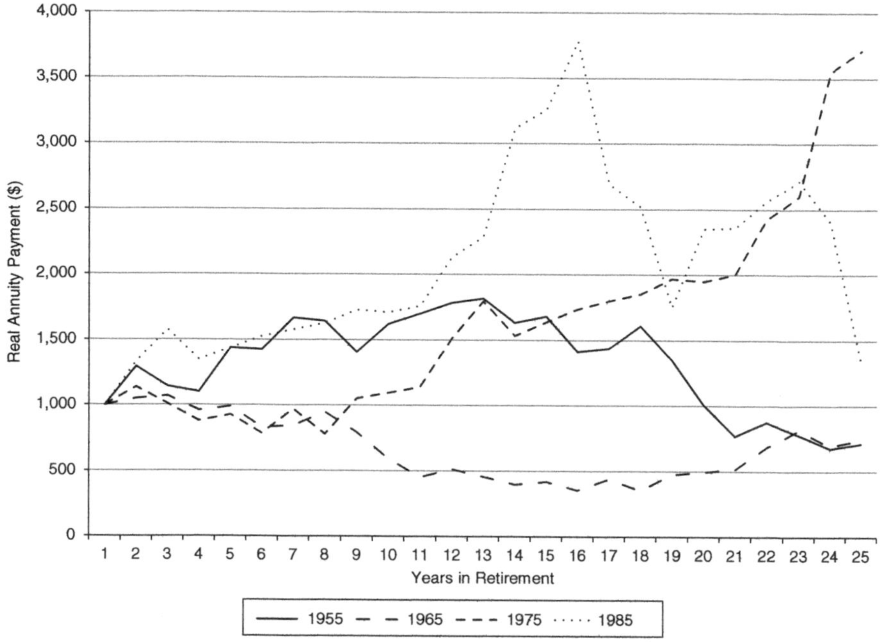

Figure 8.4 Real CREF stock annuity payments for various cohorts
Source: Authors' calculations.

hybrid system. Participants had only a simple investment menu of two choices—TIAA and CREF Stock—when deciding how to allocate contributions and assets. During that time, the TIAA-CREF system also offered a single form of retirement benefit: the immediate life annuity. Today, by contrast, participants can choose from an investment menu that includes mutual funds along with CREF variable annuity funds and the TIAA Traditional fixed annuity. Participants have a wide range of non-annuity income distribution options including Systematic Withdrawals and Transfers (SWAT), Minimum Distribution Options (MDO), Transfer Payout Annuities (TPA), and Interest Payment Retirement Options (IPRO).[23] Moreover, participants can choose from a menu of variable and guaranteed fixed annuities. So to participants, while the system today retains components of the co-operative hybrid system, it also offers more flexibility during both the accumulation and distribution phases.

Participation patterns have also changed over time. Table 8.6 shows asset class participation and proportion of contributions invested from 1993 to 2013. Here, participation rates are split between people who allocated all contributions to an asset class (100 percent), and those who allocated a fraction of contributions to an asset class (0.1 percent to 99 percent).

TABLE 8.6 Asset class participation and proportion of contributions invested from 1993 to 2013

	1993	1996	1999	2002	2005	2008	2011	2013
TIAA guaranteed								
100%	16.1	11.2	6.7	7.5	6.2	4.9	5.7	5.1
0.1–99%	65.2	56.5	48.5	54.8	56.6	49.6	41.0	34.9
Equity								
100%	11.5	22.2	29.6	20.0	11.3	8.9	7.6	7.3
0.1–99%	65.2	61.8	55.8	61.9	67.7	62.4	53.2	46.9
Fixed income								
100%	3.8	4.2	5.4	6.8	8.9	8.2	8.6	8.2
0.1–99%	24.5	23.8	25.2	26.0	34.1	37.1	34.0	29.6
Real estate								
100%	–	0.0	0.1	0.2	0.4	0.4	0.3	0.6
0.1–99%	–	0.7	9.0	26.5	39.9	39.8	32.9	29.9
Multi-asset*								
100%	–	–	–	–	1.2	10.7	20.1	27.6
50.1–99%	–	–	–	–	13.6	14.3	13.6	13.3
	81.3	67.7	55.2	62.3	62.8	54.5	46.7	40.0
	76.7	84.0	85.4	81.9	79.0	71.3	60.8	54.2
	28.3	28.0	30.6	32.8	43.0	45.3	42.6	37.8
		0.7	9.1	26.7	40.3	40.2	33.2	30.5
					14.8	25.0	33.7	40.9

Notes: Analyses prior to 2005 included the CREF Social Choice fund in the Equity Class.
Sources: Americks (2002), Rugh (2004), Richardson (2014), and authors' calculations.

In 1993, the investment menu was limited to TIAA and five CREF funds; then, 81 percent of participants contributed to TIAA, 77 percent contributed to CREF equity accounts, and around 28 percent contributed to CREF fixed income accounts. As the investment menu expanded, the proportion of participants allocating any contributions to TIAA declined, and in 2013, only about 40 percent contributed to TIAA. As noted in Rugh (2004), equity class participation peaked in the early 2000s and steadily declined since the 2001 recession. This drop in participation in the guaranteed and equity classes has been offset by a strong increase in participation in the multi-asset class, a shift almost completely attributable to increasingly strong participation in auto-diversified life cycle fund investments first offered in 2004 (Richardson 2014).

Figure 8.5 shows initial income choices by TIAA-CREF participants over the 1988–2012 period. As discussed earlier, 1988 was the last year that the TIAA-CREF could be considered a true hybrid system. Among participants choosing an income stream that year, about 56 percent opted for a joint life annuity and 44 percent a single life annuity. Over the next eight years, TIAA-CREF expanded the distribution menu. In 1989, the Interest Payment Retirement Option (IPRO), which allows participants to receive interest income from their TIAA asset accumulations, became the first non-annuity payment option offered by TIAA-CREF. The Minimum Distribution Option (MDO) was first offered in 1991 to help retirees satisfy their federally required minimum distributions. In 1996, Systematic Withdrawals and Transfers (SWAT) were automated. Figure 8.5 shows that SWATs and MDOs in particular have become relatively popular initial distribution choices, now accounting for over 50 percent of new income distribution. Figure 8.5 also shows that the decline in first-time annuitization rates was strongly correlated with long-term interest rates. We also note the drop in demand for joint life relative to single life annuities. Moreover, the demand for IPROs, in which a participant receives the interest payment from the annual crediting rate while leaving the asset untouched, has been sensitive to declines in market interest rates. While the relative demand for annuities has fallen within the TIAA-CREF system, the proportion of new retirees annuitizing part of their retirement wealth remains high relative to

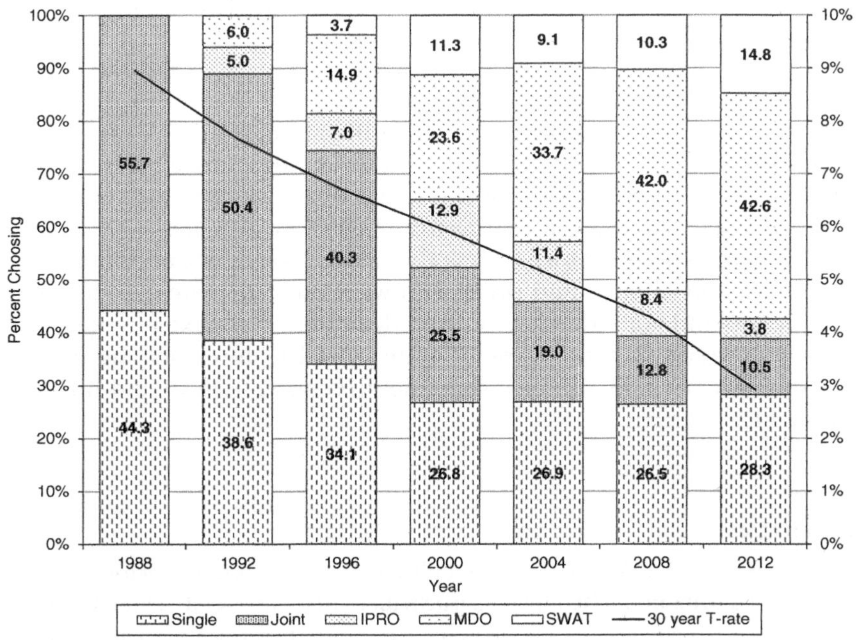

Figure 8.5 Initial income choices by TIAA-CREF participants: 1988–2012

Source: Ameriks (2002) and Brown et al. (forthcoming).

experience in the broader economy; only about 10 percent of workers leaving their job after age 65 annuitize any assets (Burman et al. 2004).

Conclusion

In theory, hybrid retirement plans can combine the best features of DB and DC plans. Co-operative pensions are designed to provide adequate risk sharing and treat different age cohorts fairly. These plans can provide an efficient and equitable method of ensuring the retirement security of workers. Nevertheless, few private sector workers are currently covered by these types of plan. The TIAA-CREF system, which began in 1918 and covers millions of workers in the non-profit sector, provides an example of how to incorporate features of hybrid, co-operative pensions into a retirement plan design. The hybrid features, along with an expanded menu of investment and distribution choices, provide participants with more flexibility. They may also result in workers and retirees increasing their retirement risk exposure. Nevertheless, many participants continue to customize their portfolios by including TIAA Traditional and CREF in their retirement planning.

Particularly for a mobile workforce, including hybrid products like TIAA Traditional within a DC plan investment menu can provide greater retirement security than a plan structure with a primary DB plan and supplemental DC plan. This is especially true for individuals who stop working early, 'job hop,' and have short life expectancy. Participants who allocate part of their contributions to a co-operative hybrid product will benefit from the risk pooling and full interest experience of the annuity.

Much work remains to be done to help current and future retirees make more effective retirement income and estate planning decisions. One area for future research is to apply lessons from behavioral finance to retirement plan distribution design. More work is also needed to better understand how to frame annuity choices and prices in a way that participants understand the trade-offs and consequences of their decisions. The next generation of life cycle products might also incorporate hybrid features helping participants diversify risk and enhance retirement security, both to and through retirement.

Endnotes

1. Department of Labor (2013) data indicate that, for private sector workers, defined contribution (DC) plan participation first surpassed defined benefit (DB) plan participation in 1992. There were more than twice as many total DC participants as DB participants and more than four times as many active DC participants in 2011.

2. Benartzi and Thaler (2007) provide a good overview on how behavior biases may affect retirement. Lusardi and Mitchell (2014) discuss the importance of financial literacy to improving decision-making.
3. Many of the institutions within the TIAA-CREF system have multiple retirement plans and the system includes 401(a), 401(k), 403(b), 415, and 457 type plans.
4. See Greenough (1990) and the TIAA-CREF website.
5. A guaranteed interest rate of 3 percent is applied to all premiums remitted since 1979. When declared, additional amounts remain in effect for a twelve-month period beginning March 1 of each year. Some newer contracts have an index guarantee rate that can be between 1 percent and 3 percent.
6. Previous studies by Ameriks (2000) and Rugh (2004) did not consider this a distinct asset class.
7. Or a participant may choose to transfer part of their existing stock of other retirement investment assets into TIAA.
8. There are actually eight versions of TIAA which differ primarily by type of retirement plan. The versions vary by guaranteed return and liquidity of the asset. Generally, the greater the liquidity of the account, the lower the guaranteed minimum rate of return.
9. A certainty period guarantees payment for a specific number of years regardless of annuitant mortality. Because the payment can be made as a lump sum at annuitant's death, it is akin to a declining value term life insurance policy.
10. The length of the TPA period will depend on which version of TIAA the participant holds. The typical transfer period is ten payments over nine years and one day. Some employers' plans do not allow TPAs.
11. The guarantee is determined by the five-year Constant Maturity Treasury (CMT) less 125 basis points with a minimum bound of 1 percent and a maximum guarantee of 3 percent.
12. This is especially true since the early 1980s.
13. $\$100 \times 1.03^{10} = \$134.39$; $100 * 1.05 * 1.03^{9} = 137$.
14. We reduce the Barclays return by 18 basis points as a proxy for bond fund expenses.
15. Participants can log into their accounts on the TIAA-CREF website and see their current TIAA accumulations by vintage as well as their overall average earning rate.
16. The annuity settlement crediting rate is the interest rate used, in conjunction with the mortality rate assumption, to determine the amount of income an annuity generates.
17. 'Contingency reserves' are rainy day funds, and all insurers need to have some level of these reserves. These reserves come from the spread that companies earn on the money invested.
18. The latter option is similar to a ten-year annuity certain.
19. Guaranteed minimum rates have been fairly stable through this period.
20. See Benartzi and Thaler (2007) and Lusardi and Mitchell (2014).

21. See Benartzi et al. (2011) for a discussion of annuity puzzles.
22. See Greenough (1990) for a discussion of the creation of CREF.
23. See Ameriks (2002) for a discussion of different income distribution options.

References

Ameriks, J. (2000). *Trends in TIAA-CREF Participant Premium and Asset Allocations: 1986–2000,* TIAA-CREF Institute Research Dialogue, 65. New York: TIAA-CREF Institute.

Ameriks, J. (2002). *Recent Trends in the Selection of Retirement Income Streams by TIAA-CREF Participants,* TIAA-CREF Institute Research Dialogue, 74. New York: TIAA-CREF Institute.

Brown, J., J. Poterba, and D. P. Richardson (forthcoming). *Trends in the Selection of Retirement Income Distributions by TIAA-CREF Participants: 2002–2013.* New York: TIAA-CREF Institute.

Benartzi, S. and R. Thaler (2007). 'Heuristics and Biases in Retirement Savings Behavior.' *Journal of Economic Perspectives,* 21(3): 81–104.

Benartzi, S., A. Previtero, and R. Thaler (2011). 'Annuity Puzzles.' *Journal of Economic Perspectives,* 25(4): 143–64.

Burman, L. E., R. W. Johnson, and D. I. Kobes (2004). *Annuitized Wealth at Older Ages: Evidence from the Health and Retirement Study.* Final Report to the Employee Benefits Security Administration. Washington, DC: Urban Institute. <http://www.urban.org/UploadedPDF/411000_annuitized_wealth.pdf>.

Greenough, W. C. (1990). *It's My Retirement Money, Take Good Care of it: The TIAA-CREF Story.* Boston, MA: Irwin.

Lusardi, A. and O. S. Mitchell (2014). 'The Economic Importance of Financial Literacy: Theory and Evidence.' *Journal of Economic Literature,* 52(1): 5–44.

Richardson, D. P. (2014). *Trends in Premium and Asset Allocation by TIAA-CREF Participants: 2005–2011,* TIAA-CREF Institute Research Dialogue, 112. New York: TIAA-CREF Institute.

Rugh, J. S. (2004). *What Happened to TIAA-CREF Participant Premium and Asset Allocations from 2000 to 2004?* TIAA-CREF Institute Research Dialogue, 80. New York: TIAA-CREF Institute.

United States Department of Labor (DOL) (2013). *Private Pension Plan Bulletin Historical Tables and Graphs.* Washington, DC: Employer Benefits Security Administration.

Chapter 9

Retirement Shares Plan: A New Model for Risk Sharing

Donald E. Fuerst

Traditional defined benefit (DB) plans burden a plan sponsor with three principal risks: investment risk, interest rate risk, and longevity risk.[1] Traditional defined contribution (DC) plans place these three risks with the individual. This chapter explores the effects of these risks on the plan sponsors and the individuals, and it also proposes a plan design that allocates these risks differently. The Retirement Shares Plan (RSP) allocates investment risk to the individual, longevity risk to the plan sponsor, and eliminates interest rate risk.

Interest Rate Risk

Sponsors of traditional DB plans must reflect on their balance sheets a liability representing the present value of accrued pension benefits. These accrued benefits are payments due to participants in future years. For financial statement purposes, these fixed future payments are considered similar to debt. The future payments must be discounted to the financial statement date with an interest rate that reflects the yield on high-quality fixed-income securities with duration similar to that of the estimated benefits. The plan's current year expense includes the present value of additional benefits expected to be accrued during the year discounted in the same manner. The market yields on which the discount rate is based can be volatile and change significantly from one year to the next. As a result, the liability and current year costs associated with the DB promise can be volatile. This volatility of the liability and costs we refer to as the interest rate risk.

In a traditional DC plan, the sponsor's commitment is to make a contribution each year to the plan on behalf of participants: the sponsor thus records as a cost the actual contribution. Contributions for future years are not considered accrued at the financial statement date because they are dependent upon the employees providing service in the future, and because the sponsor usually has the right to cease making contributions at any time. Accordingly, the sponsor does not record a liability on its balance sheet other than for accrued but not yet paid contributions. Because the sponsor's cost and liability (if any) does not involve discounting future payments, there is no interest rate risk.

The participant in a DC plan holds an asset equal to the account balance. Since the participant has no obligation to make any payments or transfer these assets to any other party, the participant has no liability, does not discount any future cash flows, and has no interest rate risk as we have defined it. The participant may experience volatility in investment returns due to changing interest rates, but we consider that under investment risk.

Investment Risk

Sponsors of DB plans contribute assets to the plans to meet their current and accrued costs. These assets are invested and are used to pay benefits due in the future. Plan assets are reflected on the sponsor's balance sheet as an offset to the plan's liabilities. In the US, plan assets are reported at market value and thus subject the plan sponsor to investment risk: the volatility of the investment portfolio is directly reflected on the sponsor's financial statement.

Sponsors of DC plans also contribute assets to the plan to meet their commitments, but plan assets are not reflected on the sponsor's financial statement because they are not offsetting any liability for future payment. The assets transferred to the plan generally discharge the sponsor's financial commitment. As a result, the sponsor of a DC plan is not subject to any volatility associated with investment risk.

The DC plan participant has an invested asset, and the benefit he will ultimately derive from the plan depends on his investment experience. The entire investment experience is immediately reflected in the participant's account balance, thus the participant bears the full investment risk of the account. In most DC plans, the participant can manage this risk by selecting the investments from a broad array of funds with varying risk characteristics.

The investments in a DB plan are generally managed by investment professionals and the asset allocation decisions are made by the plan sponsor (usually with the advice of investment professionals). Investments in DC plans are also managed by investment professionals, usually through mutual funds, but the asset allocation decisions are usually made by individual employees rather than investment professionals.

Longevity Risk

The sponsor of a DB plan promises to pay benefits for the lifetime of the plan participant (and possibly the participant's spouse or beneficiary). Actuaries estimate the value of these benefits using mortality tables. Since life expectancies have been rising, liabilities can be understated if the mortality tables do not reflect anticipated future improvements in longevity. All DB sponsors have exposure to risk due to systemic improvement in longevity experience.

DB plans are also exposed to the mortality experience of their participants. For small plans, this experience can be erratic. Small plans often mitigate this risk by paying lump sum benefits at retirement or by purchasing annuities from an insurance company. A lump sum payment transfers the longevity risk to the individual and, because the lump sum is usually based on a static mortality table, eliminates longevity risk for the sponsor. Large plan experience tends to be less erratic, with trends gradually emerging over many years. Liabilities seldom change by more than 1 percent per year unless a change in the mortality table is adopted. Although these plans have exposure to long-term systemic changes in mortality experience, the year-to-year changes in liability are generally far less volatile than investment or interest rate risk. Large plans generally fund toward the average life expectancy of the population, recognizing that some will live longer, offset by others that do not.

The individual in a DC plan is subject to longevity risk of a different sort. While a large DB pension plan can pool the longevity experience of many participants, the DC participant must manage longevity experience of just one person (or one couple). The individual generally does not know how long he will live or how long his assets must last. Planning for the average life expectancy is generally insufficient since there is a 50 percent likelihood of exceeding this. An individual can transfer this risk to an insurance company by purchasing an annuity, but few individuals do so. Longevity risk poses a challenge to the individual that is difficult to manage: spend less to accommodate a long life, or spend more and risk exhausting the funds.

Variable Annuity Plans

A variable annuity plan is a form of DB plan that allocates risk differently than traditional DB plans or DC plans.[2] A variable annuity plan is generally a career accumulation plan: it accumulates benefits for each year of service rather than basing benefits on final average pay. Benefits can accrue as a percent of pay, say 1 percent of actual earnings each year payable as an annual annuity at normal retirement, or as a dollar amount, say X dollars per month for each year of service, also payable as an annuity at normal retirement.

Unlike a traditional DB plan, the sponsor does not promise to pay a fixed amount throughout retirement. Instead, the benefit is 'indexed' and generally changes every year, both while the participant is working and accruing benefits, and after the participant retires and is receiving benefits. Indexing is usually associated with cost-of-living increases. Many public sector pension plans have benefits that are at least partly indexed to the cost-of-living index for retirees in pay status. A few career accumulation plans index accruals during employment (indexed career accumulation plans): those plans may or may not also index retiree benefits.

A variable annuity plan indexes benefits to investment results rather than a cost-of-living index. The plan document must state the methodology used to determine the indexing. Usually the plan defines an investment return benchmark, sometimes referred to as a 'hurdle rate' or an assumed investment return, which determines the investment return needed to keep benefits constant. If actual investment returns exceed this rate, benefits are increased by the excess rate. If the actual investment return falls short of the benchmark, benefits are decreased by the shortfall. For example, if a plan defined the benchmark investment return as 4 percent and the actual return for a year is 7 percent, benefits would be increased by approximately 3 percent.[3] Likewise, if the actual return for the year was only 1 percent, all accrued benefits would be decreased by approximately 3 percent.

To facilitate recordkeeping, variable annuity plans often convert benefit accruals into variable annuity units. Each variable annuity unit entitles the participant to a lifetime income commencing at normal retirement age equal to the unit value at the time of payment. Variable annuity unit values are adjusted each year by the indexing formula defined in the plan. Tracking the accrued benefits as variable units rather than dollar amounts does not change the nature of the plan or the benefits due the participant, but it can make plan administration easier. Individuals familiar with mutual funds should be able to easily understand this concept.

A variable annuity plan meets the requirement for 'definitely determinable benefits' under the law, provided that the plan states the methodology for the indexing and uses a recognized investment method or investment index. A variable annuity plan does not violate the ERISA requirement that the sponsor cannot amend the plan to decrease benefits. This is because a decrease due to investment underperformance is not an amendment decreasing benefits: rather it is a decrease necessitated by existing plan provisions.

Variable annuity plans have risk characteristics quite different from traditional DB plans. Because investment gains or losses directly change the amount of accrued benefits, volatile investment results have little or no effect on the sponsor's net obligation. An investment gain increases liabilities by an offsetting amount and an investment loss decreases liabilities by an offsetting amount. Essentially, the investment risk borne by the plan sponsor in a traditional DB plan is transferred to the participant in a variable annuity plan via the indexing of the benefit to investment results.

Like DC plans, variable annuity plans have no interest rate risk for the plan sponsor or the participant. Fixed interest rates are used to discount future fixed payments. Benefits that vary based on actual investment returns have a present value that is independent of changes in interest rates. All obligations can be valued at a fixed rate equal to the benchmark investment return or hurdle rate defined by the plan. The sponsor's obligation is to fund all benefits based on this rate of return and this amount will be sufficient regardless of the actual return on plan assets or any changes in market interest rates (Fuerst 2006).

Variable annuity plans maintain the longevity risk with the plan sponsor as in traditional DB plans. Variable annuity plans also have other demographic risks to which the sponsor is exposed including turnover and early or late retirement. Variable annuity plans can develop unfunded liabilities or surplus assets similar to traditional DB plans due to demographic gains and losses, or due to the sponsor's funding policy.

To minimize risk, the full costs of the plan need to be funded promptly and demographic gains or losses need to be managed promptly. If the full costs are not promptly covered, any unfunded liability or surplus assets can produce investment gains and losses. For instance, if the plan is 90 percent funded and then experiences a 10 percent investment gain, liabilities will increase by 10 percent but only 90 percent of that increase will be offset by the investment gain, thus the unfunded liability will grow. In other words, to keep the sponsor free of any investment risk, the plan must be fully funded. Any unfunded liability or surplus assets expose the sponsor to investment risk on the deficit or excess. Nevertheless, regardless of any such deficit or excess, the sponsor is not exposed to interest rate risk.

Hurdle Rate Characteristics

The hurdle rate is a key component of plan design that affects both benefits and costs. The lower the hurdle rate, the more valuable the benefits are to participants, because they are more likely to increase in the future. For a given plan formula, say 1 percent of compensation accrual per year, a plan with a lower hurdle rate is more expensive to fund for the plan sponsor. For example, if two plans, A and B, have the same accrual formula, but A uses a 3 percent hurdle rate and B uses a 5 percent hurdle rate, plan A will be more expensive to fund. In each year, accrued benefits in plan A will grow about 2 percent more (or decrease 2 percent less) than plan B.

Hurdle rates in the United States are seldom less than 3 percent because such a plan would likely violate the minimum distribution rules of ERISA (ERISA 1974). A plan with a hurdle rate less than 3 percent is presumed to deliver an increasing annuity that would violate the minimum distribution rules.

Plans subject to ERISA with hurdle rates less than 5 percent are deemed to be statutory hybrid plans and must use three-year vesting. Plans with higher hurdle rates have lower cost for the plan sponsor, but they also increase the risk that benefits may decrease. For example, a hurdle rate of 10 percent would produce a very low cost plan, but benefits for participants would be highly likely to decrease in most years, probably resulting in much dissatisfaction with the program. Also, high hurdle rates may expose the sponsor to other compliance issues. There are currently no regulations addressing this issue.

Investment Risk Transfer

Variable annuity plans generally index benefits based on the entire assets of the plan, a designated portion of the plan assets, a specific investment index, or the return of a specific registered investment company. All plan benefits are indexed exactly the same way. As a consequence of this, all plan participants experience the same volatility in their accrued benefits. This can produce conflict among participants with varying risk characteristics and difficulty for trustees responsible for setting the plan's investment policy.

Young participants who are actively accruing benefits are not immediately affected by volatility of investment results. Volatile investment returns may actually benefit them in a way similar to dollar cost averaging. Young participants with many years until retirement may prefer a very aggressive investment policy in the expectation that their benefits could grow substantially by retirement.

By contrast, employees approaching retirement may prefer a less aggressive investment policy, since they have a more immediate need for the plan payments. A very aggressive investment policy would make these projections less reliable.

Retirees are likely to be even less risk tolerant. Retirees may be dependent on their benefits to pay fixed expenses. As a result, they would likely prefer a conservative investment policy which attains the hurdle rate each year with little likelihood of a loss.

The trustees of the plan must act on behalf of all participants and find a way to balance these various interests. Many variable annuity plans do so by adopting balanced portfolios, often with no more than 50 or 60 percent equity exposure with the balance in fixed income or other stable investments. The result is a compromise portfolio that will not meet the exact needs of most participants but is deemed reasonable. Of course, this compromise still exposes retirees to the potential loss of income if the balanced portfolio does not consistently earn the investment hurdle rate. So some plan sponsors, highly desirous of the stable cost and low volatility of the variable annuity plan, are nevertheless reluctant to adopt such a plan because of the possibility of declining benefits for retirees.

The Retirement Shares Plan

The Retirement Shares Plan (RSP) is a concept that enables participants to tailor their plan risk exposure to their own risk tolerance. In its simplest form, the Trustees can partition the plan assets into two subaccounts, we here call the 'Diversified Account' and the 'Stable Account.' The Diversified Account would have an investment policy designed for long-term growth with its objective to exceed the hurdle rate return by a margin equal to the inflation rate. If the investment account attained this objective, benefits backed by the Diversified Account would increase similar to a cost-of-living adjustment and benefits would retain constant purchasing power.

The Stable Account would have an investment policy designed for consistent income and stable pricing. Investments would generally be in high-quality fixed income investments with only small, if any, exposure to equity markets. The goal of the Stable Account would be to attain or exceed the hurdle rate in most years. Such a plan would need to have a relatively low hurdle rate, probably not higher than 4 percent.

In such a plan, the Diversified Account and the Stable Account would each establish a share value at inception. The initial share value of both accounts is arbitrary and could be set at, say, $10.00; thereafter, the two share values will experience different growth rates based on the actual return of each account. The Diversified Share and the Stable Share each entitles the participant to a lifetime income at normal retirement age equal to the share value at the time of payment. These shares would be equivalent to the unit accounting in most variable annuity plans.

The Diversified Account would be the default fund for all participants. All benefit accruals would be converted to 'shares' of the Diversified Account. A share entitles the participant to a lifetime income commencing at normal retirement age equal to the share value at the time of payment, just as variable units do in a typical variable annuity plan. A participant in the plan who stays with the default until retirement would be entitled to a lifetime income at normal retirement age based on the number of Diversified Shares accumulated at retirement and the share value at that time.

An example helps illustrate how this can work. Assume a plan has an annual accrual of 1 percent of pay. Pat, a participating employee, earns $50,000 in a particular plan year. At the end of that plan year, Pat has accrued a benefit of $500 as a variable annuity at normal retirement age. If the Diversified Share value at the end of that plan year is $12.50, Pat's benefit accrual is converted to 40 Diversified Shares.

Pat continues to work and earn more Diversified Shares each year. At his normal retirement age he has accumulated 1,200 Diversified Shares and the Diversified Shares have grown to a value of $16.00. Pat would be entitled to an annual benefit of $19,200 (1,200 x $16.00). In each subsequent year, Pat's benefit would be based on the new share value. The benefit would always be 1,200 multiplied by the then-current value of a Diversified Share. Following a year like 2008, Pat's benefit amount might drop significantly. On the other hand, following a year like 2013, the benefit would increase significantly.

To this point, the example is similar to any variable annuity plan. But we suppose that at retirement Pat looked at projected expenses and income carefully, and he decided that the Diversified Shares had more risk and volatility than he felt appropriate. In a Retirement Shares Plan, Pat could choose to convert all or part of the Diversified Shares to Stable Shares. Suppose that Stable Shares at Pat's retirement had a value of $10.80. Pat could convert the 1,200 Diversified Shares with an annuity value of $19,200 to 1,777.777 Stable Shares that also have an annuity value of $19,200. Assuming the plan allowed partial transfers, Pat could convert any number of the Diversified Shares to Stable Shares so that some of the annual income would be stable while the rest would vary with Diversified Shares. Pat could structure the retirement income volatility to appropriate levels for Pat.

To keep the plan sponsor protected from investment risk, the sponsor would transfer the actuarial value of Pat's benefit from the Diversified Account to the Stable Account. The actuarial value would be the life annuity for Pat evaluated at the hurdle rate of interest.

This simple example is based on two types of shares, Diversified and Stable, with the Diversified Share being the default. Transfer to the Stable fund was illustrated at the time of retirement. While this is a simple example, there are many variations that could be adopted if the sponsor is willing to invest in the administration system to handle a more complex retirement shares program. A few alternatives are considered here.

When to permit transfers

To facilitate recordkeeping and ease of transferring money between accounts, permitting transfers once per year will minimize efforts and probably be sufficient to accomplish most risk mitigation for participants. Allowing transfers at benefit commencement is the most obvious time, but plans could offer other opportunities. Retirees in pay status could be offered an opportunity to transfer shares once per year. Our initial example illustrated a transfer from Diversified to Stable, but a participant might subsequently be in different circumstances and like to transfer from Stable to Diversified. Such a transfer poses no financial risk to the sponsor, provided the appropriate actuarial reserve is also transferred between accounts.

Participants nearing retirement age might like to transfer some of their accrual to the Stable Shares before actually retiring. Again, provided the appropriate reserve is transferred, this poses no risk to the plan sponsor and could be permitted. In fact, in the extreme, participants of any age could be permitted to transfer shares from one account to the other. However, allowing daily transfers among funds is probably inappropriate, in that a variable annuity DB plan is usually not intended to be an investment vehicle for frequent trading. The Retirement Shares Concept is intended to permit participants to avoid inappropriate risk for their retirement income, and not to create an investment trading platform.

Multiple accounts

The two-account model with a diversified and a stable account, together with the ability to transfer all or part of the benefit between accounts, can provide participants with a wide range of risk exposure. In this model, the upper end of risk exposure is capped based on what the plan trustees select for the diversified account. The lower level of risk is attained if 100 percent of the benefit is transferred to the Stable Fund.

While this two-fund model provides a wide range of risk exposure, it is conceivable that some participants might be willing to experience more volatility to attain greater growth. This might be particularly true of young participants who are many years from retirement. Greater risk exposure could be attained by adding a third account invested entirely in equities, designated as the Equity Shares. Participants wanting more growth than the Diversified Shares provide could transfer some of their benefit to Equity Shares. To prevent participants from taking excessive risk with retirement funds, sponsors might consider placing limits on the proportion of benefit transferred to Equity Shares.

Although it is conceivable to envision a plan with many more classes of shares, there seems little to be gained by the addition of more funds. Even the addition of Equity Shares as a third fund offers marginal utility at greater administrative expense and the risk of creating a confusing plan that participants will not understand nor appreciate.

Illustrations

The hypothetical Retirement Shares experience can easily be constructed for past years based on investment indexes. The S&P 500 Index total return (including dividends) and the Barclays Aggregate Index (also total return) were obtained from the Society of Actuaries Investment Statistics for Pension Actuaries for the years 1970 through 2013. For illustrative purposes, we assume that a Diversified Share consists of 70 percent S&P 500 and 30 percent Barclays Aggregate. A stable share is 100 percent Barclays Aggregate.

Figure 9.1 plots the changes in the Diversified Share value through a 43-year period. Several features stand out. First, the share value generally increases. Unlike a fixed pension benefit, the pension benefit amounts are growing due to aggregate investment experience that exceeds 4 percent. Second, the growth generally exceeds that of the consumer price index. Third, although the trend is generally increasing, there are three periods in which benefits decline significantly: from 1972 to 1974 benefits declined 32 percent, from 1999 to 2002 benefits declined 28 percent, and from 2007 to 2008 benefits declined 29 percent. In each of these occurrences, the Diversified Share value recovered and exceeded its previous high within five years. Over this period, a retiree who could sustain a temporary decline of income of about 30 percent was rewarded with an income that on average increased faster than inflation as measured by the Consumer Price Index.

Not all retirees would be willing to take the risk of a 30 percent decline in income, and there is no assurance that future declines would not be greater than 30 percent. A risk averse retiree unwilling to experience the potential volatility of the Diversified Shares could transfer all or part of his benefit to Stable Shares. Figure 9.2 shows the growth of a Stable Share backed by the Barclays Aggregate Index over this same time period. The stable share value fulfills its name, with generally little volatility over the 43-year period, but it falls far behind inflation, as does a fixed pension benefit. In periods of low fixed income returns, the Stable Share may decline as it did in 2011–13.

Why Retirement Shares?

The Retirement Shares design offers distinct differences from traditional DB or DC plans. Like a DC plan, the Retirement Shares design eliminates

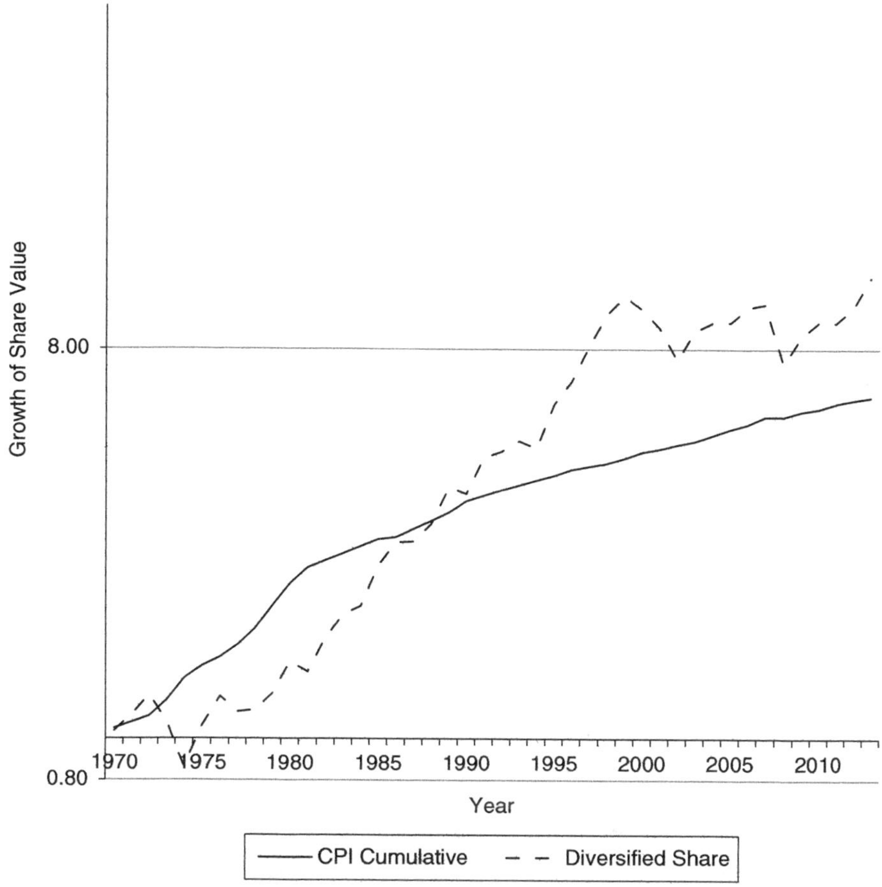

Figure 9.1 Diversified share vs. CPI 4 percent hurdle rate 1970–2013 logarithmic scale

Source: Author's computations.

interest rate risk and transfers investment risk to the individual, thus providing the sponsor a stable cost pattern without major balance sheet effects. Also like a DC plan, the benefits are portable: individuals continue to receive the full investment performance of the underlying funds even after they leave employment. Like a DB plan, the Retirement Shares plan provides lifetime income and creates the efficiencies of pooling longevity experience over large groups.

There are drawbacks to the Retirement Shares design; for instance, benefit payments are less certain under a variable annuity plan design than in a fixed DB plan. Sponsors or individuals who highly value the

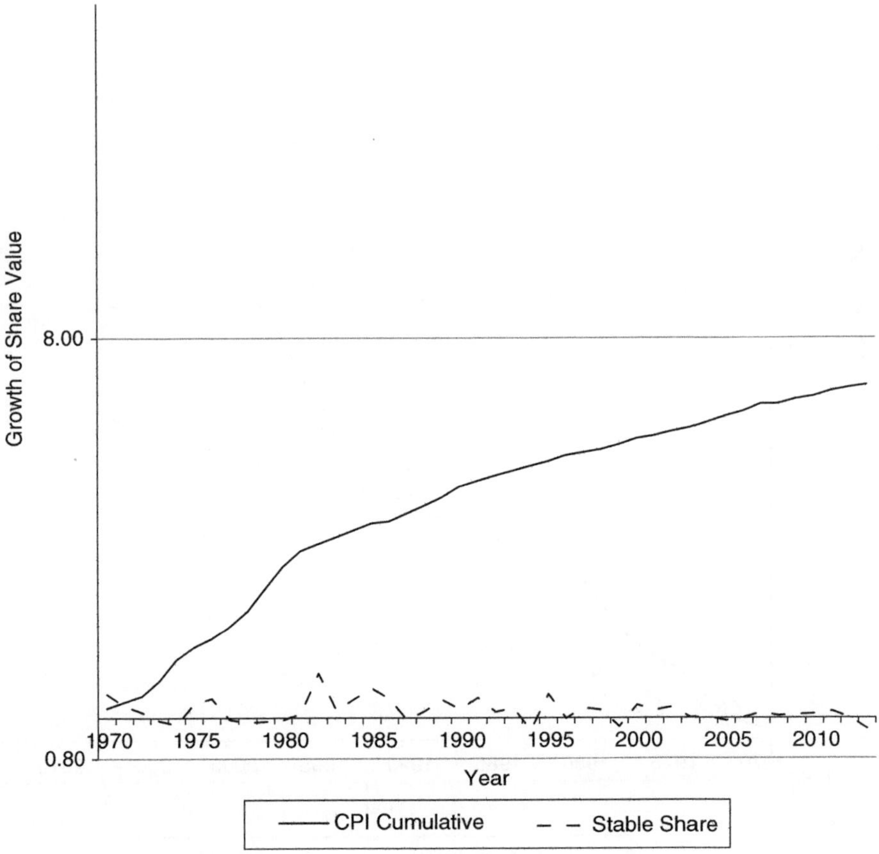

Figure 9.2 Stable share vs. CPI 4 percent hurdle rate 1970–2013 logarithmic scale
Source: Author's computations.

certainty of a fixed benefit will not appreciate the volatility of the diversified shares and see no advantage to the stable shares that still vary. Highly portable benefits do not provide the strong retention value of the traditional final pay DB pension.

The benefit accrual pattern of the Retirement Shares plan increases with age similar to that of a career accumulation DB plan. Those who prefer the level accrual pattern of a DC plan or cash balance plan may not like the upward sloping accrual pattern of the Retirement Shares design. Level accrual could be attained by a cash balance design with a variable annuity payout rather than a fixed annuity payout.

Conclusion

Variable annuity plans can provide lifetime income to participants without the risk of running out of money at advanced ages. In exchange for such a guarantee of continued income, the participant accepts the risk and reward that the actual investment returns provide. Variable annuity plans provide the sponsor with cost stability and predictability similar to DC plans, but the sponsor accepts the risk of longevity which is generally increasing but not volatile. The Retirement Shares Plan enhances a typical variable annuity plan by allowing participants to elect a more stable benefit than that from a traditional variable plan. This feature allows the trustees to adopt a more aggressive investment portfolio for the default portion of the fund, thus potentially providing greater growth in retirement income for participants and the potential to maintain purchasing power.

Endnotes

1. Plan sponsors bear several other risks including compliance risk, fiduciary risk, administrative risk, etc., but investment, interest rate, and longevity are the principal risks associated with the financial commitment to deliver the promised benefit.
2. Variable annuity plans should not be confused with the variable annuity products commonly offered by insurance companies which are primarily investment vehicles with certain tax advantages.
3. Most plans base the indexing on a ratio of returns where the change in benefits is equal to $(1+i)/(1+h) - 1$ where i is the actual return and h is the benchmark or hurdle return. In the example, this would result in an increase slightly less than 3 percent.

References

ERISA (1974). Employee Retirement Income Security Act 1974. P.L. 93–406, 88 Stat. 829.

Fuerst, D. (2006). *Actuarial Supplement to The Retirement Shares Plan: A Breakthrough in Retirement Plan Design.* Washington, DC: Society of Actuaries. <https://www.soa.org/library/monographs/retirement-systems/re-envisioning-retirement/m-as06-2_supplementXI.pdf>.

Chapter 10

The Portfolio Pension Plan: An Alternative Model for Retirement Security

Richard C. Shea, Robert S. Newman, and Jonathan P. Goldberg

This chapter describes a proposed new defined benefit (DB) pension design known as a *portfolio pension plan.* This design falls within a larger category of so-called 'shared risk' pension plans. In the United States, shared risk pension plans address a need created by the limitations of existing retirement plan designs. An alternative is needed because DB plans to date have concentrated risk on plan sponsors in a way that makes them financially unsustainable in many, if not most, circumstances. Moreover, existing defined contribution (DC) retirement plans impose risk on employees in a way that is challenging for most individuals to manage. In the past, many employers shared risk with employees by providing *both* a DB and a DC plan.[1] Nevertheless, this chapter argues that a new model can provide an alternative that better serves employers and employees in the United States.[2]

The Shared Risk Pension

Shared risk pensions offer a design that is more sustainable for employers than existing DB plans, yet they also provide greater retirement security for employees than stand-alone DC plans. Rather than concentrating risk on either employers or employees, shared risk pension plans (as their name implies) allocate risk across the parties. Done right, these new designs promise to allocate risk more efficiently, in a way that delivers both greater sustainability *and* improved retirement security.

A portfolio pension plan accomplishes this result by allocating a significant portion of the investment risk to employees and leaving the remaining investment risk and the longevity risk with the employer.[3] Under this model, employee benefits are expressed in the form of account balances, which are adjusted up or down in response to investment performance. At the same time, the employer guarantees a cumulative minimum rate of return of at least 0 percent (in effect, a minimum benefit that protects principal) as well as retiree payments in the form of life annuities. Above these minimums, employers are free to allocate more risk to themselves by offering additional investment guarantees (such as a higher minimum rate of return) or by subsidizing benefit distributions to employees and their beneficiaries.

In contrast to most existing DC plans, the portfolio pension plan does not require or permit employees to contribute to the plan or to direct their investments. Instead, the employer makes all contributions (which could be in lieu of employer contributions to a DC plan), and the plan manages all investments in employee accounts. Such investment management is designed to automatically adjust the level of investment risk the employee bears to his or her changing circumstances over time, in accordance with modern portfolio theory (hence the name 'portfolio' pension plan). A fundamental principle of the portfolio pension plan is that (1) employees are not asked to bear investment risk, unless the risk is appropriate to their individual circumstances, and (2) they are not asked to bear the additional responsibility of managing the investments in their accounts—a critical responsibility that most lack the financial acumen and time to handle.

Background

In the United States, we have moved from a world in which most significant retirement risks were borne by employers offering DB plans, to a world in which DC-covered employees must bear these risks largely on their own.[4] Yet the conventional assumption that an employer who provides access to a retirement plan must assume either all or none of the significant risks associated with retirement benefits has become dysfunctional. Specifically, many employers have concluded that they are no longer willing or able to bear the risks associated with providing retirement benefits through DB plans.[5] Nevertheless, many individuals are ill-equipped to assume those risks on their own, as they must in DC plans.[6] As a result, employers face fewer options to move individuals reliably from active employment to retirement, just as employees are becoming increasingly pessimistic about their ability to provide for a secure retirement on their own.[7]

Risk allocation in traditional DB pensions

The traditional DB plan promises workers that the employer will provide a specified level of retirement income benefit. Accordingly, an employer's funding obligations to the plan hinge on how well the plan's assets perform in the investment markets.[8] In turn, the DB plan's investment experience depends on two factors: actual investment performance to date, and expected investment performance in the future.

To reflect expected future investment performance, and to ensure that the plan has sufficient assets to provide promised benefits, financial accounting and regulatory funding rules, in effect, require the plan's promised benefits to be discounted to the present using an interest rate reflective of future risk-adjusted investment expectations.[9] Changes in the investment environment thus affect not only past investment performance reflected in the value of plan assets, but also expectations about future investment performance reflected in the interest rate used to discount promised benefits to present value. As a result, changes in the investment environment cause important shifts in the spread between the value of the plan's assets and the present value of its promised benefits. When the present value of benefits exceeds the value of plan assets, the plan is underfunded, and the employer is expected to make up the shortfall (sooner or later). Here we refer to the risk that plan asset values will not keep up with the present value of promised benefits as 'investment' risk.

Furthermore, when benefits are promised for the lifetime of retirees, the liabilities of the plan depend on how long the retirees are anticipated to live. The risk that retirees might live longer than expected is known as 'longevity' risk. In a DB plan, this risk is measured at the plan level over the entire plan population, rather than at the level of the individual retiree.

Investment risk can cause substantial swings in employers' funding obligations, as plan assets and plan benefits are periodically revalued and compared to one another. Longevity risk tends to be perceived as slower to change, absent major unexpected improvements in cohort life expectancy. Under US regulation, DB plan financial accounting and regulatory funding rules generally require the value of plan assets and plan benefits to be remeasured and compared annually, and thereafter reflected in the company's financial statements and regulatory funding requirements. The potential for dramatic swings in these obligations (stemming largely from investment risk) has led many employers to reduce their exposure to traditional DB plans. As a result, DC plans have become the design alternative most employers turn to.

Risk allocation in DC plans

DC plans, and especially participant-directed pensions such as 401(k) plans, place both investment and longevity risks squarely on employees' shoulders as individuals. The retirement income individuals receive from these types of plans depends on several factors. First, employees may fail to contribute, or save enough. Second, after contributions are made, individuals' investment choices determine returns earned on the savings over the work life, which generate the assets used to provide retirement payouts. Third, the timing of retirement can significantly affect the value of individuals' DC accumulations. A disability or early retirement, for example, can curtail individuals' ability to save as well as to time retirement to favorable market conditions.

Fourth, retirees must also manage their accounts to provide retirement income for their own and perhaps their partner's lifetime. Not knowing how long one is going to live poses a challenge difficult for any one individual (or couple) to bear. Whereas the DB model pools longevity risk across the employee and retiree group, the DC plan does not offer protection against such longevity risk.

While many people may be able to determine their own retirement plans, risk tolerance, and health conditions, investment expertise is not widespread. Indeed many individuals would find it challenging to assume the investment risk of managing their own retirement savings, and the longevity risk of planning retirement distributions over their own unpredictable lifespans.[10]

Reducing Risk by Sharing it

Plan design options that better share risk between employers and employees would enhance the retirement system in the US for several reasons. First, such options offer a middle ground between the polar extremes of allocating all significant risks to either employers or employees. Second, while many employers may not wish to bear all the risks imposed on them by traditional DB plans, they may still be willing and able to bear some of those risks. Third, employees may be willing to share investment risk with employers in a way that would relieve the plan sponsor of dramatic swings in financial liability. For instance, an employer could still guarantee some minimum retirement benefit, giving participants the chance to share in investment upside returns with reduced risk on the downside. Additionally, the investment risk could be professionally managed and tailored to workers' investment horizons and tolerance for risk. This would obviate the need for each participant to develop investment expertise.

Fourth, such risk sharing would permit diversification across a large group by having employers retain it, sharing it collectively among participants, or some combination of these two approaches. And fifth, by allocating each risk to the party best able to bear or diversify it (i.e. to the least cost avoider—see Coase 1960; Calabresi 1970) in a way that minimizes moral hazard and adverse selection, risk sharing would enhance the retirement system's efficiency.

The Portfolio Pension Plan

The Portfolio Pension Plan ('PPP') is a DB plan modeled on the cash balance plan design. A cash balance plan is a DB plan that promises a benefit based on the balance in a hypothetical account. Each year, a participant's account is credited with an amount typically based on the participant's pay (while the participant remains employed), and the balance in the account is credited with interest (regardless of whether the employee remains employed), typically at a rate based on the current yield on US Treasuries. In contrast, each employee's account balance in a PPP is adjusted over time based on the return on an investment portfolio tailored to the employee's expressed preferences and changing circumstances.

The PPP has many characteristics in common with a conventional cash balance plan. It is financed solely by the employer, and over the work life, each employee's balance is credited during employment with pay credits (typically a percentage of current pay). Each participant's accrued benefit is expressed as an account balance. Like a conventional cash balance plan, a PPP provides employees with a minimum guaranteed benefit which is generally equal to the cumulative pay credits in the employee's account accrued over his or her career (or it can be higher, if the employer wishes to provide a more generous guarantee).[11] Additionally, the plan offers at least actuarially equivalent annuities for employees and surviving spouses; and the plan sponsor is permitted to subsidize benefit distributions, to provide, for example, in joint and survivor annuities, disability benefits, death benefits, and plant closing and lay-off benefits. (For this purpose, a subsidized benefit means a benefit that has a greater actuarial value than the employee's current account balance.)

The defining feature of the PPP, and where it differs from a conventional cash balance plan, is how it credits earnings to the notional account balance ('interest credits' in conventional cash balance plans). A conventional cash balance plan provides 'interest credits' which adjust the account for the time value of money until the employee begins receiving benefits under the plan. In a conventional cash balance plan, a single rate is credited for all participants, usually the current yield on a specified government security, such as 30-year Treasury bonds. In a PPP, by contrast, each individual's account balance adjusts based on the return his or her individually-tailored retirement investment portfolio earns. This rate therefore reflects and adjusts to employees' changing circumstances over time.

As a result, employees will likely earn different returns on their accounts. For example, an employee could be placed in a cohort with other participants of like age and risk tolerance. This cohort would then start with an age- and risk-appropriate diversified portfolio that adjusts automatically over time, akin to a properly designed target date fund. As the employees approach retirement, their investment allocations would change accordingly. Taking this approach a step further, the PPP could employ an individual managed account approach, which takes into account additional variables specific to the employee, such as other retirement benefits, non-retirement assets, health condition, marital status, expressed risk tolerance, intended retirement date or work phase-down period, and so on. This investment mix could adjust to reflect changes in these variables over time. PPP investments are professionally and automatically managed, so the PPP does not rely on participant direction or education to achieve a balanced portfolio. Although individuals do not bear the burden of allocating investments, they can improve the fit of their investment portfolio to their individual circumstances by voluntarily providing additional information of the types just described.

The PPP also allocates risks between employers and individuals that could advantage both parties. Participants still bear investment risk, but the PPP tailors the level of risk to participants' individual circumstances. Furthermore, the PPP gives participants the ability to participate in the upside potential from taking on investment risk, while still enjoying a minimum benefit guaranteed by employers. And in turn, employers can invest in instruments to hedge against the minimum benefit, so funding volatility from the investment risk employers still retain would be minimized. More importantly, the investment risk and associated funding volatility for employers from sponsoring a PPP would be a tiny fraction of that they currently experience from sponsoring a traditional DB plan, or even a conventional cash balance plan.

Because the PPP plan offers an annuity benefit, employers continue to bear longevity risk. Nevertheless, we believe that the sponsor may be in a better position to assume longevity risk than individual participants. The sponsor can spread the risk across its workforce and retirees, and the plan might have the opportunity to invest in instruments that hedge against changes in mortality (meaning payments are made to the plan if plan participants receiving life annuities live longer than expected). The arrangement also enhances retirement security by avoiding the need for individual retirees to manage distributions and investments based on guesses about their own and partner longevity.[12]

Conclusion

Traditional 'all or nothing' approaches to allocating risks can be intelligently rethought. Doing so offers the potential for improving retirement outcomes for both employers and participants, in ways that have seemed impossible under traditional DB and DC plan designs. The portfolio pension plan adapts principles of both DC and DB pensions, seeking to rebalance the allocation of risks in a fresh approach to future retirement plan design.

Endnotes

1. The past approach of providing employees both a DB and a DC plan no longer works in the growing number of instances where employers have frozen or terminated their DB plans. See GAO 2008: 1–4 (stating that plan sponsors terminated over 61,000 sufficiently funded DB plans between 1990 and 2006 and that an estimated 3.3 million active participants are affected by plan freezes).
2. The pension plan design described in this chapter was first presented in Feb. 2012 at a conference in Washington, DC, hosted by the United States Senate Committee on Health, Education, Labor and Pensions and co-sponsored by the Pension Rights Center, the Urban Institute, and Covington & Burling LLP. The conference brought together senior policymakers from seven federal agencies, six Congressional committees, state and local governments, labor unions, employers, think tanks, retiree advocacy organizations, trade associations, professional actuarial organizations, and academia, as well as members of the press who cover retirement issues. The focus of the conference was on innovative pension plan designs to share and reduce risk, enhance coverage and adequacy, and expand lifetime income options. Excerpts from the conference are available online at <http://www.pensionrights.org/what-we-do/events/re-imagining-pensions>. Several of the designs presented at the conference (including the one described in this chapter) have been incorporated into subsequent legislative proposals and regulations. See, for example, 79 Fed. Reg. 56451 & 56463 (Sept. 19, 2014) (final Treasury regulations on hybrid retirement plans).
3. We note that the Employee Retirement Income Security Act (ERISA 1974) gives plan sponsors discretion to establish the actuarial assumptions used to convert employee account balances into annuities, including the ability to specify variable mortality assumptions that are updated periodically to reflect improvements in mortality. To the extent that the plan sponsor takes advantage of the discretion to use such variable mortality assumptions, employees could be said to bear the portion of longevity risk attributable to mortality improvements in the general population (as opposed to the portion of longevity risk attributable to the employee's own actual life span and, if relevant, that of his or her surviving spouse).
4. This shift is seen most dramatically in the replacement of the traditional DB plan by the participant-directed DC plan, as the predominant form of retirement arrangement. See Gale et al. (2005). This chapter focuses principally on tax-qualified retirement plans maintained by private employers in the US. We note, however, that this trend has characterized other nations as well. See Broadbent et al. (2006) at 11–17 (discussing the general shift throughout the OECD from DB to DC plans, with particular emphasis on Australia, Canada, the UK, and the US).
5. Plan sponsors cited the cost of plan contributions (72 percent) and the volatility of plan funding (69 percent) as the primary reasons for freezing DB plans (GAO 2008: 6–7).

6. 'The shift away from DB plans to DC plans places significant responsibility on individuals to make appropriate decisions concerning their contributions, their investments and how they will manage their money once they retire so that they will have adequate income to fund their retirement years. Unfortunately, many individuals are simply not prepared to handle these risks and responsibilities' (American Association of Retirement Persons 2011: 59).
7. The shift from DB to DC plans has had some positive effects in the labor market: traditional DB plans tend to be heavily backloaded economically, whereas DC plans (and other account-based plans like cash balance plans) tend to provide economically level benefit accruals over an employee's work life (Gale et al. 2005: 53). As a result, many workers fail to accrue significant benefits under a traditional DB model, because they do not remain in their jobs with the DB plan sponsor long enough. By contrast, DC plans (and other account-based plans like cash balance plans) penalize job changing less. The Employee Benefit Research Institute suggests that, as a result of the DB/DC shift, average vested benefits have increased for employees covered by employer-sponsored retirement plans, concluding that vesting rates rose from 24 percent in 1979 to 43 percent in 2012 (Copeland 2013: 1, 3).
8. Conventional cash balance plans (such as those modeled on IRS Notice 96–8, 1996–1 C.B. 359) behave similarly to traditional DB plans in this regard, even though they express retirement benefits in terms of an account balance as opposed to a deferred annuity.
9. See Elliott (2009). For ERISA minimum funding purposes, discount rate based on investment grade corporate bond yield curve, see 26 U.S.C. § 430(h).
10. See n. 5 of this chapter. We do not wish to minimize the considerable strides made recently permitting plan sponsors to structure DC plans as increasingly comprehensive retirement vehicles. Such strides include the advent of participant education and advice, auto-enrollment, auto-escalation, insurance to replace contributions lost due to disability, qualified default investment alternatives, target date funds, individual managed accounts, coordination with Social Security benefits, and various investment management services and insurance products designed to manage investments and payouts (including lifetime income payouts) in retirement. See American Association of Retirement Persons (2009: 115–16 (listing series of improvements to defined contribution system subsequent to the Pension Protection Act of 2006, P.L. 109–280, 120 Stat. 780).
11. See 26 U.S.C § 411(b)(5)(B)(i)(I)&(II) (cash balance plan is required to provide a minimum guaranteed rate of return of at least 0 percent cumulatively and is permitted to provide a more generous 'reasonable minimum guaranteed rate of return'); see also 26 C.F.R. 1.411(b)(5)-1(d)(2)&(6) (same).
12. One could also imagine that the PPP approach would offer continued investment management services throughout retirement, including the management of payouts to the employee, coordination with payouts from Social Security and

other sources of retirement income, continued exposure to the market to some degree, and the provision of 'so-called' longevity annuities, which would start when the retiree reached some pre-specified advanced age (e.g. 85).

References

American Association of Retirement Persons (2009). Statement at *Strengthening Worker Retirement Security: Hearing Before the House Committee on Education and Labor,* 111th Cong. Serial 111–13.

American Association of Retirement Persons (2011). 'Reduction in Rate of Benefit Accrual Under a Defined Benefit Plan, 26 C.F.R. 1.411(B)(5)-1(2014).' Statement at *Retirement Security: Challenges Confronting Pension Plan Sponsors, Workers, and Retirees: Hearing Before the Subcommittee on Health, Employment, Labor, and Pensions, House Committee on Education and the Workforce,* 112th Cong. Serial 112–28.

Broadbent, J., M. Palumbo, and E. Woodman (2006). *The Shift from Defined Benefit to Defined Contribution Pension Plans—Implications for Asset Allocation and Risk Management,* Bank of International Settlements, Working Group on Institutional Investors, Global Savings, and Asset Allocation. Basel: Bank of International Settlements. <http://www.bis.org/publ/wgpapers/cgfs27broadbent3.pdf>.

Calabresi, G. (1970). *The Cost of Accidents: A Legal and Economic Analysis.* New Haven, CT: Yale University Press.

Coase, R. H. (1960). 'The Problem of Social Cost.' *Journal of Law and Economics,* 3(1): 1–44.

Copeland, C. (2013). *Retirement Plan Participation: Survey of Income and Program Participation (SIPP) Data, 2012,* Notes, 34(8). Washington, DC: Employee Benefit Research Institute.

Elliott, D. J. (2009). *A Guide to the Pension Benefit Guaranty Corporation.* Washington, DC: Brookings Institute. <www.brookings.edu/~/media/research/files/papers/2009/5/20%20pensions%20elliott/0520_pensions_elliott.pdf>.

ERISA (1974). Employee Retirement Income Security Act 1974. P.L. 93–406, 88 Stat. 829.

Gale, W. G., L. E. Papke, and J. VanDerhei (2005). 'The Shifting Structure of Private Pensions,' in W. G. Gale, J. B. Shoven, and M. J. Warshawsky (eds), *The Evolving Pension System.* Washington, DC: Brookings Institution, 55–62.

United States Government Accountability Office (GAO) (2008). *Defined Benefit Pensions: Plan Freezes Affect Millions of Participants and May Pose Retirement Income Challenges,* GAO-08-817. Washington, DC: GPO.

Chapter 11

Cultivating Pension Plans

John M. Vine

The Internal Revenue Code (the Code) and the Employee Retirement Income Security Act (ERISA) cultivate employer-sponsored pension plans in the United States. The former does this by offering advantageous tax treatment to tax-qualified pension plans, plan sponsors, and participating employees and their beneficiaries; and the latter by facilitating employer administration of employer-sponsored pension plans. Nevertheless, the Code and ERISA do not merely cultivate employer-sponsored pension plans: they also regulate employer-sponsored pension plans. In order for an employer-sponsored pension plan to be tax-qualified and to be eligible for the tax advantages that flow from tax-qualification, the plan must meet regulatory requirements imposed by the Code. Similarly, although ERISA does not require an employer to maintain a pension plan, ERISA requires any pension plan that an employer adopts to meet ERISA's regulatory requirements.

Some believe that the cultivation provisions and the regulatory provisions are colliding. One reason for this belief is theoretical: regulatory requirements, standing by themselves, can discourage employers from sponsoring pension plans, prevent employees from earning pension benefits, and thereby defeat the objectives of the plan cultivation provisions. Another reason for this belief is empirical: corporate employers in the United States have been migrating away from defined benefit (DB) plans for the past 30 years. Since the mid-1980s, relatively few new DB plans have been established in the private sector, and many previously established DB plans in the private sector have been closed to new hires, amended to halt the accrual of benefits for some or all employees (that is, 'frozen'), or terminated. In addition, some DB plans in the private sector have transferred a portion of their liabilities to insurers. Increasingly, corporate employers have chosen to provide pension benefits exclusively through defined contribution (DC) plans (EBSA 2013).

Employers have migrated away from traditional DB plans for a variety of reasons. Employers have sought, among other things, to avoid the volatile pension expenses that DB plans impose on employers that sponsor DB plans, to provide pension benefits that employees understand, and to provide pension benefits that employees value more highly than the benefits provided by traditional DB plans. In addition, employers have sought to allocate pension benefits among participating employees more evenly than do many traditional DB plans, to reduce the risk of class action litigation challenging the design or administration of DB plans, and to avoid the need to comply with the regulatory requirements imposed on DB plans by the Code and ERISA. Also, due to the increasingly severe limits that the Code imposes on the benefits that a tax-qualified plan may provide, nonqualified plans have become responsible for an increasing share of the retirement benefits of corporate executives. As a result, top corporate executives have grown less reluctant to approve proposals to close, freeze, or terminate broad-based tax-qualified DB plans in which the top executives have a relatively small personal stake.

Notwithstanding the migration of corporate employers away from DB plans, the plan cultivation provisions in the Code and ERISA appear to have encouraged employers to establish and maintain DC plans. This suggests that, far from being stymied by the regulatory provisions, the plan cultivation provisions have succeeded in promoting the growth of DC plans. After all, these provisions are designed to allow each employer to determine what (if any) benefit plans it will adopt and what benefits it will provide, based on its assessment of what plans and benefits are in its own and its employees' best interests. It appears that, for a variety of reasons, many employers now believe that DC plans do a better job of meeting both their needs and their employees' needs than do DB plans.

Before ERISA

Federal Tax Laws

Before the enactment of ERISA in 1974, corporate pension plans in the United States were regulated principally by the federal tax laws. In general, an employer was free to decide whether to sponsor a pension plan, to determine the benefits that the plan would provide, and to establish the terms on which benefits would be provided, subject to the employer's collective bargaining obligations, if any.

Since the very early days of the federal income tax, the federal tax laws have granted favorable tax treatment to tax-qualified plans. The Revenue Act of 1921 conferred tax-exempt status on a trust that was part of an employer's stock bonus or profit sharing plan for 'some or all of [the employer's] employees' (Revenue Act of 1921: §219(f)). In 1926, this provision was expanded to include pension plans (Revenue Act of 1926: §219(f)).

The US Treasury, however, became dissatisfied with the 1921 Act's 'some or all' coverage standard. In 1937, the Treasury informed Congress that, although the Code's pension provisions had been intended to 'encourage pension trusts for aged employees,' the pension provisions had been 'twisted into a means of tax avoidance by the creation of pension trusts' covering 'only small groups of officers and directors who are in the high income brackets.' The Treasury proposed replacing the 'some or all' coverage standard with a requirement that a qualified pension plan cover a 'reasonable number' of employees (US Congress 1937: 294).

Congress did not act on the Treasury's 1937 proposal, however, and in 1942 the Treasury presented Congress with a revised proposal that gave greater emphasis to the objective of covering rank-and-file employees:

> The present treatment of pension trusts affords a tax subsidy to those trusts which meet the requirements set forth in the statute. This subsidy is at the expense of the general body of taxpayers. It was granted because of the desire to improve the welfare of employees by encouraging the establishment of pension trusts for their benefit. Our purpose in presenting our suggestions was to carry out this objective of the Congress by suggesting various provisions which would both make the present statute more effective in promoting the welfare of employees through such trusts and at the same time prevent utilization of such trusts for tax-avoidance purposes. (US Treasury 1942: 2405–6)

Congress responded favorably to this proposal, passing the Revenue Act of 1942 which required a tax-qualified plan to benefit either (1) at least 70 percent of all employees (or at least 80 percent of all eligible employees if at least 70 percent of all employees were eligible) or (2) employees who qualified under a classification established by the employer and found by the Commissioner of Internal Revenue not to discriminate in favor of employees who were officers, shareholders, supervisors, or highly compensated employees (the prohibited group). The 1942 Act also provided that a plan would not be treated as tax-qualified unless the contributions or benefits under the plan did not discriminate in favor of employees who were members of the prohibited group. The House Ways and Means Committee explained that the new requirements were designed 'to insure that [tax-qualified] plans are operated for the welfare of employees in general, and to prevent the trust device from being used for the benefit of shareholders, officials [*sic*], or highly-paid employees' (H.R. Rep. No. 2333 1942: 103–4).

The pre-ERISA version of the Code provided tax rules that encouraged employers to maintain tax-qualified pension plans. The tax rules governing tax-qualified plans provided for current deductibility (within limits) of employer contributions, deferred recognition of income by plan participants, and a tax-exemption for the plan itself. Participants in tax-qualified plans also received advantageous tax treatment for certain plan distributions. For example, the Code treated the income that was included in a lump-sum distribution from a plan as long-term capital gain rather than as ordinary income. Also, a participant who received a distribution of appreciated employer securities in a lump-sum distribution from a tax-qualified plan could exclude the appreciation from income until the securities were sold.

Before the enactment of ERISA, some employers provided pension benefits for both upper echelon and rank-and-file employees on an unfunded, pay-as-you-go basis, rather than through a funded, tax-qualified plan. Because an unfunded plan did not allow an employer to claim up-front deductions for its contributions to the plan, was not funded by a tax-exempt trust, and was not subject to the special rules for plan distributions, an unfunded plan was less tax-effective than a tax-qualified plan. The Internal Revenue Service's position at the time was that an unfunded plan could not be tax-qualified (Rev. Rul. 71–91 1971).

The Code did not require a pension plan to comply with the Code's tax-qualification requirements. However, if an employer wished to maintain a funded pension plan in which employees had vested interests, a tax-qualified plan was usually the most advantageous option. The Tax Reform Act of 1969 made it particularly unattractive for an employee to have a vested interest in a nonqualified, funded deferred compensation plan: the employee was required to include the value of his or her vested benefits in income before the plan distributed the benefits to the employee (Joint Committee 1970).

Other laws

Before the enactment of ERISA, no federal law comprehensively regulated pension plans. The Welfare and Pension Plans Disclosure Act (WPPDA) imposed only modest disclosure requirements and, at least until 1962, the WPPDA relied solely on individual employees for enforcement. The Labor-Management Relations Act applied only to employee benefit funds that were administered jointly by employers and unions. Although criminal penalties applied to theft, embezzlement, and bribery involving employee benefit plans, criminal penalties were not effective in curbing benefit plan abuses (H.R. Rep. No. 533 1973; S. Rep. No. 127 1973).

A few states also had enacted laws specifically designed to regulate the administration of employee benefit plans, but these state laws were not uniform. Moreover, although the state-law rules were generally based on the common law of trusts, it was unclear whether the common law of trusts applied to plans that were not funded by traditional trust arrangements. In any event, individual states did not appear to be up to the task of adequately protecting the interests of plan participants and beneficiaries in multi-state benefit plans (H.R. Rep. No. 533 1973; S. Rep. No. 127 1973; Bureau of National Affairs 1962).

The Prologue to ERISA

In 1962, President Kennedy called for a review of the rules governing the tax treatment and investment policies of corporate pension funds and private retirement programs, and created a Cabinet-level committee (the Committee) to review the implications of the growing array of retirement and welfare funds. The Committee was called the President's Committee on Corporate Pension Funds and Other Private Retirement and Welfare Programs, and the members of the Committee were the Secretary of Labor, the Secretary of the Treasury, the Secretary of Health, Education, and Welfare, the Director of the Bureau of the Budget, the Chairman of the Council of Economic Advisers, the Chairman of the Board of Governors of the Federal Reserve System, and the Chairman of the Securities and Exchange Commission.

The Committee's Report, issued in 1965, observed that Congress had long recognized both 'the importance of stimulating the development of private retirement plans' and 'the growing importance of establishing standards and regulations' to assure that the plans serve the public interest (President's Committee 1965: 18). The Report concluded that 'public policy should continue to provide appropriate incentives to private plan growth' and, by improving the plans' soundness and equitable character, 'set a firmer foundation for their future development' (President's Committee 1965: 25).

The Report also emphasized two aspects of the tax treatment of tax-qualified plans. The first was the mismatch between the immediate deductibility of employer contributions to the plan and the deferred recognition of income by participants until they received distributions from the plan. The second was the tax-exempt status of the plan itself. The Report concluded that taxpayers were indirectly subsidizing pension plans, and observed that, without the advantageous tax treatment of qualified pension plans, employees and employers would have to contribute far more if they wished to maintain the current level of pension benefits (President's Committee 1965).

The Report set the stage for a decade-long study of private pension plans that culminated in the enactment of ERISA in 1974. The Report recommended several steps including legislation governing such subjects as participation, vesting, funding, coverage, nondiscrimination, disclosure, limits on benefits and contributions, and limits on investments in employer securities. The Report also proposed repeal of the rules giving favorable tax treatment to lump-sum distributions and to distributions of appreciated employer securities, and recommended study of a number of other subjects, including pension portability and termination insurance (President's Committee 1965).

Although the Report was very influential, additional interest in pension reform was stimulated by other events, including evidence of corruption in the administration of multiemployer plans that emerged from Congressional investigations during the early 1950s, and the termination of the Studebaker pension plan in 1963, which caused over 4,000 workers with vested pension rights to lose some or all of their benefits (H.R. Rep. No. 533 1973; S. Rep. No. 127 1973; Wooten 2004: 73–8).

ERISA

Enacted in 1974, ERISA was designed to protect participants' interests in pension plans, not to require employers to maintain pension plans. ERISA regulated pensions by imposing minimum standards on plans (covering such matters as participation, vesting, benefit distribution, and funding), by requiring most DB plans to participate in a national plan termination insurance program, and by subjecting pension plans to reporting and disclosure, fiduciary responsibility, and enforcement provisions.

Congress was concerned, however, that regulatory provisions could do more harm than good. Congress recognized that regulatory provisions would protect employees only if employers elected to maintain pension plans for them and that employers' willingness to maintain pension plans voluntarily could not be taken for granted. Regulatory provisions could discourage employers from adopting pension plans, encourage employers to terminate existing plans, or both, reducing the number of plans, the number of covered employees, and the value of the benefits the plans would distribute. To counteract the potentially self-defeating consequences of ERISA's regulatory provisions, Congress included in ERISA provisions that were designed to cultivate pension plans. A leading account of ERISA's enactment concluded that 'Congress chose less stringent measures than it might have because legislators believed that stricter regulation would overburden plan sponsors ... Protective measures increase costs, which may lead employers to shut down a plan or reduce benefits' (Wooten 2004: 272).

In order to encourage employers to award their employees enforceable pension rights under voluntary employer-provided pension plans, Congress sought to strike a balance between plan cultivation and plan regulation. The United States Supreme Court (the Supreme Court) later observed that:

> ERISA represents a careful balancing between ensuring fair and prompt enforcement of rights under a plan and the encouragement of the creation of such plans. Congress sought to create a system that is [not] so complex that administrative costs, or litigation expenses, unduly discourage employers from offering [ERISA] plans in the first place. (*Conkright v. Frommert* 2010: 517)

Each of the four Senate and House committees responsible for the bills that became ERISA expressed its intent to foster the establishment and growth of voluntary employer-sponsored plans. (Pertinent portions of the committee reports are set forth in Appendix Table 11.A1.)

The statement of purpose in Title IV of ERISA (Plan Termination Insurance) formally proclaimed Congress's intent to cultivate pension plans:

> The purposes of this title, which are to be carried out by the [Pension Benefit Guaranty Corporation], are—(1) to encourage the continuation and maintenance of voluntary private pension plans for the benefit of their participants,
>
> (2) to provide for the timely and uninterrupted payment of pension benefits to participants and beneficiaries under plans to which this title applies, and
>
> (3) to maintain premiums established by the [PBGC] under section 4006 at the lowest level consistent with carrying out its obligations under this title. (ERISA §4002(a))

Congress's intent was also carried out by the ERISA provisions governing plan management and administration, employer securities, vesting, and preemption.

Plan management and administration

ERISA requires every employee benefit plan to be established and maintained pursuant to a written instrument that (1) provides a procedure for establishing and carrying out a funding policy and method that is consistent with the plan's objectives and ERISA's requirements; (2) describes any procedure under the plan for allocating administrative responsibilities; (3) provides a procedure for amending the plan; and (4) specifies the basis on which payments are made to and from the plan. ERISA also requires plan fiduciaries to discharge their duties in accordance with the plan's governing documents and instruments insofar as they are consistent with Titles I and IV of ERISA. Finally, ERISA permits a plan participant or beneficiary to bring a civil action to recover benefits due under the terms of the plan, to enforce his or her rights under the terms of the plan, or to clarify his or her rights to benefits under the terms of the plan (ERISA §§402(b), 502(a)).

These provisions both regulate and cultivate employee benefit plans. Because of these provisions, employees can ascertain their benefits, can enforce their benefit rights, and are protected from claims that unwritten amendments have eliminated their benefit rights under the plan. As the United States Court of Appeals for the Third Circuit observed,

> ERISA § 402(a)(1) was designed to ensure that every employee may, on examining the plan documents, determine exactly what his rights and obligations are under the plan. Employees entitled to rely on the terms of a written benefit plan should not have their benefits eroded by oral modifications to the . . . plan. Congress, in passing ERISA, did not intend that participants in employee benefit plans should be left to the uncertainties of oral communications in finding out precisely what rights they were given under their plan. (*Hamilton v. Air Jamaica, Ltd.* 1991: 78–9)

ERISA's plan document provisions also help to provide certainty to plan sponsors and plan administrators: they help to define the employer's financial obligation to the plan, facilitate efficient, reliable, and consistent plan administration, and provide a plan amendment procedure that can be invoked to make changes in the plan. The Supreme Court has stated:

> [H]aving an amendment procedure enables plan administrators, the people who manage the plan on a day-to-day level, to have a mechanism for sorting out, from among the occasional corporate communications that pass through their offices and that conflict with the existing plan terms, the bona fide amendments from those that are not. (*Curtiss-Wright Corp. v. Schoonejongen* 1995: 82)

Moreover, ERISA treats the act of amending or terminating a plan as a settlor function rather than as a fiduciary function. ERISA provides that

> a person is a fiduciary with respect to a plan to the extent (1) he exercises any discretionary authority or discretionary control respecting management of such plan or exercises any authority or control respecting management or disposition of its assets, (2) he renders investment advice for a fee . . . with respect to any moneys or property of such plan . . . , or (3) he has any discretionary authority or discretionary responsibility in the administration of such plan. (ERISA §3(21)(A))

Because ERISA's definition of 'fiduciary' focuses on plan management, plan administration, and investment advice, an employer does not act in a fiduciary capacity, and is not subject to ERISA's fiduciary standards, when it acts as the plan's sponsor or 'settlor,' such as when it decides whether to establish, amend, or terminate a plan. ERISA's definition of 'fiduciary' thus allows employers to design their plans as they see fit, subject only to the substantive requirements of ERISA and without their design decisions being made subject to judicial review for compliance with ERISA's fiduciary standards.

The settlor function doctrine—under which plan design decisions are outside the scope of ERISA's fiduciary responsibility standards—is fundamental to plan cultivation. Employers would undoubtedly be reluctant to adopt employee benefit plans if employers were treated as fiduciaries (and were subject to ERISA's fiduciary standards) when they adopt, amend, or terminate a plan and were therefore required, for example, to make design decisions solely in the interest of plan participants. Because the settlor function doctrine recognizes that ERISA's fiduciary standards do not apply to decisions to establish, amend, or terminate a plan, the settlor function doctrine advances the objective of plan cultivation by giving plan sponsors considerable latitude to design plans as they see fit.

The Supreme Court has distinguished plan design decisions (non-fiduciary decisions that ERISA leaves largely to the plan's settlor) from decisions regarding plan management and administration (fiduciary decisions that are governed by ERISA's fiduciary responsibility standards). In *Lockheed Corp. v. Spink* (1996), the Supreme Court ruled that Lockheed did not act in a fiduciary capacity when it amended its pension plan to add an early retirement incentive that was payable to employees who retired early and who released any employment-related claims they might have against Lockheed. The Court emphasized that 'only when fulfilling certain defined functions does a person become a fiduciary' under ERISA and that the functions specified by ERISA's definition of fiduciary 'do not include plan design.' The Court went on to say that 'ERISA leaves th[e] question of the content of benefits to the private parties creating the plan ... [T]he private parties, not the Government, control the level of benefits' (*Lockheed Corp. v. Spink* 1996: 887–90, 894).

In addition, ERISA's prohibited transaction rules—which bar transactions that Congress deemed potentially abusive—include an exemption that accommodates employer-administered plans. Set forth in ERISA §408(c)(3), the exemption provides that the prohibited transaction rules do not forbid the same person from serving both as a plan fiduciary and as an officer, employee, agent, or other representative of a party in interest (such as the sponsoring employer). The exemption authorizes a significant departure from the prototypical arrangement under the common law of trusts in which the trust is administered by a disinterested fiduciary.[1] Although the §408(c)(3) exemption does not relieve a fiduciary of its obligations under ERISA's general fiduciary standards, such as the duty of prudence, the exemption makes it clear that a fiduciary's status as a representative of the employer does not violate ERISA's prohibited transaction rules.

Employer securities

The President's Committee also called for changes in the treatment of plan investments in employer securities. The Committee concluded that, in assessing investments in employer securities, it was impossible to rely on the same standards of investment judgment that could be expected to prevail when a fiduciary made other investments and that investing a large percentage of a plan's assets in a single equity security subjected the plan to inappropriate risks. The Committee recommended a limit of 'perhaps 10 percent' on the portion of a pension plan's assets that could be invested in employer securities (President's Committee 1965: 76).

The Committee also criticized the income tax rules governing appreciated employer securities received in a lump-sum distribution from a tax-qualified plan. Under those rules, any increase in the value of the securities over their cost to the plan was not included in the employee's gross income until the securities were sold. The Committee recommended repeal of those rules on the grounds that (1) only a relatively small percentage of plan participants could take advantage of the rules and (2) the rules artificially encouraged investment in employer securities (President's Committee 1965: 66).

Nevertheless, Congress implemented only some of the Committee's recommendations regarding employer securities. On the one hand, ERISA's fiduciary standards imposed a duty to diversify plan assets, imposed a 10 percent limit on investments in employer securities and employer real property, and curbed self-dealing. On the other hand, ERISA modified these restrictions to accommodate investments in employer securities by eligible individual account plans (EIAPs) and employee stock ownership plans (ESOPs). In general terms, ERISA defined an EIAP as (1) an individual account plan that explicitly provides for the acquisition of employer stock and that is a profit-sharing, stock bonus, thrift, or savings plan, (2) an ESOP, or (3) a money purchase pension plan that was in existence on September 2, 1974, and that on that date invested primarily in employer stock. ERISA defined an ESOP as an individual account plan that is a stock bonus plan, or stock bonus plan and money purchase plan, that is tax-qualified, that is designed to invest primarily in employer stock, and that meets any other requirements imposed by Treasury Department regulations (ERISA §407(d)(3) & (6); Treas. Reg. §54.4975–11; 29 C.F.R. §2550.407d–6).

ERISA exempted EIAPs (including ESOPs) from both ERISA's diversification requirements and its 10 percent limit on the portion of plan assets that may be invested in employer securities. In addition, ERISA exempted an EIAP's purchases and sales of employer securities from ERISA's generally applicable ban on party-in-interest transactions and permitted an ESOP to borrow from the employer in order to invest in employer securities (*White v. Marshall & Ilsley Corp.* 2013).[2] Moreover, ERISA did not change the income tax treatment of unrealized appreciation on employer securities, as the President's Committee had recommended. Instead, ERISA reduced the disparity between the income tax treatment of distributions of appreciated employer securities and the income tax treatment of other distributions by making many other distributions eligible for tax-free rollover.

Vesting

ERISA's vesting provisions both regulate and cultivate benefit plans. Although ERISA's detailed vesting and benefit accrual requirements are regulatory measures, ERISA's vesting requirements apply to a benefit only if the benefit is classified by ERISA as an accrued benefit (ERISA 203(a)). As a result, many valuable pension benefits, such as early retirement subsidies and disability benefits, are exempted from ERISA's vesting requirements.

ERISA's plan cultivation provisions played a central role in the Supreme Court's 1981 ruling regarding the application of ERISA's vesting provisions to an offset provision in a pension plan's benefit formula (*Alessi v. Raybestos-Manhattan, Inc.* 1981). The offset provision reduced a participant's gross pension benefit by the amount of any workers' compensation payments that the participant was entitled to receive. The Court ruled that the offset did not violate ERISA's vesting standards. According to the Court, the plaintiffs' vesting claim overlooked the fact that the private party creating the plan (the settlor) typically 'defines the content of the benefit that, once vested, cannot be forfeited... Rather than imposing mandatory pension levels or methods for calculating benefits, Congress in ERISA set outer bounds on permissible accrual practices' (*Alessi v. Raybestos-Manhattan, Inc.* 1981: 511–12).

ERISA also cultivated welfare benefits, such as severance benefits and retiree health benefits, by exempting welfare benefits from its vesting and benefit accrual requirements. The welfare benefit exemption was motivated by Congress's concern that the application of the vesting and benefit accrual requirements to welfare benefits would significantly complicate plan administration, increase the cost of providing welfare benefits, and discourage employers from maintaining welfare benefit plans. As the United States Court of Appeals for the Third Circuit observed,

> Congress plainly did not impose as stringent vesting requirements as it might have. We can hardly attribute that decision to oversight, however. Having made a fundamental decision not to require employers to provide *any* benefit plans, Congress was forced to balance its desire to regulate extant plans more extensively against the danger that increased regulation would deter employers from creating such plans in the first place. In other words, although ERISA was clearly designed to promote the interests of employees and their beneficiaries in employee benefit plans, the statute was also designed to minimiz[e] the adverse impact of cost increases imposed on employers by the tougher regulation... Congress's concern with minimizing employers' compliance costs is especially evident in ERISA's accrual and vesting provisions. Before determining appropriate minimum vesting requirements for pension plans, the Senate Subcommittee on Labor commissioned an independent actuarial study to determine the range of estimated costs to private pension plans resulting from compliance with minimum vesting requirements under several proposed minimum vesting standards. (*Hozier v. Midwest Fasteners* 1990: 1160; *Gable v. Sweetheart Cup Co.* 1994: 859–60)

The courts have found that the welfare plan exemption furthered the interests of employees because the knowledge that they could reduce or eliminate welfare benefits made employers more willing to provide those benefits, and because employees remained free to bargain with their employers for the vesting of welfare benefits (*Hamilton v. Air Jamaica, Ltd.* 1991).

Preemption

ERISA's preemption provision states that ERISA 'shall supersede any and all State laws insofar as they may now or hereafter relate to any employee benefit plan' (ERISA §514(a)). The Supreme Court has interpreted this provision to advance ERISA's plan cultivation agenda. The Supreme Court observed that '[a] patchwork scheme of regulation would introduce considerable inefficiencies in benefit program operation, which might lead those employers with existing plans to reduce benefits, and those without such plans to refrain from adopting them. Pre-emption assures that the administrative practices of a benefit plan will be governed by only a single set of regulations' (*Fort Halifax v. Coyne* 1987: 11).

For example, in 1987, the Supreme Court considered whether ERISA preempted a Mississippi common-law cause of action alleging improper processing of a benefit claim under an insured employee benefit plan. In ruling that ERISA preempted the Mississippi law, the Court relied on ERISA's comprehensive civil enforcement scheme which, the Court said, 'represents a careful balancing of the need for prompt and fair claims settlement procedures against the public interest in encouraging the formation of employee benefit plans.' The Court concluded that ERISA's enforcement regime would be undermined if a participant were free to obtain remedies under state law that were not available under §502 of ERISA. (*Pilot Life Ins. Co. v. Dedeaux* 1987: 54; *Aetna Health Inc. v. Davila* 2004 (holding that ERISA preempted a Texas cause of action that duplicates or supplements an ERISA cause of action)).

In 1990, the Supreme Court held that ERISA preempted a Texas wrongful discharge statute that had been construed to apply to an employee who allegedly was terminated because the employer sought to avoid making pension contributions on his behalf. Based on ERISA's broad preemption provision and its larger purpose in 'encouraging the formation of employee benefit plans,' the Court ruled that ERISA preempted such state-law claims (*Ingersoll-Rand Co. v. McClendon* 1990: 143–4).

In 2001, the Supreme Court also held that ERISA preempted a State of Washington statute providing that the designation of a spouse as the beneficiary of a nonprobate asset is automatically revoked upon divorce. The

Court ruled that the Washington statute subverted two key features of ERISA's plan cultivation provisions: the plan document requirement and nationally uniform plan administration (*Egelhoff v. Egelhoff* 2001).

The United States Court of Appeals for the Second Circuit also has invoked ERISA's cultivation objectives to support its ruling that ERISA does *not* preempt malpractice actions against actuaries and other professionals who provided services to employee benefit plans. The court of appeals observed that 'immunizing actuaries could harm the financial integrity of the plans Congress intended to protect' (*Gerosa v. Savasta & Co.* 2003: 329).

Post-ERISA Legislation

Following ERISA's enactment, Congress continued to encourage employers to maintain or contribute to pension plans via three important pieces of legislation. One was the Multiemployer Pension Plan Amendments Act of 1980 (MPPAA), which declared it to be federal policy 'to alleviate certain problems which tend to discourage the maintenance and growth of multiemployer pension plans' (MPPAA 1980: §3(c)(2)). The second was the Single-Employer Pension Plan Amendments Act of 1986 (SEPPAA), which declared it to be federal policy 'to encourage the maintenance and growth of single-employer defined benefit pension plans' (SEPPAA 1986: §11002 (c)(2)). And the third was the Pension Protection Act of 2006 (PPA), which encouraged the adoption of hybrid pension plans (cash balance and pension equity plans) by, among other things, settling the long-standing dispute over whether a DB plan may express a participant's benefit on the basis of the participant's account balance and by explaining how an account-based DB plan can comply with statutory restrictions on forfeitures and age discrimination (PPA 2006).

In addition, the Tax Reform Act of 1986 overhauled the Code's coverage and nondiscrimination provisions to advance the objective of providing pension benefits to rank-and-file employees. The Senate Finance Committee report for the 1986 Act explained that, although the coverage provisions were originally intended as anti-abuse measures, the Committee's current intent was to assure that the tax incentives provided by the Code's qualified plan provisions encouraged employers to sponsor plans that covered rank-and-file employees:

> For many years, the committee has supported measures that provide tax incentives designed to encourage employers to provide retirement benefits for rank-and-file employees. It has been the committee's intention that these tax incentives, which are more valuable for individuals with high levels of income because of their marginal

tax rates, should be available to employers only if their plans provide benefits for rank-and-file employees.

Coverage tests for qualified plans originally were provided by remedial legislation in 1942 to prevent abuses. The committee is now concerned that current interpretations of the coverage tests for qualified plans, by permitting large disparities in the coverage of highly compensated employees and nonhighly compensated employees, are not sufficient to ensure broad, nondiscriminatory coverage of rank-and-file employees. The coverage rules provided by the bill are intended by the committee to deny tax benefits to plans in which the percentage of highly compensated employees who benefit under a plan is unreasonably in excess of the percentage of other employees benefiting under the plan. (S. Rep. No. 313 1985: 578)

After enacting ERISA, Congress has continued to enact legislation encouraging employers to offer employer securities as investments or investment options under ESOPs.[3]

Employer Migration

In the past 30 years, very few private sector employers have adopted new DB plans, and many sponsors that had previously adopted DB plans have now shut them down to one extent or another. Some employers have terminated their DB plans, while others have closed their DB plans to new entrants. Yet others have frozen accruals under their DB plans for some or all participants. Of late, some DB plans have reduced their liabilities (and their assets) by purchasing annuities (and thereby transferring a portion of their liabilities to insurance companies) or by allowing retired participants to take their benefits as lump-sum cash payments.

According to the Employee Benefits Security Administration (EBSA), the number of DB plans in the US reached its peak in the mid-1980s, when there were approximately 170,000 single-employer DB plans in the private sector. (See Tables 11.1 and 11.2.) By 2011, only 44,000 or so were left (roughly 25 percent of the corresponding mid-1980s number). In 1984, there were approximately 24 million active participants in single-employer DB plans, but in 2011, there were about 12 million (about 50 percent of the corresponding 1984 number) (EBSA 2013).[4] While the numbers for single-employer DB plans have plummeted, the corresponding numbers for single-employer DC plans have skyrocketed, as shown by Tables 11.1 and 11.2. A DC plan with an elective deferral feature, the 401(k) plan, is now the predominant form of retirement plan. About 75 percent of all corporate retirement plans (513,496 out of a total of 680,899 in 2011) are designated as 401(k) plans, and 401(k) plans cover about 75 percent of all active retirement plan participants. (EBSA 2013).

TABLE 11.1 Number of plans

Type of plan	1985	2001	2011	Increase (Decrease) 1985–2011
DB plan	167,911	45,159	43,813	(124,098)
DC plan	461,158	685,375	637,086	175,928
Total	629,069	730,534	680,899	51,830

Source: EBSA 2013: 1.

TABLE 11.2 Number of active plan participants

Type of plan	1985	2001	2011	Increase (Decrease) 1985–2011
DB plan	23,336,000	17,105,000	12,327,000	(11,009,000)
DC plan	32,237,000	50,090,000	70,278,000	38,041,000
Total	55,573,000	67,195,000	82,606,000	27,033,000

Source: EBSA 2013: 9.

Moreover, many of the remaining DB plans look quite different from the traditional 'final average pay' plan. Under a final average pay plan, a participant's accrued benefit is typically expressed as an annuity commencing as of the participant's normal retirement age, with the size of the annuity based on the participant's years of service and final average pay. Many employers have now converted their traditional DB plans to cash balance or other hybrid forms, such as pension equity plans. Under a typical cash balance plan, for example, a participant's benefit is expressed as an account balance, and the participant's account is credited each year with a pay credit (a percentage of the participant's current compensation) and an interest credit (a percentage of the participant's account balance). According to a Towers Watson report, only seven of that year's Fortune 100 companies offered new hires a traditional DB plan (down from 89 in 1985), and only 30 of that year's Fortune 100 companies offered a DB plan of *any kind* to new hires (down from 90 in 1985) (McFarland 2013). See Table 11.3.

Although there is no doubt that employers have migrated away from DB plans, it is not clear why this migration has occurred. It seems unlikely that a single explanation could possibly account for the behavior of thousands of unaffiliated employers—publicly owned and closely held, for-profit and non-profit, large and small—over a thirty-year period. Indeed, there may be no single explanation that accounts for the behavior of many individual employers. Several explanations have been offered, including a desire to

TABLE 11.3 Fortune 100 company offerings to new hires

Type of retirement plan for new hires	1985	2002	2013
Traditional DB plan	89	48	7
Hybrid DB retirement plan	1	35	23
Total DB plans	90	83	30
DC plan only	10	17	70

Source: McFarland (2013): 1.

accommodate employee preference for a benefit that is expressed as, and that can be paid as, a portable lump-sum amount and lack of employee appreciation for the value of a pension benefit that is expressed as an annuity. In addition, some explain the migration away from DB plans by pointing to employer and employee preference for a benefit that is allocated more evenly across the covered workforce than is a traditional DB plan benefit. Others point to employers' desire to shed the economic and financial accounting risks associated with DB plans, including the volatility and unpredictability of both the contribution requirements and the financial accounting expense associated with DB plans, and to employers' need to compete effectively with (1) foreign companies whose governments provide most of the pension benefits for their employees, (2) newer domestic companies that have never maintained a DB plan, and (3) other companies that have already frozen or terminated their DB plans. Other explanations that have been offered relate to employers' desire to adjust compensation expense in response to mounting health care costs and to top executives' increasing reliance on top-hat plans for retirement benefits. Others point to concerns about potential for class action litigation and to excessive regulation of DB plans (Towers Watson 2012; GAO 2009; Kennedy 2008; VanDerhei 2006; Munnell et al. 2006; *Cooper v. IBM Personal Pension Plan* 2006).

Surveys often identify the regulatory burden on DB plans as one of the reasons why employers have migrated away from DB plans. Yet published survey reports generally do not identify which specific regulatory burdens have been most onerous, nor do they identify excessive regulation as the only reason, or even as the principal reason, for employer migration. The US GAO found that employers' principal reasons for freezing DB plans were their funding volatility and the effects on employers' cash flows (GAO 2008: 6–7). Another GAO report regarding the nation's largest private DB plan sponsors found that the top three reasons for changing their DB plans for *non-bargained* employees were (1) the unpredictability or volatility of the funding requirements, (2) competitive economic pressures, and (3) trends in employee demographics (toward an older or younger workforce) (GAO

2009). The responses for DB plans for *collectively bargained* employees were somewhat different. Here the top three reasons were (1) competitive economic pressures, (2) changes in bargaining unit demographics, and (3) increase in contributions to DC plan as a trade-off (GAO 2009).

The vast majority (74 percent) of plan sponsors that had frozen their pension plans reported that they could not conceive of any conditions that would make them consider adopting a new DB plan. Only 26 percent of plan sponsors reported that there *were* conditions under which they would consider adopting a new DB plan, the top six being (1) change in accounting treatment, (2) greater effectiveness as a retention tool, (3) reduced volatility in funding requirements, (4) DB plans becoming industry standard, (5) an increase in the tax-deductibility of contributions to DB plans (as compared to contributions to a DC plan), and (6) reduced regulatory/administrative requirements (GAO 2009).

A 2012 Towers Watson survey elicited similar responses. Plan sponsors that had closed, frozen, or terminated their DB plans reported that reducing cost and cost volatility were their two principal objectives in closing, freezing, or terminating the plan. Simplifying plan administration was near the bottom of the list of reasons given (Towers Watson 2012).

Plan regulation appears to have contributed to the migration of employers away from DB plans. Major employers initially displayed considerable interest in offering hybrid plans to their employees: the number of Fortune 100 companies offering a hybrid plan to new hires increased from one in 1985 to 35 in 2002. But this period of growth was followed by a marked decline in the popularity of hybrid plans. Between 2002 and 2013, the number of Fortune 100 companies offering a hybrid DB plan to new hires fell from 35 to 23, and during the same period, the number of Fortune 100 companies offering only a DC plan to new hires increased sharply (from 17 to 70) (McFarland 2013).

While there may be no single explanation for the peaking of interest in hybrid plans in 2002 and for the pronounced decline of interest thereafter, the views of regulators at the Treasury Department and Internal Revenue Service on hybrid plans cannot have helped. In December of 2002, the Treasury and the Service proposed highly controversial regulations regarding the age discrimination provisions of the Code. Employer-commenters asserted, among other things, that the proposed regulations would (1) impose an intricate mathematical approach that was inconsistent with the text of the statute and Congressional intent; (2) outlaw many commonplace pension plans, including plans that could not reasonably be considered age-discriminatory; (3) saddle cash balance plans with an excessively rigid 'safe harbor'; (4) subject plans and employers to the risk of years of costly litigation; (5) impose enormous economic costs on employers that sponsor DB plans; and (6) threaten the future of all DB plans (ERIC 2003).

As a long-term financial arrangement, an employer-sponsored DB plan is subject to a variety of significant risks. A number of those risks—such as investment and interest rate risks—are potentially costly, difficult to foresee, and largely beyond the control of an individual employer and its employees. The design of a plan can affect how these risks are allocated between the sponsoring employer and participating employees. Table 11.4 identifies the principal risks that apply to pension plans and how traditional DB plans and DC plans have allocated those risks.

The impact of investment and interest rate risks was evident during the 2000–10 decade. Because of stock market and interest rate fluctuations, that decade witnessed volatile and unpredictable swings in the values of DB plan assets and liabilities. Low equity prices reduced the value of plan assets, and low interest rates increased the present value of plan liabilities. During this period, employers did not simply migrate away from DB plans; many migrated away from DB plans to DC plans, while others migrated away from traditional DB plans to hybrid plans.

Aaronson and Coronado (2005) found that, although there was a general shift away from DB plans due to factors affecting all employers and employees, certain industries experienced significantly larger increases in DC plan coverage than others. They concluded that some employers and employees preferred more flexible, short-term employment arrangements, and therefore favored pension plans that, unlike traditional DB plans, provided for even rates of benefit accrual and did not penalize job change. Employers preferring more flexible employment relationships included companies finding that, due to the pace of technological change, their future success did not depend on long-term employment relationships. Employees preferring more flexible, short-term relationships included mobile employees who moved from employer to employer in search of better opportunities, members of two-earner couples whose employment decisions were affected by the other member's employment opportunities, and parents who had young children and who moved in and out of the workforce depending on the needs of their children.

Plan Design Options

Although DC plans have some advantages over DB plans, and particularly over traditional DB plans, some employees may not be prepared to handle the risks that DC plans impose on plan participants. Several design options are among those available to employers concerned with employees' ability to bear the risks that DC plans impose on plan participants. These design options include the following:

TABLE 11.4 Allocation of risks under DB and DC plans

Risk	Traditional DB plan	DC plan
Investment risk: the risk that the plan's investments will not perform as well as expected.	The employer bears all of the investment risk.	Plan participants bear all of the investment risk.
Interest rate risk: the risk that a change in interest rates will cause the present value of retirement plan liabilities to change.	The employer bears all of the interest rate risk. For example, all other things being equal, a decline in interest rates tends to increase the present value of the plan's liabilities (and to increase the employer's funding obligations and financial accounting expense). To some extent the effect on the present value of liabilities may be offset by the effect of the change in interest rates on the value of the plan's assets.	Because the value of the plan's liabilities equals the value of the plan's assets, there generally is no interest rate risk independent of investment risk (the risk that interest rate changes will affect the value of the plan's assets). (An exception: a money purchase pension plan with a funding waiver.)
Inflation risk: the risk that inflation will erode the value of the benefits provided by the plan.	Unless the plan provides for an automatic COLA, participants bear the risk of inflation. If benefits are based on the participant's final pay, and the participant receives pay increases that keep up with (or surpass) inflation, the plan can help the participant to keep up with *pre-retirement* inflation. The employer bears the cost of any increases in benefits that are attributable to a COLA or to increases in employees' pay levels.	Participants bear the risk of inflation. To the extent that appreciation in the value of the plan's investments keeps up with (or surpasses) inflation, the plan can help a participant to cope with inflation.
Accrual/contribution rate risk: the risk that the rate at which benefits are earned will decline.	Participants bear this risk, but the employer typically determines whether the accrual rate declines. If the plan accepts participant contributions, participants also determine whether the contribution/accrual rate declines.	Participants bear this risk, but the employer typically determines whether the contribution rate declines. If the plan accepts participant contributions, participants also determine whether the contribution rate declines.

(*continued*)

TABLE 11.4 Continued

Risk	Traditional DB plan	DC plan
Annuity purchase rate risk: the risk that the rate at which annuities may be purchased will change.	An annuity is typically provided by the DB plan itself rather than by an insurer. If, however, the plan provides annuity benefits by purchasing annuity contracts from insurers, the plan and the employer bear the annuity purchase rate risk. Annuity purchase rates are affected by interest rates and other factors, such as supply and demand conditions. Annuity purchase rate risk can be borne by participants who intend to receive benefits from the plan in a lump sum and to use the proceeds to purchase an annuity from an insurer.	Participants typically bear this risk. The annuity purchase rate risk typically applies under a DC plan that offers an annuity as an optional payment method.
Employment termination risk: the risk that a participant will terminate employment before (or after) reaching the point at which the participant is eligible for the benefit with the highest value under the plan.	The employer and plan participants bear this risk. Traditional DB plans provide meaningful retirement benefits only to long-service employees. For example, under a traditional DB plan with an early retirement subsidy, the value of the employee's retirement benefit can increase substantially once the employee attains early retirement age. An employee who would otherwise be eligible for early retirement can suffer a significant loss in value if the employee terminates employment before (or after) early retirement age.	Under a DC plan, all other things (such as compensation) being equal, benefits accrue evenly over a participant's career, so that there is less risk to an employee's retirement savings if a participant switches jobs in mid-career. Some employers provide a matching or other contribution only to plan participants who are employed on the last day of the year (Yang 2014).
Plan termination risk: the risk that the plan will terminate without sufficient funds to meet its benefit obligations.	If the plan is covered by the termination insurance program in Title IV of ERISA, both the employer and plan participants share this risk. Depending on the employer's financial condition, the employer may bear some of the risk, and plan participants may bear the risk for benefits in excess those covered by PBGC insurance.	There is a risk that the plan will terminate before the employer makes all of the contributions that are then due under the plan (for example, the contributions for the then-current year). Depending on the employer's financial condition, the employer and/or the plan participant may bear the risk.
Longevity risk: the risk that the participant (and any	The presumptive form of distribution is required to be an annuity under a DB plan. If a participant in a DB plan	

survivor) will live longer than anticipated and exhaust the participant's retirement savings.	receives his or her benefits from the plan as an annuity, the plan, rather than the participant, bears the longevity risk.	The risk falls on the participant unless the participant transfers the risk to an insurer by using the lump sum to purchase an annuity contract. Typically, it is more expensive to purchase an annuity from an insurer than it is to obtain an annuity directly from a DB plan.
	DB plans are permitted, however, to allow a participant to elect (with spousal consent) to receive the actuarial equivalent of the participant's accrued benefit in a lump sum. If a plan distributes benefits in the form of a lump sum, the participant bears the longevity risk—and runs the risk that the participant will spend the entire lump sum before the participant dies—unless the participant transfers the longevity risk to an insurer by using the lump sum to purchase an annuity contract.	

Source: Author's analysis.

- DC Plan Equity Fund with a Rate-of-Return Guarantee. Concerns about the incidence of investment risk under a DC plan might be addressed by offering investment options that provide participants with more downside protection, such as an investment-linked variable annuity with an investment guaranty offered by an insurance company. However, such offerings come at a price, typically in the form of higher fees, lower investment returns, or both.
- A DB/DC Floor-Offset Arrangement. Depending on the DC plan's contribution formula, the DB plan's benefit formula, and the plans' investment policies, a floor-offset arrangement might offer participants both the upside potential of a DC plan and the downside protection of a DB plan. Nevertheless, the funded status of the DB component of a floor-offset plan can be even more volatile than the funded status of a stand-alone DB plan.
- A Cash Balance Plan Offering an Investment Return. An employer might adopt a cash balance retirement plan under which much of the investment risk is allocated away from the employer and to plan participants, subject to the zero cumulative floor mandated by the Pension Protection Act of 2006, in accordance with the current proposed and final Treasury cash balance plan regulations. In this case, the plan's assets can be invested in a fashion that mirrors the investments used to determine the investment performance of the plan's account balances. This approach addresses employers' concerns regarding the volatility and unpredictability of employer contributions and expenses under a DB plan, but it does not offer an employee much more than what is already available under a DC plan (except that the relevant deduction and benefit limits would be the limits for DB plans).
- A Cash Balance Plan Offering an Investment Return with a Floor Exceeding the Zero Cumulative Floor Mandated by the PPA. Under current proposed and final Treasury regulations, cash balance plans are required to operate like DC plans and to shift *all* of the investment risk to plan participants (subject to the zero cumulative floor mandated by the PPA). If anticipated forthcoming Treasury Department regulations so permit, an employer might adopt a cash balance retirement plan under which investment risk is shared by the employer and plan participants. It remains to be seen whether the Treasury responds affirmatively to the objection made in the comments to the proposed regulations. By combining the best features of DB and DC plans, cash balance plans could offer participants an account-based benefit that includes a market-based rate of return with lower investment risk than a traditional DC plan. For example, a DB plan can provide annuities at lower cost, subsidized disability and death benefits, and subsidized early

retirement (or early retirement window) benefits. Moreover, plan fiduciaries could find it easier to reduce funding volatility by matching plan investments with their plans' future benefit obligations (Shea et al. 2011).

- Investment education. It is difficult to quarrel with the desirability of providing investment education to participants in DC plans that allow them to determine how the funds in their accounts will be invested. The US Department of Labor's interpretive bulletin on investment education explains how an employer can provide investment education without providing investment advice. By contrast, the provision of investment advice to plan participants might qualify as fiduciary conduct and might therefore subject the employer and others to potential liability as fiduciaries under ERISA (I.B. 1996).
- Investment advice. The US Department of Labor has also published a regulation that allows fiduciaries to provide investment advice to participants in participant-directed individual account plans without violating the conflict-of-interest rules in the Code and ERISA. Designating an investment advisor in accordance with the regulation is a fiduciary act, however, and compliance with the regulation does not relieve the party making the designation of the obligation to make the designation in accordance with ERISA's fiduciary standards (Investment Advice Regulation 2011).
- Payout education. If a plan offers a lump-sum option, employees strongly favor taking their benefits in the form of a lump-sum payment when they leave the firm, regardless of whether the plan is a DB or a DC plan. Employees who take their benefits in the form of a lump-sum payment, however, incur the risk that they will exhaust their retirement savings before they die. A growing body of research indicates that employees would be well-advised to address the risk that they will outlive their retirement savings by including annuities in their investment portfolios. Many employees do not understand annuities, however, and are concerned that they don't know enough about them to make informed decisions. Employers are in a position to educate their employees about annuities, but some employers remain concerned that any assistance that they provide will expose them to fiduciary liability under ERISA (Purcell 2009).

Conclusion

The basic policy decision that the US Congress made in the Code and ERISA was that the employer, not the government, should decide whether the employer will offer benefit plans to its employees and, if so, that the employer, not the government, should select the benefit plans and the benefits that will be offered. Moreover, the plan cultivation provisions in ERISA and the Code apply to both DB and DC plans and are designed to encourage employers to maintain the benefit plans that they prefer, not to require employers to maintain a particular type of plan. If the plan cultivation provisions were fundamentally flawed, one would expect to observe migration away from *both* DB and DC plans. Nevertheless, during the period from 1985 to 2011, the number of active participants in single-employer DC plans has more than doubled. During the same period, the percentage of *Fortune* 100 companies offering new hires some form of retirement plan has remained constant at 100 percent.

The differences between DB and DC plans, and between traditional pension plans and hybrid plans, suggest that the migration away from traditional DB plans was attributable primarily to employers' desire to avoid volatile and unpredictable swings in contribution requirements and financial accounting expenses, paired with employers' and employees' preference for plans that allocate benefits more evenly than do traditional DB plans. Although concerns about the burdens imposed by the regulatory provisions of the Code and ERISA appear to have influenced employers' decision-making, particularly with respect to the movement away from DB plans during the past decade, such concerns do not appear to have been the primary cause of the migration away from traditional DB plans in general.

Appendix

Appendix table 11.A1 ERISA committee reports

Committee	Report Text
Senate Committee on Labor & Public Welfare S. Rep. No. 127 1973: 8, 13, 18–19	'Although the need for legislative reform has been and continues to be widely acknowledged among all persons and sectors affected, governmental supervision of mandated and essential improvements has been resisted due to the belief that such legislation might impede plan growth. However, as the Committee has progressed in its inquiries and made public disclosures of its analysis and findings, it has been discerned that some resistance has been dissipated and various opponents have now acknowledged that such reforms will not deter the establishment or the improvement of pension plans.' 'The enactment of progressive and effective pension legislation . . . should serve to encourage rather than diminish efforts by management and industry to expand pension plan coverage and to improve benefits for workers.'

'The Committee also concluded that an exemption for plans of small size was necessary in order to prevent discouraging small employers from establishing pension plans.... While reasonable men may differ in their judgment as to whether a small plan exemption would encourage greater expansion of private pension plans among small businessmen, it is the Committee's judgment that subjecting all plans, regardless of size, to the standards of this Act could have an inhibiting effect on future private pension expansion.'

Senate Committee on Finance
S. Rep. 383 1973: 1, 10–11, 18–19

'The [bill] as reported by the committee is designed to make pension, profit-sharing, and stock bonus plans more effective in providing retirement income for employees who have spent their careers in useful and socially productive work. It encourages provision for the retirement needs of many millions of individuals. At the same time, the committee recognizes that private retirement plans are voluntary on the part of the employer, and, therefore, it has carefully weighed the additional costs to the employer and has minimized them to the extent consistent with the minimum standards for retirement benefits.'

'A fundamental aspect of present law, which the committee bill continues, is reliance on voluntary action by employers (and employees under contributory plans) for the establishment of qualified retirement plans. The committee bill also continues the approach in present law of encouraging the establishment of retirement plans which contain socially desirable provisions through the granting of tax inducements. In other words, under the new legislation as under present law, no one is compelled to establish a retirement plan. However, if a retirement plan is to qualify for the favorable tax treatment, it will be required to comply with specified new requirements which are designed to improve the retirement system. Since the favorable tax treatment is quite substantial, presently involving a revenue loss of over $4 billion a year, it is anticipated that plans will have a strong inducement to comply with the new qualification rules and thereby become more effective in fulfilling their objective of providing retirement income.'

'[T]he committee is aware that under our voluntary pension system, the cost of financing pension plans is an important factor in determining whether any particular retirement plan will be adopted and in determining the benefit levels if a plan is adopted, and that unusually large increases in costs could impede the growth and improvement of the private retirement system. For this reason, in the case of those requirements which add to the cost of financing retirement plans, the committee has

(*continued*)

Appendix table 11.A1 Continued

Committee	Report Text
	sought to adopt provisions which strike a balance between providing meaningful reform and keeping costs within reasonable limits.' 'If employers respond to more comprehensive coverage, vesting and funding rules by decreasing benefits under existing plans or slowing the rate of formation of new plans, little if anything would be gained from the standpoint of securing broader use of employee pensions and related plans.'
House Committee on Education & Labor H.R. Rep. No. 533 1973: 1–2	'The primary purpose of the bill is the protection of individual pension rights, but the committee has been constrained to recognize the voluntary nature of private retirement plans. The relative improvements required by this Act have been weighed against the additional burdens to be placed on the system. While modest cost increases are to be anticipated when the Act becomes effective, the adverse impact of these increases have been minimized. Additionally, all of the provisions in the Act have been analyzed on the basis of their projected costs in relation to the anticipated benefit to the employee participant. In broad outline, the bill is designed to: (1) establish equitable standards of plan administration; (2) mandate minimum standards of plan design with respect to the vesting of plan benefits; (3) require minimum standards of fiscal responsibility by requiring the amortization of unfunded liabilities; (4) insure the vested portion of unfunded liabilities against the risk of premature plan termination; and (5) promote a renewed expansion of private retirement plans and increase the number of participants receiving private retirement benefits.'
House Committee on Ways & Means H.R. Rep. No. 807 1974: 2	'The bill encourages provisions for the retirement needs of many millions of individuals. At the same time, the committee recognizes that private retirement plans are voluntary on the part of employers, and, therefore, it has weighed carefully the additional costs to employers and minimized those costs to the extent consistent with minimum standards for retirement benefits. . . . The bill continues to rely primarily on the tax laws to secure needed improvements in pensions and related plans. In general, it retains the tax incentives granted under present law for the purpose of encouraging the establishment of plans which contain socially desirable provisions. However, it also improves the effectiveness of these tax incentives by extending or increasing them in certain cases where this is warranted and by pruning them where they have given rise to problems.'

Sources: As indicated in this table.

Acknowledgements

The author acknowledges with thanks the constructive comments received from Amy N. Moore and Richard C. Shea.

Endnotes

1. See *Pegram v. Herdrich* (2000: 225): 'Professor Scott's treatise admonishes that the trustee "is not permitted to place himself in a position where it would be for his own benefit to violate his duty to the beneficiaries." Under ERISA, however, a fiduciary may have financial interests adverse to beneficiaries'. Langbein (2007: 1327): 'This concession to employer interests, which departs notably from the trust tradition, was motivated by the concern that without it employers would be less likely to sponsor benefit plans. Because pension and welfare benefit plans entail major expenditures, the sponsor community prefers to have its own managers administering and monitoring plan operations for cost containment, a traditional management function' (footnotes omitted).
2. 'To preserve and encourage ESOPs, Congress exempted fiduciaries of ESOPs from the duty to diversify and limited the duty of prudence so as not to require diversification for such plans.'
3. See, for example, *Fifth Third Bancorp v. Dudenhoeffer* (2014: 21): 'Congress, in seeking to permit and promote ESOPs, was pursuing purposes other than the financial security of plan participants'; *In re Citigroup ERISA Litig.* (2011: 137): 'Due to the risk inherent in employees' placing their retirement assets in a single, undiversified stock fund, Congress has expressed concern that its goal of encouraging employee ownership of the company's stock could "be made unattainable by regulations and rulings which treat employee stock ownership plans as conventional retirement plans"'; (*Steinman v. Hicks* 2003: 1103): 'Congress, believing employees' ownership of their employer's stock is a worthy goal, has encouraged the creation of ESOPs both by giving tax breaks and by waiving the duty ordinarily imposed on trustees by modern trust law (including ERISA) to diversify the assets of a pension plan' (citations omitted); *Moench v. Robertson* (1995: 568): 'Under their original rationale, ESOPs were described as ... devices for expanding the national capital base among employees—an effective merger of the roles of capitalist and worker. Thus, the concept of employee ownership constituted a goal in and of itself. To accomplish this end, Congress ... enacted a number of laws designed to encourage employers to set up such plans' (internal quotation marks and citations omitted).
4. For years preceding 2005, EBSA used data that excluded (1) individuals who were eligible to participate in a §401(k) plan but who did not elect to have contributions made on their behalf and (2) non-vested former employees who had not yet completed the plan's break-in-service period. For 2005 and subsequent years,

EBSA has relied on data that treat these individuals as 'active participants.' EBSA has stated, however, that because these individuals are not contributing to the plan and are not entitled to receive benefits under the plan, EBSA has adjusted the reported active participant counts to provide more meaningful statistics. 'In a purely economic sense, and for research purposes, individuals in these groups should not be included in the count of active participants' (EBSA 2013: 40–1).

References

Aaronson, S. and J. Coronado (2005). *Are Firms or Workers Behind the Shift Away from DB Pension Plans?* Finance and Economics Discussion Series, Divisions of Research & Statistics and Monetary Affairs (2005–17). Washington, DC: Federal Reserve Board. <http://www.federalreserve.gov/pubs/feds/2005/200517/200517pap.pdf>.

Aetna Health Inc. v. Davila (2004). 542 U.S. 200.

Alessi v. Raybestos-Manhattan, Inc. (1981). 451 U.S. 504: 511–12.

Bureau of National Affairs (1962). *Federal-State Regulation of Welfare Funds*, Washington, DC: Bureau of National Affairs.

In re Citigroup ERISA Litig. (2011). 662 F.3d 128 (2d Cir.): 137.

Conkright v. Frommert (2010). 559 U.S. 506: 517.

Cooper v. IBM Personal Pension Plan (2006). 457 F.3d 636 (7th Cir.): 642–3.

Curtiss-Wright Corp. v. Schoonejongen (1995). 514 U.S. 73: 82.

Egelhoff v. Egelhoff (2001). 532 U.S. 141: 147–8.

Employee Benefits Security Administration (EBSA), United States Department of Labor (2013). *Private Pension Plan Bulletin Historical Tables and Graphs.* <http://www.dol.gov/ebsa/pdf/historicaltables.pdf>.

ERISA (1974). Employee Retirement Income Security Act 1974. P.L. 93–406, 88 Stat. 829.

ERISA Industry Committee (ERIC) (2003). *Initial Comments of the ERISA Industry Committee on Proposed Treasury Department Regulations on Age Discrimination and Nondiscrimination Cross-Testing* (Jan. 30). Washington, DC: ERISA Industry Committee.

Fifth Third Bancorp v. Dudenhoeffer (2014). 2014 U.S. LEXIS 4495: 21.

Fort Halifax Packing Co. v Coyne (1987). 482 U.S. 1: 11.

Gable v. Sweetheart Cup Co. (1994). 35 F.3d 851 (4th Cir.): 859–60.

Government Accountability Office (GAO) (2008). *Defined Benefit Pensions: Plan Freezes Affect Millions of Participants and May Pose Retirement Income Challenges*, GAO-08-817. Washington, DC: GPO.

Government Accountability Office (GAO) (2009). *Defined Benefit Pensions: Survey Results of the Nation's Largest Private Defined Benefit Plan Sponsors*, GAO-09-291. Washington, DC: GPO.

Gerosa v. Savasta & Co. (2003). 329 F.3d 317 (2d Cir.): 329.

Hamilton v. Air Jamaica, Ltd. (1991). 945 F.2d 74 (3d Cir.): 78–9.

H.R. Rep. No. 533 (1973). Employee Benefit Security Act of 1973, 93d Cong., 1st Sess: 3–4.

H.R. Rep. No. 807 (1974). Report [To accompany H.R. 12855], 93d Cong., 2d Sess: 2.

H.R. Rep. No. 2333 (1942). The Revenue Bill of 1942, 77th Cong., 2d Sess: 103–4.

Hozier v. Midwest Fasteners, Inc. (1990). 908 F.2d 1155 (3d Cir.): 1160.

Ingersoll-Rand Co. v. McClendon (1990). 498 U.S. 133: 143–4.

I.B. 1996. Interp. Bulletin 96–1, 29 C.F.R. §2510.96–1.

Investment Advice Regulation. 76 Fed. Reg. 66,136 n. 8 (Oct. 25, 2011).

Joint Committee (1970). Staff of Joint Committee on Internal Revenue Taxation, *General Explanation of the Tax Reform Act of 1969* (H.R. 13270, 91st Cong., P.L. 91–172): 109–14.

Kennedy, K. (2008). 'The Demise of Defined Benefit Plans for Private Employers.' *Tax Notes,* 179 (Oct. 13): 200–2.

Langbein, J. (2007). 'Trust Law as Regulatory Law: The Unum/Provident Scandal and Judicial Review of Benefit Denials under ERISA.' 101 *Northwestern. University Law Review,* 1315: 1327.

Lockheed Corp. v Spink (1996). 517 U.S: 882, 887–90.

McFarland, B. (2013). 'Retirement Plans Offered by 2013 *Fortune* 100.' *Towers Watson Insider* (Nov. 14). <http://www.towerswatson.com/en-US/Insights/Newsletters/Americas/insider/2013/retirement-plans-offered-by-2013-Fortune-100>.

Moench v. Robertson (1995). 62 F.3d 553 (3d Cir.): 568.

MPPAA. The Multiemployer Pension Plan Amendments Act of 1980, P.L. 96–364, 94 Stat. 1208.

Munnell, A., F. Golub-Sass, M. Soto, and F. Vitagliano (2006). *Why are Healthy Employers Freezing their Pensions?* Issue in Brief, 44 (Center for Retirement Research). <http://crr.bc.edu/briefs/why-are-healthy-employers-freezing-their-pensions>.

Pegram v. Herdrich (2000). 530 U.S. 211: 225.

PPA. The Pension Protection Act of 2006, P.L. 109–280, 120 Stat. 780.

Pilot Life Ins. Co. v. Dedeaux (1987). 481 U.S. 41: 54.

Purcell, P. (2009). *Pension Issues: Lump-Sum Distributions and Retirement Income Security* (RL30496). Washington, DC: Congressional Research Service. <http://digitalcommons.ilr.edu/key_workplace/586>.

President's Committee on Corporate Pension Funds and Other Private Retirement and Welfare Programs (1965). *Public Policy and Private Pension Programs: A Report to the President on Private Employee Retirement Plans.* Washington, DC: President's Committee.

Revenue Act of 1921. 42 Stat. 227.

Revenue Act of 1926. 44 Stat. 9.

Revenue Act of 1942. P.L. 77–753, 56 Stat. 798.

United States Treasury (1942). *Revenue Revision of 1942: Hearings Before the House Comm. on Ways and Means,* 77th Cong., 2d Sess. (Apr. 10, 1942).

Rev. Rul. 71–91 (1971). 1971–1 C.B. 116.

S. Rep. No. 127 (1973). Retirement Income Security for Employees Act of 1973, 93d Cong., 1st Sess.

S. Rep. No. 313 (1985). Tax Reform Act of 1986, 99th Cong., 2d Sess: 578.

S. Rep. No. 383 (1973). Private Pension Plan Reform, 93rd Cong., 1st Sess: 1, 10–11, 18–19.

Shea, R., R. Newman, and K. Mineka (2011). 'Hybrid Plans at the Crossroads: Will Treasury and the IRS Allow Them to be Defined Benefit Plans?' *Pensions and Benefits Daily* (BNA, Inc.), 107. <http://www.bna.com/uploadedFiles/Content/Press/Hybrid_Plans_at_the_Crossroads.pdf>.

SEPPAA. The Single-Employer Pension Plan Amendments Act of 1986, Title XI of the Consolidated Omnibus Budget Reconciliation Act of 1985, P.L. 99–272, 100 Stat. 82,237.

Steinman v. Hicks (2003). 352 F.3d 1101 (7th Cir.): 1103.

Towers Watson (2012). *Pensions in Transition: Retirement Plan Changes and Employer Motivations.* <www.towerswatson.com/en/Insights/IC-Types/Survey-Research-Results/2012/05/Pensions-in-Transition-Retirement-Plan-Changes-Survey-2012-Report>.

United States Congress (1937). Tax Evasion and Avoidance, *Hearings Before the Joint Comm. on Tax Evasion and Avoidance,* 75th Cong., 1st Sess. (July 2): 294.

VanDerhei, J. (2006). *Defined Benefit Plan Freezes: Who's Affected, How Much, and Replacing Lost Accruals,* Issue Brief, 291. Washington, DC: Employee Benefit Research Institute.

White v. Marshall & Ilsley Corp. (2013). 714 F.3d 980 (7th Cir.): 986.

Wooten, J. (2004). *The Employee Retirement Income Security Act of 1974: A Political History.* Berkeley-Los Angeles: Univ. of California Press.

Yang, J. L. (2014). 'At AOL, Backlash over 401(k) Cuts—and Rationale.' *Washington Post,* Feb. 8: A1.

Part III

Pension Reform: Lessons from Abroad

Chapter 12

The Promise of Defined Ambition Plans: Lessons for the United States

A. Lans Bovenberg, Roel Mehlkopf, and Theo E. Nijman

This chapter explores defined ambition (DA) schemes that provide variable annuities to participants. These schemes are based on occupational pension schemes in the Netherlands in which participants—rather than an external sponsor—bear the balance sheet risks of pension funds. These Dutch schemes have evolved from traditional defined benefit (DB) schemes with employers as external risk sponsors. The government of the United Kingdom is looking at DA schemes as one of the ways to strengthen occupational pension provision in the UK (Department for Work and Pensions 2013). Also some public sector pension schemes in the United States are considering risk sharing among participants as a way to reduce plan costs and risks imposed on taxpayers as external risk sponsors (e.g. Novy-Marx and Rauh 2013). Our analysis addresses the key issues associated with a move from the DB design towards DA schemes.

The chapter is structured as follows.[1] First, we describe the Dutch pension system, followed by an investigation of the major strengths of Dutch occupational schemes. Next, we analyze the major weaknesses of Dutch occupational systems as revealed by the financial crisis. These weaknesses originate in the legacy of the DB design in terms of (1) communicating and setting risk exposures; (2) valuing annuities; and (3) accruing new benefits and determining pension contributions. These weaknesses led to proposals for DA schemes. We then describe the key features of these schemes and describe the Dutch policy debate on occupational pensions in general and DA schemes in particular. This includes a review of various obstacles to the actual implementation of DA plans. Subsequently, we draw lessons for the United States by comparing DA schemes with mainstream defined contribution (DC) schemes. Finally, we offer conclusions on the promise of DA for the United States, including for public sector plans.

Dutch Occupational Pensions

Three-pillar system

The Dutch pension system consists of three pillars. The first is a pay-as-you-go public pension scheme. This Beveridge-type public system provides a uniform, flat pension to all residents at a level that is related to the minimum wage rather than individual earnings. Most other continental EU countries, by contrast, feature Bismarckian earnings-related public pensions. Accordingly, compared to other EU governments, the Dutch government provides only a relatively small part of pension income for workers who earn middle and higher incomes. If these workers want to maintain their standards of living in retirement, they need additional pension provisions. This is where the second pillar of pension provision (i.e. occupational pensions) enters the picture. In contrast to the first pillar, the second pillar is earnings-related, and it aims to maintain the standard of living of middle-class workers during retirement. The third pillar consists of voluntary personal pension provisions, which are tax-favored up to a ceiling. This last pillar is especially important for self-employed individuals who lack occupational pension provisions.

Occupational pensions

Our chapter focuses on the occupational pension schemes in the second pillar. These are typically part of labor contracts negotiated between unions and employers in collective labor agreements; employees are thus obliged to participate in the negotiated pension scheme. As a result, occupational schemes cover more than 90 percent of the labor force. These schemes are funded, and the value of assets in the second pillar currently amounts to about €1 trillion (140 percent of GDP).

Dutch pension funds are independent trusts with their own governance and administrative structures. The governing board of a pension fund has traditionally consisted of equal representatives of employers and unions, although recently retirees and independent specialists have also been able to become board members. These representatives act as fiduciary trustees. Industry-wide pension funds arrange pensions for workers in a specific sector of the economy. These sectoral funds own more than two-thirds of the assets in the second pillar, and account for more than 80 percent of active participants. A company can opt out of an industry fund only if it offers a better pension plan than the plan offered by the sectoral fund.[2] This mandatory participation of firms in sectoral arrangements contributes to the high coverage of occupational pensions in the Netherlands.

Benefit entitlements in terms of annuities

The occupational plans seek to generate a specific lifetime income stream during retirement, and property rights are defined in terms of a (deferred) annuity. Years of service and a reference wage typically determine the benefit entitlement level. In the past, the reference wage was the final rate of pay, but over the last decade, most funds have moved to career-average schemes. In the latter schemes, entitlements to deferred annuities accrue based on a percentage of the average wage level during the career. These schemes typically aim at an annuity level of about 75 percent of average pay (including the flat public benefit) after 40 years of service. The benefit accrual (in terms of annuity level) is uniform across age groups. Hence, if the aim is to provide 75 percent of average pay after a working career of 40 years, the annual accrual rate is 1.875 percent (75/40). The uniform accrual rate of annuity units implies that benefits are backloaded, because the time value of money implies that the value of the (deferred) annuity (as a percentage of the wage) rises with age. Industry funds charge the same premium rate for the annuity units irrespective of age. Hence, firms with a younger workforce subsidize firms with an older workforce.[3]

The goal is to index the deferred annuity to the development of contractual wages during the accumulation phase. Some funds also aspire to link annuities to the development of contractual wages during the payout phase. Other funds aim to provide cost-of-living adjustments during the decumulation phase.

Payout conditional on performance

The aspired annuity levels represent the plans' ambitions rather than a guarantee. That is, a pension fund aims to index the pension rights, but the bonus payments are conditional on the financial performance of the fund. Not only is indexation conditional on fund performance, but also the nominal (or 'base') pension can be cut if the assets of a fund fall below the value of the nominal liabilities (i.e. the value of the annuities excluding indexation).[4] Dutch solvency regulation requires that a funding shortage (calculated on the basis of the value of nominal liabilities) is resolved within a three-year period in expectation. The length of the recovery period has temporarily been increased to five years in the aftermath of the recent financial crisis. In calculating the scope for recovery, funds can use expected returns on assets. Hence, risk premiums on risky assets are assumed to contribute to the potential for recovery. But funds are not allowed to increase mismatch risk if they are in a recovery program.

Nominal liabilities computed with market interest rates

For the purpose of solvency regulations, Dutch pension funds must calculate nominal liabilities on the basis of the term structure of nominal interest rates (based on European swap rates) published by the Dutch Central Bank. This market-based valuation method, introduced in 2007, thus assumes that nominal liabilities are guarantees.[5] Before 2007, pension funds discounted their liabilities against a fixed discount rate of 4 percent. The introduction of valuation on the basis of market interest rates did not have a substantial effect on funding rates at the time, as market interest rates in 2007 were close to 4 percent.

Strengths of Dutch Occupational Plans

This section explores the main strengths of Dutch occupational pension schemes compared to mainstream DC schemes.

Advanced risk management and protection against behavioral biases

Workers in the Netherlands are automatically enrolled in pension plans, which reduces marketing and other transaction costs, and protects individuals against myopia and other behavioral biases. Such co-operative pension plans allow individuals with limited financial capabilities to delegate complex saving, investment, payout, and insurance decisions to professionals. In fact, the plans assist individuals to properly exploit their long-run investment horizons and to gain access to complex investment strategies at low costs.

Pension funds also manage interest-rate and inflation risk, seeking to realize their ambition to index retirement income to wages and/or prices. Hence the hedge portfolio is defined in terms of income streams during retirement. Indeed, the main risks (e.g. investment risk, inflation risk, and interest-rate risk) are managed so as to hedge risks on behalf of households while at the same time exploiting the risk premiums on various risk factors by optimizing the trade-off between return and risk. This asset-liability management thus results in liability-driven investment. More sophisticated, illiquid, and long-term investments by institutional investors help to stabilize financial markets and facilitate macroeconomic stability.

Protection against agency issues

The board of trustees of a Dutch pension fund contracts out several financial services to asset managers and other providers of financial services.

Accordingly, with the employer as a distribution platform, competition occurs on a wholesale level rather than a retail level. By joining forces in a professionally run co-operative pension fund, workers in effect strengthen their buying power in financial markets and markets for financial services. This also permits them to exploit scale economies and discipline commercial financial service providers to act in the interests of pension fund members, who tend to lack sufficient expertise to contract complex financial services.

Pooling of idiosyncratic longevity risk and completion of financial markets

In addition to addressing agency and governance issues, Dutch pension funds reduce selection in longevity insurance through compulsory risk pooling. This facilitates the pooling of idiosyncratic longevity risk, thereby reducing the costs of providing lifetime income streams. Collective risk-pooling not only combats adverse selection in insurance of idiosyncratic longevity risk, but it also allows fund members to trade systematic risks that are not (yet) traded in financial markets. In particular, young members can share in systematic longevity risks faced by older cohorts. To illustrate, if a cohort lives longer than expected, the resulting lower funding rate harms the indexation of the deferred annuities offered to younger cohorts. Moreover, by linking pension benefits to the wages of workers, pension funds allow retirees to share in the wage risks of workers.[6]

Weaknesses of Dutch Occupational Plans

The major weaknesses of Dutch occupational pension plans were exposed by the financial crisis. They relate to the legacy of a DB design with external risk sponsors. A first weakness involves the risk profiles of retirement income. In particular, funds' investment policies do not originate from participants' desired risk profiles. That is, the pension contract does not allow much scope to tailor the risk profile to the needs of different generations. A second main weakness concerns the valuation of pension rights. This valuation is based on the fiction of guaranteed pensions, even though pension funds in fact offer variable annuities whose actual value depends on investment policy, funding rates, and the rules for distributing surpluses and deficits. Next, we investigate how the ambiguity surrounding risk profiles and valuation gives rise to intergenerational conflicts about the investment profile of the fund and the ownership of the assets.

Ambiguous risk profiles and liabilities for communication and investment

Lack of risk-bearing capital

As the ratio of pensioners to workers rises due to aging and the maturation of pensions systems, pension liabilities have increased compared to the premium base. As a direct consequence, large changes in contributions are now required to absorb the risk of mismatch between assets and liabilities. Indeed, for many companies, the risks of their DB pension schemes have started to dominate those of the core business. These firms therefore no longer wish to underwrite the risks of their pension funds. Another reason why contributions can no longer absorb shocks is that contribution rates to occupational pensions have reached rather high levels due to low interest rates, increased longevity, and additional recovery contributions aimed at reducing funding shortages (Figure 12.1). Moreover, volatile contributions that are inversely related to the funding rates of pension funds impact the economy in a pro-cyclical fashion. As a result of these developments, employers and workers supply less risk-bearing capital to pension funds in the form of contributions that stabilize funding rates. Accordingly, participants must supply more risk-bearing capital through pension rights that absorb mismatch

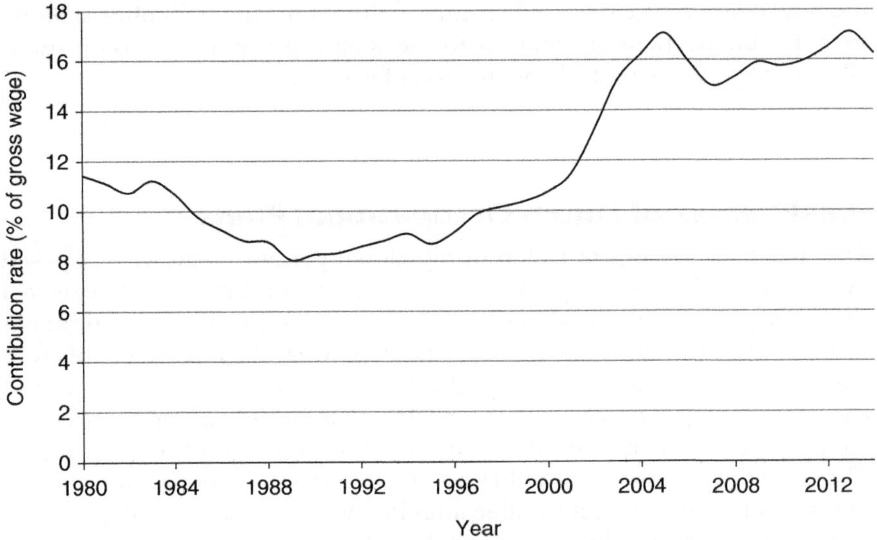

Figure 12.1 Average total (employee plus employer) contributions to Dutch occupational pensions as percentage of gross wage income, 1980–2013

Source: CPB (2014).

on the balance sheet of pension funds. Participants rather than contributors have, in fact, become the residual risk bearers of pension funds.

Substantial mismatch risk due to macroeconomic shocks

Pensions funds' increased financial risks became quite apparent during the financial crisis, which generated a substantial mismatch between the funds' assets and liabilities. Figure 12.2 displays the development of the average nominal funding rate of Dutch pension funds during the last 25 years.[7] Prior to the onset of the financial crisis in 2007, the average nominal funding rate amounted to about 145 percent. The financial crisis in 2008 caused the average nominal funding ratio to decrease substantially to a low of about 90 percent in the first quarter of 2009.

Three main factors contributed to the fall of funding rates. First, in combination with the use of the term structure of nominal interest rates to compute the value of nominal liabilities, the sharp decline in nominal interest rates during the financial crisis boosted the present value of nominal pension liabilities. Indeed most of the decline in the funding rate between 2007 and 2011 can be attributed to lower nominal interest rates. The second factor behind the drop in funding rates was lower mortality. Following major healthcare reforms in 2001, retirees' mortality rates dropped more substantially than anticipated. Upward revisions of life expectancy have depressed average funding rates by about 5 percent. The

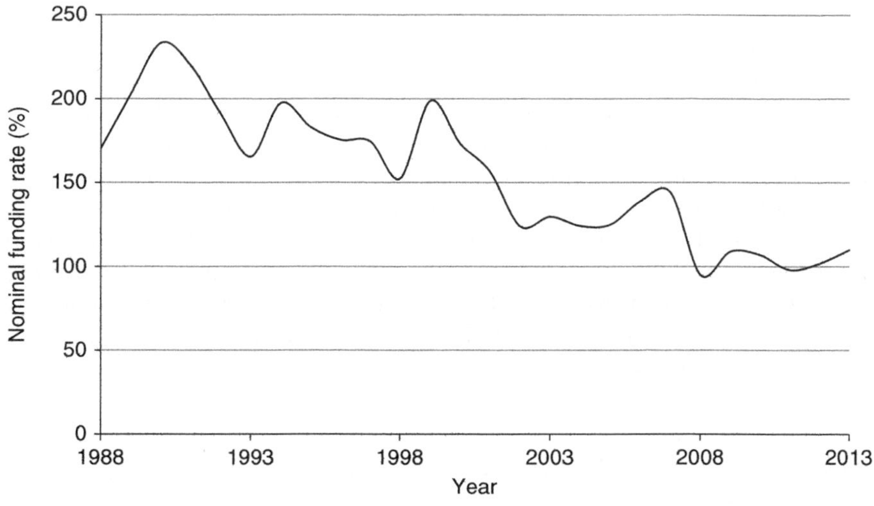

Figure 12.2 Average nominal funding rate of Dutch occupational pension funds, 1988–2013

Source: CPB (2014).

final factor affecting funding rates involves the asset side of the balance sheet. In particular, the worldwide collapse of share prices in the immediate aftermath of the financial crisis reduced asset values dramatically.

The rise in pension liabilities as a result of lower interest rates was not sufficiently compensated by the increase in the value of bonds (or interest derivatives) on the asset side of the pension balance sheet. This was because the funds did not fully hedge nominal interest-rate risk after the 2007 move to employ nominal interest rates in computing liabilities. On average, Dutch pension funds hedge only around 45 percent of the nominal interest rate risk on their liabilities through positions in nominal bonds and interest derivatives. Moreover, there is substantial heterogeneity in the degree to which funds have hedged interest rate risks. Additionally, funds differ in how they define their liabilities for their own risk-management purposes, even though the public supervisor uses the construct of nominal guaranteed liabilities to compute funding rates. In particular, in the face of fluctuating (wage) inflation expectations, funds must choose which kind of income liability to hedge: either a nominal pension benefit or a (wage) indexed pension income stream. In particular, short-term debt instruments allow funds to take advantage of rising nominal interest rates if wage inflation expectations increase so as to protect the real value of pensions. This investment policy, however, leaves the fund vulnerable to the risk that falling nominal interest rates will worsen the nominal funding rate, necessitating a cut in nominal pension rights. In the aftermath of the financial crisis, this tension between hedging *nominal* and *real* liabilities has become especially stark, depending in part on whether one believes that changes in nominal interest rates are primarily driven by changes in real interest rates, or by changes in expectations about inflation and the inflation risk premium.

As regards investment risk, various funds have also taken rather different decisions. Indeed, supervisory authorities do not force pension funds to match their nominal liabilities if capital buffers become low.[8] The supervisory rules thus leave substantial discretion to the pension funds on how to respond to low funding rates in terms of their investment risk. Some pension funds chose to defend nominal pension rights by not only matching these nominal obligations through hedging nominal interest-rate risk but also by cutting back on investment risk. Other pension funds, by contrast, continue taking investment risk in order to retain upside potential.

Insufficient scope for tailor-made risk profiles gives rise to intergenerational conflict

The trade-off pension funds face in setting their investment policies can also be regarded as a trade-off between the interests of young and old participants. As many authors advocating life cycle investing have shown (e.g. Bodie et al. 1992; Cocco et al. 2005), taking substantial investment risk is more attractive for young participants than for retirees. Similarly, protecting nominal guarantees by hedging nominal interest rate risks is primarily in the interest of the elderly. The current Dutch occupational pension plans impose uniform investment and adjustments in pension rights (indexation and cuts in nominal pensions) for all participants. This limits the scope to attune risk exposure to the needs of various cohorts (Ambachtsheer 2013), although intertemporal smoothing of shocks allows for limited age differentiation between the risk exposures of various generations (Boelaars et al. 2014). The limited scope for tailor-made risk profiles may lead to suboptimal risk profiles and result in intergenerational conflicts over the investment policy of the pension funds.

Nominal cuts of pensions in payment due to materialized interest-rate risk

Many pension funds that had deliberately chosen to continue to take mismatch risk at low nominal funding rates saw their nominal funding rates fall below 100 percent when interest rates sank during the financial crisis and the subsequent Euro crisis. Most of these pension funds were unable to recover from their funding shortage within the maximum period of five years without cuts in nominal pension rights, including pensions in payment.

The biggest wave of cuts in pensions in payment occurred in 2013: in that year, 68 pension funds (of 415) were required to cut nominal pension rights. These cuts affected around 2 million active participants (who pay contributions), 1.1 million retired participants, and 2.5 million inactive participants who neither paid contributions nor received benefits.[9] Figure 12.3 shows a bar chart displaying the size of pension cuts. Around 2 million participants faced a relatively large cut of 6 or 7 percent. A cut of 7 percent is observed frequently because the Dutch government allowed pension funds to cap the level of pension cuts in 2013 at 7 percent and defer the remainder to 2014.[10]

Most pension funds have been unable to provide (full) indexation in recent years. Table 12.1 illustrates that actual indexation to retirees has lagged indexation ambitions: on average, retirees have experienced a decline of around 10 percent of their replacement rates as a consequence of inadequate indexation. This decline is expected to grow because the current low funding rates will not allow pension funds to provide full indexation in the near future.

Inadequate communication about risks profile

Pension funds in the Netherlands typically communicate to participants in terms of nominal pension rights, but they are rather silent on future

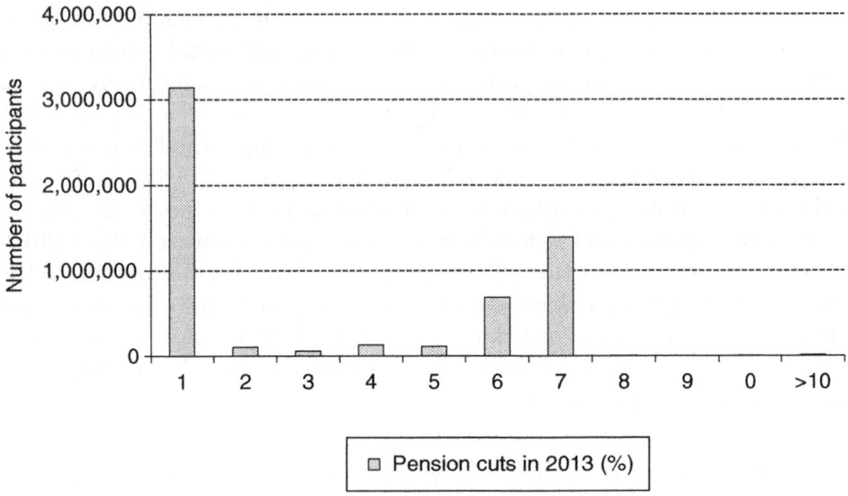

Figure 12.3 Number of participants affected by cuts in Dutch occupational pensions in 2013

Source: DNB (2015).

TABLE 12.1 Average indexation shortfall, 2008–14

	2008	2009	2010	2011	2012	2013	2014
Indexation ambition	1.84	3.76	1.66	1.2	1.35	1.47	1.11
Actual indexation	2.91	0.17	0.42	0.02	0.02	0.08	0.18

Source: DNB (2015).

indexation prospects and the possibilities of future cuts in nominal pension rights. Communication to participants has not yet adapted to the new reality of participants being the main risk bearers.[11] Hence, the fact that pension payouts could be cut came as an unpleasant surprise to many pensioners and eroded the confidence of active members. Table 12.2 shows that the percentage of people expressing 'some or a lot of trust' in pension funds declined from 64 percent before the crisis to 42 percent after the crisis.[12]

Pension funds aren't 'walking the talk': incomplete investment policy

The cuts in pension payouts have made it clear that the pension contract does not provide guarantees, even though pension funds continue to communicate in terms of nominal pension rights. Indeed, pension funds do not 'walk the talk.' Whereas they suggest that they supply fixed annuities, they

TABLE 12.2 Confidence in pension funds, the government, banks, and insurers (% of Dutch people that have some or a lot of confidence)

	2004 (%)	2006 (%)	2009 (%)	2011 (%)
Pension funds	53	64	44	42
Government	37	42	45	41
Banks	32	37	25	34
Insurers	32	37	18	20

Source: Van Dalen and Henkens (2011).

actually provide variable annuities because they continue to deliberately take mismatch risk at low funding rates in the absence of the possibility of raising contributions to make up funding deficits. The financial crisis thus exposed a major weakness of the Dutch pension system: the ambiguity of the risk profiles of future pension payments on account of incomplete investment policy, and a mismatch between the communicated risk profile and the funds' investment policy. In particular, risk profiles are not specified and communicated ex ante, and supervisory authorities do not force pension funds to make their investment policies consistent with their communicated risk profiles.

To address this weakness, pension funds would have to change their ways. One solution ('do what you currently say' or 'walk your current talk') would imply a so-called 'combination-contract' in which there is a 'base' level of guaranteed pension payments and a remainder that is conditional on performance.[13] A combination-contract, which involves both debt-like and equity-like claims, would require solvency rules to force pension funds to defend the guaranteed part of obligations through dynamic investment policies reducing investment risks and interest-rate risks at low funding rates.[14] A second solution ('say what you currently do' or 'talk about your current walk') would change the funds' communicated liability structure by communicating that all pension rights have become uncertain in a particular statistical sense.

Lack of economic valuation and fair pricing: ambiguous property rights

Lack of economic valuation

Valuation of pension rights in the Netherlands is still based on an outdated DB design, which opens the door for a non-transparent redistribution of wealth across various stakeholders. In particular, pension rights are valued as guaranteed nominal annuities, rather than variable annuities resulting from the funds' investment policies in combination with the withdrawal of external risk bearers. By contrast, an economic valuation of pension rights would take into account the option value of individuals' claims on collective buffers. These conditional claims depend on the rules for distributing surpluses and funding shortages across stakeholders. Next we explain how the lack of economic valuation (and thus fair pricing of pensions entitlements) leads to ambiguity about ownership rights when the pension contract and investment policies are changed, or if annuity units are bought and sold.

Incomplete pension fund policies

A necessary condition for determining the economic value of individual property rights is that the pension contract must be complete, in the sense that the rules for distributing risk are known in advance and are not subject to discretionary changes. Yet most pension contracts do not offer transparency ex ante about the rules for allocating the mismatch risk on the balance sheet of pension funds across stakeholders ex post. Although pension funds have recently strived to make risk sharing contracts more complete, these contracts usually offer little more than guidelines for the governing board. Indeed, the pension governing boards still retain substantial discretion in redistributing resources across stakeholders. For example, most contracts tend to stay silent on what happens in the situation of a funding deficit. It is also unclear what happens if the buffers rise above the levels necessary to fully finance indexed pensions. Discretionary decision-making by pension fund boards may alter the value of individual annuities and thus redistribute wealth positions across stakeholders, if the different variable annuities produced by a change in distributional rules or investment policy are not exchanged at fair prices (see also Kocken 2012). This politicizes decision-making in pension funds.

Incomplete government policies

In addition to pension fund board discretion, the policies of the government are another source of ambiguity about the distribution of risk and thus the economic value of pension ownership rights. The Dutch government regularly adjusts the rules for pension funds and thereby alters how mismatch risk is allocated across stakeholders. If the original and new variable annuities as a result of a change in government policy are not exchanged at fair prices, the government in effect redistributes economic value across participants.

The discount rate is particularly important in allocating the distribution of resources across stakeholders, because it determines the financial position of a pension fund. This in turn determines pension payments to retirees in the short run, and also the resources remaining for pension payments in the long run. Starting in 2007, discounting was no longer based on a fixed discount rate of 4 percent but on the term structure of nominal interest rates. This new discounting method caused the funding position to be highly sensitive to changes in nominal interest rates. The low interest rates during the Euro crisis led to proposals for a more stable discount rate. The current valuation method is also controversial because it is still based on guaranteed nominal annuities. Alternative valuation methods have been proposed that aim to provide a better representation of the risk characteristics of the variable annuities that are actually being provided. A key property of these proposals is that they all embody reduced sensitivity to fluctuations in interest rates. Proponents of these alternative valuation methods argue that fluctuations in the risk-free rate are less relevant for the valuation of variable annuities, so that the price of new annuities should be less sensitive to time-variation in the market price of certainty as reflected in interest rates of safe assets (SER 2013).

In 2012, the Dutch government adopted the so-called 'Ultimate Forward Rate' (UFR) method for discounting liabilities with long maturities discussed in Solvency-II proposals. The introduction of UFR with fixed annuity units led to an instantaneous 3 percent increase in the funding rate of the average Dutch pension fund. Improved finances have allowed the pension funds to provide more indexation or reduce the size of required pension cuts.[15] Hence the introduction of the UFR methodology shows how adjustments in regulation can lead to redistribution of market value across stakeholders. Another example of an adjustment in government regulation is the 2008 temporary increase in the maximum number of years that pension funds are allowed to be underfunded, from three to five years. Frequent changes in the rules for computing and distributing mismatch risk have led to intergenerational conflicts and politicized pensions.

To minimize political conflicts, the Dutch government has asked CPB (an independent government body for economic policy analysis) on several occasions to calculate the redistributive effects between generations that result from proposed changes in regulation (CPB 2012a, 2012b, 2013). CPB applied generational accounting to calculate the change in the value of pension rights. These calculations employ stochastic discounting of projected stochastic cash flows instead of valuation based on nominal guarantees.

Intergenerational conflict about investment policy due to asymmetric contract

A valuation based on guaranteed nominal annuities, which the pension funds currently report, fails to recognize that the economic value of individual annuities depends on the pension fund's investment policy. In particular, the relatively short recovery period of five years for a funding shortfall implies that the downside risk associated with risk taking is allocated primarily to the older generations. The upward potential, by contrast, is used to build up collective buffers, which primarily benefit the younger generations. With the old in effect providing a put option to the young participants, an intergenerational conflict emerges about the investment profile of the fund. The old will seek to hedge nominal interest rate risk and reduce investment risk, the young will prefer to take more interest rate and investment risk in order to increase the economic value of their pension entitlements. Due to this asymmetry in the current pension contract (another legacy of the DB approach), in order to protect the value of individual property rights, one should make the contract complete in terms not only of distributional rules but also investment policy.

Non-transparent redistribution when selling and buying annuity units

The lack of fair pricing of annuity units due to inadequate valuation leads to redistribution of wealth if annuity units are bought and sold. In particular, failure to conduct economic valuation of pension rights implies that transfers of pension rights across funds may hurt either those who transfer the rights or the remaining participants. This distorts decisions to transfer value across funds. Moreover, since the price charged for new pension rights does not reflect the economic value of these rights, the accumulation of new pension entitlements by workers causes non-transparent redistribution between retirees and inactive participants, on the one hand, and workers who are accumulating new (deferred) annuities, on the other. This problem has worsened due to another legacy of the DB schemes: a fixed accrual rate for newly accrued entitlements. A fixed accrual rate implies that the economic costs of pension accruals vary over time as a result of fluctuations in the price of the annuity units. With fair prices, this system of a fixed accrual rate independent of the price of the accrued annuity units is pro-cyclical because the price of annuity units tends to be high in recessions (with low interest rates) and low in booms (with high interest rates). To prevent such pro-cyclicality, the present Dutch system allows for smoothing of the price over time but this leads to non-transparent redistribution between existing participants and active workers. The pro-cyclicality could be mitigated without these value transfers, either by moving to a more stable discount rate (as proposed by SER 2013) or by employing variable accrual rates that fluctuate inversely with the price of the annuity units.

Difficulties in introducing elements of individual choice

With risks increasingly being shifted onto participants, interest has grown in giving individuals a greater say in how much risk they want to bear. However, inadequate valuation hinders the introduction of more elements of individual choice, not only in risk profiles but also contribution levels. In particular, individual choices will be distorted as a result of inadequate valuation.[16]

Characteristics of DA Plans

The weaknesses of Dutch occupational DB plans, which became more apparent in the aftermath of the financial crisis, led to proposals to address these weaknesses through the introduction of so-called DA schemes. In this section we describe key features of DA plans, and also explore how these schemes address the shortcomings of DB contracts, and protect the desirable features of traditional occupational schemes described.

Employer as distribution platform for annuities rather than as risk sponsor

DA schemes are similar to DC plans in that they both lack outside risk sponsors: mismatch risk on the fund balance sheet is borne by the participants of the scheme rather than a corporate sponsor. Participants can thus trade risk with outsiders only through tradable financial instruments. This is in the interest of workers for two reasons: first, workers are not exposed to their employer's or industry's credit risk. This is an important advantage because the expected lifetime of firms and industries is declining in the face of ever-more dynamic and competitive economies. Second, by relieving firms of their role as risk sponsor, workers keep firms involved as a distribution platform for occupational pensions. In this way, employers can continue to help address the behavioral factors, agency issues, and the imperfections of insurance and financial markets identified above.

Pension entitlement as (deferred) annuity

Pension entitlements in the DA environment are defined in terms of deferred annuity units (i.e. lifetime income streams beginning at a particular retirement age). Conversion of capital into annuities occurs when contributions are paid, so participants share idiosyncratic longevity risk within the fund's insurance pool. DA schemes thus preserve the advantage of current Dutch contracts in which collective risk-pooling combats selection in longevity insurance.

Risk sharing with complete contract in mutual insurer yields variable annuities

Participants in DA schemes also share the systematic risks associated with joint asset and liability pools on the basis of complete contracts. In particular, if the value of the fund's aggregate liabilities deviates from the value of aggregate assets, the pension contract specifies how annuity units will be adjusted over time so that the aggregate value of individual pension rights continues to match the value of the assets in the fund. The fund can thus be viewed as a stand-alone mutual insurer: all risks within the collective are allocated to plan members, so there is no residual balance sheet risk left to outside shareholders or sponsors. Risk sharing within this fund thus results in variable annuities: annuity units vary with financial and biometric risks in the common asset and liability pools.

Fund liabilities may also include other non-traded risk factors such as (wage) inflation risk.[17] In this way, participants hold claims on notional assets that are not traded in financial markets. DA contracts thus preserve the benefit of traditional collective occupational pension schemes, in that they allow participants to exchange systematic risk factors which are not externally traded.

Innovation in occupational pension schemes

The DA model with variable annuities also offers an innovation in the area of funded occupational pension schemes, just as non-financial defined contribution (NDC) schemes did for pay-as-you-go public schemes (Holzmann et al. 2012). In particular, by replacing DB schemes where corporate risk sponsors absorb risk, both NDC and DA schemes lack external risk sponsors; here, in fact, funding gaps do not affect contribution levels. Both of these schemes allocate risk of joint asset and liability pools across participants on the basis of complete contracts that specify how liabilities must be adjusted if the value of aggregate assets deviates from the value of aggregate liabilities.

Specific forms of risk sharing contracts

The mechanism for allocating mismatch risk in proposed Dutch DA contracts involves some specific features. First of all, the contract is symmetric, so positive shocks in funding are allocated in the same way as are negative shocks. Second, proportional adjustments of annuity units are uniform across individuals, which imposes restrictions on participants' risk exposure. Annuities are all variable, varying with the financial and biometric risk of the common asset and liability pool. Third, income streams provided by the variable annuities are adjusted gradually after an unexpected shock causes a mismatch between assets and liabilities. Accordingly, retirees do bear investment risk but they have some time to adjust their standards of living after an unexpected event. Such smoothing of adjustment of consumption to shocks is consistent with habit formation.

Communication and risk management on basis of consumption frame

Pension rights are communicated not just in terms of capital, but also in terms of the risk profile of an income stream in retirement. In particular, the pension contract specifies how sensitive real income in retirement will be with respect to the various risk factors. These risk profiles for each horizon are the starting point for risk management (Figure 12.4), and specifying this risk profile is the main responsibility of the pension fund board. The fund's investment policy is then determined endogenously such that the risk

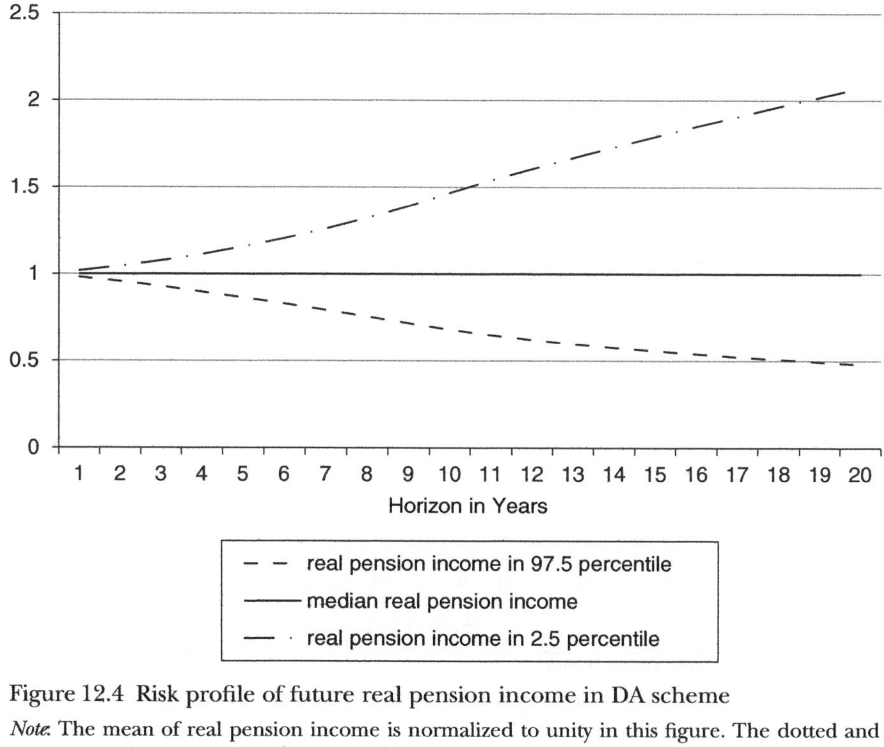

Figure 12.4 Risk profile of future real pension income in DA scheme

Note: The mean of real pension income is normalized to unity in this figure. The dotted and dash-dotted lines illustrate real pension income in the 97.5 and 2.5 percentiles, respectively.

Source: Bovenberg et al. (2015).

surrounding projected pension payments matches desired risk profiles. In this way, the idea of liability-driven investment based on asset-liability management familiar from DB schemes is generalized to stochastic liabilities with risk budgets. In this way, the contract is complete not only in terms of the allocation of mismatch risk across participants, but also in terms of investment policy, so that participants obtain the risk exposures that have been communicated to them. Pension funds 'walk their talk': assets match liabilities.[18] The desired liabilities discipline the investment policy.

As a result of employing a consumption frame for risk management, interest rate risk is actively managed during both the accumulation and payout phases. In addition, contribution levels can be set so as to reach a particular goal for retirement income. In this regard, we can distinguish between a DC scheme which fixes the premium, and a DA scheme which adjusts the premium level so as to attain a particular objective for retirement income.

Economic valuation

Economic valuation of individual property rights over annuity units can be derived endogenously from the stochastic pension promises (i.e. the pension ambitions), which represent the liabilities of the DA scheme. In particular, the deferred stochastic annuities provided by the DA scheme are priced on the basis of the term structure of interest rates amended by a horizon-dependent risk premium that rises with the investment horizon, as illustrated in Figure 12.5 (see Bovenberg et al. 2015).

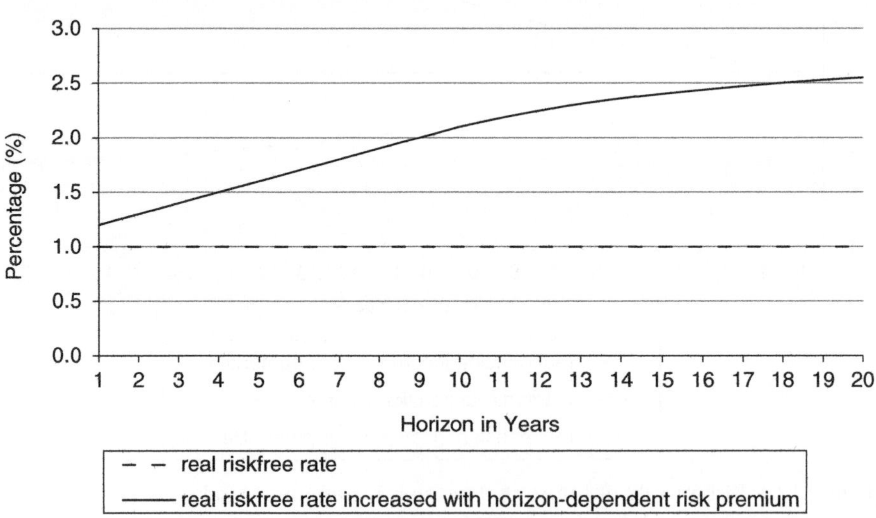

Figure 12.5 Horizon-dependent discount rate of a DA scheme
Source: Bovenberg et al. (2015).

Non-traded risk factors in the common liability pool complicate valuation, since the DA schemes cannot be valued objectively on the basis of prices in financial markets. This gives rise to a trade-off between completing financial markets versus being able to make an objective economic valuation. On the one hand, these schemes allow participants to trade risk factors among themselves that are not yet traded on financial markets, thereby potentially creating value. On the other hand, the prices of these risk factors are difficult to determine objectively, which may give rise to political risk.

The symmetric nature of the pension contract implies that the investment policy of the fund does not affect the market value of individual pension rights for given annuity units (see Bovenberg et al. 2015). The separation between risk exposures and the value of the individual annuities allows trustees to change the risk profile of given annuity units without changing their value. In this way, DA pension funds may be allowed more discretion to modify risk profiles.

Proper valuation is needed to give participants some limited freedom of choice in selecting their own risk profiles or saving levels. In particular, by allowing participants to exchange various types of variable annuities at fair prices, pension funds can provide individuals discretion in selecting their own risk profile and contribution level without imposing externalities on the other participants of the fund.

Market-consistent valuation is also relevant for determining the prices for buying and selling the annuities that do not impose externalities on existing owners of annuity units. In particular, required pension contributions can be derived endogenously from the stochastic pension promises (i.e. the pension ambitions). This is reminiscent of traditional DB schemes in which the pension contributions are determined on the basis of the guaranteed income stream during retirement. Similarly, the value of the variable annuities can be determined in the DA context when individuals want to transfer their pension rights to another pension fund.[19] This avoids distortions.

Economic valuation also helps protect property rights and generational fairness when the risk sharing contract is changed. In particular, the value of property rights should remain constant if a change in the pension contract implies that participants may exchange one type of variable annuity for another. Exchanging variable annuities at fair prices avoids mixing up a change in the pension contract with intergenerational redistribution. This condition of neutrality in market value in case of contract changes allows one to value the contract on a market-consistent basis, even though the contract is incomplete in the sense that it may be changed over time in the face of new information. To illustrate, a single annuity may be transformed into a joint-and-survivor annuity, leaving the total value of the pension right unaffected. Another element that may be subject to change is the way in which discount rates and hence liabilities are computed. In particular, how sensitive the discount rates should be to the nominal interest rate is a controversial issue, and pension funds may differ in how they want to define liabilities. By enforcing fair pricing when the definition of the liabilities changes, supervisors can allow pension funds more discretion in how the funds define liabilities.

It is debatable as to whether changes in the way discount rates are computed should lead to intergenerational distribution. It could be argued that changes in the discount-rate methodology set by the government, based on advice from experts, should lead to similar intergenerational risk sharing as when interest rates change (at given annuity units). To illustrate, a higher assumed risk premium (at a given risk) raises expected future rates of return and thus reduces the current cost of funding an uncertain future pension with a given expectation. The pension contract thus allows generations to share risk factors that are not traded on financial markets (namely, the subjective estimates of experts on the equity risk premium). But allowing changes in the estimated risk premium to redistribute market value across generations may well lead to intergenerational conflicts about the unobservable risk premium. Moreover, pension funds cannot hedge discretionary changes in the assumed risk premium.

Current Status of Pension Reform in the Netherlands

In the Dutch pension agreement of 2010, social partners (i.e. the unions and the national association of employers) proposed moving towards DA-type contracts in occupational pensions. The goal was to allow pension income to adapt to unexpected changes in life expectancy and returns on financial markets. In this way, unexpected biometric and financial shocks would be absorbed in pension rights (i.e. annuity units) rather than in additional contributions from employers and workers. The move towards DA contracts provided risk-bearing capital to the pension funds, given employers' withdrawal as external risk sponsors. The goal was to make the new pension contracts transparent and complete, and to have pension funds communicate the risks implied by the pension contract (including investment policies) to participants. As regards systematic longevity risk, it was proposed that the eligibility age for the public pension and the accrual rate in occupational pensions would both be linked to life expectancy. In particular, the average number of pension years for each generation would be set equal to the average expected pension years for generations who started to collect the public pension between 2000 and 2009.

Government's response

The Dutch government adopted the proposal to increase the retirement age, implementing legislation in 2012 linking the eligibility age for the public pension and the accrual rate for tax-privileged occupational pensions to life expectancy. The eligibility age for the public pension will gradually increase from 65 to 66 during the period 2013–19 and will be further increased to 67 during 2020–3. After 2023, this age will be permanently linked to longevity.

The proposals to move towards DA contracts in the funded pension pillar are still under consideration. It is unclear whether the government will adopt the full set of proposals for DA or whether it will only implement rather small changes to current pension structures.[20] Three main factors complicate the actual implementation of a DA model and explain why the government is reluctant to adopt DA schemes: namely transitional problems, disagreements about risk profiles, and intergenerational conflicts about annuity valuation.

Regarding transitional problems, the proposal anticipated that the new contracts would apply not only to newly accrued pension rights, but also to existing pension rights. Yet this retrospective change in pension contracts could be challenged in court. The Dutch government is reluctant to take on these legal risks and is therefore unwilling to mandate a wholesale conversion to DA contracts. Instead, it advocates that a choice to retrospectively change the pension contract would be the responsibility of the pension funds, and many smaller pension funds fear possible legal risks, though some larger sectoral funds seem willing to accept them.

Two factors complicate the conversion of existing 'DB' rights into 'DA' rights, and they make the outcome of court cases uncertain. First, individual property rights under the current contracts cannot be valued objectively because the contracts are incomplete. Among other things, the economic value of pension rights depends on the portfolio mix because of the asymmetric nature of pension contracts. For this reason, it is not so clear who would gain and who would lose from a transition to DA. Second, the risk profile under current contracts is ambiguous and not clearly specified, nor has it been communicated ex ante. Accordingly, the extent to which the move toward DA changes the risk profile of pension entitlements is unclear. If existing pension rights were interpreted as guarantees, then the move towards DA contracts could be viewed as a debt-equity swap. But as explained above, most pension funds do not match nominal liabilities in their investment policy even though they lack external risk sponsors. For this reason, nominal pension rights are in fact already risk-bearing.

The proposals for DA contracts have also led to heated discussions about the desired risk profile of pension payments. To illustrate, the extent to which pension funds should offer nominal guarantees is controversial. On the one hand, some people argued that guarantees should not be provided, because real guarantees cannot be purchased (the supply of safe inflation-linked bonds is very limited in the Euro area) and are too expensive, especially for workers. On the other hand, some argued in favor of including some form of nominal guarantee to offer some certainty, which also makes the pension product easier to communicate. Moreover, the funds' investment policy can also be better disciplined. Some proponents of the second view denounced contracts without guarantees as 'casino pensions.' At the same time, those who supported nominal guarantees were accused of exploiting participants' money illusions.

A third explanation for why DA plans have not yet been adopted has to do with the combination of the subjective and unstable character of the contracts, and the legacy of the traditional DB mindset with fixed annuity units. In particular, fair pricing is difficult to adopt when the contract (including the discount methodology for computing liabilities) is changed, because then the number of annuity units would have to change.[21] With fixed annuity units, however, a change in the pension contract (including the discounting methodology) results in redistribution of wealth across participants and therefore yields intergenerational conflicts. The experience of the last couple of years shows that smoothing periods and discount rates are, in fact, changed frequently. Some argued that economic valuation under DA would reduce political risks, by increasing transparency about intergenerational redistribution associated with changes in the contract. Others, by contrast, maintained that the discount methodology in DA contracts might be changed even more frequently because the risk premium and expected inflation in the discount rate are difficult to estimate. For this reason, DA contracts might give rise to even more intergenerational conflict than the current DB contracts. Concerns about political risk intensified when the social partners proposed employing the expected return on the portfolio of pension funds as the discount rate for calculating pension liabilities. Critics pointed out that using the expected return as discount rate would result in intergenerational redistribution from older to younger participants, if pension funds were to raise their expected return by investing in riskier assets while not raising the annuity units for young participants.

Market pricing of a variable annuity is hard to adopt because of the legacy of DB thinking in terms of fixed annuity units, not only when contracts are changed but also if new annuity units are bought. Social partners seek to maintain a fixed annual accrual rate (in terms of annuity units) even though they are unwilling to tolerate fluctuations in the contribution rates as a consequence of changes in the economic value of the annuity units. The goals of stabilizing both accrual rates and contribution levels have led to heated discussions about the interest sensitivity of the discount rate. The social partners argued that discount rates should be more stable than nominal interest rates, to ensure that the interest sensitivity of contribution rates does not affect the economy in a pro-cyclical fashion. The discounting methodology debate together with an unwillingness to modify either the fixed accrual rate or annuity units when the discounting methodology is changed has intensified concerns about political risks surrounding DA contracts.

Companies are considering individual defined contribution

Other proposals for pension reforms look beyond DA and focus instead on individual accounts in which entitlements are defined in terms of claims on tradable financial assets without joint liability pools that are difficult to value (see PJO 2013 and WI CDA 2014). Several large companies who operate their own pension funds have lost patience with the slow reform process, and they are now considering a move towards individual DC schemes. Here, entitlements would be defined in terms of claims on tradable financial assets in the accumulation phase, while annuities will be provided in the payout phase.[22] These companies will continue to play a role as a distribution platform, setting defaults and collectively contracting out a pool of insured participants to the financial service industry. Hence, these individual contribution schemes can retain a collective wrapping.

These individual DC schemes do not rely on fixed accrual rates of deferred annuities and thus they reconcile a fixed contribution level with the absence of external effects on the value of existing pension rights. Other advantages are that property rights are defined in terms of capital rather than difficult-to-value annuities. Hence DC plans are less subject to political risk than are DA plans. Moreover, DC plans allow for more tailor-made risk exposures because they are not constrained by a uniform definition of liabilities along with the associated discounting methodology, including the interest rate sensitivity of discounting, prescribed by the government and uniform adjustments of annuity units.

The firms considering a move to a defined contribution plan face three obstacles. First, Dutch tax privileges for individual DC schemes are less generous than those for schemes that define entitlements in terms of deferred annuities. Second, the tax regime is modeled after the fixed accrual rate in DB schemes, which implies that the accrual of pension benefits is backloaded. Hence tax deductible contribution rates are low for young workers and rise sharply with age. Third, legislation stipulates that capital must be converted at retirement into a fixed nominal annuity bought from an insurance company, and guidelines require investment and interest rate risks to be shut down even prior to retirement. Together with the relatively low contribution rates for young workers, this makes it difficult for workers to benefit from the equity risk premium. These regulations also expose workers to inflation risk. Regulatory changes to allow variable annuities for Dutch DC pensions are currently under consideration.

Lessons of DA for DC Schemes in the United States

This section explores the relevance of DA plans for mainstream DC schemes in the United States.

'Consumption frame' during the accumulation phase

Traditional DC schemes can allow a more conservative portfolio when retirement approaches. In doing so, these schemes recognize that taking investment risk is more attractive for young workers than for older workers and retirees. Nevertheless, they are typically based on a 'capital frame,' which fails to recognize the importance of interest rate management for providing a stable lifetime income stream during retirement. Indeed, since interest rates affect expected future returns, rational investors should engage in intertemporal hedging. For this reason, DC risk management could be improved if investments can be 'liability-driven' by adopting the 'consumption frame' of DA.

In DC plans, liabilities are used only to conduct individual asset-liability risk management; unlike in DA, liability risks are not shared with others in a mutual insurance framework. An advantage of the individual approach is that one need not confront controversial valuation issues of joint liabilities and the associated political risks (including changing the valuation methodology of the joint liabilities). A disadvantage of not sharing liability risks is that individuals cannot share risks that are not traded on financial markets.

If all risk factors determining the value of liabilities could be traded in financial markets, then a DC scheme that based its investment strategy on a properly defined individual liability could, in theory, mimic the risk exposures of a DA scheme that defines entitlements in terms of annuity units purchased and sold on the basis of fair economic pricing. The practical advantage of the DA model, however, is that the 'consumption frame' is inherently integrated in its design because individual entitlements are defined in terms of annuity units, and thus income streams. This contrasts with DC schemes which define entitlements in terms of capital, rather than a consumption frame. As a result of this difference in framing, DA schemes typically feature more advanced risk management with more intertemporal hedging. A disadvantage of the 'consumption frame' in DA schemes, however, is that the economic value of individual entitlements may be less well protected in DA schemes than in DC schemes, in which property rights are based on easy-to-value financial assets and thus do not involve controversial valuation methods. In theory, redistributing wealth across individuals can be ruled out in a DA contract if fair pricing were applied in the event that contracts are changed, including the valuation methodology of the joint liabilities. In practice, however, individual ownership rights may be subject to political risk because annuity units may not be adjusted when contracts are changed.

Managing interest rate risk is complicated for three reasons. First, during the accumulation phase, an investor may not yet know which fraction of wealth he intends to use to buy an annuity (as opposed to a lump-sum payment), and what the desired risk profile of the income stream will be (nominal or real, guaranteed or variable). In this case, it may not be clear which 'liability' needs to be hedged during the accumulation phase. Second, if one continued to take investment risk during retirement, the assumed relationship between interest rates and expected returns on risky investments becomes relevant for intertemporal hedging demands. Yet this relationship is difficult to estimate and is subject to substantial model risk. Third, if the aim is to provide an income stream linked to wage inflation in the absence of wage inflation-linked bonds, then the optimal intertemporal hedging strategy in terms of hedging nominal interest rate risk depends on whether one believes that changes in nominal interest rates are driven primarily by changes in real interest rates or by changes in expectations about wage inflation.

Communication in mainstream DC schemes is typically based on the accumulated wealth (the 'capital frame') rather than in terms of a future income stream. Nevertheless, communication in terms of income streams can improve people's understanding of their financial situation, particularly when it provides information on the uncertainty and purchasing power of future consumption streams.[23]

Dealing with longevity risk

Annuitization of pension wealth is mandatory in the Dutch second pillar, as well as for individual DC schemes. The level of annuitization in the United States, by contrast, is relatively low: few retirees voluntarily annuitize their retirement savings. Rational models of risk-averse consumers have difficulty explaining limited annuity demand in view of the potential for mortality credits (especially at the end of life) to reduce the costs of lifetime income. The DA consumption frame may help boost the demand for annuities. In particular, Brown et al. (2008) show that people value annuities more highly in a consumption frame. In a capital frame, by contrast, annuities are seen as a risky asset because the payoff depends on one's uncertain lifespan. Moreover, annuities can help reduce the costs of means-tested public healthcare because they protect individuals from running out of money at the end of life, when people tend to need care (Peijnenburg et al. 2010).

Individual pension plans also must deal with macro longevity risk. When annuities are bought for the payout phase, systematic longevity risk can be (re)insured by an insurance company. One disadvantage of this solution is default risk of the insurer. Insurance also tends to be costly due to required solvency buffers in the absence of a natural hedge against macro longevity risk.[24] An alternative solution, which does not require insurance by a third party, is mutual insurance with collectively owned solvency buffers for the purpose of absorbing unexpected shocks in longevity. Examples of mutual insurance companies offering fixed annuities include TIAA in the US and mutual insurers in Scandinavia. A disadvantage of this form of mutual insurance is that the prices for insurance and the property rights of the mutually owned buffer are not well defined, which may give rise to non-transparent redistribution of wealth within the mutual across various parties. Moreover, younger participants may have to bear substantial longevity risk due to mutual insurers having a large number of old participants that must be shielded from systematic longevity risk.

A DA solution for sharing macro longevity risk within a joint liability pool can provide an attractive alternative. Indeed, DA resembles the CREF annuity scheme in the United States, which adjusts the annuity units of its retired participants in response to longevity shocks (including changes in projected mortality). CREF differs from DA in that unexpected shocks are not smoothed but immediately absorbed in payouts. In view of habit formation, a smoothing procedure in the spirit of DA may be more attractive because it results in gradual adjustment of income streams.

A DA solution with joint liabilities to deal with systematic longevity risk can be restricted to the payout phase. This limits difficult valuation issues, as well as the associated political risks and potential intergenerational conflicts, in the face of substantial uncertainty regarding future retiree mortality. Moreover, workers can absorb changes in remaining life expectancy by working to a later age, whereas retirees cannot. Hence it does not seem to make sense to have retired generations share in workers' systematic longevity risks. One might even want to restrict sharing the risks of joint liabilities to only the oldest cohorts (e.g. cohorts of age 75 and older). In this way, capital is not completely converted into annuity units at the retirement age, and until the age of full annuitization, retirement income comes in part from capital.[25] Indeed, longevity insurance is most valuable at old ages when mortality credits are substantial (Scott 2008).

Workers can also insure the macro longevity risk of older participants in the annuity pool if their capital has not been converted to an annuity. This form of intergenerational risk trading may be welfare-improving because workers can exploit their remaining human capital to absorb shocks (Bodie et al. 1992). A disadvantage is that the risk premium workers require to take on longevity risk of the oldest cohorts is not observable in financial markets and therefore may give rise to intergenerational conflicts.

Heterogeneity in terms of life expectancy within cohorts can lead to intra-generational transfers in collective pools that insure longevity risk at uniform prices: for example, transfers from men to women, or from low earners to high earners. If some forms of redistribution between groups with different mortality rates were to be considered undesirable, these could be ruled out by differentiating prices for annuities based on observed heterogeneity in life expectancy or by forming homogeneous pools. If such transfers were deemed desirable, by contrast, one could employ risk-equalization schemes to reconcile solidarity between groups with free entry in insurance pools.

Variable annuities: smoothing investment risk

Most annuities purchased from accumulated wealth in individual DC schemes currently take the form of guaranteed lifelong income streams. The conversion of wealth into an annuity thus prevents the annuitant from taking advantage of risk premiums. DA schemes, by contrast, allow participants to continue taking investment risk after annuitization. Gradual adjustments after unexpected investment shocks protect retirees from large discrete changes in their consumption levels. Smoothing of shocks in effect leads to life cycle investments beyond the moment of retirement: investment risk is gradually reduced after the retirement age.[26] Smoothing and the associated life cycle investment distinguish DA from most variable annuities in the United States, including the CREF annuities already referred to.

Role of the employer to deal with behavioral and market imperfections

By discharging employers from their role as risk sponsor, DA makes it more attractive for employers to continue to play a role as a distributional platform for occupational pensions. In this way, employers help address (1) behavioral imperfections by setting defaults; (2) agency issues in financial markets by collective procurement of financial services from commercial suppliers; and (3) selection in insurance by pooling longevity risks.

Conclusion: Are DA Schemes Suitable for the United States?

This chapter has explored the strengths and weaknesses of DA pension schemes. In overview, four features of DA hold promise for the United States.

First, the consumption frame used by DA schemes can improve communication and risk management compared to DC schemes. Communication in terms of lifetime income streams may assist individuals to better understand their financial situations. Among other things, it may boost the demand for annuities. Regarding risk management, viewing income streams as liabilities encourages financial providers to engage in better intertemporal hedging.

Second, the DA model addresses systematic longevity risk in annuity provision through risk sharing within a joint liability pool. Collective risk sharing does not suffer from the drawbacks of external insurance (i.e. default risk and costly solvency buffers) or mutual insurance with collective buffers (i.e. non-transparent ownership).

Third, the DA approach allows retirees to continue to benefit from risk premiums without being subject to large discrete fluctuations in consumption, because of the smoothing mechanism that leads to a continuation of life cycle investment throughout retirement. This design for variable annuities reconciles insurance of idiosyncratic longevity risk with taking investment risk.

Fourth, DA schemes allow employers to play an important role in addressing behavioral imperfections, agency issues, and imperfections of insurance and financial markets.

Collective DA plans with joint liabilities may be especially useful during the payout phase for DC schemes. To limit valuation problems, risk sharing of joint liabilities could be limited to the oldest group (e.g. 75 years and older) only.

DA schemes may also be attractive for DB schemes in the public sector, as the latter must reduce risks and costs to taxpayers. Nevertheless, risk sharing with a common liability pool of retirees and workers can lead to intergenerational conflicts about the contract. Additionally, choosing the discount methodology for valuing joint liabilities can be contentious if annuities are not priced and exchanged fairly in the event the contract is changed or when the annuities are bought. In any case, the current underfunding of public sector pension funds in the US must be addressed. Framing entitlements as annuity units results in volatile contributions, unless accruals move inversely with the price of the variable annuities. Moreover, the DA model does not allow for sufficient tailor-made risk management if adjustments of annuity units are uniform across cohorts. For instance, asking retired cohorts to share the longevity risk of the working generations is probably not optimal. Accordingly, a DA plan can be attractive for the payout phase but it holds promise for the accumulation phase only if annuity units are priced fairly, benefit accrual varies with the price of the annuity units, and risk exposure of the annuity units can differ across cohorts.

In sum, for the US, a hybrid solution may be attractive. This would employ a DC frame (defining entitlements in terms of capital) during the accumulation phase and a DA frame (defining entitlements in terms of annuity units) during the payout phase. Such a hybrid combines the strengths of individual DC, including individual ownership, actuarially neutral pension accruals, and scope for tailor-made risk management and individual choice, with the strengths of DA, namely insurance of idiosyncratic longevity risk, sharing of systematic longevity risk, and utilization of the employer as a platform for addressing behavioral and market imperfections.

Endnotes

1. The analysis in this chapter is descriptive in nature; for a theoretical treatment, see Bovenberg et al. (2015), who formalize DA schemes, including the market valuation of variable annuities provided by these schemes.
2. In terms of active participants, the other most important type of pension fund is a company pension fund. To provide pension benefits to its workers, a company does not have to set up its own company pension fund but can also contract out its pension scheme to an insurance company.
3. The combination of uniform accrual and a uniform contribution rate in industry funds implies that occupational pensions are in effect financed in part on a pay-as-you-go basis, as younger workers subsidize older workers. CPB (2014) estimates that the implicit debt, due to the backloading of benefits is approximately 10 percent of total assets.
4. Several Dutch pension funds had to cut pensions in payments in nominal terms in Apr. 2013.
5. This valuation method was amended in 2012 with the Ultimate Forward Rate (UFR) methodology to determine discount rates beyond a horizon of 20 years.
6. In principle, one could share financial market shocks not only between currently living generations but also with generations not yet participating in the pension scheme. From an ex-ante point of view, this intergenerational trade is actually welfare-improving. In practice, however, the scope for such risk sharing is limited by the ability to commit generations to the contract (see Bovenberg and Mehlkopf 2013). As a result, the welfare gain associated with risk sharing with future participants is rather limited in Dutch occupational pension schemes (see Boelaars et al. 2014).
7. Nominal liabilities in Figure 12.2 are calculated on the basis of the term structure of interest rates, also before 2007 when pension funds in fact still employed a fixed discount rate of 4 percent to compute their liabilities.
8. They do, however, prohibit funds that face a nominal funding shortage taking more mismatch risk.

9. These numbers include some double-counting for people who have pension entitlements in more than one pension fund, for example, people who are active participants in one pension fund and who are inactive participants in another pension fund (i.e. people who did not transfer their pension wealth when moving to another company or sector).
10. The wave of pension cuts in 2014 is smaller compared to the year before: 29 pension funds are required to cut pensions. The cuts in 2014 affect around 200,000 retirees, 300,000 active participants, and 600,000 participants who neither pay contributions nor receive benefits. The size of cuts is on average 1.3 percent.
11. The government has announced that, starting in 2015, pension funds should communicate to individual participants projected pension incomes in real terms for both the median outcome and a 'bad weather' scenario.
12. The recent cuts in nominal pension rights in 2013 and 2014 were not measured in this survey, and they are likely to have resulted in a further decline in confidence levels.
13. At current asset levels and interest rates, nominal guarantees would have to be lower than current pension rights if pension funds would maintain enough upward potential for indexing pension rights to (wage) inflation. Such a 'debt-equity swap' would especially necessary for (younger) workers.
14. Ambachtsheer (2013) contains a proposal for the introduction of a two-fund solution in the Netherlands that is based on a similar idea. In Ambachsheer's proposal, young participants start accumulating wealth in a return-seeking mutual fund with a long investment horizon and gradually convert their wealth into an annuity fund during the life cycle.
15. This wealth transfer from workers to retirees through pension payments is partially offset by the impact of the discount rate on the contributions that workers have to pay for new accruals (CPB 2012b).
16. Individual choice in contribution levels is distorted also by the combination of backloading of pension benefits in combination with the uniform pricing of annuities.
17. The supply of inflation-linked bonds is limited in the Euro area. Moreover, these bonds use Euro inflation rather than Dutch price inflation used by pension funds.
18. Even though assets match liabilities ex ante, liabilities may diverge from assets ex post because liabilities are stochastic. Hence, mismatch risk is zero ex post only if liabilities are guaranteed (i.e. non-stochastic).
19. In the present Dutch context, transferring pension rights between pension funds is possible only if workers change jobs. Market valuation, however, would in principle allow workers to select their own pension fund, and hence would allow more competition in pension provision. Drawbacks of this freedom of choice between pension providers are additional transaction and marketing costs as well as less scope for pension funds to benefit from liquidity premiums by investing in illiquid assets.

20. These changes would be aimed at making cuts in nominal annuities after adverse shocks in a more gradual way, in order to prevent large abrupt cuts in pensions during economic downturns.
21. In the payout phase, one could smooth the adjustment in the annuity units to prevent large discrete changes in income levels.
22. These companies are inclined to close the DB fund for new entrants without converting existing rights.
23. This typically requires subjective assumptions about expectations and volatilities of future returns (to calculate future asset values) as well as inflation (to calculate future liabilities). Hence, model risk complicates communication in terms of uncertainty and purchasing power.
24. A more attractive solution may be that the government could issue longevity bonds to cover the tail risk of mortality for the very oldest cohorts, especially if longevity risk on the government balance sheet is limited because the eligibility age for public pension benefits is linked to longevity.
25. To avoid selection issues, one may want to buy the lifetime income stream after age 75 already at age 65. Risk sharing within a single cohort (i.e. generational accounts or 'tontine') may also be possible in large pension funds, but may be problematic at high ages (when the number of surviving participants is small) and the insurance pool is no longer large enough for the 'law of large numbers' to hold.
26. Life cycle investment can alternatively be organized as an escalating annuity that provides nominal guarantees and uses risky investments to provide conditional cost-of-living adjustments (van Bilsen et al. 2013). These solutions do not rebalance equities and risk-free bonds after a negative investment shock. An advantage of these schemes is that nominal income never declines on account of investment risk. A disadvantage is that expected bonuses may fall short of expected inflation after an adverse shock.

References

Ambachtsheer, K. P. (2013). *Towards Individual Solidarity in Pension Design: Why the Dutch Can and Should Lead the Way. The Ambachtsheer Letter.* Toronto, ON: KPA Advisory Services Ltd.

Bilsen, van, S., R. Laeven, and T. Nijman (2013). *Escalerende Garantietoezeggingen,* Netspar Working Paper, 21. Tilburg, the Netherlands: Netspar.

Bodie, Z., R. C. Merton, and W. F. Samuelson (1992). 'Labor Supply Flexibility and Portfolio Choice in a Life-Cycle Model.' *Journal of Economic Dynamics and Control,* 16: 427–49.

Boelaars, I., R. Cox, M. Lever, and R. Mehlkopf (2014). *Risk Sharing in Funded Pension Systems,* Netspar Discussion Paper. Tilburg, the Netherlands: Netspar.

Bovenberg, A. L. and R. J. Mehlkopf (2013). *The Optimal Design and Regulation of Funded Pension Schemes,* Netspar Working Paper, 08/2013–026. Tilburg, the Netherlands: Netspar.

Bovenberg, A. L., R. J. Mehlkopf, and S. Van Bilsen (2015). *Variable Annuities in Pension Schemes with Risk Sharing, Valuation, Investment and Communication*, Netspar Discussion Paper. Tilburg, the Netherlands: Netspar.

Brown, J. R., J. R. Kling, S. Mullainathan, and M. V. Wrobel (2008). 'Why Don't the People Insure Late Life Consumption? A Framing Explanation of the Under-Annuitization Puzzle.' *American Economic Review*, 98(2): 304–9.

Centraal Planbureau (CPB) (2012a). *Generatie-effecten Pensioenakkoord.* The Hague: CPB. <http://www.cpb.nl/publicatie/generatie-effecten-pensioenakkoord>.

Centraal Planbureau (CPB) (2012b). *Aanpassing Toezicht Pensioenfondsen.* The Hague: CPB. <http://www.cpb.nl/publicatie/aanpassing-toezicht-pensioenfondsen-septemberpakket>.

Centraal Planbureau (CPB) (2013). *Premie-effecten Herzien FTK en Versobering Witteveenkader.* The Hague: CPB. <http://www.cpb.nl/publicatie/premie-effecten-herzien-ftk-en-versobering-witteveenkader>.

Centraal Planbureau (CPB) (2014). *Eindrapportage 'Voor- en nadelen van de Doorsneesystematiek'.* The Hague: CPB. <http://www.cpb.nl/publicatie/eindrapportage-voor-en-nadelen-van-de-doorsneesystematiek>.

Cocco, J. F., F. J. Gomes, and P. J. Maenhout (2005). 'Consumption and Portfolio Choice over the Life Cycle.' *Review of Financial Studies*, 18: 492–533.

De Nederlandsche Bank (DNB) (2015). *Macroeconomic Statistics Pension Funds.* Amsterdam: DNB.

Holzmann, R., E. Palmer, and D. Robalino (2012). *Non-financial Defined Contribution Pension Schemes in a Changing Pension World.* Washington, DC: World Bank. <http://hdl.handle.net/10986/9378>.

Kocken, T. (2012), 'Pension Liability Measurement and Intergenerational Fairness: Two Case Studies.' *Rotman International Journal of Pension Management*, 5(1): 16–24.

Novy-Marx, R. and J. D. Rauh (2013). *Linking Benefits to Investment Performance in US Public Pension Systems*, NBER Working Paper, 18491. Cambridge, MA: National Bureau of Economic Research.

Peijnenburg, K., T. Nijman, and B. Werker (2010). *Health Cost Risk and Optimal Retirement Provision. A Simple Rule for Annuity Demand*, Netspar Working Paper, 05/2010–018. Tilburg, the Netherlands: Netspar.

PJO (2013). *Een Nieuw Pensioenstelsel!* <http://nieuwpensioenstelsel.nl>.

Scott, J. (2008). 'The Longevity Annuity: An Annuity for Everyone?' *Financial Analyst Journal*, 64(1): 40–8.

Sociaal-Economische Raad (SER) (2013). *Naar Macrostabiele Pensioenen.* The Hague: SER. <http://www.ser.nl/nl/publicaties/adviezen/2010–2019/2013/macrostabiele-reele-pensioenen.aspx>.

UK Department of Work and Pensions (2013). *Reshaping Workplace Pensions for Future Generations.* Cm 8710. London: The Stationery Office.

van Dalen, H. and K. Henkens (2011). 'Hoe herwinnen pensioenfondsen, banken en verzekeraars het vertrouwen?' *MeJudice*, 30 June. <http://www.mejudice.nl/artikelen/detail/hoe-herwinnen-pensioenfondsen-banken-en-verzekeraars-het-vertrouwen?forceFullWebsite=true>.

Wetenschappelijk Instituut van het CDA (2014). *Naar een Solide en Solidair Pensioenstelsel, bouwstenen voor hervorming.* The Hague: Wetenschappelijk Instituut voor het CDA.

Chapter 13

Insights from Switzerland's Pension System

Monika Bütler

Old age insurance systems around the world face similar challenges. Rising life expectancies and low birthrates produce a greater proportion of elderly—and potentially frail—individuals in the population. Most social security systems suffer from excessive promises made in the past, generating substantial burdens on the active population. Recent turbulence in the capital market increased funding gaps of pension plans. Reforms, though necessary, are increasingly difficult to implement. Immediate cuts harm the elderly, as they cannot adjust quickly enough. Workers and firms are more mobile than in the past, not only in a geographic sense, but also over the life cycle. New patterns of work life have also emerged in part due to higher female labor market participation. Last, but not least, individuals want more autonomy in managing the provisions for old age. At the same time, they are often not sufficiently informed about the functioning of social insurance and the capital market.

Why look to Switzerland to examine how it is meeting this global challenge? Together with the Netherlands, Switzerland stands out as having a strong reliance on its second pillar for old age income. In contrast to most other countries with younger funded pension schemes, lessons can be drawn from decades of experience. Two main policy concerns are addressed in this chapter. First, while there is certainly evidence that policy is challenged by behavioral anomalies, it can also be plagued by strategic behavior: 'too much' rationality. Using the example of Swiss annuitization patterns in retirement, we show that strategic decumulation of assets, given a generous means-testing cushion, poses a serious threat to the system. Since first pillar benefits are below the level of subsistence, full cash-outs of occupational pension capital jeopardize the adequacy of retirement income and may in turn be costly for the government.

Second, the chapter discusses often-neglected political constraints in reforming the old age system. As people live longer and have fewer children, the median voter ages very quickly and the number of policy options shrinks. This problem is even more visible in a country like Switzerland, where the population has a factual line-item veto on policy proposals. Potentially painful pension reforms cannot simply be integrated into a larger package, but have to be approved separately. However, political constraints are also prevalent in representative democracies, albeit to a lesser extent. The evolution from decentralized provisions of income in old age with little government involvement to a more institutionalized and supervised pension scheme brought many advantages such as transparency, equal treatment, and economies of scale. But this larger and more institutionalized system is much more difficult to reform and more susceptible to political pressure. The chapter also presents another aspect of the Swiss system that is of interest for other countries: the treatment of families and couples in the accumulation of claims to the pension system.

In Switzerland, a large fraction of retirement income stems from mandatory fully funded occupational pension plans, which provide generous income guarantees. While individuals cannot choose the pension provider, retirees have a number of withdrawal options upon retirement. Annuitization rates are still comparatively high, but they also vary greatly over time and between pension providers. Interestingly, Switzerland's second pillar had been the primary source of retirement income for many decades, long before the first pillar of old age security was introduced in 1948. When the second pillar became legally mandatory in 1985 (following a change in the constitution approved by the Swiss electorate in 1972), almost 60 percent of the Swiss workforce was covered by an occupational pension fund. This high coverage rate was not only present for paternalistic reasons, but also because pension plans have always been a tool to attract qualified workers in a low unemployment environment.

Several authors have addressed features of the Swiss social security system. Detailed analysis of the strengths and weaknesses of the Swiss pension system can be found in Queisser and Vittas (2000) and Queisser and Whitehouse (2003). A World Bank report on annuity markets in Switzerland (Bütler and Ruesch 2007) provides a comprehensive description of the Swiss system with a focus on the second pillar. Bütler and Staubli (2011) take a closer look at annuitization of pension wealth, while Bütler (2009) focuses on the labor market.

The present chapter revisits the Swiss social security system in view of upcoming challenges. We begin with an overview of the institutional structure with a focus on the occupational pension pillar, and then we discuss the current demographic and economic situation in Switzerland. The following section illustrates the choice to annuitize or cash out pension wealth. Finally, we turn to a discussion of recent pension system reforms, with an emphasis on the political process. We conclude with a summary and lessons to be drawn for other countries from Swiss pensions.

The Swiss Pension Scheme: Institutions and Outcomes

Key elements

The two main pillars of Switzerland's pension system are more or less of equal importance. The first pillar AHV/AVS is a pay-as-you-go (PAYG) system and strives to provide a basic subsistence income level to all retired residents. The second pillar is an employer-based, fully funded occupational pension scheme, mandatory for all employees whose annual income exceeds a certain threshold. Means-tested supplemental benefits may be claimed if a retiree's total income does not cover his or her basic needs in old age. A voluntary third pillar, which is an individual tax-deductible savings account for retirement, complements the scheme (see Table 13.1).

TABLE 13.1 Features of the Swiss old age pension system

Second pillar: occupational pension system	
Payment type	**Size of the payment**
Old age pension	Depends on contribution history and average lifetime earnings. The minimum and maximum full old age pensions are CHF 1,170 and CHF 2,340 per month, respectively; average old age pension is CHF 2,013 per month (BSV 2013a).
Old person's child's pension (paid for dependent children)	40% of corresponding old age pension.
Survivor benefits	Depends on contribution history and average lifetime earnings of deceased person. If the person has died before the age of 45, prospective lifetime earnings are calculated. Survivor benefits are paid for widows and widowers with children and additionally widows that meet certain criteria. Orphans (full and half) are eligible as well until the age of 18 (25 if still in education). Widow and widower benefits are between CHF 936 and CHF 1,872, orphan children's benefits are between CHF 468 and CHF 936.
Supplementary benefits	Covers difference between basic living expenses (i.e. rent, health insurance, nursing or other care, and other essential needs) and the sum of old age pensions and other income. Means-tested benefits guarantee an income of roughly CHF 3,000 per month for singles and CHF 4,500 for married couples. In 2012, the average means-tested benefits were CHF 901 per month for people living at home and CHF 2,893 for people living in a nursing home (BSV 2013b)
Second pillar: occupational pension system	
Payment type	**Size of the payment**
Old age pension	Proportional to accumulated second pillar wealth at retirement. From 2014, the annual full old age pension is 6.8% of the total old age assets for both men and women in the mandatory coverage (up to an annual income of 84,240 CHF). Conversion rates are lower on income exceeding 84,240 CHF. Average second pillar old age benefits conditional on coverage were CHF 2,519 per month (BFS 2013).

(continued)

TABLE 13.1 Continued

Second pillar: occupational pension system	
Payment type	Size of the payment
Old person's child's pension	20% of corresponding old age pension per child; lower percentage for high wage earners.
Survivor benefits	Proportional to accumulated second pillar wealth at the time of death of the insured person. Eligible for survivor benefits are widows and widowers with children or over the age of 45 if married for 10 years or more. Most pension providers also offer benefits for non-married couples. Orphan (full and half) children are eligible as well until the age of 18 (25 if still in education). Widow and widower benefits are 60% of the ordinary second pillar invalidity (if person deceased before pension age) or old age pension. Invalidity pensions are calculated by extrapolating the final old age assets, assuming that the individual contributes at the same level with an interest rate of 0. Orphan benefits are 20% of the ordinary invalidity or old age pension.
Third pillar 3a: voluntary provision	
Payment type	Size of the payment
Capital from voluntary contributions	As of 2013, the maximum contribution per year is CHF 6,739 for individuals covered by a second pillar plan, and CHF 33,696 for those not covered. Contributions can be deducted from taxable income, but they can only be disposed of after pension age or when buying real estate. Upon reception of the capital, the amount is taxed at a reduced rate.

Sources: BSV (2013a, b); BFS (2013).

Taking the first and second pillar together, an individual with an uninterrupted working career can expect a replacement rate of approximately 50–60 percent. The net replacement rate after taxes often amounts to 70–80 percent even for higher levels of income, and it can reach 100 percent for beneficiaries with dependent children. In contrast to other countries, Swiss replacement rates are similar for both lower and higher incomes due to a careful integration of the first and second pillars. In addition to retirement income, the first and second pillars also provide disability insurance, benefits to surviving spouses and children, and to dependent children, even if the main claimant is still alive.

First pillar benefits depend weakly on income and in a linear way on the number of contribution years, including those granted for childcare. Conditional on having contributed at least 45 years to the system, a minimum pension of 13,680 CHF (approx. US$15,000) per year is payable. A majority of retirees qualifies for a pension close to a maximum benefit level, which is equal to twice the minimum pension (i.e. 27,360 CHF). The statutory retirement age is 64 for women and 65 for men. The earliest age at which first pillar benefits can be claimed is 62 for women and 63 for men, subject to an actuarially fair benefit reduction of 6.8 percent per year. Working beyond age 64/65 is possible, but most work contracts specify a retirement age that coincides with the statutory age of retirement. First pillar benefits are financed by a proportional tax on earned income, without a cap. They account for approximately 70 percent of AVS/AHV revenue. The remaining financing comes from earmarked value-added taxes and a fixed share of additional funds paid from general government revenues (see Table 13.1).

Since 1966, means-tested supplemental benefits may be claimed as part of the first pillar when total income does not cover basic needs in old age. Eligibility for benefits is limited to individuals who receive an old age or disability pension, live in Switzerland and have Swiss or EU citizenship, or have been living in Switzerland for at least 10 years. These additional benefits usually result in an income that is above the poverty threshold. The guaranteed total income is approximately 36,000 CHF for singles and 51,000 CHF for couples (without children).

A voluntary third pillar of individual savings complements the first and second pillars for retirement. Given the already high replacement rate provided by the first and second pillar, the third pillar is primarily important for the self-employed (who are not covered by the second pillar), and for individuals with contribution gaps. Since contributions are fully tax-deductible up to a certain amount, the third pillar has also become a popular instrument for middle- and high-income earners to save taxes.

Occupational pension scheme

The second pillar in Switzerland is based on occupational pensions, mandated by law, but organized by employers. Several possible organizational forms vary by the degree the pension sponsor handles risks, the two polar cases being autonomous pension funds with little or no outside insurance for risks such as longevity and investment risks, and collective organizations which sub-contract all risks with an insurer. Typical examples of autonomous funds are pension schemes directly related to a company, but legally independent. Typical examples of collective organizations are insurance companies that offer standard contracts to employers to organize the second pillar in both the accumulation and decumulation phase. Table 13.2 gives an overview of the type and size of different pension plan structure.

The accumulation of retirement assets and their withdrawal as annuities or lump sums are usually organized by the same pension provider. The

TABLE 13.2 Size and structure of occupational pension plans

Type of risk coverage	No. of pension sponsors	No. of covered individuals	women (%)	DC (%)
Autonomous (with & without reinsurance)	838	2,316,785	44.9	74.9
of which private	758	1,675,155	40.6	83.3
Partly autonomous (pension guaranteed by insurance and reinsurance)	1,058	588,665	37.6	91.8
of which private	1,050	586,070	37.5	91.8
Collective (all risks with an insurance)	163	1,003,579	37.0	91.5
of which private	161	1,002,970	37.0	91.5
Total (without savings account)	2,059	3,909,029	41.8	81.7
of which private	1,969	3,264,195	38.9	87.4

Source: BFS (2014a).

strong link between the accumulation and decumulation phases is an important feature of the Swiss system. The institutions that implement occupational pension schemes according to the terms of the BVG/LPP law (Bundesgesetz über die berufliche Alters-, Hinterlassenen- und Invalidenvorsorge) must be registered. The managing body must include as many representatives of employees as of employers, having the same rights.

Individual contributions and benefits

Participation in the occupational pension scheme is mandatory for all employees with annual earnings of 21,060 CHF or more. Approximately 96 percent of working men and 83 percent of working women are covered by the second pillar. The insured income above the threshold and below an upper threshold (at present 82,080 CHF) is called the *mandatory part*. The income above the upper threshold is called the *super-mandatory part* of the second pillar. While the mandatory part is subject to stringent regulation—minimum contribution rates, minimum interest rates, and the conversion rate—there are few restrictions on the contract conditions offered by the insurance companies in the super-mandatory part. By law, pension plan providers are required to insure the mandatory share. They are free to provide insurance for the super-mandatory part as well, and most do because the second pillar is important in attracting a well-educated workforce. Both mandatory and super-mandatory pension contributions are tax-exempt.

Contributions to the occupational pension plans correspond to a certain fraction of an employee's salary (depending on his age), of which the employer has to pay at least half. When an employee starts working at another company, all of the accumulated contributions (including the employer's part) are transferred to the new fund. The total amount of assets at retirement is thus accumulated over the entire working life and is a good proxy for lifetime income. A majority of individuals are covered by DC plans, though given the stringent regulation and income guarantees for all plans, the difference between DB and DC plan is small. Even in DB plans, in which benefits are based on a final salary, contribution gaps must be closed to qualify for full benefits in retirement. For example, an individual's pay increase triggers the need for additional payments to the plan. On the other hand, extensive income guarantees for DC—a minimum interest rate on accumulated assets, a minimum conversion rate, reinsurance of pension income up to 150 percent mandatory coverage, no obligation for retirees to cover financial shortfalls—make DC plans look very much like DB plans.

The occupational pension wealth can be withdrawn either as a monthly lifelong annuity, a lump sum, or a combination of the two components. In some plans, the cash-out limit is equal to 50 or 25 percent of accumulated capital (the legal minimum). In most plans, individuals must declare their choice between three months and three years prior to the effective withdrawal date, depending on the insurer's regulations. Many pension insurers define a default option if the beneficiary does not make an active choice. In 2012 approximately 30 percent of new retirees (which includes individuals not covered by the second pillar) got a lump sum payment at retirement (up from 24 percent in 2004).

Occupational pension annuities are proportional to the accumulated retirement assets (contributions made during the working lifetime plus accrued interest). Retirement capital K is translated into a yearly nominal annuity B using the conversion rate γ: $B=\gamma*K$. The conversion rate is independent of marital status, income, or gender (at least in the mandatory part), but it does depend on the retirement age. By law, the annuity option includes dependent children's benefits of up to 20 percent of the main claimant's benefit for each child younger than 18 (or below the age of 25 if still dependent), as well as survivor benefits equal to 60 percent of the deceased's pension. Combined with a uniform conversion rate, these additional benefits create a sizeable redistribution between married and non-married male annuitants. On average, female annuitants create the same costs as males, with their longer life expectancy compensated by low expected survivor benefits. Pension funds are requested to index annuities to inflation, if the fund's financial situation allows it to do so. At present, only a few funds are actually able to index pensions to inflation, due mainly to the great liabilities created by a very high conversion factor in the mandatory part.

The annuity is subject to normal progressive income tax rates. Additional income from other sources, for example from the first pillar, increases the effective marginal tax rate under the annuity option. The lump sum, on the other hand, is taxed only once (at retirement). The tax rate applied to the capital option varies greatly across Swiss cantons. The present value of the tax bill is almost always smaller under the lump sum option compared to the annuity option, particularly for average and higher levels of second pillar pension wealth. Therefore, the differential tax treatment is expected to reduce the demand for an annuity.

Regulation

The BVG/LPP law specifies minimum requirements along several dimensions. While a regulation of the contribution rates and certain restrictions on payout options are not uncommon in an international context, the law also mandates the minimum interest rate for old age credits and the conversion factor at which the accumulated pension capital has to be translated into a lifelong annuity. The minimum interest rate on accumulated old age balances is determined by the federal council and is periodically adjusted taking into account market data. Figure 13.1 depicts the evolution of the minimum interest rate together with market interest rates and the so-called technical interest rate (not regulated by law) used to discount future liabilities of the plan. Figure 13.1 also contains the returns of a fictional pension fund portfolio containing 40 percent shares. This portfolio proxies the returns of a typical pension fund investment portfolio pretty well. It illustrates the high volatility of market returns in recent years. Minimum interest requirements thus greatly smooth the accumulation of old age balances, but create risks for the sponsors.

The conversion rate (the annuity factor) is fixed by law. As a consequence, it is even more open to political pressure than the minimum interest rate, as will be demonstrated in this chapter. Until 2004 and despite large changes in market conditions over the previous 20 years, the minimum conversion rate in the mandatory part was fixed at 7.2 percent. With the aim of improving the stability of the second pillar, the Swiss government implemented a series of changes in 2004, 2005, and 2006. An integral part of these changes was that the minimum conversion rate in the mandatory part was successively lowered to 6.8 percent by 2015. Pension funds are free to set the conversion rate in the less-regulated super-mandatory part of the second pillar, but until 2003, conversion rates in the mandatory and super-mandatory part were virtually identical. In 2004, several large pension funds started to reduce the conversion rate in the super-mandatory part to 5.4 percent for women and 5.8 percent for men. Since then most other pension funds have followed. Surprisingly, there is little variation over time in the conversion rate not only for the tightly regulated mandatory part, but

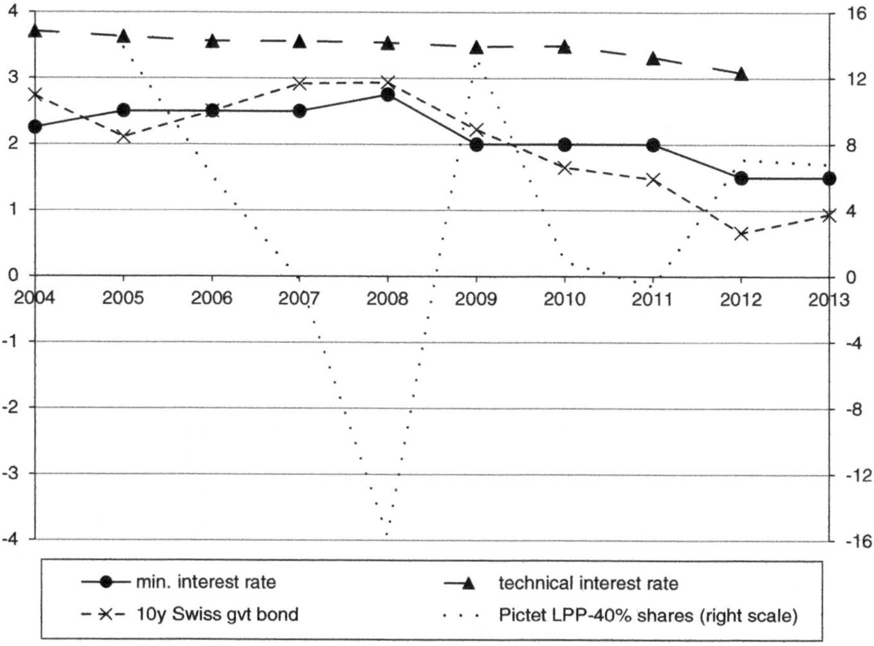

Figure 13.1 Interest rates for Swiss occupational pension plans

Notes: The minimum interest rate is determined by the Swiss federal council and is periodically adjusted. The technical interest rate is used to discount future liabilities of a pension plan. Pictet LPP-40% represents a synthetic investment with 40% shares, a typical portfolio of sufficiently funded pension plans.

Sources: D. Cecil, Fondation Pictet (personal communication, June 19, 2014); SNB (2014); Swisscanto (2014); Schweizerische Eidgenossenschaft (2014); J. Steiger, BSV (personal communication, June 16, 2014).

also in the virtually unregulated super-mandatory part. This is another informal indicator for the high utility value attached to policy smoothing, which is typical for Switzerland's high-stability environment.

The pension funds also have to meet certain requirements on the degree of funding, their investment structure, as well as on transparency issues. There is little regulation (and even less reliable representative data) on the asset and liability management of the different pension funds.

Current demographic and economic situation and labor markets

As in other industrialized countries, the demographic situation in Switzerland has seen a substantial increase in life expectancy and a low fertility rate. As shown in Table 13.3, the total fertility rate declined from 2.1 children per

TABLE 13.3 Demographic trends in Switzerland

	1970	2000	2030	Change
Total fertility rate	2.1	1.5	1.52	−0.58
Life expectancy at age 65				
Men	13.3	17.3	21.8	+8.5
Women	16.2	21.1	24.7	+8.5
Old age dependency ratio	17.7	25	43	+25.3

Notes: Old age dependency ratio is the number of individuals aged 65 and over relative to the number of individuals aged 20 to 64.

Source: BFS (2014d), numbers according to middle scenario A-00-2010.

woman in 1970, to 1.5 children per woman in 2000. Over the same period, the remaining life expectancy at age 65 increased for men from 13.3 to 17.3 years and for women from 16.2 to 21.1 years. This rise in life expectancy is projected to continue at the same rate until 2030. This demographic transition is producing a substantial increase in the old age dependency ratio. The proportion of individuals age 65+ to those age 21–64 has grown from approximately 18 percent in 1970 to 25 percent in 2000 and it will increase further to 43 percent in 2030.

Despite the country's low fertility rates, the Swiss population is aging at a slower rate than most other European nations, due to high rates of immigration. Nonetheless, the rising old age dependency ratio has a direct impact on the financial stability of the first pillar. If the current levels of contributions and benefits are left unchanged, the scheme will start running a sustained deficit very soon (see Table 13.3).

Employment of elderly workers as a way to alleviate the pension problem

Switzerland has a flexible labor market, a low unemployment rate as well as a low implicit tax rate on working beyond the age of 65 (for most individuals). Moreover, retirement at 65 or 64 is not legally mandatory, but represents eligibility for full public pension benefits. Individuals are free to postpone payment of benefits for up to three years at actuarially fair rates. Nevertheless, most labor contracts specify a retirement age—in most cases still mandatory—that coincides with the age of eligibility.

The positive work incentives are diluted to some degree by income effects due to high replacement rates even for high-income earners and generous means-tested supplementary benefits (Bütler and Teppa 2007; Bütler et al. 2013a, 2013b). These and widespread early retirement plans provided by occupational pension plans in the 1990s and early 2000s have shrunk the

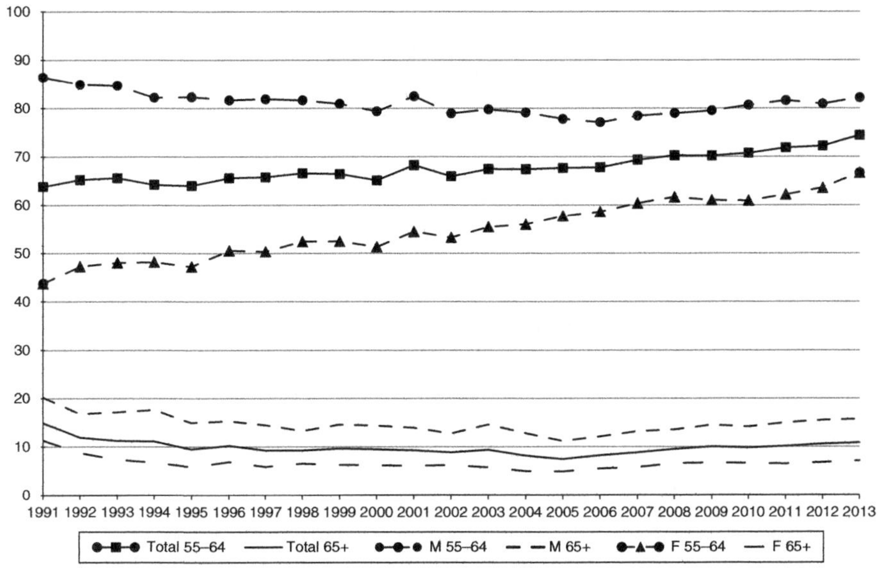

Figure 13.2 Labor force participation of elderly individuals in Switzerland

Notes: M = men, F = women.

Source: BFS (2014b).

traditionally high labor force participation rate of elderly workers (see Figure 13.2). Since the turn of the millennium, the employment rate of older men has been more or less stable and may even be seen to increase slightly again.

An equally interesting fact is that the participation rate of women over age 50 has risen in the last decades, most dramatically for those of age 60–4. This can be attributed in part to the increase in the statutory age of retirement from 62 to 64, although the increase was weakened by a transitory decrease in the actuarial adjustment for early retirement from 6.8 percent to 3.4 percent. Hanel and Riphahn (2006) show that despite the relatively small reduction of retirement benefits by 3.4 percent during the transition period, more than 70 percent of females decided to postpone benefit take-up to the new retirement age. Turning to employment rates beyond the normal retirement age of 65, Switzerland saw a decrease in participation for quite some time until a reversal of the trend around 2005. This date coincided with the reform of the second pillar and the tightening of early retirement conditions in most plans. The increase in labor participation of individuals older than age 65 has hardly been affected by the financial crisis (see Figure 13.2).

Employment of older people may also encounter difficulties due to other factors, such as health and working conditions. Using SHARE data, Bütler and Engler (2008) showed that although incentives still dominate all other aspects, health and working conditions also play a role in the labor market participation of elderly individuals. Employed persons in Switzerland are less often afflicted with health problems than in other European countries. Individuals with favorable working conditions as measured by job satisfaction, appreciation for work performance, and adequate pay and career opportunities are less likely to retire early.

Adequacy of retirement income for spouses

Adequacy of pension income is an important policy concern not only for the primary earner, but also for the surviving spouse in old age, most importantly for the partner who took care of children, and for the frail elderly during the accumulation phase. Decisions such as marriage, having children, and employment over the life cycle influence not only current disposable income, but also long-term financial resources of household members.

The provision of adequate consumption in old age had traditionally been a task of the family. Interestingly, it was the lack of income for widows that drove the political process to adopt a public pension system in Switzerland. With the emergence of formal pension plans, the dominant family-based income provision model was replaced by a pension rights based approach. The Swiss first pillar, AHV/AVS, started from the assumption of a permanent marriage in which the husband had the role of the breadwinner while the wife mainly took over unpaid childcare and household work. Married couples received a so-called couple pension, amounting to 150 percent of a single pension, which was related to the pension contributions of the husband. The wife could not claim her own pension, but she received a generous widow's pension in the event of her husband's death.

Social liberalization seen in the later twentieth century changed the character of family ties and a multitude of lifestyles weakened the traditional family arrangements. While the nuclear family continued to form the social reference model and the number of marriages remained high, divorce rates also increased sharply in the late 1980s.

To adapt the pension system to societal change, both main pillars were reformed in the 1990s, based on a separation of premarital acquired pension rights and the division of acquired claims during marriage. The tenth AHV revision created a separate pension for both spouses based on individual notional accounts, where individual accounts record all pensionable contributions over the entire working life of a person. During marriage, spouses' contributions are equally split, including care credits. The latter is a fictitious income equal to three times the minimum pension granted for the total number of years in which the family takes care of children younger than age 16. Nonetheless, to maintain the character of a basic income and for financial reasons, total benefits of a couple remained capped at 150 percent of maximum individual pension benefits. While the reform promoted independence of the wife, it also created unintended incentives. For many women the generosity of childcare credits and the splitting of contributions led to a situation in which future pensions did not depend on their work income. This reduced the incentive of the secondary earner to work. For medium and higher incomes (roughly 60 percent of all couples), moreover, the cap creates a marriage penalty in retirement.

As a second change, a major reform of the divorce law regulated the mutual claims of the partners with respect to the accumulated pension assets in the second pillar during marriage. In case of a divorce, each spouse is now entitled to half the partner's accumulation during marriage, including interest earned. The split of the pension credits is mandatory and is outside the marital property consideration in the divorce case. In contrast to the first pillar reform, the mandatory split of funded plan balances did not impact labor supply of the secondary earner directly. If at all, it created a positive incentive to take up paid work, as employment-related pension plans provide better protection and higher benefits than stand-alone pension plans.

While the reforms of the two pillars hardly changed the material situation for intact marriages in retirement, they had an impact on the bargaining power of the spouses in retirement, and the income of both partners in case of divorce. The changes not only shifted some retirement income from the primary to the secondary earner, but also increased combined retirement income for a majority of divorced spouses. Figure 13.3 depicts the evolution of divorce rates before and after the reforms. The changes in the divorce law as well as the pension reforms are mirrored by the data. Obviously, the reforms affect both timing and likelihood of divorce. First, the divorce rates fluctuate around the time of the revision of the divorce law, going down prior to, and rebounding after the change. It seems that some couples anticipated divorce in view of the changes, while others waited until the reform was in place. Second, the relative difference in divorce rates between older couples and the total population decreased significantly after the period of social reforms. This pattern suggests that the change in individual claims as a consequence of the pension reforms might have led to an economic reevaluation of marriage and divorce (see Figure 13.3). In the last few years, divorce rates of elderly couples have almost reached the average divorce rate of the population, suggesting that factors other than pensions play a role. Nonetheless, the magnitude of the relative and discontinuous change in divorce rates around the period of reform remains very large.

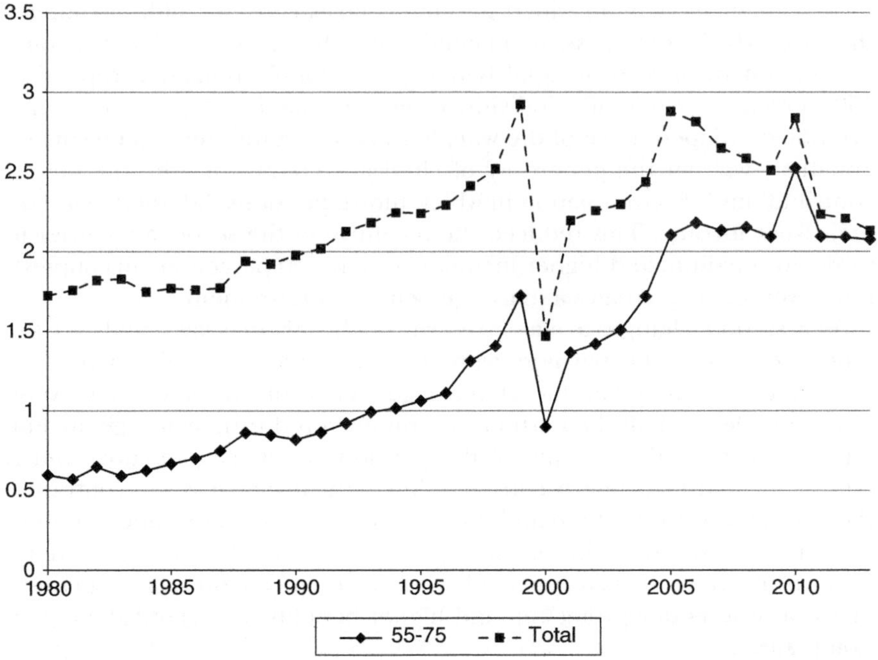

Figure 13.3 Divorce rates for couples between 55 and 75 and total Swiss divorce rates
Source: BFS (2014c).

Annuitization: Not Rational, or Rather Too Rational?

Making decisions for many decades ahead is a difficult task, so it comes as no surprise that behavioral anomalies in retirement planning abound. While some of the mistakes that individuals could make are taken care of by public pension plans and regulation, others remain. The shift from a highly regulated first pillar with little choice to a more individual pension plan, often with many options to choose from, makes mistakes more costly for both individuals and the government. Behavioral mistakes have sparked a huge literature analyzing the anomalies and coming up with better alternatives. While there is certainly evidence that policy is challenged by behavioral anomalies, it might be equally challenged by strategic behavior, or 'too much' rationality. Strategic behavior could be as costly for the government as investment or spending mistakes. Undersaving, for example, might be caused by individuals underestimating their income needs in old age, or it might equally likely be caused by individuals who anticipate the government footing the bill in case of financial shortfalls in old age.

Behavioral anomalies and rational behavior often go hand in hand as illustrated in the following example. Bütler et al. (2013b) exploit the large and sudden cutback in the conversion rate in the super-mandatory part to examine how changes in annuity values impact the annuitization decision. This can be identified by comparing the annuitization behavior of individuals who were affected by the reduction in the conversion rate with observably similar individuals who were covered by an insurance company that did not reduce the conversion rate. The 20 percent reduction in the annuity value led to an approximately 14 percentage point drop in the annuitization rate. Interestingly, this policy change also triggered substantial anticipatory behavior: individuals who had planned to retire after the policy change shifted their retirement to earlier dates to take advantage of the favorable conditions prior to the change. In particular, there was a large spike in the number of retirees in the month prior to when the lower conversion rates became effective. The pattern suggests that individuals were well aware of the large loss in the annuity value.

Bütler et al. (2013b) also showed that almost all beneficiaries chose a polar option and did not distinguish between the mandatory and super-mandatory part, although implicit annuity prices were dramatically different after the reduction in the conversion rate in 2004. Taking out the super-mandatory capital as a lump sum and annuitizing the mandatory part should have been the dominating strategy for a majority of individuals who took out the full lump sum. That they did not do so is consistent with the proposition that many retirees do not make fully informed choices.

Using as an example the Swiss annuitization patterns in retirement, this section illustrates the tension between not-rational-enough behavior and potentially 'too rational' strategies. Cash-out decisions are influenced by three main factors: money's worth ratios, behavioral anomalies, and generous means-tested supplemental benefits that act as a supplementary longevity insurance. While the impact of generous income guarantees have been discussed elsewhere (Bütler and Staubli 2011; Bütler and Ruesch 2007), we will focus on the latter two factors illustrated by individual retirement decisions from Swiss occupational pension plans.

Not so rational: behavioral factors in annuitization decisions

The behavioral economics literature has been able to account for many aspects of retirement planning, such as participation in employer-provided pension plans (Duflo and Saez 2003), contribution rates (Beshears et al. 2008), and portfolio allocation decisions (Choi et al. 2009). The recent literature on the determinants of individual cash-out behavior suggests

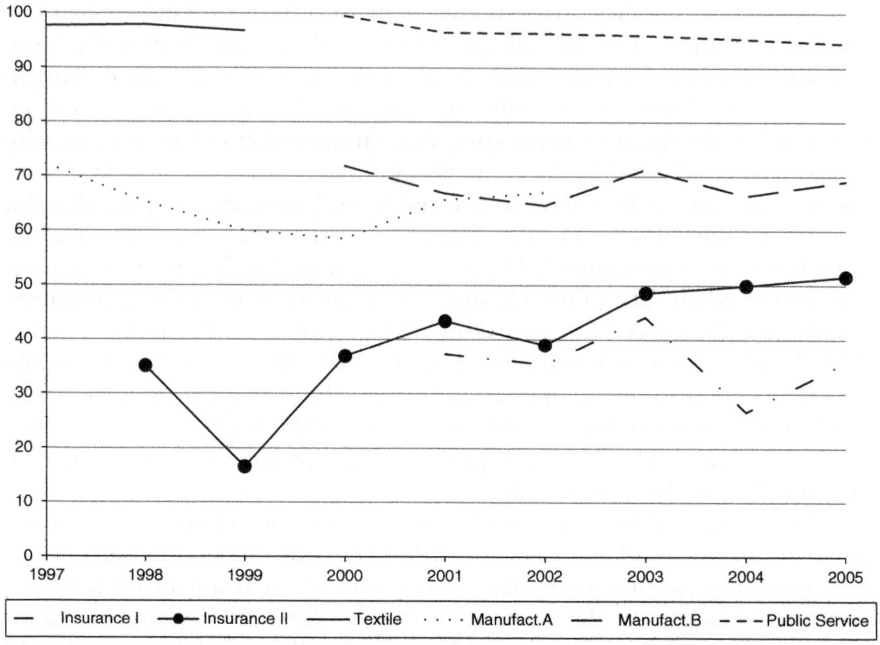

Figure 13.4 Annuitization rates for six pension providers prior to the reform of the occupational pension law in 2005 (which triggered a number of changes). Stable parameters (exception: decrease in supermandatory conversion rate for Insurance I in 2004)

Source: Individual data from Swiss pension plans.

that behavioral biases also play an important role in the annuitization decision (Benartzi et al. 2011; Brown et al. 2013). Brown et al. (2008), for example, show that framing matters for the annuitization decision. Under an 'investment frame' that focused on risk and return, only 21 percent of the individuals preferred a life annuity over a savings account. On the other hand, under a 'consumption frame' that highlighted the consequences for lifelong consumption, 72 percent chose the life annuity. More recent contributions in the field try to come up with recommendations to improve individual decision-making using nudges and defaults, thus increasing the likelihood that people will choose the annuity (Beshears et al. 2014).

Figure 13.4 provides graphical evidence of how Swiss defaults influenced the fraction of capital cashed out at retirement. While good aggregate statistics are hard to get, on average 60 to 70 percent of all individuals annuitize their accumulated pension wealth. Figure 13.4 presents the fraction of capital cashed out at retirement based on administrative records from several pension funds and large insurance companies. On average and consistent with aggregate numbers, annuitization rates are high, but there are also large and persistent differences between different plan sponsors. A part of the difference can be attributed to a composition effect: individuals covered by collective funds tend to earn less and to be poorer, as measured by their accumulated pension wealth. Nevertheless, annuitization patterns remain virtually unchanged after controlling for composition. More importantly, there are differences in the standard cash-out option at retirement for otherwise almost identical pension plans. Only between 10 to 30 percent of all individuals covered by an autonomous pension plan cash out all or a fraction of their pension wealth, but even for these autonomous pensions plans, annuitization patterns differ. Interestingly, the two companies with the highest annuitization rates are companies in the tradition of defined benefits (Textile and Public Service in Figure 13.4). The next two companies (Manufact A and B in Figure 13.4), on the other hand, have a defined contribution tradition. In all four companies mentioned, individuals were allowed to cash out their full or partial retirement balances. But they had to take the initiative if they wished to choose this option, informing the pension sponsors six to 36 months prior to retirement.

The insurance companies, labeled Insurance I and II, take another approach. The sponsor takes the initiative and actively informs the contributors ahead of time about the choices they can make. The difference between Insurance I and Insurance II is that the former forces individuals to make an active decision (no default), while the latter has an annuity default option, which is also communicated to the individuals. This seemingly small difference triggers a stable gap in annuitization rates of approximately 10 percentage points (after controlling for composition effects) between the two very similar plans (Bütler et al. 2013b).

The annuitization behavior in Swiss occupational pension plans is in line with our previous research on the role of behavioral factors in cash-out decisions at retirement (Bütler and Teppa 2007). For instance individuals mostly stick with the sponsor's default option, rather than making an active decision. In particular, the likelihood to cash out pension wealth is significantly higher in companies that provide the (partial) lump sum as a default. Interestingly, several small pension funds displayed almost no variation with respect to the annuitization decision: all retirees chose either the lump sum or the annuity. Pension fund managers usually explain the phenomenon by referring to peer effects and an implicit standard option ('it has always been done like that').

The high rate of annuitization in Switzerland may also be attributed to the *framing of the scheme*: occupational pension benefits were traditionally framed as annuities, and very recently, many contributors to the system were unaware of the sum of money they had accumulated, though they knew the approximate amount of their monthly payments. To improve transparency, starting in 2005 all pension funds were required to provide insured participants with a yearly statement (many funds offered such statements already before the mandatory introduction). The statement declares the amount of capital accumulated to date and reports the expected approximate annuity stream (based on an extrapolation of current earnings and interest rates). Interestingly, with respect to framing, for most plans the space on the paper given to annuity streams (which also include survivor benefits and benefits in case of disability) is much larger compared to the space given to the accumulated capital. The statement on an individual's occupational pension benefits thus comes close to what Brown et al. (2008) call a 'consumption frame,' which they found was likely to induce beneficiaries to choose the annuity.

'Too' rational: means-tested benefits and annuitization

Approximately 12 percent of all Swiss retirees receive means-tested benefits as part of the first pillar, because their total income does not cover basic needs in old age. These very generous supplemental benefits have contributed to a low poverty rate among the elderly in Switzerland, but they may also have had unintended consequences for the annuitization decision. In particular, because means-tested benefits provide an implicit insurance against outliving one's assets, older individuals have a strong incentive to cash out their accumulated pension wealth. For the government, strategic decumulation of assets in view of a generous means-testing world can be very costly.

The yearly amount of means-tested benefits is obtained by summing up all applicable expenditures and subtracting all pension income, investment income, and earnings, plus one-tenth of wealth exceeding a threshold level of 25,000 CHF for singles and 40,000 CHF for married claimants. Applicable expenditures include a cost of living allowance, health insurance expenditures, and rent payments. Given that pension income is fully taken into account in the calculation of means-tested benefits, an annuity offsets the means-tested benefits one for one. By contrast, a lump-sum payment has no effect on supplemental benefits as long as the total wealth (including the lump sum) is below the threshold level. Even if the total wealth does exceed the threshold, only one-tenth of wealth is credited against means-tested benefits. Moreover, since the eligibility age for benefits in pension plans is typically younger than the statutory retirement age, the lump sum can be used to finance early retirement. Once the statutory age of retirement is reached, means-tested benefits can be claimed.

The incentive to cash out their pension in order to apply for means-tested benefits later is particularly strong for those having little pension wealth.

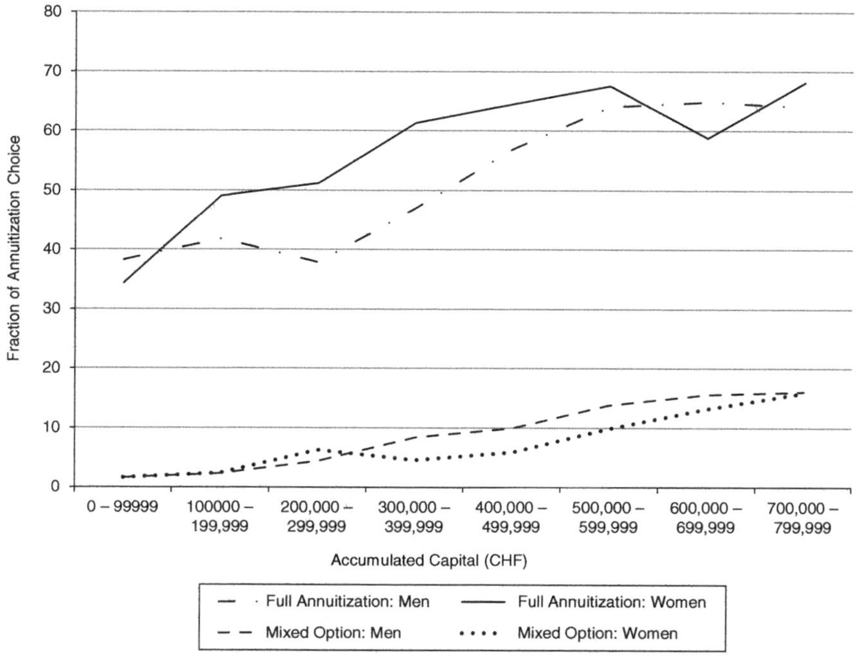

Figure 13.5 Percentage of capital annuitized as a function of accumulated second pillar wealth (upper curves). Percentage of individuals opting for a mixed payout (10% capital or more, plus 10% annuity or more)

Source: Individual data from Swiss pension plans.

Middle-income individuals, by contrast, have to weigh the benefit of taking a lump sum and later receiving generous supplemental benefits, against the disadvantage of not being able to smooth consumption optimally. Maximal first pillar benefits amount to roughly 2,000 CHF per month. The means-tested benefits increase total income to approximately 3,000 CHF a month. Thus an individual with a monthly second-pillar benefit of less than 1,000 CHF a month (which corresponds to accumulated occupational pension wealth of approximately 170,000 CHF) and little non-pension wealth is always better off withdrawing the accumulated capital upon retirement, spending it quickly, and then applying for means-tested benefits.

Figure 13.5 plots the fraction of individuals who annuitized at retirement as a function of the level of old age capital. Clearly, the frequency of taking an annuity is low for people with small capital stocks, and it increases with higher levels of second pillar wealth. This pattern is also in line with Bütler and Teppa (2007) who showed that the probability of annuitizing increases with accumulated wealth. In Bütler et al. (2013a), it is shown that optimal annuity demand and consumption patterns derived from a realistic life cycle model under a social security scheme calibrated to the Swiss scheme comes close to the observed payout pattern. A comparison of model results and real-world data suggests that means-tested benefits do substantially decrease annuity demand for individuals with low or medium levels of pension wealth.

These findings do not preclude other explanations for the increase in annuitization rates with accumulated capital. For instance, less wealthy individuals may favor the lump sum because they tend to have a higher mortality risk. However, the likelihood to annuitize continues to increase even for relatively high levels of pension wealth where health is not an important factor. The same is true for women, for whom differential mortality is very small. Moreover, it is well known that financial literacy is positively correlated with income and wealth (see e.g. Lusardi and Mitchell 2007). Therefore, annuitization rates may increase with accumulated capital just because wealthier individuals make more informed choices. The increasing frequency of taking a mixed option with accumulated capital may be interpreted as indirect evidence for a positive relationship between investment skills and (pension) wealth. On the other hand, tax incentives to opt for a split between the lump sum and the annuity instead of a polar option also go up for increasing levels of pension wealth.

Strategic decumulation of retirement savings not only influences individual consumption profiles, but it also generates costs to the government via two channels. The first arises because of the direct financial costs of boosting retirement incomes to the subsistence level. The second channel results from an induced change in behavior. If individuals switch from an annuity to a cash-out option, the government provides insurance to those with a higher expected income, while the unused assets of those with a premature death fall to the heirs and not the insurance provider. Bütler et al. (2013a) show the benefits and costs of various reforms to limit government expenditures. A first reform might ban cash-outs altogether, while a second would mandate annuitization only to a level corresponding to the subsistence level at retirement. In the latter case, the government still picks up the bill for those with a lump sum in case of low capital returns or high inflation. As a last reform option, a tightening of the asset test is considered, which would eliminate the possibility of claiming means-tested benefits before one's capital is completely exhausted. As before, this policy change would decrease the burden for society directly via a later claiming time when people have to run down assets completely, and indirectly through higher annuitization rates so people avoid low consumption in old age. The indirect effect would be strong enough to halve the wedge between optimal and observed annuitization rates. While limiting cash-outs seems like the obvious solution to the problem of strategic decumulation, one has to keep in mind distributional aspects. Low-income people would suffer the most from limiting cash outs, also because they usually have a lower life expectancy.

Swiss annuitization patterns suggest that individuals navigate some complex decisions in ways that are highly rational. At the same time, people are also influenced by behavioral factors such as defaults. But what determines whether and when individuals act very rationally or not rationally enough? There is of course almost no direct empirical evidence for potential reasons for either of the two behavioral patterns. A first indication might be the surprisingly large differences in individual decisions between companies (as is clear from Figure 13.5 and is also discussed in Bütler and Teppa 2007). It seems that at least some implicit or explicit advice is taken from discussions and information at the workplace. Due to the tight link between accumulation and payout phase, formal advice from financial intermediaries plays a minor role. The public debate around means-tested benefits in old age might have induced individuals to think more clearly through the consequences of choosing between a lump sum and an annuity at retirement.

Future Reforms Under Political Constraints

While the three pillar structure of the Swiss old age insurance system is generally undisputed, both the first and second pillars will have to tackle the problem of too-generous benefits combined with insufficient contributions. Attempts to stabilize the Swiss pension system have proven to be difficult, not least because the Swiss political system is based on direct democracy. Swiss policymakers face strong political constraints for potential reforms, as the public possesses what amounts to veto power (Bütler 2009). Any change in the law can be (and usually is) challenged by a facultative referendum.

The last time the first pillar was reformed was in 1997, when the female retirement age was raised from 62 to 64. All further attempts to reform the system have failed so far either in parliament or at the ballot. There have been few fundamental changes in the second pension pillar. In view of the increase in life expectancy at age 65 of about three years since 1985, and the fall in capital market returns, the conversion factor should have been reduced by approximately 15 to 20 percent. Nevertheless, minimum interest rates and the conversion factor have remained constant for almost 20 years. The illusion of perpetual stability was only squashed after the stock market downturn at the beginning of 2000. At that time, market returns fell below the 4 percent minimum return requirement and many pension funds became underfunded. After an intense political debate, the Swiss Federal Council agreed to reduce the minimum return requirement to 3.25 percent as of January 1, 2003. Since then, the interest rate has been adjusted several times and now follows market interest rates more closely than before (see Figure 13.1).

The Swiss parliament also changed the occupational pension scheme in 2005, including new regulations concerning transparency, an extension of the coverage of the second pillar to low-income and part-time workers, and a step-wise, but small reduction of the conversion rate in the mandatory part to 6.8 percent by 2015. The adjustments in the second pillar proved too weak to trigger any serious political opposition, but also far too weak to secure long-run sustainability of the scheme.

How difficult it can be to change the public's vested interests can be illustrated by a recent vote on the conversion rate (or annuity factor). As a consequence of the impact of the financial crisis, the government proposed another reduction, on top of the already implemented reform. But in March 2010, 73 percent of Swiss voters chose not to reduce the second pillar conversion rate. Since most national votes are evaluated by a telephone survey of individuals who participated in the ballot (the so-called VOX database), we are able to analyze results. Table 13.4 presents the results of a simple regression analysis on the potential determinants of this outcome on individual survey data (first column in Table 13.4), complemented by an analysis of community level data in which the approval rate of the initiative is regressed on similar socio-economic variables.

In the first specification of Table 13.4 we regress the outcome 'approve the reduction in the conversion rate' (1 = approval) on individual demographic and socio-economic variables taken from the survey. In the second specification, the approving vote share of 2,400 Swiss communities is regressed on similar aggregate indicators. The results are informative: French- and Italian-speaking individuals and communities were significantly less willing to approve the conversion rate cut than the German-speaking individuals/communities, in line with previous research (Eugster et al. 2011). The most likely interpretations are cultural differences between the regions (as economic variables play a minor role), or minority groups voicing a concern against social insurance cuts imposed by the dominant language group (German). A second interesting result has to do with trust. For the analysis on individual data, distrust was one of the most influential variables shaping the vote.

Surprisingly, approval of a cut in benefits increases in a more or less linear way with age (in several specifications tested). While individuals already retired or who are close to retirement age soon would have been grandfathered (and might have benefited indirectly from the reform in the form of more secure income streams), the ranking of middle-aged and young voters is surprising. Given that the young would have benefited most from a reduced conversion rate (and thus lower forced redistribution), the low support of the reform by this group is a puzzle.

Other demographics had the expected signs. Better educated voters were more likely to approve the reform. Richer individuals and those owning an

TABLE 13.4 Political support for a reduction in the conversion rate (annuity factor), individual data from telephone survey after the ballot

	Individual	Community
	Dependent variable:	Dependent variable:
	Yes (=1) in ballot)	Percentage yes-votes in Community
Person aged 65 and over	0.189*** (0.035)	
Share of population aged 65 and older		0.299*** (0.019)
Person aged 45–64	0.047 (0.031)	
Share of population aged 45–64		−3,986 (4.701)
French/Italian-speaking person	−0.082*** (0.026)	
French/Italian-speaking community		–6.187*** (0.369)
House owner	0.063** (0.028)	
Taxable income per capita in 1'000 CHF		0.088*** (0.018)
Person with secondary education	0.169*** (0.031)	
Share of persons with secondary education		0.271*** (0.023)
Person with tertiary education	0.220*** (0.032)	
Share of persons with tertiary education		0.294*** (0.030)
Distrust in government	−0.092*** (0.027)	
Adjusted R2	0.249	0.912
Number of observations	881	2,401

Notes: The dependent variable is the decision taken in the vote (approval of annuity reduction=1, decline annuity reduction=0,
*** $p < 0.01$ ** $p < 0.05$ * $p < 0.1$

apartment or house (as a proxy for wealth) were slightly more likely to favor the reform (though the effect is not significant). Individuals with a high income (and presumably better education) already face lower de facto annuity rates and would consequently have been less affected by the reform, since the politically fixed annuity rate only concerned contribution on income below a certain threshold.

Overly generous nominal income guarantees implicit in the high conversion rate also limit the ability of pension funds to adjust pensions to the rate of inflation. Surprising to an economist, this aspect was almost completely ignored in the public discussion preceding the vote. A plausible explanation is that voters' perceptions and preferences might be influenced by past experiences. Not having had significant inflation during the past three decades, the Swiss may have forgotten just how important indexing annuities is.

Taken together, these results demonstrate not only the difficulty of reforming a generous pension system with large vested interest, but also the importance for the government (or private pension sponsors) of gaining trust and coming up with convincing proposals. That people vote in their own interest need not make reforms more difficult. In our example, the grandfathering of the elderly brought important support for the reform. That the proposal was not accepted, nonetheless, also reflects the failure to convince an important group of potential beneficiaries, the younger voters.

Conclusion

The Swiss three pillar retirement system provides policymakers with a rich context to explore policy revisions. Switzerland has a very comprehensive pension scheme based on two main pillars, in which a large element of retirement income comes from a mandatory occupational pension scheme. While individuals in Swiss occupational pension plans do not have much choice during the accumulation phase, they have considerable freedom in choosing how their capital will be paid out at retirement. This feature has the potential to undermine the adequacy of retirement income, especially for low- and middle-income earners and may lead to additional governmental expenditures in the form of means-tested benefits. Nonetheless, Switzerland still has relatively high annuitization rates compared to other countries, with only approximately 30 percent of individuals cashing out their second pillar. Payout choices are significantly influenced by default options and peer effects. While behavioral anomalies have attracted quite a bit of attention and research in recent years, a bigger challenge for policymakers may be what to do when individuals behave rationally, strategically exploiting the interactions between the different income schemes in old age. The annuitization pattern in Switzerland supports the interpretation of rational individuals taking into account the possibility of claiming means-tested social assistance once wealth is depleted. The impact of the divorce law's new treatment of pensions provides another piece of evidence on the prevalence of rational decision-making at advanced ages.

In view of institutional peculiarities and a strong impact of historical and societal context, it is difficult to come up with straightforward lessons for another country. A general finding from our analysis is that individual pension decisions involve both rational and behavioral factors. As in Switzerland, and unlike in many European countries, US individuals are used to taking large financial decisions concerning their pension wealth. It would thus be surprising to see completely different decision patterns in the US. Recent evidence on long-term care by Brown and Finkelstein (2008) supports the interpretation that individuals come up with choices that look close to the predictions from rational forward-looking optimization models. These findings lend support to the view that improving financial literacy is a very important component in policymaking with regard to pension reforms. Nudging might do the trick when it comes to technical points or some tactical decisions, but it cannot replace education and information in an increasingly complex pension world.

The Swiss experience also demonstrates that political constraints should be taken seriously in reforming the pension system. Our small example illustrates that gaining a majority for a painful reform to the pension system is not an easy task. While many determinants of a reform support are not surprising, our results show the importance of cultural and historical factors as well as general trust in the government. In view of fast population aging, it seems easier to implement reforms that grandfather individuals already in retirement, such as an increase in retirement age.

References

Benartzi, S., A. Previtero, and R. H. Thaler (2011). 'Annuity Puzzles.' *Journal of Economic Perspectives*, 25(4): 143–64.

Beshears, J., J. J. Choi, D. Laibson, and B. Madrian (2008). 'The Importance of Default Options for Retirement Saving Outcomes: Evidence from the United States,' in S. J. Kay and T. Sinha, *Lessons from Pension Reform in the Americas*. Oxford: Oxford University Press, 59–87.

Beshears, J., J. J. Choi, D. Laibson, B. Madrian, and S. P. Zeldes (2014). 'What Makes Annuitization More Appealing?' *Journal of Public Economics*, 116(C): 2–16.

Brown, J. R. and A. Finkelstein (2008). 'The Interaction of Public and Private Insurance: Medicaid and the Long-Term Care Insurance Market.' *American Economic Review*, 98(3): 1083–102.

Brown, J. R., A. Kapteyn, and O. S. Mitchell (2013). 'Framing and Claiming: How Information-Framing Affects Expected Social Security Claiming Behavior.' *Journal of Risk and Insurance*. Forthcoming.

Brown, J. R., J. R. Kling, S. Mullainathan, and M. V. Wrobel (2008). 'Why Don't People Insure Late Life Consumption? A Framing Explanation of the Under-Annuitization Puzzle.' *American Economic Review: Papers and Proceedings*, 98: 304–9.

Bütler, M. (2009). 'Switzerland: High Replacement Rates and Generous Subsistence as a Barrier to Work in Old Age.' *The Geneva Papers*, 34: 561–77.

Bütler, M., K. Peijnenburg, and S. Staubli (2013a). *How Much Do Means-Tested Benefits Reduce the Demand for Annuities?* NRN working paper 2013-11. Linz, Austria: Austrian Center for Labor Economics and the Analysis of the Welfare State, Johannes Kepler University of Linz.

Bütler, M. and M. Ruesch (2007). *Annuities in Switzerland*, Policy Research Working Paper, 4438. Washington, DC: World Bank.

Bütler, M. and S. Staubli (2011). 'Payouts in Switzerland: Explaining Developments in Annuitization,' in O. S. Mitchell, J. Piggott, and N. Takayama (eds), *Securing Lifelong Retirement Income: Global Annuity Retirement Payouts*. Oxford: Oxford University Press, 195–213.

Bütler, M. and F. Teppa (2007). 'The Choice between an Annuity and a Lump Sum: Results from Swiss Pension Funds.' *Journal of Public Economics*, 91: 1944–66.

Bütler, M., S. Staubli, and M. G. Zito (2013b). 'How Much Does Annuity Demand React to a Large Price Change?' *Scandinavian Journal of Economics*, 115(3): 808–24.

Bundesamt für Sozialversicherungen (BSV) (2013a). *AHV-Statistik 2012*. Berne: BSV.

Bundesamt für Sozialversicherungen (BSV) (2013b). *Statistik der Ergänzungsleistungen zu AHV und IV 2012*. Berne: BSV.

Bundesamt für Statistik (BFS) (2013). *Die berufliche Vorsorge in der Schweiz: Pensionskassenstatistik 2011*. Neuenburg: BFS. <http://www.bfs.admin.ch/bfs/portal/de/index/themen/13/22/publ.html?publicationID=5180>.

Bundesamt für Statistik (BFS) (2014a). *Die berufliche Vorsorge in der Schweiz. Pensionkassenstatistik 2012*. Neuenburg: BFS. <http://www.bfs.admin.ch/bfs/portal/de/index/themen/13/02/03/dos/01.html>.

Bundesamt für Statistik (BFS) (2014b). *Swiss Labour Force Survey (SLFS)*. Neuenburg: BFS. <http://www.bfs.admin.ch/bfs/portal/en/index/themen/03/02/blank/data/00.html#parsys_0006>.

Bundesamt für Statistik (BFS) (2014c). *Vital Statistics (BEVNAT)*. Neuenburg: BFS. <http://www.bfs.admin.ch/bfs/portal/en/index/infothek/erhebungen__quellen/blank/blank/bevnat/01.html>.

Bundesamt für Statistik (BFS) (2014d). *Zukünftige Bevölkerungsentwicklung—Daten, Indikatoren—Schweiz Szenarien*. Neuenburg: BFS. <http://www.bfs.admin.ch/bfs/portal/de/index/themen/01/03/blank/key/intro.html>.

Bütler, M. and M. Engler (2008). *Arbeitsfähigkeit und Integration der älteren Arbeitskräfte in der Schweiz - Studie II*, SECO Publikation Arbeitsmarktpolitik, 25. Berne: SECO.

Choi, J. J., D. Laibson, and B. C. Madrian (2009). 'Mental Accounting in Portfolio Choice: Evidence from a Flypaper Effect.' *American Economic Review*, 99(5): 2085–95.

Duflo, E. and E. Saez (2003). 'The Role of Information and Social Interactions in Retirement Plan Decisions: Evidence from a Randomized Experiment.' *Quarterly Journal of Economics*, 118: 815–42.

Eugster, B., R. Lalive, A. Steinhauer, and J. Zweimüller (2011). 'The Demand for Social Insurance: Does Culture Matter?' *Economic Journal*, 121(556): F413–48.

Hanel, B. and R. T. Riphahn (2006). *Financial Incentives and the Timing of Retirement: Evidence from Switzerland*, IZA Discussion Paper, 2492. Bonn: Institute for the Study of Labor (IZA).

Lusardi, A. and O. S. Mitchell (2007). 'Baby Boomer Retirement Security: The Role of Planning, Financial Literacy, and Housing Wealth.' *Journal of Monetary Economics*, 54: 205–24.

Queisser, M. and D. Vittas (2000). *The Swiss Multi-Pillar Pension System: Triumph of Common Sense?* World Bank Policy Research Working Paper, 2416. Washington, DC: World Bank.

Queisser, M. and E. R. Whitehouse (2003). *Individual Choice in Social Protection: The Case of Swiss Pensions*, OECD Social, Employment and Migration Working Paper, 11. Paris: OECD.

Schweizerische Eidgenossenschaft (2014). *Verordnung über die berufliche Alters-, Hinterlassenen- und Invalidenvorsorge* (BVV 2). Berne: Schweizerische Eidgenossenschaft. <http://www.admin.ch/opc/de/classified-compilation/19840067/index.html>.

Swiss National Bank (SNB) (2014). *Monthly Statistical Bulletin, June 2014.* Zurich: Swiss National Bank. <http://www.snb.ch/en/mmr/reference/stat_monatsheft_2014_06/source/stat_monatsheft_2014_06.en.pdf>.

Swisscanto (2014). 'Studie "Schweizer Pensionskassen," 2000–2013.' <http://www.swisscanto.ch/ch/de/berufliche-vorsorge/publikationen/pkstudie/studien.html>.

Chapter 14

The Australian Retirement Income System: Comparisons with and Lessons for the United States

Rafal Chomik and John Piggott

Typical retirement income systems across the developed world comprise multiple pillars with (1) some form of welfare poverty alleviation payment, sometimes part of a non-age related welfare policy; (2) an unfunded, pay-as-you-go, defined benefit (DB), earnings-related, income replacement scheme, which requires contributions and a substantial vesting period; and (3) income tax-preferred voluntary retirement saving, with the tax break contingent on these savings being preserved to some specified access age. While parametric settings vary widely, this basic structure is widely deployed, and it is also being adopted by newly maturing economies such as Korea, or emerging ones such as Thailand.

By contrast, the Australian structure comprises a non-contributory tax-free[1] pension payment available at a given age, generous enough to provide a modest standard of living when combined with ownership of a dwelling, and means-tested to exclude the affluent; a mandatory tax-preferred defined contribution (DC) plan for employees, with substantial employer contributions; and voluntary, tax-preferred (often workplace-based) contributions.

This chapter provides a partial account of the design and operation of the Australian retirement income system, with a view to emphasizing the lessons for US institutions. To establish how the two countries are comparable we begin with some relevant facts and figures about their economies and demographics. We then describe Australian policy and practice, with special emphasis on its two most important elements: the age pension and mandatory pre-funded superannuation. We also discuss the role and interpretation of incentives in the Australian structure and suggest that this structure has incentive effects which are less distortionary in a modern mixed economy than a more conventional structure has. As an aside, we provide some information about how public sector employee plans have evolved in this environment.

Australia and the US: Demography and Economy

Australia and the US are vastly different countries. Australia is a small, open economy with a population of about 23 million people, slightly smaller than Texas (Figure 14.1). The US population is 14 times larger. Adjusted for purchasing power parity, Australia's GDP was $1 trillion (USD) in 2012,

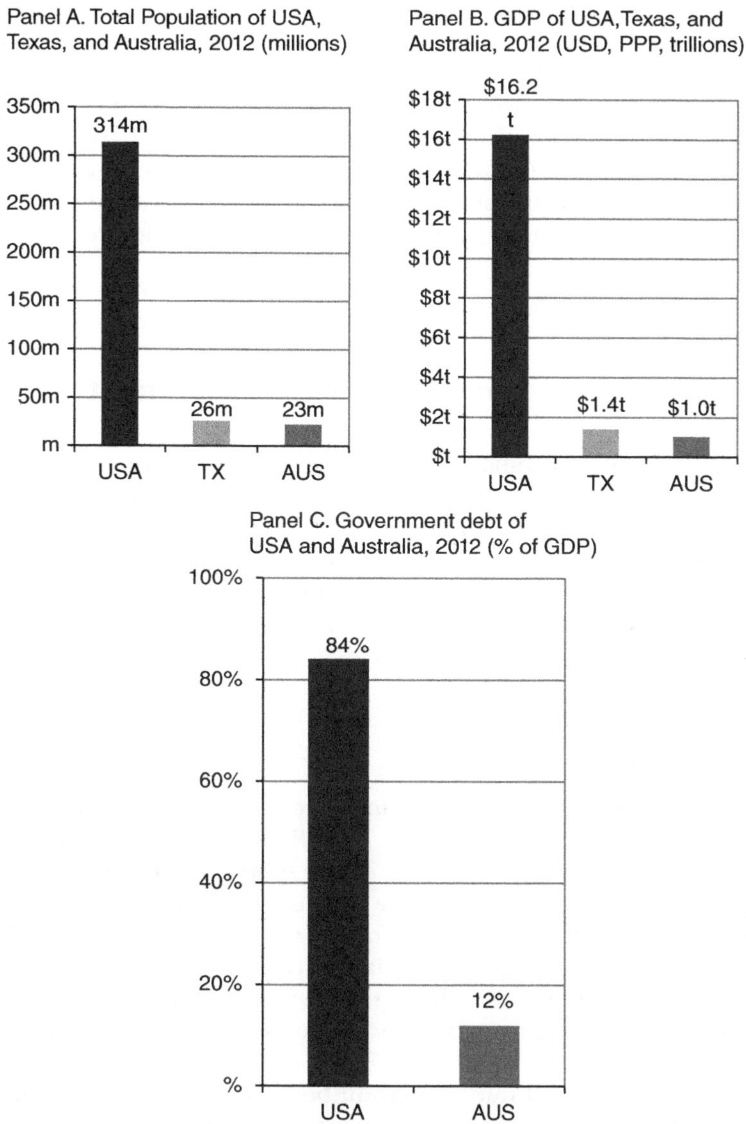

Figure 14.1 Comparison of population, economy, and government budget
Source: OECD (2014); IMF (2014).

just over 6 percent of the US figure. In 2012, net government debt stood at 12 percent of GDP in Australia; the US figure was 84 percent of GDP. The Australian budget deficit was about 3.5 percent of GDP, while the US government budget deficit was about 9.3 percent of GDP.

When we adjust for population size, the countries resemble each other more closely. Average per capita income, adjusted for purchasing power parity, is slightly higher in the US but of the same order, at approximately $52,000 (USD), compared to Australia's $44,000. Median incomes are also slightly higher in the US, as is income inequality (Figure 14.2).

In spite of these differences, the fundamentals relevant to retirement provision are reasonably similar. Australia and the US have similar age structures (Figure 4.3). On average, Australians live longer and have fewer children than Americans, but higher migration rates and gentler fertility declines mean Australia's current and projected age structure is similar to that of the US.

The Australian Retirement Income System Structure

A much-used framework for retirement provision posits three 'pillars' of old age support.[2] The first pillar operates as a non-contributory transfer program, which means it can pay benefits to all.[3] The second pillar offers payments related to pre-retirement labor income, on some mandatory basis—typically, some proportion of wages or salary, paid either by employer, employee, or both. The third pillar comprises voluntary retirement saving. This structure is depicted in Figure 14.4, in which the Australian and US structures are highlighted.[4]

The age pension

The mainstay of Australian government retirement provision is the age pension, first introduced in 1909. This flat rate benefit is potentially available to all, regardless of work history, subject to access age and residency requirements. It operates as a means-tested support payment. It is not tested to target the destitute but rather to exclude the affluent. Almost 80 percent of the age-eligible population receive some age pension payment, and 50 percent receive a full age pension, in sharp contrast to the US means-tested programs (see the later section on Comparative Retirement Outcomes).

Means test withdrawal rates, based on both income and asset tests, were incorporated into the age pension at its inception. Since the late 1960s, they have undergone repeated modification and reform. The means tests are

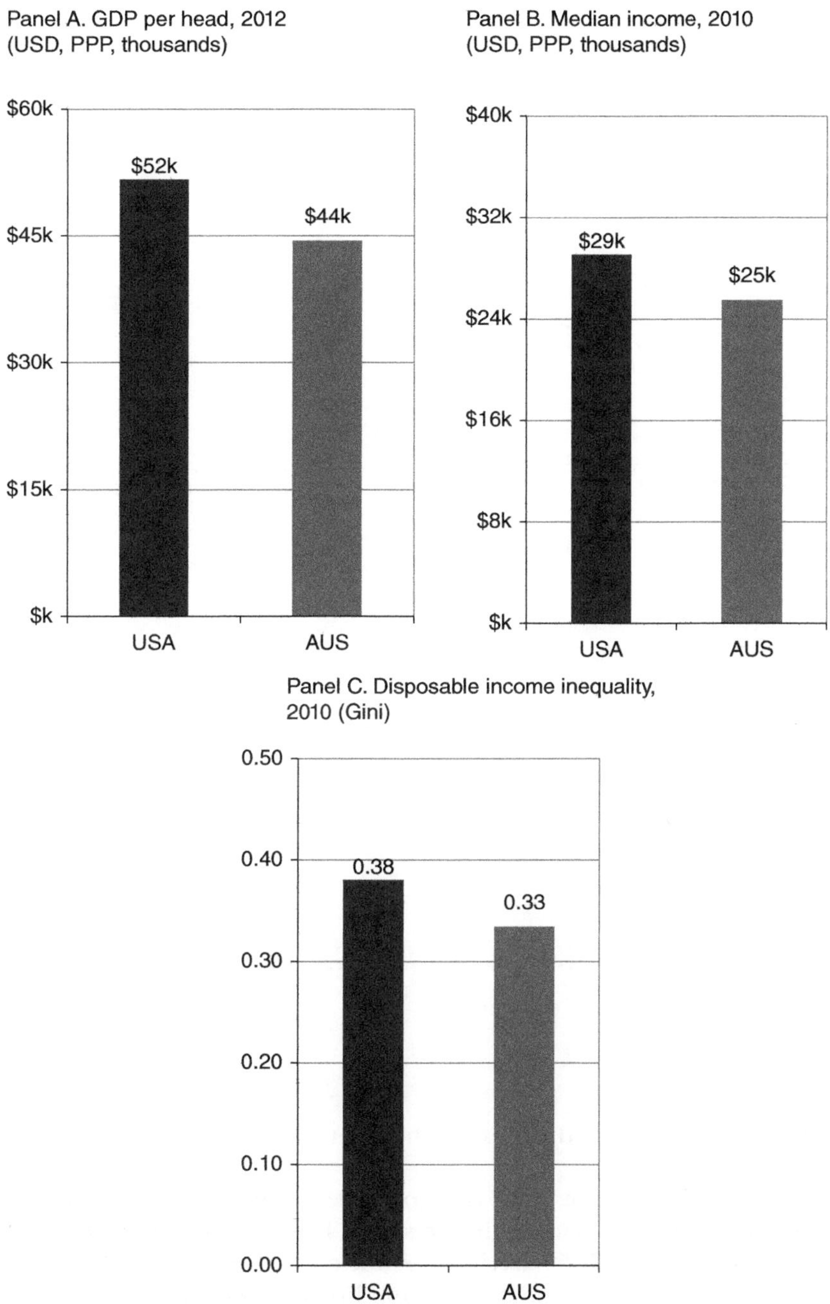

Figure 14.2 Comparison of population incomes
Source: OECD (2014).

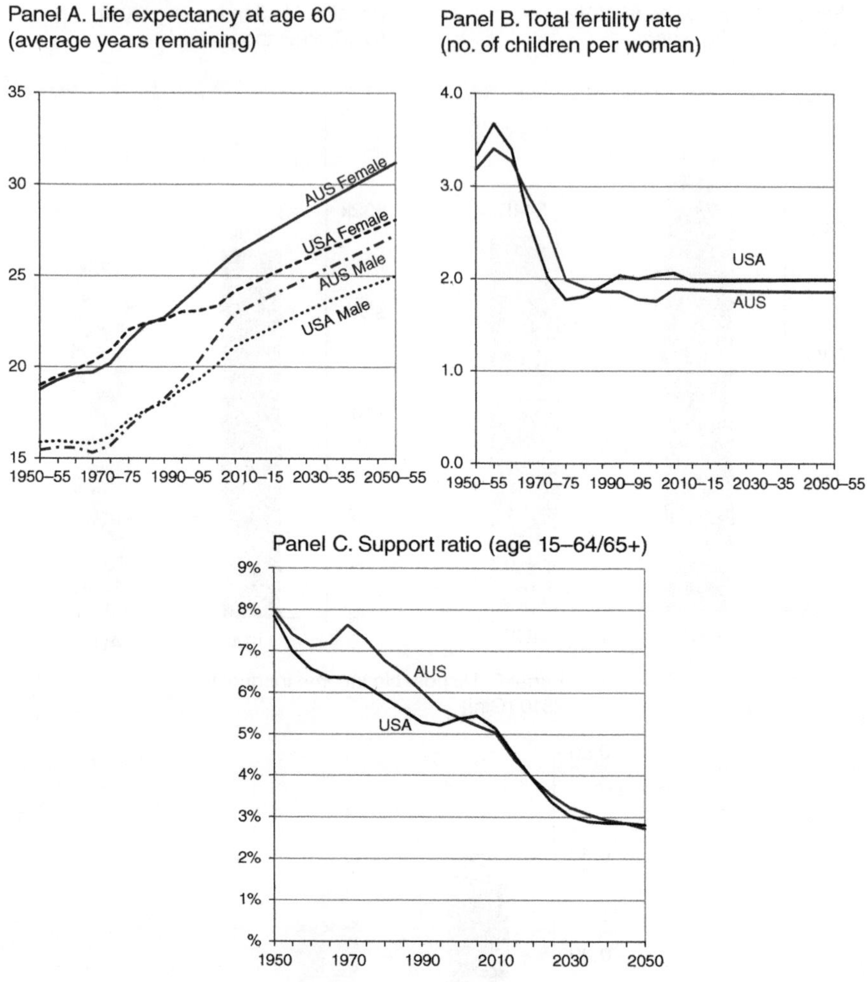

Figure 14.3 Comparison of demography
Source: UN (2013).

comprehensively defined, although the asset test excludes owner-occupied housing.[5]

Currently, the income taper rate (or benefit reduction rate) is set at 50 percent for income over a certain threshold. The asset taper reduces the age pension amount by $1.50 (AUD) per fortnight, for every $1,000 over a threshold that differs by family status and homeownership.

The age pension is financed from general revenue and (including a related disability pension) costs approximately 3.6 percent of GDP (see

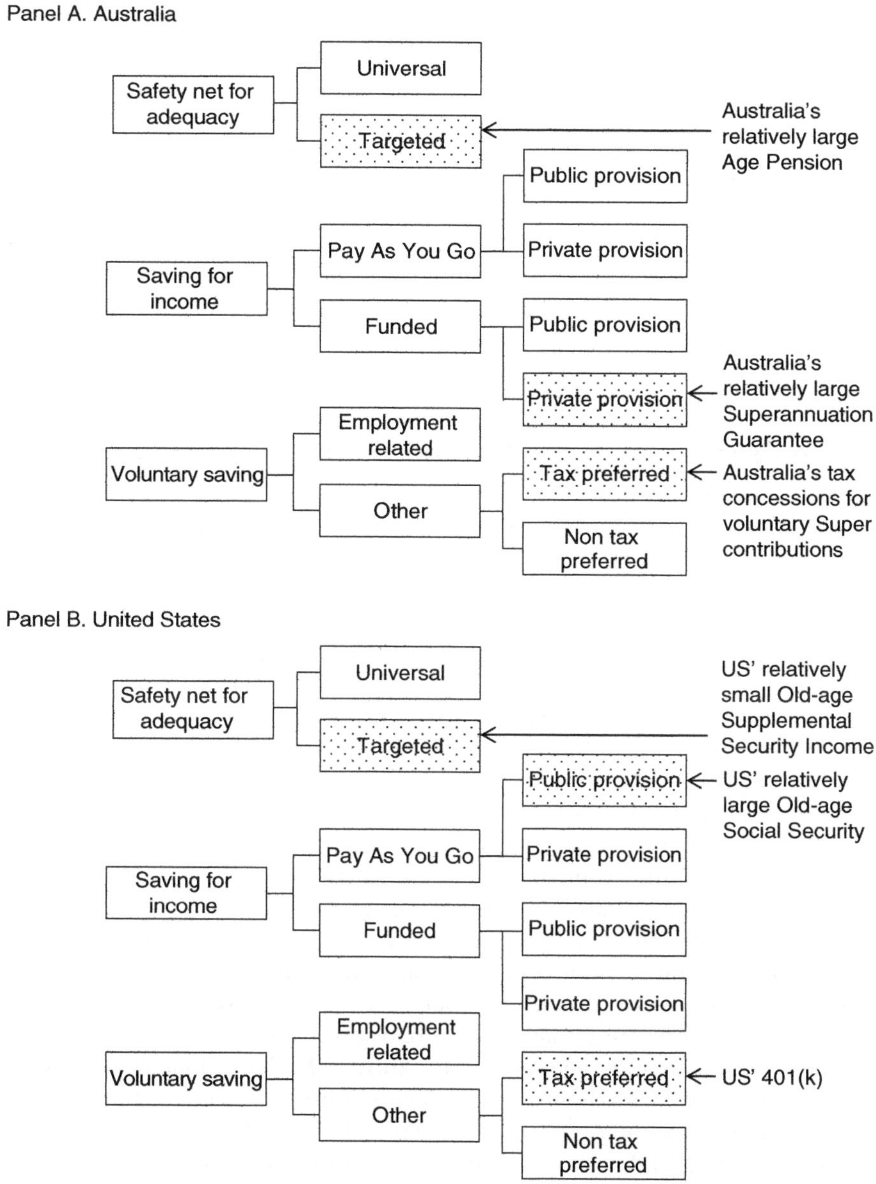

Figure 14.4 Comparison of pension system structure

Source: Adapted by authors.

section on Comparative Retirement Outcomes). A full age pension benefit is equivalent to 27.7 percent of male average full-time earnings for single pensioners and 41.3 percent for couples. Net replacement rates (the comparison of net income before and after retirement) are relatively high because no income tax is payable on the age pension.[6]

This benefit level is indexed to the greater of the increase in male average earnings, the consumer price index (CPI), and a pension and beneficiary living cost index (PBI).[7] As a result, the age pension keeps up with wages in the rest of the economy, and by implication with standards of living. The eligibility age is currently 65 but will increase to age 67 between 2017 and 2023 (Commonwealth of Australia 2009).[8]

Compulsory saving: the Superannuation Guarantee

Australia also mandates significant employer contributions to DC pension funds, known as Superannuation Funds. This 'Superannuation Guarantee' corresponds to government-based income replacement policies such as US Social Security. While tax-preferred, it does not generate government liabilities.

In essence, the Superannuation Guarantee guarantees only that the employer will contribute 9.25 percent of wages to a superannuation fund of the employee's choice; this rate is set to rise to 12 percent over the next several years. Fees and a fund tax are payable on these contributions, so the net contribution to the account is probably closer to 7 percent, increasing to a little less than 10 percent. Some 90 percent of Australian employees are now covered by the superannuation system, about double the level of coverage seen at the time mandatory arrangements were introduced in the late 1980s (Australian Bureau of Statistics 1999, 2011b).

Employees may choose to have the contributions deposited into an account with a range of investment options, managed by any open fund, although 'choice of fund' is not much exercised. All DC funds offer an investment menu and all must nominate a low-management-cost default, known as *MySuper* (which may be age-based), for those (the large majority) who do not actively engage with their superannuation fund. Many people have also set up and self-manage their own superannuation funds, which must comply with various reporting and auditing requirements overseen by the tax authority.

Benefits from superannuation savings can be accessed as early as age 55, the statutory preservation age, which is rising to 60 for those born after June 1964. The form of retirement benefits is not mandated, and these are often taken as lump sums, although there has been a recent trend toward phased withdrawal type income streams (account-based pensions or annuities). At present, very few lifetime annuities are purchased (Bateman and Piggott 2011b).

The lack of policy structure around drawdowns is seen by many as a major flaw in the Australian policy. The Australian Treasury estimated that a fully mature superannuation guarantee after 40 years' contributions, along with the means-tested age pension, can be expected to deliver a retirement replacement rate of around 90 percent for a worker with median male earnings and 78 percent for a worker with average weekly earnings (Gallagher 2011; see section 4 for OECD analysis and US comparisons). But for these outcomes to be realized, retirement income products must be purchased. In practice, the annuity market is very thin, the product range is limited, and there is little in the way of regulatory structure to support its development. In addition, average accumulation balances at retirement are currently relatively small, around $100,000 (AUD) for women and $200,000 for men in 2011–12 (Clare 2014).[9]

How the Superannuation Guarantee was introduced

A brief history of the Superannuation Guarantee may be of interest from a political economy perspective.[10] Until the 1990s, Australians relied mainly on the age pension for retirement income provision. Tax breaks for voluntary superannuation (the third pillar) were introduced in 1915 and subsequently strengthened in 1936. Nevertheless, preservation and coverage were low. By the mid-1980s, only about one-third of workers in the private sector and fewer than half of all workers were covered by superannuation.

Unlike many other OECD countries, a government-provided earnings- or employment-related retirement income scheme has never been introduced in Australia, despite several attempts to do so. Draft legislation for such a plan was developed in 1939, but the outbreak of war meant that it was never introduced into Parliament. In the 1970s, a government-commissioned report recommended a more or less standard social security plan, but a change of government in 1975 meant the report was never acted upon.

In the early 1980s, an era when centralized wage fixing still existed in Australia, a Labor government found itself committed to maintaining real wages in the face of an economy with significant excess demand and the threat of a wage-price spiral. This was resolved by granting an increase equal to the inflation rate of 6 percent, with half being put into industry-based superannuation funds. Following the introduction of 'Productivity Award Superannuation,' coverage increased markedly. This was particularly true for workers in private sector industries dominated by women, and for casual and part-time workers, such as in the retail industry, where coverage increased from 24 percent in 1986 to 82 percent in 1993 (Australian Bureau of Statistics 1999, 2011a, 2011b).

But a contribution system built into the national wage award structure, which was itself being dismantled, was costly and difficult to enforce. In

1991, an attempt supported by government and the unions to increase contributions by a further 3 percent was rejected by the Australian industrial court. The government response was to introduce legislation that would enshrine what is now known as the Superannuation Guarantee. Starting in 1992, it required employers to make contributions on behalf of their employees into an approved superannuation fund, with contribution rates phased to increase to 9 percent by 2002. In 2012 the government initiated a phased increase in the mandatory contribution rate to 12 percent.

Voluntary retirement saving

The first and second pillars of Australia's retirement income system are supplemented by voluntary long-term savings that include superannuation, property, shares, managed investments, and homeownership. The last is the most important non-superannuation asset for most Australians: net equity in home ownership in 2009/10 was worth 40 percent of household wealth and over 80 percent of retirees are owner-occupiers (mostly with no mortgage) (Australian Bureau of Statistics 2011a).

Voluntary contributions fall under the same policy structures as mandatory contributions. Voluntary contributions from employees or employers result in about one-third of superannuation fund members enjoying contribution rates of over 9 percent of earnings (Australian Bureau of Statistics 2009).

Structure and function of the superannuation industry

The superannuation industry comprises a range of fund categories, ranging from public sector employee funds through 'industry' funds, institutionally close to the union movement, corporate and retail funds, and self-managed superannuation funds (SMSFs). Except for SMSFs, superannuation funds are managed by a board of trustees. Their operations are overseen by the Australian Prudential Regulatory Authority (APRA) which provides prudential oversight for banks, insurance companies, and superannuation funds.

Overall, administration costs and charges have tended to be slightly higher than in the US. This may be because of more complex taxation and other arrangements which have been 'grandfathered' with policy change. High fees may also reflect a lack of competition, given, for example, that the mandatory contributions are made not 'into the account' but 'from the employer,' which generates less cost competition to service providers. On latest available figures, average overall fees are about 0.97 percent of managed assets (Cooper 2010) compared to 0.93 percent in the US (Deloitte 2009).

Comparative Retirement Outcomes

The structure and parameters of a retirement income system are influential for retirement outcomes for individuals and government budgets, even if causality is difficult to tease out. In the following, we look at the profile of older people in Australia and the US in relation to poverty alleviation and income replacement from pensions and other sources.

As noted above, Australia's first pillar is more prominent than in other countries, and certainly in comparison to the US. While 78 percent of the Australian population age 65 and over relies on the targeted age pension, in the US only 7 percent are eligible to receive old age Supplemental Security Income (SSI; Figure 14.5A). The value of the Australian age pension is also higher: approximately 29 percent of average earnings, compared to 18 percent for the US SSI (Figure 14.5B). Pension eligibility and generosity arrangements are reflected in elderly poverty rates. Based on a poverty line at 40 percent of the population-wide median income,[11] poverty rates in Australia are significantly lower than in the US—around 5 percent of people aged 65 and older are below the poverty threshold, less than half of the US rate (Figure 14.5C).

Comparing income replacement outcomes is also instructive. While Australian and US workers with average earnings are estimated to pay similar taxes and Social Security contributions, taxes are higher for US pensioners (Figure 14.6A, which shows income tax and social contributions rates for average workers compared with non-working pensioners with pension amounts at the two different levels).

Most of the older US population relies on Social Security for income. Coverage for private pension schemes is about half of the rates seen in Australia where membership is compulsory (Figure 14.6B). So future net replacement rates may be lower for US pensioners. Using mandatory schemes only, the OECD (2013) calculates net replacement rates for hypothetical full-career workers with average earnings to be 68 percent in Australia and 47 percent for those in the US. Replacement rates for those on low incomes are higher, but much more so in Australia, which has a more progressive pension structure (Figure 14.6C).

Older peoples' standards of living depend on a number of factors. For example, homeownership can result in lower reported rates of poverty if rent is imputed in the calculation of income. The level of homeownership is slightly higher in Australia than the US, with 84 percent of people age 65 and over owning their homes, compared to 81 percent in the US (Figure 14.7A). The average older Australian has a greater reliance on capital income (which includes private pensions) than is true for older Americans, who source more of their household income from work (Figure 14.7B). In recent history, the US has had much higher mature age

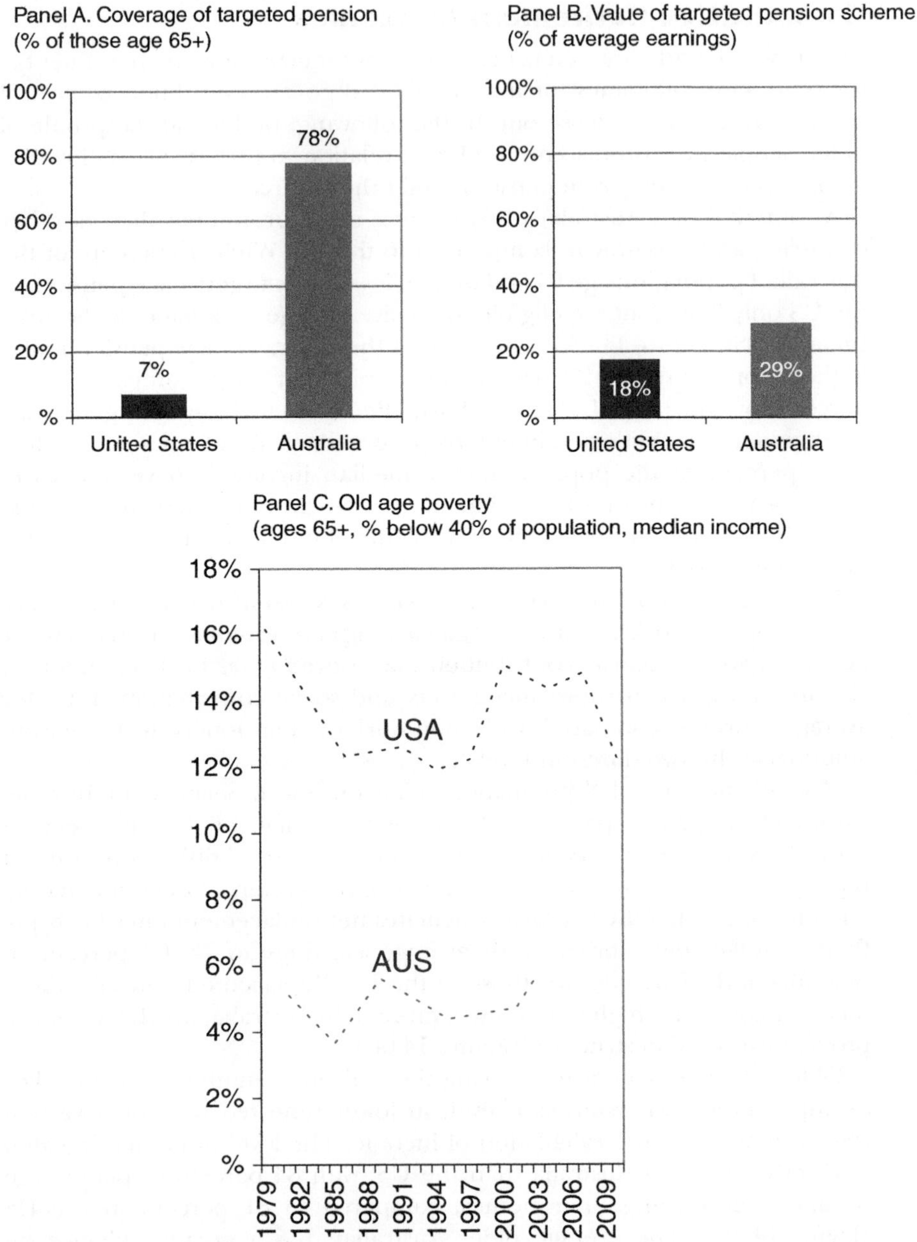

Figure 14.5 Comparison of targeting and poverty

Note: More recent comparable data for old age poverty in Australia is unavailable but it is worth noting that the value of the age pension was increased considerably in 2009.

Source: OECD (2013); LIS (2014).

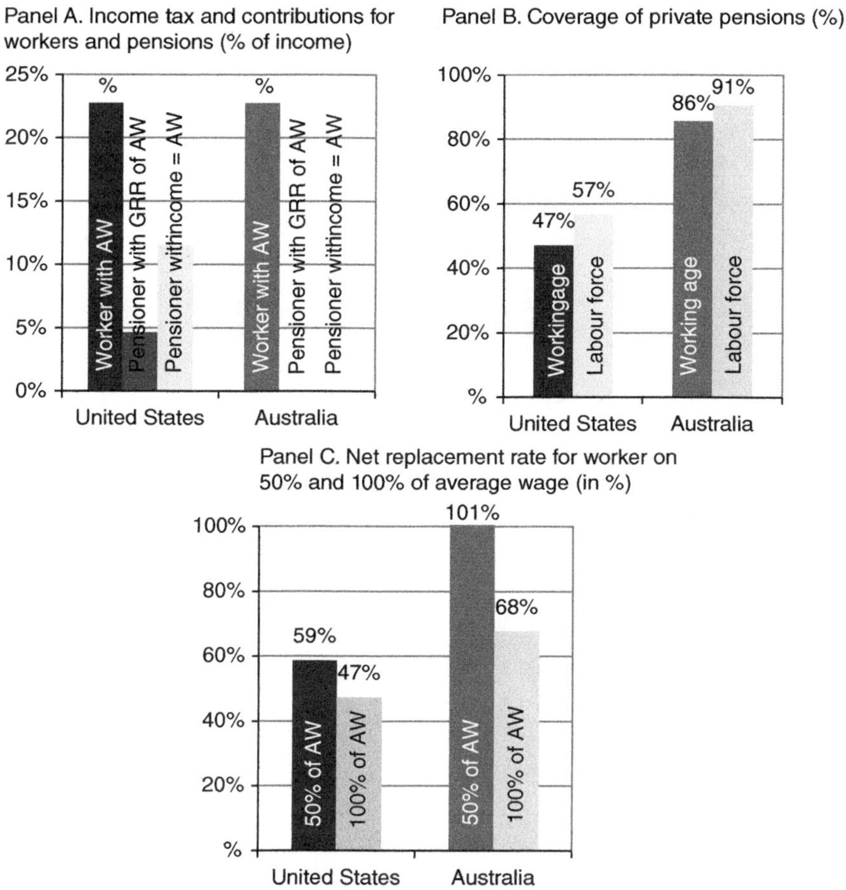

Figure 14.6 Comparison of income replacement

Note: AW denotes average wage. GRR denotes gross replacement rate.
Source: OECD (2013).

labor force participation rates than Australia. Nevertheless, the participation rate in Australia has been increasing at a faster rate than is the case in the US, in part due to increases in the pension access age for Australian women. Australian men between ages 55 and 64 now have higher participation rates than their American equivalents (Figure 14.7C).

A final comparison relates to public expenditure on old age pensions. The cost of age-related public pensions as a proportion of GDP is considerably lower in Australia than the US—3.6 percent versus 4.8 percent of GDP. Official projections from the US Congressional Budget Office and the Australian Treasury suggest that as population aging affects both countries and spending increases, these relative differences will remain. By 2050, fiscal spending is expected to reach 4.9 percent of GDP in Australia and

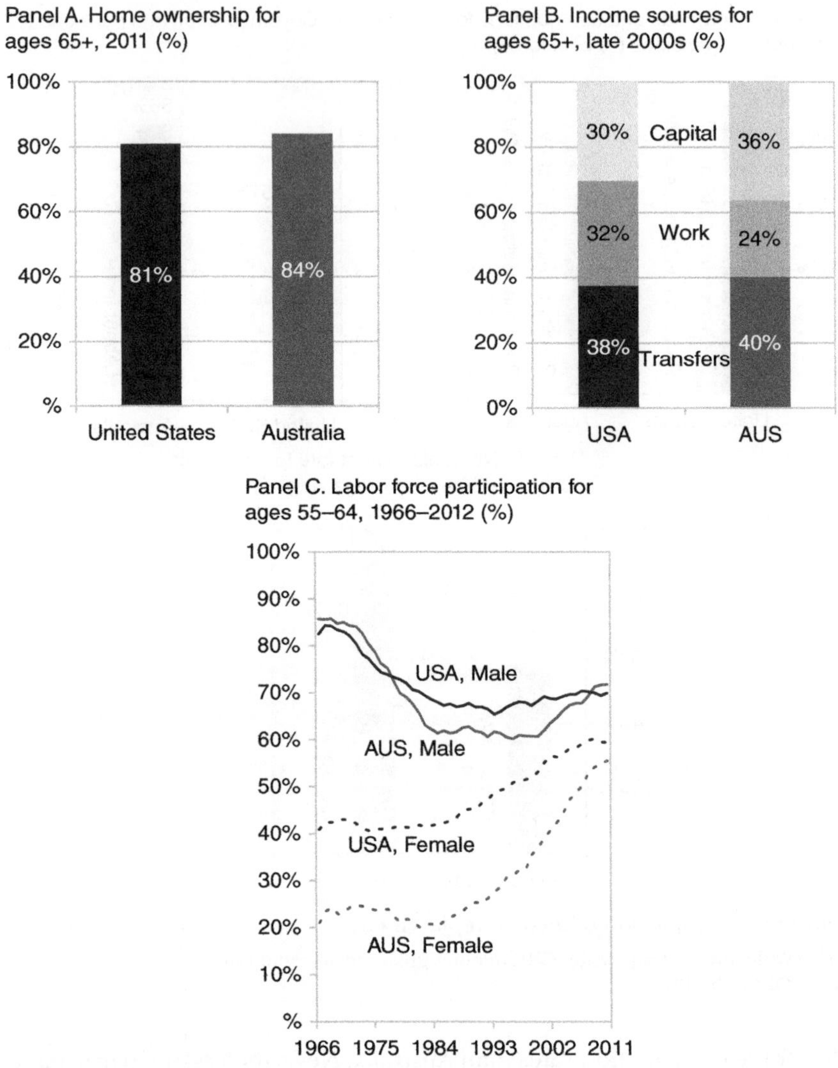

Figure 14.7 Comparison of alternate sources of income

Source: OECD (2013, 2014).

6 percent in the US (Figure 14.8). Much of this difference in public spending comes back to the structural differences between the two retirement income systems. That is, Australia's age pension scheme is much larger and more important than SSI in the US but more modest than US Social Security, while Australia's second pillar is run as a funded DC scheme independent of government.[12]

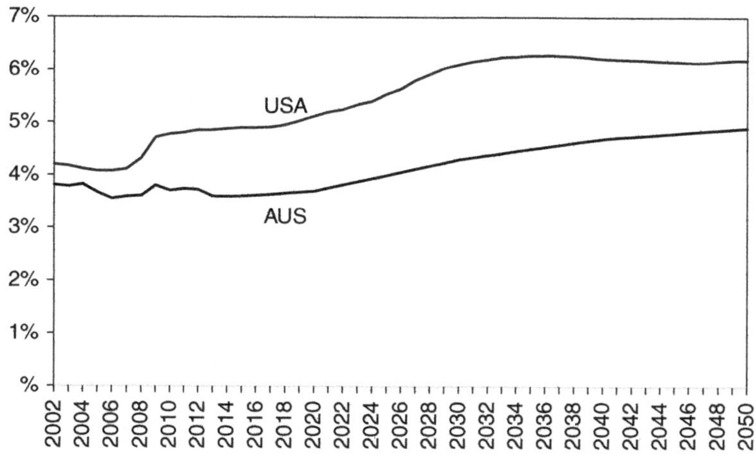

Figure 14.8 Comparison of fiscal projections: central government expenditure on age-related pensions, 2002–2050 (% of GDP)

Source: Commonwealth of Australia (2010); CBO (2013).

Means-Testing and Incentives[13]

Retirement income transfers have the potential to distort incentives at two different points: when tax to fund the transfer is levied and when the transfer itself is received. Both need to be considered when analyzing the economic efficiency of tax-funded transfers.[14] In addition to evaluating effective marginal tax rates (EMTRs) of those being taxed to finance transfers and those eligible to receive them, a complete analysis must include dynamic inter-temporal effects. That is, the promise of transfers in retirement can affect labor supply and savings decisions in working life. Greater entitlement to retirement income, whether or not it is targeted, will have an impact on labor supply and savings rates since the same standard of living can be maintained with less work and saving.

So how can an analysis of effective marginal tax rates (EMTRs) help with understanding the incentive effects of targeted retirement income transfers? The most commonly cited examples are the large EMTRs affecting those on the margin of eligibility. For example, the financial incentives created by the retirement income system and related to EMTRs have been shown empirically to have an effect on labor force participation and retirement decisions (Gruber and Wise 1999). Since efficiency costs increase disproportionately with EMTRs, their assessment is an obvious focus for analysis. But EMTRs need to be balanced against other related explicit taxes in the economy.

To understand the trade-offs between EMTRs, the proportion of the population affected, and other explicit taxes, it is instructive to compare a universal social pension with one that is targeted. The targeted pension will result in high EMTRs for those on the margin of eligibility whose pension is withdrawn but will not affect the wider population in the way that a universal pension will. The proportion of the population that is on the margin of eligibility and the level of their EMTR will depend on the level of benefit, the scope of resources being means-tested, and importantly, the taper rate at which the pension is withdrawn. For example, lower taper rates will mean that a greater proportion of the population is affected but their EMTRs will be lower.[15] Yet having lower taper rates (and EMTRs), or zero taper rates in the case of a universal pension, means that the cost of the program and the resulting revenue requirement requires higher tax rates in the rest of the economy. If the tax burden falls on workers who already pay high taxes, then the lower EMTR for those receiving transfers may be outweighed by high marginal tax rates on employment. Efficiency will therefore depend on an appropriate trade-off between EMTRs of targeted schemes and the tax burden of alternative programs.

Over recent decades, the analysis of means testing has received a boost from new analytical literature on optimal taxation. Since the 1980s, the received wisdom has been that it is inefficient to tax capital since it distorts saving and investment decisions (e.g. see Judd 1985). But more recently this outcome has been challenged. In particular, the advantages of leaving capital income untaxed may not materialize if markets are incomplete or there are liquidity constraints; for example, losses from taxing capital must be weighed against the losses suffered by constrained individuals from taxing labor *instead* of capital.

Erosa and Gervais (2002) show that it may be optimal to impose a positive tax on capital income. This is because an individual's optimal consumption-work plan can vary over the life cycle, and governments pursuing economic efficiency as a goal would therefore want to make use of age-based consumption and labor income tax rates. If these are not available, then capital taxes may be efficient. In a well-known paper, Conesa et al. (2009) use an OLG model to estimate optimal capital and labor income tax rates in the US. The model assumes that individuals face permanent productivity differences and uninsurable idiosyncratic income shocks, which the authors conclude leads to an optimal capital income tax rate of 36 percent. Since true age-based consumption and labor income tax rates are politically impractical, the positive capital income tax rate acts as a second-best solution.

In the present context, however, the most important implication of this research is that means-testing now can be rationalized on economic efficiency grounds. That is, a retirement income transfer with a means test on capital income or assets can act as a tax on capital. In fact, such a means test is better targeted than a standard capital income tax since it is effectively an age-based tax, directly addressing the complementarity between retirement saving and retirement leisure.

So far as we are aware, no country has drawn on the age-based tax literature (e.g. Alvarez et al. 1992; Erosa and Gervais 2002) to inform the construction of means test withdrawal rates. Indeed, there are variations of taper that could be investigated, including rates that depend on the value of assets and age of benefit recipients. The literature itself is deficient in this field. To take just one example, to the authors' knowledge, no study has investigated economic effects of non-linear taper rates.

Some research suggests that economic efficiency is better served by withdrawal rates which are quite significant. An early study by Sefton et al. (2008), focused on the UK pension system, suggested a 'desirable' withdrawal rate of about 40 percent. Kumru and Piggott (2010), using an overlapping generations model incorporating liquidity constraints and stochastic wages, found efficiency improvements from even higher taper rates. These findings contrast with the partial equilibrium analysis of high taper rates examined in isolation from interactions with the economy as a whole and its taxation system, which typically suggest that lower taper rates are welfare-improving. Hence the research agenda is lengthy.

Compulsory Participation?

Mandatory retirement saving can be justified by appeal to economic efficiency on two grounds. First, if retirement transfers are to be provided to less well-off households in retirement, then some form of mandatory saving will offset free-riding behavior induced by the transfer (Hayek 1960). Second, there is much evidence that people under-save for retirement, relative to what would be predicted by a standard life cycle model as optimal. Behavioral economics and finance attribute departures from this benchmark not only to lack of competence, but to inertia, confusion, short-termism, and lack of self-control (Mitchell and Utkus 2003). In such circumstances, mandating contributions can be seen as efficiency-improving.[16] Mandatory contributions were successfully implemented in Australia in part because no mandatory contributory pension plan had been previously in place. Where a contributory earnings-related social security system already operates, mandating savings is a more problematic option.

In many countries, enrollment in an earnings-related pension offered by an employer is not mandatory, which affects coverage. An international comparison of private pension coverage shows that countries with voluntary enrollment into private pensions have consistently lower levels of participation (Figure 14.9A).

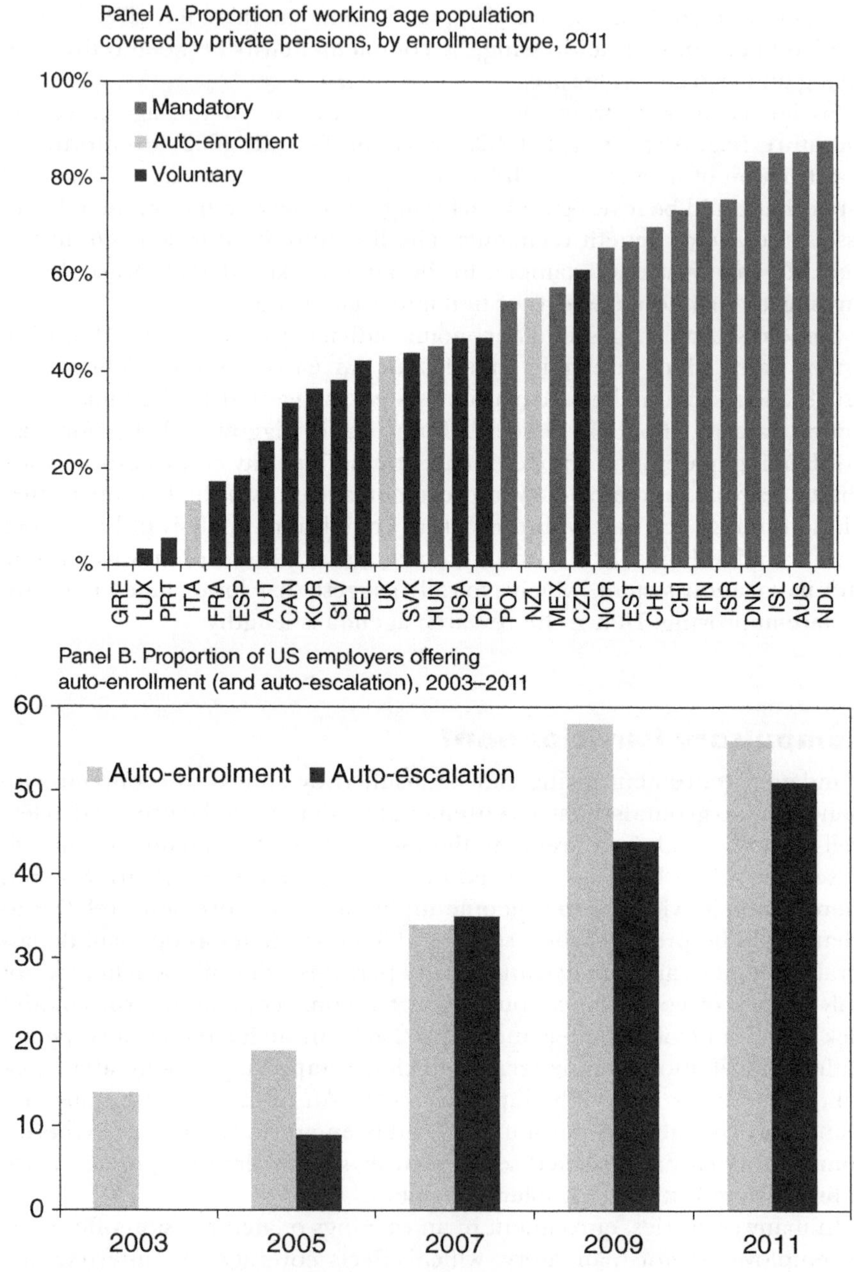

Figure 14.9 Comparison of coverage rates of private pensions

Note: The UK introduced automatic enrolment after the data for 9A was collected; 9B data may over-estimate rates given focus on larger plans/employers.

Source: UN (2013); Benartzi and Thaler (2013).

In place of mandating savings, policymakers are increasingly seeking to use inertia and procrastination by developing defaults related to enrollment and other choice parameters. Some countries such as New Zealand have found success in auto-enrollment, where a new employee is automatically enrolled to contribute to a private pension unless they actively opt out. In the UK, auto-enrollment for occupational pensions was proposed in 2008 and recently implemented. Johnson et al. (2010) submitted a further series of recommendations aimed at making auto-enrollment work in the UK, including changes to eligibility thresholds, portability, and flexibility around re-enrollment. There have also been recent calls in the UK to introduce auto-escalation policies, where the rate of contribution increases over time or is contingent on a future pay rise.

Some employers in the US are also beginning to use such strategies (Figure 14.9B). These have been shown to work well in the US setting. Madrian and Shea (2001) found that 401(k) enrollment was significantly higher under auto-enrollment and that defaults related to contribution rates and investment mix had a substantial influence on changing saving patterns.

Defaults in Australia focus on fund and portfolio choice. A 2010 review of the Superannuation Guarantee recommended that each fund develop a default investment portfolio (Cooper 2010). This recommendation was made in the context of compulsory enrollment for all employees, and a minimum contribution as a percentage of wages.

Table 14.1 shows how a range of countries position policy with regard to choice, within a context where membership of a DC plan is either mandatory or effectively so. Minimum contributions are therefore also mandatory. However, there is considerable variation in the extent of suggestion and persuasion with regard to fund allocation, choice of provider, and benefit. Interestingly, none of these countries promotes taking advice through default settings.

Defaults are now seen as a policy instrument. But because individual circumstances vary so much, standard defaults can be crude and sometimes miscalibrated. In principle, the Australian model allows defaults to be determined on an individual basis, taking wealth, salary, age, and other information held by the pension fund into account, although in practice only age is taken into account within a fund's default settings. Auto-enrollment, auto-investment, auto-escalation of contributions, and auto-annuitization, are all possible settings that should be considered when designing and evaluating a well-structured DC pension plan. For the private sector, these are also important human resource management strategies (Mercer 2013).

TABLE 14.1 Choice in defined contribution schemes in OECD countries, 2013

	No soft or hard compulsion[a]	Default	Tax preference only	Mandated/highly restricted choice
Enrollment				AUS, CHI, DNK (ATP), DNK (OCCUP), EST, ISR, MEX, NOR,[j] POL, SVK, SWE (PPM)
Contribution				AUS, CHI, DNK (ATP), DNK (OCCUP), EST, ISR, MEX, NOR, POL, SVK, SWE (PPM)
Allocation	SVK	AUS, CHI, DNK (Occup.),[e] MEX, EST, NOR, SWE (PPM)		DNK (ATP), ISR, POL
Provider	CHI, EST, SVK	AUS, POL, MEX, ISR		DNK (ATP), DNK (Occup.), NOR, SWE (PPM)
Advice	AUS, CHI, DNK (ATP), DNK (OCCUP), EST, ISR, MEX, NOR1, POL, SVK, SWE (PPM)			
Retirement phase[b]	CHI,[c] MEX[h]			AUS[d], DNK (ATP), DNK (OCCUP), EST, ISR, NOR, POL, SVK, SWE (PPM)
Benefit	AUS, MEX,[i] SVK[k]	DNK (Occup.)[e]		DNK (ATP), CHI[l] EST,[f] ISR,[g] NOR,[f] POL, SWE (PPM)

Notes: [a] Only actuarial adjustment. [b] For retirement decisions, the existence of a minimum age represents a mandated choice. [c] Requires a DC benefit of at least 80% of the maximum targeted benefit and a replacement rate of at least 70%. [d] Tax incentive to delay until 60 until 2024, then mandated to no earlier than 60. [e] Choice with respect to allocation and benefit can differ by scheme and is decided when first becoming a member, but annuities are often the default option. [f] Choice among types of annuities. [g] Once annuity is purchased up to a certain level, left over funds can be taken as lump sum. [h] Members may retire at any age if the accumulated capital in their account allows them to buy an annuity that is at least 30% higher than the minimum guaranteed pension. In this case, the member does not have to complete the 1,250 weeks of contributions. [i] Choice is between phased withdrawal or annuity. Lump sums can be taken only if 1,250 weeks of contributions is not reached. [j] Employer must pay minimum contribution; employee may contribute but does not have to. [k] Annuity or phased withdrawal. No lump sum. [l] Chile allows restricted choice of phased withdrawal, price indexed life annuity or a combination of withdrawals and immediate or deferred annuity, while lump sums are allowed for funds beyond those required to provide a specified level of pension.

Source: Authors' compilation of various sources.

Public Employee Pensions

For a substantial minority of Australian workers, the Superannuation Guarantee had no immediate consequence, because they were already members of a public employee pension plan. In the US, solvency issues have become critical in many state plans and a source of fiscal stress at the state level (Novy-Marx and Rauh 2012). In some countries, particularly emerging economies such as India and China, rapidly aging populations have exacerbated the issue of financing civil service pensions, which are sometimes seen as a source of fiscal stress on their own.

Public sector pensions in Australia are unusual: currently all new members of public sector schemes (except the judiciary and the military) are enrolled in DC plans. While many countries still offer final salary schemes to public sector workers, over the past 20 years Australia has transitioned these from unfunded or partially funded DB to fully funded DC schemes. Admittedly, legacy costs are large, totaling about 15 percent of GDP. However, projections see these declining over time (Bateman and Piggott 2011b).

A recent comparison of Australian and US sub-sovereign pension credit risk commends the switch of Australian states and territories to the more predictable and less risky DC plans (Moody's 2013). Australia also adopted more conservative discount rate assumptions tied to government bond rates. Such policies have contributed to the fact that, according to Moody's, all Australian states (and the Northern Territory) have the highest available credit ratings of AAA or AA1, compared to only 29, or 60 percent, of US states.

Bateman and Piggott (2011a) argue that the introduction of the Superannuation Guarantee in the private sector provided the impetus for reform of public sector pensions. It is part of a long-term trend of private and public sector workers becoming subject to similar policies: as the framework for Superannuation Guarantee developed, it was natural that workers from both sectors were subject to it.

The main remaining challenge for public sector superannuation funds in Australia is dealing with the unfunded liabilities of the now closed pay-as-you-go schemes across the Commonwealth, State, and Territory governments (Bateman and Piggott 2011a). This challenge is being addressed via legislation stipulating regular contributions that will see a gradual fall in unfunded liabilities. In addition, specific funds have been established to finance future liabilities that will come due at a time period when population aging is likely to place significant pressure on government budgets. For example, the Commonwealth government established the Future Fund in early 2006. Sometimes referred to as Australia's 'sovereign wealth fund,' the Future Fund is expressly devoted to financing previously unfunded superannuation liabilities of Commonwealth government employees (including defense personnel). The arm's-length Future Fund was started with contributions from budget surpluses as well as large asset sales, particularly the sale of the previously government-owned telecommunication company, Telstra.

Conclusion

This chapter has outlined Australia's somewhat idiosyncratic system of retirement provision, with its means-tested, flat-rate age pension along with mandatory, pre-funded income replacement. We have also related that structure to the US experience. We speculate that some limited means testing of Social Security might be possible, reducing the system's unfunded liabilities. Although the structure is unusual, Australia is not alone in having a means-tested social pension at the heart of its retirement structure—Denmark is another. Canada moved some distance toward this structure by legislating a tax claw-back of its basic pension, payable by the affluent; this is a possible implementation mechanism which would leave social security entitlements intact.

Mandatory pre-funded pension contributions seem a more difficult reform to implement in an environment which already delivers graduated Social Security benefits. Defaults appear to be expanding 401(k) plan membership in the US. It may be possible to contemplate an initiative such as the UK's by mandating auto-enrollment, at some acceptable contribution rate. Changes in private sector pension provision may make reforms of public sector pensions more palatable.

Endnotes

1. In practice age pension payments are counted in assessable income but the senior and pensioners tax offset means that it is effectively tax-free.
2. The idea of 'three pillars' originated in the seminal World Bank publication, 'Averting the Old Age Crisis' (World Bank 1994), and has also been used in OECD analysis (e.g. OECD 2013).
3. It may only be available subject to a means test, since its function is to ensure the elderly are adequately provided for.
4. The discussion of Australia's retirement income system draws on Bateman and Piggott (2011a) and Bateman (2011).
5. An age service pension is available to veterans. It is paid on the grounds of age or invalidity, and to eligible partners, widows, and widowers. Benefit level is the same as the age pension and the means test also applies. The access age is 60.
6. Recipients of the age pension also gain access to other benefits such as subsidized medication and assistance with rent.

7. Announcements made in the 2014 Australian government budget foreshadow a future change in indexation of benefits to prices only. This would undermine the relative importance of the age pension in Australia. Projections presented in this chapter assume the age pension retains its long-term value relative to wages.
8. Age pension access age for women increased from 60 to age 65 by 2014. Subsequent increases to age 67 will apply to both males and females. Announcements made in the 2014 Australian government budget foreshadow a future rise in the pension access age to 70.
9. The Superannuation Guarantee has not yet fully matured—the initial 9 percent contribution target was phased in, and applied from 2002.
10. See Bateman and Piggott (1997, 1998) for a detailed discussion of the historical evolution of the Australian system.
11. A poverty line at 40 percent of population-wide median income approximates the relevant poverty threshold used by the US government while allowing for comparability across countries. In 2010, the official US poverty thresholds for households with one and two older people were 36 percent and 45 percent of median (unequivalized) income, respectively (authors' calculations based on OECD 2014 and US census data).
12. Note that the comparison of expenditure does not include tax expenditures. In both cases spending on disability pensions is included.
13. This material draws heavily on Piggott et al. (2009).
14. For a discussion of links between redistribution and incentives see Robalino et al. (2007).
15. This point was first made by Blinder and Rosen (1985). Sefton et al. (2008) makes the same point in the context of means-tested pensions in the UK.
16. While Strotz (1956) did not explicitly mention retirement saving, he understood clearly the role of commitment devices: 'We are often willing even to pay a price to pre-commit future actions (and to avoid temptation).'

References

Alvarez, Y., J. Burbidge, T. Farrell, and L. Palmer (1992). 'Optimal Taxation in a Life-Cycle Model.' Canadian Journal of Economics, 25: 111–22.

Australian Bureau of Statistics (ABS) (1999). *Employee Earnings, Benefits and Trade Union Membership*. Canberra: ABS.

Australian Bureau of Statistics (ABS) (2009). *Employment Arrangements, Retirement and Superannuation*. Canberra: ABS.

Australian Bureau of Statistics (ABS) (2011a). *Australian Social Trends*. Canberra: ABS.

Australian Bureau of Statistics (ABS) (2011b). *Employee Earnings, Benefits and Trade Union Membership*. Canberra: ABS.

Commonwealth of Australia (2009). *Secure and Sustainable Pensions*. Canberra: ABS.

Commonwealth of Australia (2010). *Australia to 2050: Future Challenges*. Canberra: ABS.

Bateman, H. (2011). 'Structuring the Payout Phase in a Defined Contribution Scheme in High Income Countries: Experiences of Australia and New Zealand,' presented at the conference, Selected Issues in Strengthening Social Protection in East Asia, Singapore, Mar.

Bateman, H. and J. Piggott (1997). *Private Pensions in OECD Countries—Australia,* OECD Labour Market and Social Policy Occasional Papers, 23. Paris: OECD.

Bateman, H. and J. Piggott (1998). 'Mandatory Retirement Saving in Australia.' *Annals of Public and Cooperative Economics,* 69(4): 547–69.

Bateman, H. and J. Piggott (2011a). 'Civil Services and Military Retirement Income Provision in Australia,' in N. Takayama (ed.), *Reforming Pensions for Civil and Military Servants.* Tokyo: Maruzen Publishing, 29–54.

Bateman, H. and J. Piggott (2011b). 'Too Much Risk to Insure? The Australian (Non-) Market for Annuities,' in O. S. Mitchell, J. Piggott, and N. Takayama (eds), *Securing Lifelong Retirement Income: Global Annuity Markets and Policy.* Oxford: Oxford University Press, 139–76.

Benartzi, S. and R. H. Thaler (2013). 'Behavioral Economics and the Retirement Savings Crisis.' *Science,* 339(1): 1152–3.

Blinder, A. and H. Rosen (1985). 'Notches.' *American Economic Review,* 75(4): 736–47.

Clare, R. (2014). *An Update on the Level and Distribution of Retirement Savings,* ASFA Research and Resource Centre, The Association of Superannuation Funds of Australia Limited. Sydney: ASFA.

Congressional Budget Office (CBO) (2013). 'The 2013 Long-Term Projections for Social Security: Additional Information' (updated 17 Dec. 2013) <http://www.cbo.gov>.

Conesa, J. C., S. Kitao, and D. Krueger (2009). 'Taxing Capital? Not a Bad Idea After All!' *American Economic Review,* 99: 25–48.

Cooper, J. (2010). *Super System Review: Final Report.* Canberra: Commonwealth of Australia.

Deloitte (2009). *Defined Contribution/401(k) Fee Study.* Conducted by Deloitte for the Investment Company Institute. New York: Investment Company Institute.

Erosa, A. and M. Gervais (2002). 'Optimal Taxation in Life-Cycle Economies.' *Journal of Economic Theory,* 105: 338–69.

Gallagher, P. (2011). 'Treasury Measurement of Retirement Income Adequacy,' presentation to FEAL Pre-Forum Discussion, Feb. 9.

Gruber, J. and D. A. Wise (1999). *Social Security and Retirement around the World.* Chicago: University of Chicago Press.

Hayek, F. A. von (1960). *The Constitution of Liberty.* Chicago: University of Chicago Press.

International Monetary Fund (IMF) (2014). *World Economic Outlook.* Washington, DC: IMF.

Johnson, P., D. Yeandle, and A. Boulding (2010). *Making Automatic Enrolment Work: A Review for the Department for Work and Pensions.* London: Department for Work and Pensions. <www.dwp.gov.uk>.

Judd, K. L. (1985). 'Redistributive Taxation in a Simple Perfect Foresight Model.' *Journal of Public Economics,* 28 (Oct.): 59–83.

Kumru, C. and J. Piggott (2010). *Should Public Retirement Pensions Be Means-Tested?* UNSW Working Paper. Sydney: University of New South Wales.

Luxemburg Income Study, Cross National Data Center (LIS) (2014). *Key Figures Database.* <http://www.lisdatacenter.org>.

Madrian, B. C. and D. F. Shea (2001). 'The Power of Suggestion: Inertia in 401(k) Participation and Savings Behavior.' *Quarterly Journal of Economics,* 116(4): 1149–87.

Mercer (2013). 'Corporate Retirement Plans: What's the Point?' <www.mercer.com/dc>.

Mitchell, O., and S. Utkus (2003). *Lessons from Behavioral Finance for Retirement Plan Design,* Working Paper 03-34. Philadelphia, PA: Wharton Financial Institutions Center.

Moody's (2013). 'Moody's on Pensions: Sub-Soverign Credit Risk.' <http://www.moodys.com>.

Novy-Marx, R. and J. D. Rauh (2012). 'Fiscal Imbalances and Borrowing Costs: Evidence from State Investment Losses.' *American Economic Journal: Economic Policy,* 4(2): 182–213.

Organisation for Economic Co-operation and Development (OECD) (2013). *Pensions at a Glance.* Paris: OECD.

Organisation for Economic Co-operation and Development (OECD) (2014). *OECD Stat Extracts Database.* Paris: OECD.

Piggott, J., D. Robalino, and S. Jimenez-Martin (2009). 'Incentive Effects of Retirement Income Transfers,' in D. Robalino, D., R. Holzmann, and N. Takayama (eds), *Closing the Coverage Gap: The Role of Social Pensions and Other Retirement Income Transfers.* Washington, DC: World Bank.

Robalino, D., G. V. Rao, and O. Sluchinsky (2007). *Preventing Poverty among the Elderly in MENA Countries: Role and Optimal Design of Old-Age Subsidies.* Washington, DC: Human Development Department, Middle East and North Africa Region, World Bank.

Sefton, J., J. van de Ven, and M. Weale (2008). 'Means Testing Retirement Benefits: Fostering Equity or Discouraging Savings.' *Economic Journal,* 118: 556–90.

Strotz, R. H. (1956). 'Myopia and Inconsistency in Dynamic Utility Maximisation.' *Review of Economic Studies,* 23(3): 166–80.

United Nations (UN) (2013). *World Population Prospects: The 2012 Revision.* New York: United Nations. <esa.un.org/wpp>.

World Bank (1994). *Averting the Old Age Crisis.* New York: Oxford University Press.

Chapter 15

Singapore's Social Security Savings System: A Review and Some Lessons for the United States

Benedict S. K. Koh

Singapore is one of the world's fastest aging nations, due primarily to its low fertility rates and long life expectancy.[1] In the next two decades, it may overtake every country except Japan in its elderly fraction of the population. This demographic trend places a heavy burden on its pension system to be the main vehicle to prepare citizens for old age.

Singapore's social security savings system was set up with the primary goal of helping citizens prepare for retirement. Unlike the defined benefit Social Security system adopted by the United States and European nations, Singapore operates a defined contribution (DC) savings system administered by a government statutory board, the Central Provident Fund (CPF). The CPF was established even before Singapore became independent from the British colonial rule. Under this system, members have their own individual retirement accounts and assume sole responsibility for providing for their own retirement needs. When originally conceived, CPF's main focus was retirement adequacy. However, over the years, it has evolved into a system with multi-faceted objectives.

The CPF Board states that it aims to achieve five objectives, helping its members accumulate sufficient savings to (1) finance retirement, (2) own a home, (3) pay for health care, (4) provide insurance protection for family, and (5) enhance assets for future consumption. The CPF calibrates its policies to only provide for basic needs. This means that individuals who wish to have a lavish retirement must rely on private savings to fund needs beyond the basic level. The income groups targeted by policymakers are the 10th to 80th percentile of the working population, with the lowest income group receiving financial assistance from the government.

This chapter reviews the key features of Singapore's social security savings system and evaluates whether the five key objectives set by the CPF have been successfully achieved. We show that Singapore's system is generally successful in meeting the needs of citizens for home ownership, health care, and protection but it requires reforms to secure retirement adequacy and asset enhancement for its members. We go on to make specific suggestions for the types of reforms that might be undertaken to improve retirement security.

In what follows, we first outline the structure of Singapore's social security savings system, focusing on the links between the Central Provident Fund's schemes and its five key objectives. Next, we show how the CPF system has been liberalized to cater to the changing needs of its members. Subsequently, we identify gaps in the current system and suggest reforms that can be made to improve it. We conclude by identifying some lessons Singapore's pension system can provide for the United States.

The Central Provident Fund (CPF)

The Central Provident Fund was first established in 1955 as a mandatory retirement savings scheme. As of the end of 2013, the scheme covered 3.51 million members, of whom 1.85 million were active (Table 15.1).[2] The CPF's defined contribution plan is funded by mandatory contributions from members' monthly wages. Table 15.2 shows the contribution rates made by employees (age 35 and below) and employers to the CPF Board. At inception of the scheme, the contribution rate was 10 percent; it subsequently rose to a peak of 50 percent in 1984–5. The contribution rate fluctuated between 35 and 40 percent during the thirteen-year period between 1986 and 1998, before declining to a low of 30 percent in 1999. It held steady at 36 percent over the period 2011 to 2014.

The CPF Board initially channeled all contributions into a single account, but over the years this has expanded to four accounts: the Ordinary Account (OA), the Special Account (SA), the Medisave Account (MA), and the Retirement Account (RA) (Figure 15.1). Cash savings in these accounts earn interest on their balances. The savings in the Ordinary Account (OA) can be withdrawn to purchase homes, service mortgage payments, finance premiums for insurance protection, pay for children's tertiary education, and to invest in financial products to grow savings. The Special Account, introduced in 1977, holds savings primarily for retirement, which cannot be withdrawn before the age of 55. Members can deposit them with the CPF Board to earn interest, or they can invest in a smaller set of lower risk financial products. The Medisave account, created in 1984, holds savings for members to pay inpatient hospital bills, selected outpatient treatments, and premiums for insurance against catastrophic illness and disabilities. All working adults have only three accounts until they turn 55 years old, when savings earmarked for retirement are deposited into the Retirement Account (RA). Since 2013, it is mandatory for all CPF members to invest

TABLE 15.1 Contributions and balances in Singapore's Central Provident Fund (CPF) system

	2008	2009	2010	2011	2012	2013
Total Number of CPF Members (mil)	3.23	3.29	3.34	3.38	3.42	3.51
Total Number of Active CPF Members (mil)	1.61	1.64	1.7	1.74	1.79	1.85
Total Contributions (S$m)	20,294	20,125	21,993	24,628	26,048	28,530
Ordinary Account (OA) Balance (S$m)	65,341.10	70,593.80	77,939.50	85,084.80	91,862.00	98,336.20
Special Account (SA) Balance (S$m)	30,547.30	35,389.20	40,392.70	46,533.70	53,191.90	60,142.60
Medisave Account (MA) Balance (S$m)	42,928.20	46,238.00	50,671.20	55,329.30	60,024.40	65,576.00
Retirement Account Balance and Others (RA) (S$m)	12,490.50	14,583.00	16,884.60	20,597.70	25,079.30	28,913.80
Total Members' Balance (S$m)	151,307.10	166,804.00	185,880.00	207,545.50	230,157.70	252,968.60

Source: Singapore's CPF (2014).

their RA savings in life annuities (CPF life) to provide a stream of income from age 65 until their deaths.

The CPF contribution rates and allocation into the three accounts are not uniform but decline with age as shown in Table 15.3. In 2014, those age 35 and below had to contribute 20 percent of their monthly wages, and their employers 16 percent, to the CPF Board. Of the total 36 percent contribution, 23 percent is deposited into the Ordinary Account, 6 percent into the Special Account, and 7 percent into the Medisave Account. At the other end of age band, contributions from elderly workers over 65 and their employers decline sharply to 5 percent and 6.5 percent respectively; the allocations into Ordinary, Special, and Medisave accounts are 1, 1, and 9.5 percent respectively. These contribution rates apply to wages up to an income ceiling of S$5,000 per month.[3] For workers earning more than S$5,000 per month, both the employer and employee contributions are computed based on the income ceiling.[4]

Members' contributions into their CPF accounts over time have resulted in substantial asset accumulation. Aggregate contributions to the OA, SA,

TABLE 15.2 Singapore CPF contribution rates by employers and employees age 35 and under (% of monthly wage)

Year	Contribution rate (for monthly wages $\geq$ \$750)			Credited to			
	Contribution by employer (% of wage)	Contribution by employee (% of wage)	Total contribution (% of wage)	Ordinary Account (% of wage)	Special Account (% of wage)	Medisave Account (% of wage)	Income ceiling for CPF contributions (S$)
1955 to 1967	5	5	10				500
1970	8	8	16				1,875
1975	15	15	30				2,000
1984	25	25	50	40	4	6	5,000
1986	10	25	35	29	0	6	6,000
1990	16.5	23	39.5	30	3.5	6	6,000
1995	20	20	40	30	4	6	6,000
1999	10	20	30	24	0	6	6,000
2000	12	20	32	24	2	6	6,000
2005	13	20	33	22	5	6	5,000
2010	15	20	35	23	5	7	4,500
2014	16	20	36	23	6	7	5,000

Source: Singapore's CPF (2014).

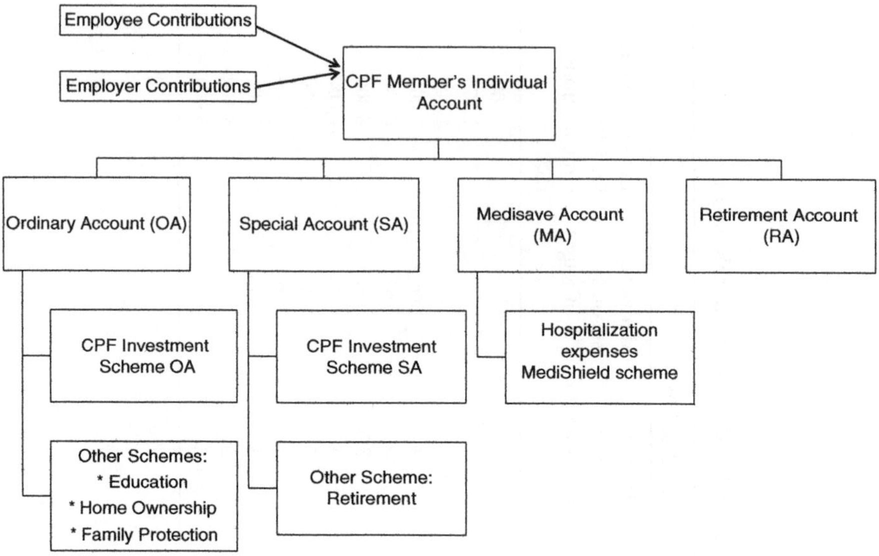

Figure 15.1 Central Provident Fund (CPF): overview
Source: Singapore's CPF (2014).

TABLE 15.3 2014 contribution rates for various age groups (% of monthly wage)

	Contribution Rate (for monthly wages ≥ $750)			Credited to		
Employee Age (Years)	Contribution by Employer	Contribution by Employee	Total Contribution	Ordinary Account	Special Account	Medisave Account
35 & below	16	20	36	23	6	7
Above 35–45	16	20	36	21	7	8
Above 45–50	16	20	36	19	8	9
Above 50–55	14	18.5	32.5	13.5	9.5	9.5
Above 55–60	10.5	13	23.5	12	2	9.5
Above 60–65	7	7.5	14.5	3.5	1.5	9.5
Above 65	6.5	5	11.5	1	1	9.5

Source: Singapore's CPF (2014).

and Medisave accounts in 2013 totaled S$28.5 billion, and CPF balances stood at S$253 billion (Table 15.1). Retirement savings of members have grown 67 percent over the last five years.

Currently, CPF savings in the Ordinary Account (OA) and Special Account (SA) are paid a government-set interest rate of 2.5 percent and 4 percent per annum respectively. This interest rate is not fixed but can fluctuate over the years, as shown in Table 15.4. The highest interest rate

TABLE 15.4 Singapore CPF interest rates paid over time

A. Interest Rate Paid on All CPF Accounts: 1955–1995

Year	CPF Interest Rate Per Annum (%)
1955–1962	2.5
1963	5
1964–1966	5.25
1967–1969	5.5
1970–1973	5.75
1974–Feb. 1986	6.5
Mar.–June 1986	5.78
July–Dec. 1986	5.38
Jan.–June 1987	4.34
July 1987–Dec. 1987	3.31
Jan.–June 1988	3.19
July–Dec. 1988	2.96
Jan.–June 1989	3.1
July–Dec. 1989	3.39
Jan.–June 1990	3.77
July–Dec. 1990	3.88
Jan.–June 1991	4.85
July–Dec. 1991	4.54
Jan.–June 1992	4.59
July–Dec. 1992	3.31
Jan.–June 1993	2.62
July 1993–Dec. 1994	2.5
Jan.–June 1995	3.1

B. Higher Interest Rates Were Paid from Mid-1995 on Special, Retirement, and Medisave Accounts

Year	Interest Rate Per Annum (%)	
From 1 July 1995		
	Ordinary and Medisave Accounts	Special and Retirement Accounts
July–Dec. 1995	3.82	5.07
Jan.–June 1996	3.52	4.77
July 1996–June 1998	3.48	4.73
July–Dec. 1998	4.29	5.79
Jan.–June 1999	4.41	5.91
July 1999–Sept. 2001	2.5	4
From 1 October 2001		
	Ordinary Account	Medisave, Special and Retirement Accounts
Oct. 2001–Dec. 2006	2.5	4

Notes:

a) The Special Account, Medisave Account, and Retirement Account were introduced in July 1977, Apr. 1984, and Jan. 1987 respectively.

b) From 1955 to 1976, CPF interests were credited and compounded annually.

c) From 1977 to 1985, CPF interests were credited quarterly and compounded annually.

d) From 1986 to present, CPF interests are computed monthly and compounded and credited annually.

e) From 1 July 1999, CPF interests are reviewed quarterly.

Source: Singapore's CPF (2014).

paid was 6.5 percent during the thirteen-year period from 1974 to 1986. Since then, the OA rate has declined gradually to 2.5 percent, in line with the global interest cycle. The actual return paid on Ordinary Account balances is computed as the maximum of 2.5 percent or the average deposit rate paid on the twelve-month fixed deposit and savings deposits by major local banks.[5] This means that the CPF Board guarantees a minimum nominal return of 2.5 percent per annum (stipulated by the CPF Act) and it provides members the opportunity to earn a higher return should bank deposit rates rise. The interest rate paid on balances in Special, Medisave, and Retirement Accounts is computed as the twelve-month average yield of ten-year Singapore Government Securities plus 1 percent. However, the rate has a floor of 4 percent, set at 1.5 percent above the OA rate. There has been no change in the OA rate of 2.5 percent and SA rate of 4 percent since 1999. To help members grow their savings further, the CPF Board announced that it would pay an extra 1 percent on the first S$60,000 of combined savings, including up to S$20,000 in the Ordinary Account. As of the end of 2013, CPF members have S$253 billion in savings, of which 39 percent is allocated in the Ordinary Account, 24 percent in the Special Account, 26 percent in the Medisave Account, and 11 percent in the Retirement Account.

Review of Singapore's Social Security Savings System

Currently, the CPF operates a comprehensive social security savings system providing funding for retirement, health care, home ownership, family protection, and asset enhancement. These objectives were achieved through various schemes introduced from 1968 to 2009, as shown in Table 15.5. On the program's inception, all CPF savings were defaulted into a single account earning a prescribed interest rate for retirement. Over time, the CPF system has liberalized to permit savings to be used for other purposes. The Home Ownership Scheme (HOS) was introduced in 1968 to permit members to use CPF savings to purchase public housing apartments.[6] Ten years later, in 1978, CPF liberalized further to allow members to purchase common shares in a listed company (Singapore Bus Service). In 1981 and 1986, CPF savings were permitted to be used for the purchase of private properties and commercial properties respectively. The Approved Investment Scheme (IS) was introduced in 1986 to allow members to use a restricted portion of their savings for investment in specified financial instruments. The scheme was further liberalized to allow members to invest 100 percent of OA and SA savings in 2001.[7] Over the decades, the CPF Board has introduced many new schemes such as Home Protection, Medisave Account, Minimum Sum, Dependent's Protection,

TABLE 15.5 Singapore CPF schemes

Goal	Scheme	Year introduced
1) Home Ownership	Public Housing Scheme	1968
	Residential Properties Scheme	1981
2) Protection for family	Home Protection Scheme	1981
	Dependent's Protection Scheme	1989
3) Healthcare Financing	Medisave Account	1984
	MediShield Scheme	1990
	Medifund	1993
	Eldershield	2002
4) Retirement Adequacy	Minimum Sum Scheme	1987
	CPF Top-up Scheme	1995
	CPF Life Annuity	2009
5) Asset Enhancement	CPF Investment Scheme	1986
	Non-residential Properties Scheme	1986
6) Others	Tertiary Education financing for children	1989

Note: When introduced in 1986, the CPF Investment Scheme was known as Approved Investment Scheme (IS).

Source: Singapore's CPF (2014).

Education Financing, MediShield, Medifund, Eldershield, and the CPF life annuities to enhance the social security savings system.

In the following sections, we review the key measures taken by the CPF to achieve its goals of retirement adequacy, home ownership, health care adequacy, financial protection, and asset enhancement.

Home ownership

Singapore citizens are encouraged to own their homes, to ensure that they not only have roofs over their heads but are also rooted in their country. The CPF has introduced two schemes, the Public Housing Scheme and the Residential Properties Scheme, to promote home ownership.

The Public Housing Scheme was introduced in 1968 to help members purchase public housing apartments known as HDB flats. These flats ranged in size from 807 square feet (three-room) to 1,453 square feet (five-room). The amount of withdrawals allowed from members' OA account is the minimum of either the purchase price or the market value of the flat. In addition, OA savings can be used to service the mortgage payments for the duration of the loan, which can be as long as 30 years.

The Residential Properties Scheme was introduced in 1981 to help CPF members purchase homes sold by private developers. These homes cost substantially more than public housing apartments. Under the scheme, CPF members can withdraw more than 160 percent of the value of the purchased property from their Ordinary Account to pay for the purchase price as well as service mortgage payments. In recent years, the CPF has taken steps to reduce the excessive withdrawal of CPF savings for housing, with the aim of reducing the limit gradually to 120 percent of the home's valuation.

Figure 15.2A shows a time series of home ownership rates in Singapore, which grew from 58.8 percent in 1980 to 90.5 percent in 2013. A comparison of the home ownership statistics across countries in Figure 15.2B indicates that Singapore has one of the highest home ownership rates in the world. Home ownership is much higher in Singapore (90.5 percent) compared to those in developed countries such as the United States (66 percent) and United Kingdom (64 percent). This shows that the two housing schemes have been successful in promoting home ownership in Singapore.

Pursuing high home ownership does come at a cost of diminished retirement adequacy. Figure 15.3 shows that 44 percent of cumulative CPF contributions have been invested in housing, leaving the remaining for retirement and other purposes. The decline in retirement adequacy is somewhat mitigated by the appreciation of home values over the last four decades. Figure 15.4A shows that private properties have appreciated 16 times since 1975 or 7.77 percent per annum for the last 38 years. Figure 15.4B shows that public housing apartments also registered five times appreciation since 1990, or 8.2 percent per annum over the last 23 years. The sharp appreciation in the home values allows CPF members the option of cashing out of their properties or entering in a reverse mortgage contract to generate income to finance retirement.

Financial protection for families

A key financial risk faced by families is the loss of income due to death or permanent disability of the breadwinner. To hedge this risk, the CPF Board has introduced two insurance schemes (dependent's protection scheme and home protection scheme) to cover members and their dependents against death and permanent disability.[8] The Dependents' Protection Scheme provides term insurance protection of S$46,000 up to age 60 at an affordable premium. The policy provides financial assistance to families in the first few years of the insured's incapacity or death. CPF members who wish to have insurance coverage of more than S$46,000 can utilize their OA savings to purchase private insurance. Table 15.6 shows that more than half (between 55 and 57 percent) of CPF members purchase term insurance plans to protect their families.

The Home Protection Scheme is a mortgage-reducing insurance scheme to prevent members from losing their homes in the event of death or

Panel A. Percentage of home ownership in Singapore over time.

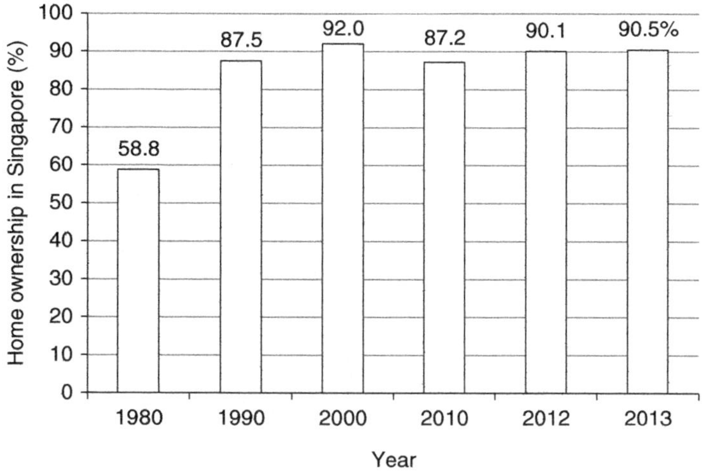

Panel B. Percentage of home ownership across countries.

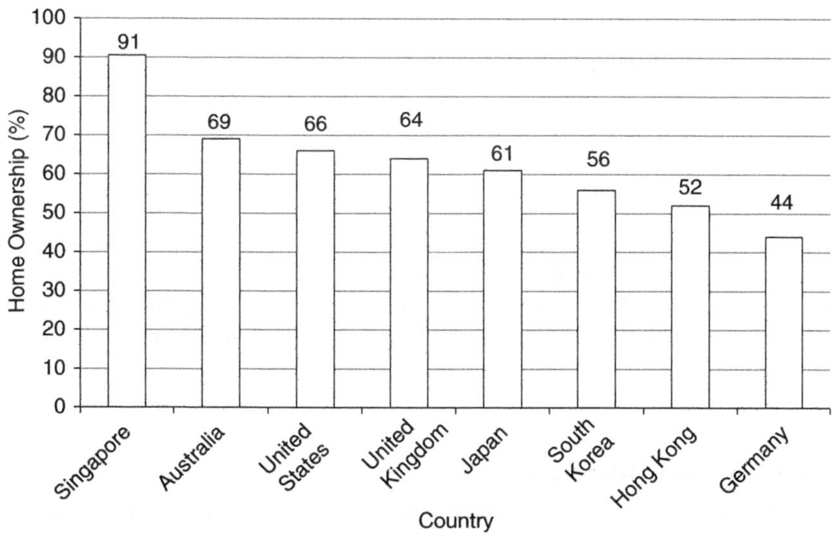

Figure 15.2 Comparative home ownership statistics

Source: Singapore's Ministry of National Development (2014) and Singapore Department of Statistics (2013).

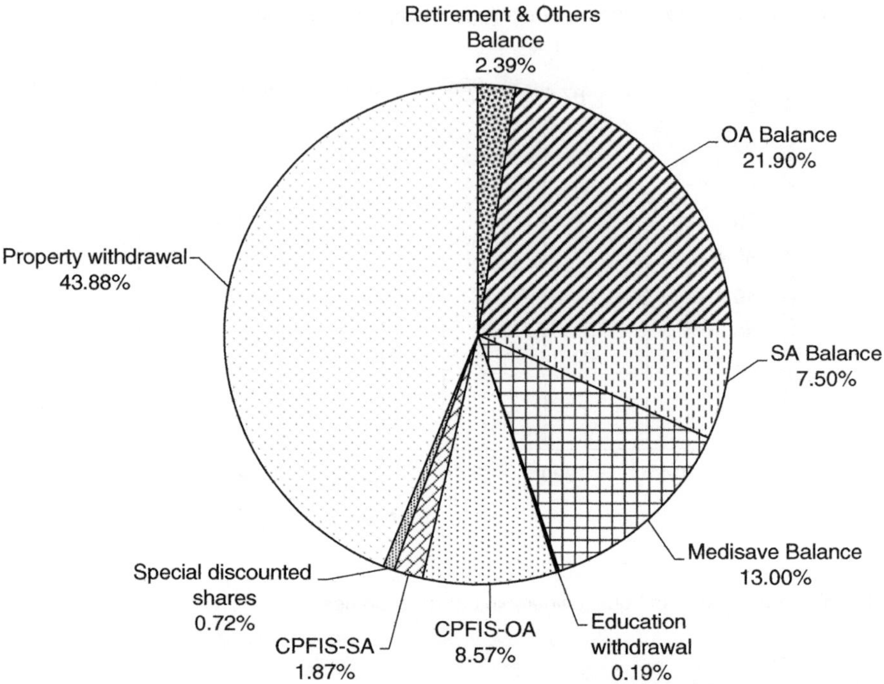

Figure 15.3 Cumulative use of Central Provident Funds. (Ordinary Account and Special Account combined)

Source: Koh et al. (2008a).

permanent disability. This scheme is mandatory for members who use CPF savings to purchase public housing. When death or permanent disability occurs, the CPF Board will pay off the insured's outstanding housing loan. The scheme covers members until age 65 or for the full duration of the housing loan.

Health care financing

As citizens age, their health care expenditures are expected to rise significantly. Such increases result from escalation in health care costs, increasing usage of sophisticated medical technology for treatment, and longer life expectancy of individuals. The CPF supports health care financing for its members through the 3-M framework: Medisave, MediShield, and MediFund. The Medisave Scheme was set up in 1984 to help members save for future medical expenditures. Initially, these savings could only be used to

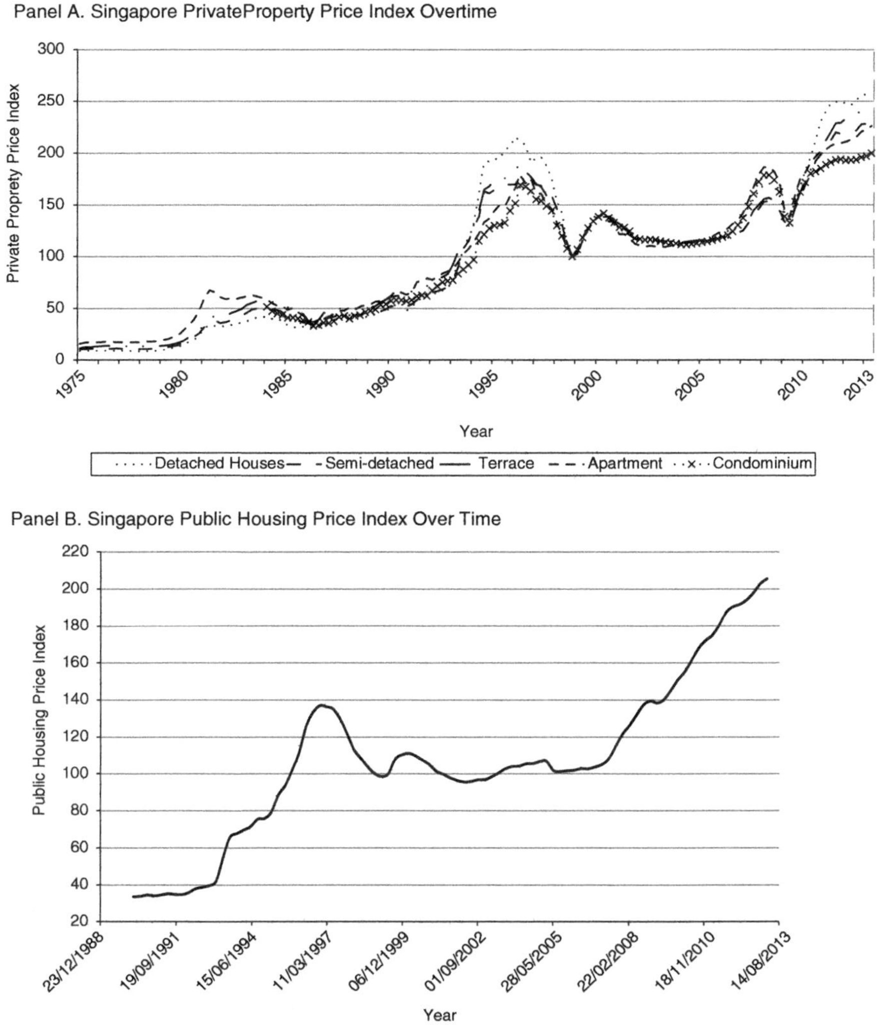

Figure 15.4 Singapore property price indexes over time

Source: Urban Redevelopment Authority (2014) and Housing and Development Board (2014).

pay inpatient hospitalization expenses incurred by members or their dependents. Over time, the scheme was expanded to permit selected out-patient treatments such as chemotherapy and radiotherapy, along with step-down care in community hospitals and hospices. Savings in the Medisave Account can also be used to pay premiums for medical insurance schemes such as MediShield and ElderShield. Table 15.7 shows contribution rates as a share of salary that go into the Medisave Account for the various age

TABLE 15.6 Dependent Protection Scheme (DPS) and MediShield Schemes under Singapore CPF over time

Dependants' Protection Scheme (DPS)	2005	2006	2007	2008	2009	2010	2011	2012
No. of persons covered by DPS	1,676,038	1,725,661	1,776,604	1,829,835	1,871,599	1,893,488	1,923,090	1,947,326
% of enrollment	55	56	56	57	57	57	57	57
No. of persons covered by Medischield Scheme	1,955,392	2,763,673	2,870,631	3,075,994	3,298,682	3,389,815	3,496,523	3,542,898
% of insured persons	56	78	78	84	88	90	92	93

Source: Singapore's CPF (2014).

TABLE 15.7 Contributions to MediSave Account by age groups (% of monthly wage)

Year	Age						
	< 35	35–44	45–9	50–4	55–9	60–4	> 65
1984	6	6	6	6	6	6	6
1990	6	6	6	6	6	6	6
1995	6	7	8	8	8	8	8
2000	6	7	8	8	8	8	7.5
2005	6	7	8	8	8	8.5	8.5
2010	7	8	9	9	9	9.5	9.5
2014	7	8	9	9.5	9.5	9.5	9.5

Source: Singapore's CPF (2014).

groups. For a young person age 35 years and below, 7 percent of monthly income is credited to his Medisave Account in 2014, while the contribution rate is higher, at 9.5 percent, for those over age 50.

To ensure that there are sufficient savings for health care, members are encouraged to build up their Medisave Account balances to $43,500. Once they attain that amount, excess savings will be transferred to their Special Accounts (below age 55) or Retirement Accounts (above age 55). In addition, members must set aside the Medisave Required Amount of $40,500 in the Medisave Account at age 55 to ensure there are sufficient savings to finance future medical expenditures during retirement.

To help members hit those targets, the CPF Board has progressively increased contributions to Medisave Accounts from 6 percent in 1984 to a range of 7–9.5 percent in 2014 for the various age groups (Table 15.7). Furthermore, since 1992, contribution rates for older age groups have increased more rapidly than those in the younger age groups.

While CPF members can rely on their Medisave savings to pay small hospital bills and outpatient treatments, they do risk depleting these savings if they are struck with prolonged or catastrophic illnesses. To help members pay these large hospital bills, the MediShield Scheme was introduced in 1990 to provide insurance coverage for costly health care expenditures. Medishield uses risk pooling to keep the cost of insurance low and provide wider coverage for participants. The scheme covers members up to 92 years of age. Those who wish to have insurance coverage for treatment in private hospitals or better class wards in public hospitals can purchase upgraded insurance plans (Integrated Shield Plan) from private insurers. The Medishield is an opt-in plan with a high participation rate of 93 percent in 2012 (see Table 15.6).

The health care needs of average CPF members are adequately covered by the Medisave and MediShield schemes. Nevertheless, a minority of people are too poor to enroll in the MediShield plan or contribute to their Medisave Accounts. The government has specifically created the Medifund to help this group with their health care bills. Applicants are means-tested to ensure that only the financially needy can tap into this fund. The government's strong support for Medifund assures citizens that they will always have access to basic medical care.

Elderly CPF members are also strongly encouraged by the government to participate in ElderShield, a disability insurance scheme that provides coverage for long-term care. This insurance scheme pays a cash payout of S$400 per month for 72 months if the insured is struck with disabilities. CPF members who reach 40 years old are automatically enrolled in the insurance plan and pay premiums until they are 65 years old. The premium is fixed at the age of entry and will not increase with age. Although premium payment ends at age 65, the insurance coverage is for life.

Retirement adequacy

Singapore is experiencing seismic changes in the demographics of its population. By 2030, approximately 900,000 workers (a quarter of citizens) will leave the workforce and go into retirement. Furthermore, these cohorts are also expected to live longer. Singapore's life expectancy was estimated to be 82 in 2010, one of the highest in the world. While the early pioneers who settled in Singapore had large families with many children to depend on for financial support during old age, more recent retirees will not be in this position. This is because they have smaller families, a trend that is prevalent in developing countries experiencing rising affluence. It is therefore crucial that Singapore's social security savings system adequately prepare workers for old age. To this end, the CPF Board set up the Special Account Scheme in 1977 to help members accumulate savings for retirement. Every working adult is required to make contributions based on a percentage of his monthly wage to his Special Account. The SA savings are strictly designated for retirement and cannot be withdrawn until age 55.

In 1987, the CPF Board also established the Minimum Sum Scheme requiring members to retain a minimum level of savings for old age. From July 2013 onwards, members must set aside S$148,000 in their Retirement Account upon reaching age 55, an amount deemed sufficient to support a subsistent level of living. The Minimum Sum was initially set at S$90,000 in 2005 but it has risen steadily to S$148,000 as of 2013 (Table 15.8). Such upward adjustments in the Minimum Sum were necessary to keep up with inflation, so that a consistent standard of living can be maintained throughout retirement.

To boost cash savings, the CPF Board has both raised SA contribution rates and paid higher interest on SA savings. The SA contribution at

TABLE 15.8 CPF Minimum Sum Scheme (MSS)

	2005	2006	2007	2008	2009	2010	2011	2012	2013
Required MSS Amount (S$)	90,000	94,600	99,600	106,000	117,000	123,000	131,000	139,000	148,000
Persons meeting MSS at age 55 (%)	37.5	36.4	36.3	33.8	37.5	40.7	45.0	48.7	

Note: S$1.25 is roughly equivalent to US$1.
Source: Singapore's CPF (2014).

inception was 1 percent and it rose to a high of 6 percent in 2011 for those ages 35 and below. A government review committee had recommended that the total contribution rate be raised from the current level of 36 percent (for those below 35 years old) to 40 percent in the future, and most of the increase is to go into the Special Account for retirement purposes. Besides the general uptrend in SA rate, the share of total contribution into the Special Account will also increase as members age.

From 1977 to 1994, the interest rate paid on SA balances was identical to that of OA balances. Since 1999, an additional 1.5 percent was paid on SA balances above the OA rate. From 2008, the CPF Board has decided to pay an extra 1 percent interest on the first S$60,000 of combined CPF balances with up to S$20,000 from the Ordinary Account to boost retirement savings. This means that the first S$20,000 in the Ordinary Account will earn 3.5 percent instead of the default 2.5 percent rate. The interest income earned in the Ordinary Account annually will be transferred to the Special Account. The remaining portion of S$40,000 from the Special Account or Retirement account will be paid an interest rate of 5 percent instead of the default 4 percent rate. The CPF Board estimated that with the extra 1 percent interest rate payment, members will earn an extra $1 billion in interest income in their retirement accounts in 2011.

Figure 15.5 shows that during the thirty-four-year period from 1980 to 2014, interest rates on SA balances were generally higher than the inflation rate.[9] This means that retirement savings were growing at positive real rates of return.

An indicator of retirement adequacy is the percentage of CPF members that meet the Minimum Sum requirement at age 55. Another indicator is the income replacement rate (IRR) of retirees, or the ratio of retirement income to pre-retirement earnings. McGill et al. (2005) and Scheiber (2004) suggested that IRR should be at least 70 percent.[10] An early estimate of Singapore's IRR by McCarthy et al. (2002) found that it was a low 28 percent. Hui (2012) estimated the IRR for three groups segmented by

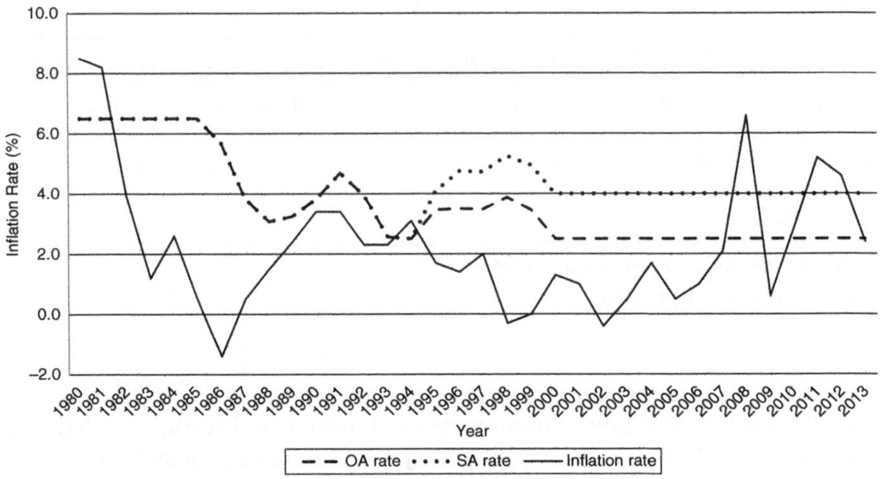

Figure 15.5 CPF interest rate and Singapore's inflation rate over time
Note: OA refers to the Ordinary Account; SA refers to the Special Account.
Source: Singapore's CPF (2014) and Singapore Department of Statistics (2013).

education level (secondary, post-secondary, and tertiary) and found that only the low-income secondary educated workers were able to achieve the target IRR of 66 percent. A recent report by Mercer (2012) found that the median income earner in Singapore achieved an IRR below 20 percent. OECD (2009) estimated that Singapore's IRR was a low 13 percent compared to the 72 percent average for 34 member countries. Nevertheless, critiques of Mercer's and OECD's IRR studies pointed to a lack of understanding of Singapore's social security savings system. For example, although both OA and SA savings can be used for retirement, these studies only used SA savings to estimate Singapore's IRR. Recently, Mercer (2013) has rectified this error and raised Singapore's IRR significantly. OECD (2009) estimated that if both OA and SA savings were used in the computation, Singapore's IRR would have been 82 percent. The latest study by Chia and Tsui (2012) found that a median male earner could achieve an IRR of 70 percent if he retires at 65, while a female earner has a slightly lower IRR of 64 percent. They concluded that a young Singaporean joining the labor force would likely have sufficient savings for retirement.

Although members do manage to save for retirement, many have insufficient cash savings to hit the Minimum Sum of S$148,000 (Table 15.9). Two groups of members are especially vulnerable to financial hardship during retirement. The first is the elderly who are above 60 and have average cash savings of only S$52,000, an amount which would be sufficient to only pay

TABLE 15.9 Singapore CPF member average balances by age and sex

Age group	Men (S$)	Women (S$)
< 20	852	1,196
20–5	6,386	12,003
25–30	33,242	40,893
30–5	59,886	61,365
35–40	85,353	85,587
40–5	105,009	93,789
45–50	100,360	88,570
50–5	109,538	92,260
55–60	100,905	81,077
60 +	51,642	33,759
Unspecified	1,888	2,205
All groups	72,421	62,264

Note: S$1.25 is roughly equivalent to US$1.

Source: Singapore's CPF (2014).

for a few years of consumption. If they lack private savings or family support, they will be in dire straits during the last stage of their lives. The second vulnerable group is women above 55 who have substantially lower savings than their male counterparts. As women tend to live longer than men, they would need more financial resources for retirement.

Given the high mandatory saving rates (36 percent of gross monthly salary for those 35 years and below), it is puzzling why so many CPF members did not accumulate even the Minimum Sum. Figure 15.3 provides a clue to this liquidity problem. Almost half of members' cumulative CPF contributions (44 percent) have been withdrawn to purchase homes and to service mortgages, leaving only 29 percent of these contributions in Ordinary and Special Accounts for retirement. These huge withdrawals meant that very little cash savings remain in the CPF OA and SA accounts. The other reason is that the contribution rate for the Special Account in past years may have been too low. Only 6 percent of the total contribution of 36 percent (for workers 35 and younger) went into the SA for retirement. The bulk of the contributions of 23 percent went to the OA and was withdrawn prior to retirement for other purposes.

In view of increasing life expectancy, retirees face the prospect of outliving their savings during old age. To hedge such longevity risk, the government in 2009 introduced CPF Life, a life annuity for retirees. Initially launched as a voluntary scheme, it is now mandatory for members to purchase CPF Life using their Minimum Sums when they reach age 55. This life annuity will pay a monthly income from the drawdown age of 65.

For members who do not have sufficient savings to enroll in the annuity scheme (less than S$40,000), they have the option to rejoin it if they accumulate S$60,000 by the drawdown age of 65. The CPF Board currently offers two plans for members: the Life Standard Plan and the Life Basic Plan. The Life Standard plan offers members a higher monthly payout of S $1,100–1,210 but a lower bequest (S$38,869 to S$177,061) to their beneficiaries.[11] The Life Basic Plan offers a lower monthly payout of S$1,008–1,112 but a higher bequest (S$67,622 to S$212,925). By purchasing CPF Life, members are assured of a subsistence level of income for the rest of their lives.

Asset enhancement

The CPF Investment Scheme was introduced in 1986 to allow members to invest their savings in a wide variety of financial instruments to grow their pension assets.[12] CPF Members can avail themselves of many investment products that could potentially earn a higher yield than the interest rate paid by the CPF Board. Currently, the CPF operates the CPFIS-OA and CPFIS-SA investment schemes which cover savings in the Ordinary Account (OA) and Special Account (SA) respectively.

Under the CPFIS-OA scheme, members can invest their OA savings in bank fixed deposits, government bills and bonds, corporate bonds, property funds, equities traded on the Singapore stock exchange, annuities and endowment insurance policies, investment-linked insurance products, unit trusts, exchange traded funds, fund management accounts, and gold. For instruments deemed as more risky, the CPF Board place limits on the maximum allowable investments. For example, a member can invest only up to 10 percent of his OA savings in gold, and up to 35 percent in shares, property funds/REITs, and corporate bonds. Such restriction ensures that members' portfolios are well diversified and take no concentrated risk in any particular asset. For the CPFIS-SA scheme, a narrower set of financial products is permitted for investment, as members are discouraged from taking high risk when investing savings meant for retirement. Members can invest in all the financial instruments in the CPFIS-OA scheme except fund management accounts, shares, property funds, REITS, corporate bonds, gold, investment-linked insurance products, unit trusts, and higher risk exchange traded funds.

Low participation in CPF Investment Scheme (CPFIS)

Prior research showed that only 12 percent of OA savings were utilized by members for investment (Koh et al. 2008a) and the situation is similar for the SA where members invested only 20 percent of their SA savings. In other words, the participation rate in CPF Investment Scheme has been low. Possible reasons accounting for members' preference to leave their savings in the Special Account are the relatively high government-paid interest rate of 4 percent per annum and the unwillingness of members to assume risk for savings meant for retirement. Nevertheless, these reasons do not adequately explain the reluctance of members to invest their OA savings, since the interest rate paid is a meager 2.5 percent per annum.

Of the OA savings committed to investment, 63 percent went into insurance products, 25 percent into shares, 11 percent into unit trusts, and a negligible amount (0.64 percent) into other instruments such as bank deposits, bonds, Exchange Traded Funds (ETFs), gold, property funds, and fund management accounts (Koh et al. 2008a). For the CPFIS-SA scheme, 86 percent were invested in insurance products and 14 percent in unit trusts. These findings suggest that, although the CPF Board offers a comprehensive menu of investment options, members are not utilizing the scheme fully. The asset allocation patterns of OA and SA savings showed that members were prepared to take more risk with their OA funds than SA funds. They seemed to put SA savings in a separate 'mental account' targeted for retirement and preferred not to take risk to actively manage it. We observed two distinct investment behaviors of a high preference for insurance products and a low preference for professionally managed funds. The low yield on whole-life and endowment policies of 2–4 percent cannot explain the preference for insurance products. A comparison of the relative investment performance of investment-linked insurance products versus unit trusts sheds light on the high investment in insurance products. There is no empirical evidence to suggest that ILPs outperform unit trusts. As the industry parlance goes, insurance policies are sold rather than bought. With a large sales force and aggressive sales strategies, insurance companies have been successful in persuading many CPF members to buy insurance products. Other possible reasons for the low interest in professionally managed unit trusts include poor investment performance, high fees and transaction costs charged by funds, and people's lack of financial literacy to select funds. CPF members who lack financial knowledge may not know how to begin to assess the 400 funds on offer. Furthermore, selecting the best fund to invest in means having to evaluate the return and risk characteristics of 400 funds, a task too onerous even for many financially savvy members.

Performance of professionally managed funds

Koh et al. (2010) studied the performance of CPFIS unit trusts over two ten-year periods, 1991–2001 and 1997–2007.[13] These two periods were chosen to coincide with the bear and bull phases of Singapore's stock market.

TABLE 15.10 Performance statistics of Singapore CPFIS-included unit trusts

A: Summary Statistics of CPFIS Unit Trusts

	10-year period ending Dec. 2001	10-year period ending Dec. 2007
Average annual return (%)	7.96	10.27
CPF OA (average) annual rate (%)	3.23	2.77
T-notes/bond yield annual rate (%)	3.73	3.02

B: Alphas and Gammas of CPFIS Unit Trusts

	Period ending Dec. 2001		Period ending Dec. 2007	
	Equity	Balanced	Equity	Balanced
Average Alpha (%)	0.35	0.62	0.32	0.07
% where Alpha > 0	14	100[a]	22.5	0
Average Gamma (%)	0	0	0	0
% where Gamma > 0	29	0	27.50	50

Note: [a] There is only one balanced fund in the sample.
Source: Koh et al. (2008b), tables 2 and 4.

The question was whether CPF-included unit trusts were successful in helping investors grow their retirement savings. The authors found that the average return of CPFIS unit trusts ranged from 7.96 to 10.27 percent per annum, higher than the risk-free and the CPF default interest rates (panel A of Table 15.10). This means that CPF members were able to grow their savings faster through investing in unit trusts than leaving them in CPF default accounts.[14]

While unit trusts' average returns were relatively high, the funds were unable to outperform their style-specific benchmarks. A common statistic to gauge the stock selection skill of fund managers is a positive Jensen alpha.[15] Panel B showed that few funds reported alphas statistically larger than zero at the 5 percent significance level. Only 14–22.5 percent of equity fund managers exhibited superior stock selection skills. The results for balanced funds were more extreme, ranging from 0 to 100 percent (the latter figure must be interpreted with care as there is only one balanced fund with a ten-year historical series ending 2001). The empirical results imply that unit trusts managers in Singapore generally did not exhibit superior stock selection skills, so CPF members at the time could not expect them to outperform the stock market.

Fund managers who do have market timing skill will report positive gamma.[16] Panel B showed that the average gamma of equity and balanced funds was zero, and only 27.5–50 percent of funds reported gammas larger than zero at the 5 percent significance level. This implies that fund managers generally did not exhibit market timing skills and they cannot be relied upon to earn superior returns.

High fees and charges for CPFIS options

The range of fees charged by CPFIS unit trusts can be bewildering to naïve investors, as it includes sales charges, transaction fees, realization charges, switching fees, annual operations fees, performance fees, and redemption charges. The sales charge (front-end load) for unit trusts can be hefty, as high as 5 percent of the amount invested. Some unit trusts do not impose a sales charge but instead levy a realization charge (back-end load) upon divestment by investors. When selling out of a fund within 90 days of purchasing it, an investor may also have to pay a redemption fee. An additional switching fee is imposed when investors switch between funds.

In addition to these charges, unit trusts also pay a wide range of fees such as management, trustee, administration, custodian, registrar, audit, accounting, and valuation.[17] Although these fees are borne by unit trusts directly, they are eventually passed on to investors through lower dividends. To help investors gauge the cost associated with investment in unit trusts, fund managers are asked to declare their *total expense ratio* which captures all their operating cost as a proportion of the fund's average Net Asset Value (NAV).[18] Table 15.11 shows that the sales load of CPFIS-included unit trusts ranged from 0.1 to 5 percent of NAV, expense ratios from 0.7 to 2.1 percent, and annual management fees from 0.5 to 1.4 percent. As observed by Mitchell (1998), the fees levied in Singapore appear to be far more diverse and complex than those of the US institutional market.

To evaluate how investment cost can impact the return of retirement savings of a CPF member who had invested in unit trusts, Koh et al. (2008a) computed the rate of return an investor would require in order to 'cost-recover' the expenses over one-year (short-term), five-year (medium-term), and ten- to twenty-year (long-term) periods. In the simulation, they assumed that the prices of unit trusts remain unchanged so the change in fund value reflects solely the cost levied by the unit trust. They also assumed that management fees and other annual operating costs were fixed at the prevailing average rates for equity, balanced, income, and money market funds.[19]

Table 15.12 shows how much $1 investment would be eroded by annual operating costs, assuming no change in the value of component securities in the unit trust. It computes the annual rate of return required for an investor to 'cost-recover' by each fund type. The values are large for short horizons. For example, transaction costs of an equity fund eroded 6.9 percent of its value in one year and 3 percent per annum over a five-year holding period.

TABLE 15.11 Summary data on costs associated with unit trust investment in Singapore

	Number of funds sampled	Average sales loads (%)	Average management fee (%)	Average expense ratio (%)
Equity funds	167	4.9	1.4	2.1
Active	164	5	1.4	2.1
Passive	3	2.1	0.7	1
Balanced funds	26	4.8	1.3	1.9
Active	22	5	1.3	2.1
Passive	4	3.5	1	1.3
Income funds	39	2.1	0.9	1.1
Cash funds	3	0.1	0.5	0.7
Sample mean		4.4	1.3	1.9

Notes:

a) The sales load comprises both front-end and back-end sales charges. Annual operating costs comprise fees for management, custodian, trustee, administration, and other major fees paid by the unit trust out of the fund's net asset value, and are estimated using the total expense ratio publicly reported by Investment Management Association of Singapore (IMAS) under its Fund Information Service website (<http://www.fundsingapore.com>).

b) There is one partially passive fund under the income funds category. However, its costs are not presented separately since one single fund is not a representative sample for analysis.

Source: Koh et al. (2008b), table 4.

TABLE 15.12 Simulation study showing the percentage of $1 investment eroded by expenses assuming zero investment return, by fund type and holding period (%)

Type of Fund	1 year	5 years	10 years	20 years
Equity	−6.90	−3.00	−2.60	−2.30
Balanced	−6.60	−2.90	−2.40	−2.20
Income	−3.20	−1.50	−1.30	−1.20
Money market	−0.80	−0.70	−0.70	−0.70

Notes: This simulation study assumes that the prices of unit trusts in Singapore remain unchanged so the change in the fund position solely reflects cost impacts on a $1 investment over 1, 5, 10, and 20 years. Costs include the one-off sales load and the annual operating costs for each of the four fund types as presented in Table 15.10. The sales load comprises both front-end and back-end sales charges. Annual operating costs comprise fees for management, custodian, trustee, administration, and other major fees paid by the unit trust out of the fund's net asset value, and are estimated using the total expense ratio publicly reported by Investment Management Association of Singapore (IMAS) under its Fund Information Service website (www.fundsingapore.com). The performance fee is excluded from the total expense ratio.

Source: Koh et al. (2008b), table 11.

The high transaction costs associated with unit trusts may explain low participation rates of CPF members in CPF Investment Scheme.

Given the numerous instruments available for investments, we would have expected CPF members to exploit them to grow their savings over the long term. Yet Table 15.13 paints a rather disappointing picture of their investment performance: almost half of CPFIS-OA investors (47 percent) incurred losses from investing, while 35 percent realized profits equal to or less than the default OA rate of 2.5 percent. Only 18 percent of the investors made net realized profits in excess of the OA interest rate. Allowing a free rein for CPF members to invest their savings may not help those lacking investment skills. Rather, what they need might be professional advice and default portfolios such as indexed portfolios or life cycle funds, which are attractive in the US to those lacking financial knowledge.

Reforming Singapore's Social Security Savings System

Our review of Singapore's Social Security Savings system in the preceding sections showed that it is generally successful in helping CPF members own their homes, pay for health care costs, and provide financial protection for their families. However, there are three areas that require reforms, namely, retirement adequacy, asset enhancement, and health care financing. The relatively low cash savings accumulated in the CPF OA and SA accounts point to low retirement adequacy faced by CPF members. In the following sections, we provide specific suggestions on the reforms that could be undertaken to improve retirement security.

Monetization of home equity

Although many Singaporeans are proud owners of their homes, they tend to lack sufficient retirement savings in the CPF accounts. This is termed the 'asset rich and cash poor' syndrome by McCarthy et al. (2002). As explained previously, this situation arose because of excessive pre-retirement withdrawals of CPF savings to acquire homes. Figure 15.6 shows that 59 percent of accumulated CPF OA savings have been channeled into property purchases. With an inelastic supply of land for housing and a rising population, home prices have been appreciating over the past few decades.[20] Furthermore, unlike the 1970s and 1980s where property was regarded as a home, many people today regard properties as a financial asset for wealth accumulation. Due to the high cost of housing and the long duration of mortgage servicing, Singaporeans found themselves diverting the bulk of their lifetime

TABLE 15.13 Realized profits/losses for investments held under the Singapore CPF investment scheme Ordinary Account (CPFIS-OA): FY04–13

	FY 2004	FY 2005	FY 2006	FY 2007	FY 2008	FY 2009	FY 2010	FY 2011	FY 2012	FY 2013	10-year avg.
Members who made net realized profits *in excess of* the OA interest rate of 2.5%	127,518	147,387	179,987	239,137	173,987	112,642	134,841	152,063	143,956	138,436	
(%) of members	17	19	23	28	20	13	14	17	16	15	18
Members who made realized profits, but *equal to or less than* OA rate	240,010	250,237	257,191	244,841	278,758	314,901	332,399	344,299	362,598	385,493	
(%) of members	33	33	32	29	31	35	37	38	41	43	35
Members who made realized losses	369,591	363,124	362,129	368,054	440,063	465,724	437,101	399,717	389,399	374,699	
(%) of members	50	48	45	43	49	52	49	45	43	42	47

Source: Author's computations.

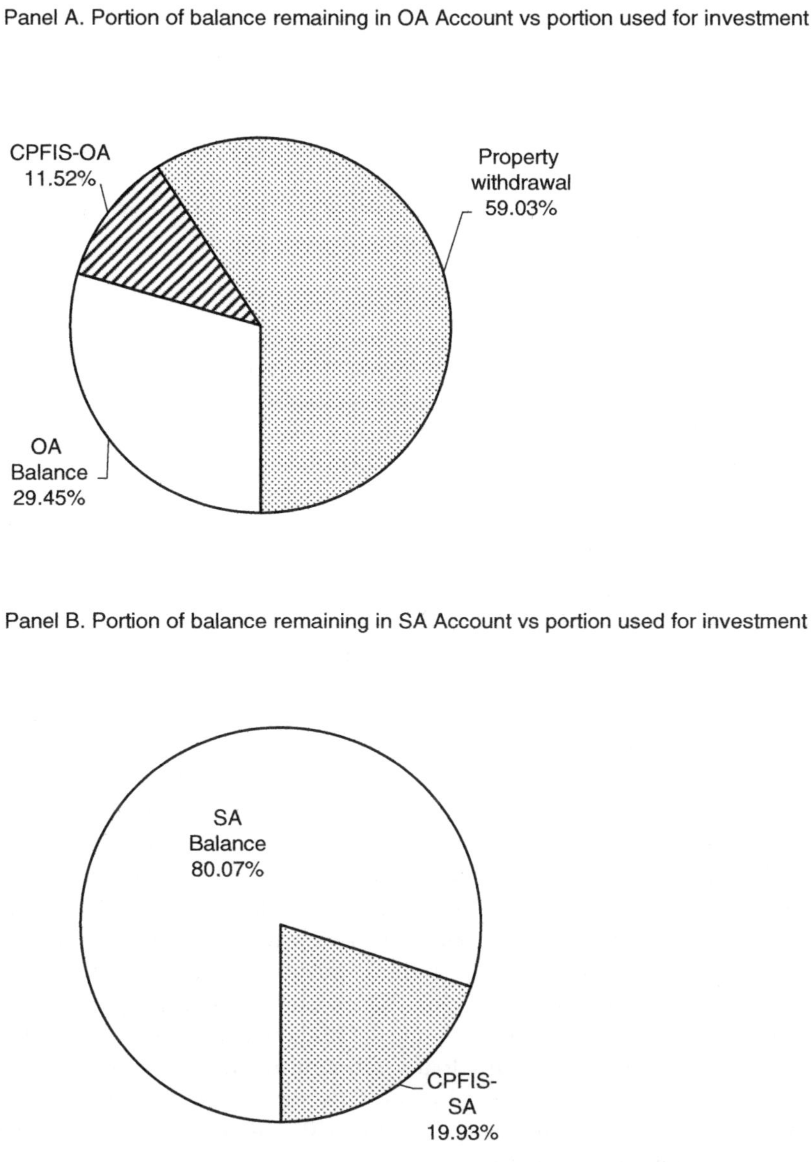

Figure 15.6 Portion invested and balance remaining in Singapore's CPF Ordinary (OA) and Special (SA) Accounts

Source: Koh et al. (2008a).

incomes to home ownership instead of preparing for retirement. This has resulted in a lack of liquidity during old age, and it suggests an urgent need to introduce mechanisms for households to unlock home equity to generate cash flow for retirement. Currently, the four ways of monetizing home equity in Singapore are reverse mortgage, subletting of home, downsizing to a smaller home, and lease and buyback (Chia and Tsui 2009). We review these mechanisms in the following sections and suggest further refinements that would make them more robust and effective.

Reverse mortgage

A reverse mortgage is a scheme whereby a home owner receives a stream of income from a financial institution for a specified period in return for progressively giving up equity ownership of his home. Upon the owner's death, the home is sold by the financial institution to recover the loan and cumulative interest due. The key appeal of a reverse mortgage is that the owner gets to stay in his own home while receiving a regular income for daily expenditures. A disadvantage is that the owner may lose ownership of his home should its market value fall abruptly below the allowable limit; this is more likely to happen during a property market crash. In recent years, commercial lenders have been encouraged to offer reverse mortgage schemes to help members unlock their home equity, though their response has been lukewarm, with very few transactions done. With the bulk of housing stock in public housing apartments, financial institutions find it difficult to offer reverse mortgages on homes with short leases.[21] The asset values are likely to depreciate as the leases approach their expiration dates.

Given the profit motive and risk aversion of financial institutions, it is unlikely that the private reverse mortgage market will thrive in Singapore in the future. If the reverse mortgage market for public housing units is to take off, HDB, the public housing board, must step in as the market maker to offer these contracts. To make the scheme attractive to owners, the lending rate should be the current HDB's loan rate which is currently pegged at 2.6 percent (0.1 percent above the OA rate). This is reasonable since that HDB is currently offering new housing loans to first-time home buyers at this rate. The risk to HDB is that the value of flats may drop to a level that is insufficient to recover the loan. This tail risk can be hedged by buying insurance against that outcome.

Subletting

Owners of public housing flats may sublet part of their homes to earn rental income. This option is appealing to older owners, as they get to stay in their homes which they can then bequeath to their children. An impediment to widespread subletting in Singapore is the concern about personal safety and privacy. Aged owners worry about their personal safety when subletting a part of their homes to strangers. A strong preference for privacy also means that owners are unlikely to accept intrusion into their family's daily routines. A recent survey carried out by the government found that 54 percent of home owners would not sublet due to concerns about privacy and 20 percent due to security concerns. The long-term solution to these two problems is to design dual-key apartments with two separate entrances. When the owner has decided to sublet his home, he can erect a wall to divide the apartment, thereby creating two smaller living units with separate entrances. This allows the owner to live in a separate area of the apartment from his tenant. Existing public housing apartment without the dual-key entrances can be renovated to have this feature.

Downsizing

Public housing units of different sizes ranging from two- to four-bedroom apartments are currently sold to citizens, and owners of larger apartments can downsize to smaller apartments to extract home equity. To encourage downsizing, the government has provided a S$20,000 cash incentive to owners. The extracted home equity can then be invested in a life annuity to provide a lifetime income. Yet some elderly members may find it difficult to adjust to new living environments after downsizing, as their new homes may be in different neighborhoods from their former homes and they may lose their social network of friends and relatives when moving to new localities. The public housing board may wish to consider building mixed housing types in the same neighborhood to allow owners to downsize to new apartments located within a couple of blocks of their old homes.

Lease and buyback

In a lease and buyback scheme, the homeowner sells away the lease period remaining beyond 30 years to the public housing authority to generate a lump-sum payment. This scheme is currently applicable to owners age 65 or older. The advantage of this scheme is that the owner gets to live in his flat for another 30 years, in addition to getting a cash payout. The key risk of the scheme is that the owner may need to vacate his home if he outlives the thirty-year lease period. Due to this uncertainty, few people have taken up this scheme, as the elderly dislike taking longevity risk during old age. To make the scheme more attractive, the public housing board might assume the tail risk of an owner outliving the thirty-year lease period. Given current mortality tables, it is relatively easy to estimate the likelihood of this occurring and the number of owners involved. If need be, this risk could be hedged through insurance.

Limiting withdrawal of CPF for housing

Excessive pre-retirement withdrawals to acquire housing is a contributing factor leading to a lack of liquidity in retirement. Although most households will have a fully paid home at retirement, they may have insufficient cash flows for daily living. And while owners can monetize their homes, the amount of home equity they can extract is subject to market risk. For example, Singapore's property market plunged 45 percent from 1996 to 1998, and 25 percent during the 2008 global financial crisis. In a depressed real estate market, retirees may be forced to sell out at fire-sale prices. An asset-based retirement strategy is therefore clearly risky. One long-term solution to the 'asset rich, cash poor' syndrome is to restrain the amount of pension savings that can be diverted into property purchases, so that CPF participants can earmark sufficient savings for retirement. When the housing schemes were first launched, CPF members could withdraw up to 160 percent of home valuation, 150 percent in 2002, and 120 percent in 2007. The CPF Board may wish to consider reducing the maximum withdrawal amount to not exceed 100 percent of home valuation.

Raising contribution rates of older age groups

Table 15.3 showed that the contribution rates decline rapidly by age from 36 percent for workers below age 50, to 11.5 percent for those above age 65. The rationale for reducing contribution rates for older workers is to enhance their employability. Besides lowering employer's contributions, employees' contribution rates also fall with age. Yet low contribution rates for aged workers can adversely affect their ability to achieve old age retirement adequacy. To boost adequacy, contribution rates for the older age groups could be raised progressively until they are at parity with the younger workers.

Hedging against inflation risk

The life annuity offered by the CPF Board has been estimated to be quite valuable (Fong et al. 2011). This is primarily due to low administrative charges and little adverse selection. In addition, due to the non-profit status of the CPF Board in managing the annuity scheme, profits typically earned by private insurers who offer similar life annuities are returned to members by the CPF. While the mandatory life annuity is useful in hedging longevity risk, its current features have some deficiencies that may benefit from refinement. First, the payouts are not predetermined at the point of purchase at age 55; the CPF Board instead only provides an indicative estimate of future payouts which are not guaranteed. The payouts are determined by prevailing interest rates as well as population mortality changes, so there is some uncertainty as to whether the annuity payouts will be sufficient to provide a subsistence level of living. Furthermore, the scheme is not hedged against inflation, which means that the payouts will have decreasing purchasing power as retirees age. Moving forward, the annuity scheme could be enhanced to provide an inflation-indexed payout. Nevertheless, this could substantially reduce early benefit payout levels.

CPF contribution rates used as a macro-economic counter-cyclical tool

Although the primary goal of CPF is to prepare members for retirement, it has been used occasionally as a cost-cutting tool to combat recession. For instance, in 1986, the Singapore government took the unprecedented action of slashing employers' contributions from 25 to 10 percent. The second time a similarly drastic reduction in employer's contribution rate occurred was during the 1999 Asian Financial Crisis, when the contribution rate was reduced from 20 to 10 percent. These cuts effectively reduced the retirement savings of individuals by 15 and 10 percent respectively. The purpose of these cuts was to reduce business costs for employers and increase their cost competitiveness so that they could recover quickly from the recession or crisis. Yet these cuts significantly reduced workers' retirement savings, as when their SA contribution rate fell to 0 percent in 1986 and 1999. This rate reduction was only partially restored in 1994. Similarly, the 10 percent reduction in employers' contribution rate was partially restored by 2 percent in 2000, another 4 percent in 2001 bringing the rate to its current level of 16 percent (previously 20 percent). In sum, the contribution rate for employers has declined by 9 percentage points from its peak of 25 percent in 1986.

The key policy issue to address is whether a country's pension system should be used as a counter-cyclical cost-cutting tool to help firms recover during economic recession. While it may help corporations cut costs, years in which contribution rates are low will adversely affect members' retirement adequacy. Ideally, the government should utilize other monetary, fiscal, or administrative measures outside the retirement system to resuscitate an ailing economy.

Extending the retirement age

Another measure to boost retirement adequacy would be to extend workers' official retirement age. Currently, the statutory minimum retirement age in Singapore is 62, though under the recently introduced Retirement and Reemployment Act, employers are required to offer re-employment to eligible employees age 62–5 and the government is mulling over extending this further to age 67. For workers who are healthy and able, they should be allowed to continue working. Employers are strongly encouraged by the government to engage older workers as long as they are healthy and able to perform in their jobs. By working longer, workers keep themselves mentally alert and have a means to support themselves financially during old age.

Healthcare Financing

The current MediShield Scheme provides insurance cover for members to pay large inpatient bills, yet our review of the scheme revealed several limitations. For example, the scheme does not cover pre-existing medical conditions and members older than 92 years of age. This means that the elderly above 92 are completely exposed to huge health care bills without insurance. With life expectancy rising, more health insurance protection will be needed. This could be achieved if the MediShield Scheme were enhanced to allow for universal and lifetime coverage. With these refinements, members would be covered throughout their lives, no matter how old they are; pre-existing illnesses could be covered as well. With better benefits, health care costs will rise, but this may be diversified by pooling those with pre-existing medical conditions with those that are healthy. The Singapore government is currently considering whether such a modified scheme (MediShield Life) would be feasible and affordable if introduced. Other refinements being considered include raising the maximum claimable limit above the current level of S$300,000, increasing the daily claim limit by 55 percent, or lowering the co-insurance payment by policy participants. With these changes, it is anticipated that the majority of Singaporeans could pay less than S$3,000 out of pocket cost for large inpatient bills, as the bulk would be paid by insurance. While a universal, lifetime medical insurance scheme ensures that health care is affordable and accessible, the premium paid can escalate rapidly if there is rampant over-utilization of health care services. Measures should be put in place to discourage unnecessary consumption of health care services and to contain the rising health care cost. This will ensure that the MediShield Life insurance scheme will be sustainable over the long run.

Asset Enhancement

Lowering transaction costs of CPFIS scheme

As noted, professionally managed funds in Singapore charge high sales loads of 4.4 percent, management fees of 1.3 percent, and expense ratios of 1.9 percent (Table 15.11). To lower transaction costs, the CPF Board announced a few policy changes in 2007 and 2008 to make it more affordable for members to invest in CPFIS-included funds. These include the capping of front-load charges of all CPF-included funds at 3 percent (as of July 1, 2007) and expense ratios at the median of existing funds from the same risk category (from January 1, 2008).[22] The revised 3 percent front-end load is significantly lower than the 5 percent front-end load previously charged by professionally managed funds. The expense ratio of equity funds will now be capped at 1.95 percent of the fund's NAV, balanced funds at 1.75 percent, fixed income funds at 1.15 percent, and money market funds at 0.65 percent.[23] A review of the US market found that the average expense ratio for equity funds was 1.13 percent and that of bond funds was 0.9 percent (ICI 2006). Compared to the US then, transaction costs of investing in CPFIS funds are still high. For a start, the CPF Board might want to omit small funds with inefficient cost structure from the CPF Investment Scheme, replacing them with larger global funds with low transaction costs.

With the myriad of fees charged by funds, investors need to comb through prospectuses carefully to estimate all the component costs. Yet, it is onerous for a naïve investor to sieve through each of the 400 CPFIS-included unit trust prospectuses to decipher their cost structure and compute overall costs before deciding whether to invest in them. To help CPF members make investment decisions painlessly, the CPF Board can consider developing a real-time, online calculator to combine all the myriad charges and fees in a single overall cost measure. This statistic would allow the investor to know the true cost of investment and thereafter decide if the unit trust is worth investing in after adjusting for all associated costs.

Offering low-cost passive default portfolios

There are more than 400 funds on offer in Singapore at present, and some CPF members are overwhelmed by the number of funds they need to evaluate. Although new funds are admitted into CPFIS after clearing a set of stringent admission criteria, there are fewer rigors in screening out existing poor performers from the scheme. It would be useful to streamline the investment menu regularly, so that only high-performing funds remain in the scheme on offer to CPF members (Koh and Mitchell 2010).

In studying the asset allocation decisions of CPF investors, Koh et al. (2008a) found that men were more proactive in investing their savings compared to women. They tended to invest more in shares and unit trusts than women, who chose to put the bulk of savings in insurance products. This finding is similar to the US, where higher income men sought riskier investments and traded more in their accounts (Mitchell et al. 2006a). Contrary to conventional wisdom that investment in risky products should decrease with age, the more mature CPF members (56+ age groups) invested a higher proportion of their savings in individual stocks and less in insurance products, as compared to those in the younger age groups. In addition, the younger working adults were more likely to delegate their investments to professional fund managers while the mature group tended to invest in shares on their own. These investment behaviors confirmed findings by Mitchell et al. (2006a) for the US, that higher income, older men were more likely to hold riskier portfolios compared to their female and younger counterparts. Koh et al. (2008a) also found that lower income earners were less likely to hold risky investments, with at least 70 percent of their investments committed to insurance products. As salary levels rose, so did the fraction invested in risky instruments.

These research findings have identified three vulnerable groups of investors needing special attention: women, the aged, and the low-income. Women and low-income members may need more guidance to select the right financial products to grow their retirement savings. For the older members, they need advice on portfolio rebalancing so that, as they age, they reduce exposure to risky financial instruments to preserve their savings.

Of the numerous funds on offer in the CPF Investment Scheme, very few are low-cost, passively managed, index-linked funds or ETFs, and there are no target maturity date life cycle funds and inflation-protected instruments.[24] Life cycle funds may appeal to financially less-savvy members as these funds automatically rebalance the portfolio based on investor age. One possible reason for the low investment in unit trusts is that CPF members do not know how to evaluate and select funds for investments. Without guidance from the CPF Board, these members simply default their savings in the OA or SA accounts. If they could access default portfolios, which have low transaction costs and are well-diversified, CPF members would stand a better chance of growing their savings substantially over the long term. Of the 400 funds, few can exploit economies of scale, and their higher cost of operations will be passed on to retail investors. One reform that the CPF Board could consider would be to invite a few large low-cost privately managed life cycle funds to participate in the CPF Investment Scheme. The CPF Board could then pool all members together to enjoy lower institutional transaction costs.

As an example, Chile is a country that has adopted life cycle funds as the default portfolios in its pension system. Private pension managers there offer up to five funds, ranging from 'Fund A,' which invests 80 percent of the portfolio in equities, to 'Fund E', which invests 100 percent in fixed income securities. Funds B to D hold intermediate weightage in equities. Chileans may select up to two funds at a time offered by a single money manager; the fund manager then automatically rebalances participants' portfolios to a more conservative one as members age (Arenas de Mesa et al. 2008). The introduction of diversified low-cost life cycle funds could appeal to many less sophisticated members and help increase participation in Singapore's CPF Investment Scheme as well.

Lessons for the United States

The pension system adopted by the United States is a multi-pillar retirement system entailing a universal social security, an employment-based pension, and voluntary savings. Increasingly, the US Social Security System faces a mounting sustainability problem of financing Baby Boomers' retirement in the future. This is due to the dwindling population of young taxpayers and longer life expectancy of post-war retirees. The pay-as-you-go pension system is expected to experience significant stress from the impending fiscal imbalance. Compounding this problem is the low US households' savings rate, which portends inadequate private savings for old age. The private pension system is predominantly employment-based and offers either a traditional defined benefit plan (DB) or an increasingly popular defined contribution (DC) plan. For DB pension plans, employers assume the responsibility of providing pensions to employees during their retirement. For DC pension plans, employers make regular contributions to employees' retirement accounts but are not responsible for providing income to retired employees. Instead, the burden of retirement adequacy is transferred to employees.

Increasing pension coverage

One of the criteria of a successful pension system is the extent of pension coverage for employees. Ideally, a good pension system should cover all employees. As US employer-sponsored 401(k) pension plans are offered to employees on a voluntary basis, this has resulted in relatively low participation rates by companies. Additionally, the decision on who is covered and how much employers should contribute in 401(k) plans vary across companies. For companies that offer such plans, many employees do not contribute the maximum or take full advantage of matching contributions by employers. Consequently, the median balance of these plans stands at a relatively low US$77,000.[25] It is estimated that currently only one out of two workers in the US has a pension (Forman 2006; Moore 2011). In contrast, the Singapore's CPF system is able to achieve full coverage for all working adults by making participation mandatory. Under the current US political environment, it is not feasible to enact laws to compel employers to offer pension plans and employees to enroll in these plans. A more viable alternative is for the US government to require all employers to offer either a 401 (k) plan or an IRA. In addition, by setting the default to automatic enrollment for both 401(k) and IRA, the participation level from employees can be raised and the level of savings can be increased (OECD 2012; Thaler and Benartzi 2007).

Expanding the scope of 401(k) plans

Unlike the US pension systems which focused solely on financing retirement, Singapore's comprehensive CPF system helps members to own homes and finance health care in addition to preparing them for retirement. The success and sustainability of Singapore's social security savings system over the last 59 years suggests that such a comprehensive pension system can be viable for the US and other countries. Some plan participants may prefer to use pension savings to finance housing or repay education loans in the early years of their working life. The US pension system currently does not support these uses as pension savings can only be withdrawn for retirement purpose.[26] Using pension savings to acquire a home has several advantages such as saving on rental payments during retirement, having the option to monetize a valuable housing asset when liquidity is required, and avoiding the need to pay high interest on mortgage loans. Singapore's CPF System currently allows members to make pre-retirement withdrawals to purchase homes, service mortgage payments, and finance tertiary education. The interest rate charged on housing loans is the default interest paid on the CPF account plus 0.1 percent. With this home financing scheme, most CPF members are able to fully own their own homes prior to retirement. For education loans, the interest levied is the default CPF interest rate of 2.5 percent. At such low interest cost, children can comfortably repay education loans that were financed by parents' CPF savings. In contrast, the educational loans taken by US college entrants are pegged to commercial loans' rates, thereby making loans costly and repayment burdensome. A key worry about making the pension system more flexible is the adverse effect on retirement adequacy. If pre-retirement withdrawals are generous and lax, pension plan participants may end up with insufficient retirement savings. Singapore's CPF system mitigates this risk by requiring recipients of education loans to repay the loan principal with interest into their parent's

CPF account upon graduation. By enlarging the scope to accommodate housing and education financing, 401(k) plans can be made more attractive for members and their participation in such plans can be expected to rise.

Enhancing the portability of pension account

Currently, all 401(k) plans are sponsored and administered by employers, and this rigid linkage between a worker and his employer can limit labor mobility. US employees stand to lose their pension benefits if they change their employers prior to the vesting period. Portability can be greatly enhanced if the US follows Singapore's system of requiring all employees to set up employees' pension accounts with an independent pension administrator (CPF Board).[27] Using a central body in pension management allows workers to retain the same pension accounts even when they change employers. With a centralized system, employers' role is dramatically simplified to being a conduit of employees' pension contributions. Portability of pension accounts can be further enhanced if the contributions made by employers and employees are standardized across all companies.

Hedging longevity risk through annuitization

401(k) plans are currently not required to offer annuities and few do. Furthermore, for plans that offer life annuities, the take-up rate is low.[28] Upon retirement, most plan participants withdraw their pension savings as a lump sum, thereby exposing them to longevity risk if they outlive their savings. By contrast, Singapore mandates annuitization of retirement savings, requiring that the Minimum Sum of $148,000 be invested in a life annuity. The income from life annuities provides approximately S$1,200 per month for a retiree to maintain a subsistence level of living. As income will be paid throughout an annuitant's life, longevity risk faced by retirees is hedged. With a partial annuitization of the Minimum Sum, the CPF member can still withdraw his remaining savings in lump sum. The unique features of Singapore's life annuity scheme are that it is mandatory and the government is its underwriter. This results in significant benefits to annuitants such as economies of scale, pooling of longevity risk, low adverse selection cost, and affordable premiums. While it is unlikely that the United States can mandate annuitization of pension assets, it can increase purchase of annuities by requiring all employers to offer life annuities in 401(k) plans and making them the default option on drawdown at retirement. This will help plan participants overcome their inertia in dealing with longevity risk.

Enhancing risk diversification through pension design

In 401 (k) plans, the onus is on plan participants to grow their pension assets through judicious investments. Given the low level of financial literacy worldwide, it would be challenging for plan participants to make informed investment decisions. Some may be overly conservative in investing while others may be overly aggressive by taking excessive risk. Singapore's CPF Investment Scheme has been carefully designed to encourage risk diversification. For example, while members can assume more investment risk when investing their OA saving, they cannot do this with their SA savings. With OA savings, members can avail themselves of the complete menu of investment instruments. However, the range of investment instruments is drastically reduced when investing SA savings that are meant for retirement. In addition, when investing OA savings, there is a 10 percent cap on investments in gold and a 35 percent cap on investments in individual common shares, REITs, and corporate bonds. With such built-in limits on investments in specific asset classes, members are more likely to end up with a broadly diversified portfolio. Like the CPF Investment Scheme, the US 401(k) plans can enhance risk diversification by placing caps on how much pension assets can be invested in each asset class.

Intergenerational transfers to enhance retirement adequacy

Singapore's CPF Board provides substantial flexibility for inter-generational transfers to enhance retirement adequacy in households. For example, a member can top up the CPF accounts of his grandparents, parents, spouse, and siblings. Such transfers are tax exempt and can enhance the retirement adequacy of household members who currently do not have sufficient pension savings. 401(k) plans currently do not accept contributions from anyone other than the employee or his employer. To enhance retirement adequacy, the rules on contributions into the 401(k) plan can be relaxed to allow for external cash injection into a worker's account. Government tax incentives can also be used to promote top-ups made to an employee's account whose balance is below a threshold level.

Conclusion

Since 1955, Singapore's social security savings system has helped citizens save for retirement. This chapter has explored its various schemes introduced through the years to help citizens own homes, gain health care coverage, attain financial protection for families, save for retirement, and grow pension assets. The CPF Board has been successful in achieving its first three objectives, of home ownership, health care coverage, and financial protection. More remains to be done for retirement adequacy and asset enhancement, since many CPF members have insufficient cash savings for retirement. Due to high transaction costs, lack of financial literacy, and inertia, many have not taken advantage of the large menu of investment instruments on offer to grow their retirement savings. Instead, they left them in their CPF OA and SA accounts earning low interest. Singapore's system could enhance the retirement security of its members by developing financial markets to facilitate monetizing home equity, limiting the withdrawal of retirement savings for home purchase, raising contributions of older workers, refining the CPF life scheme to offer inflation-indexed payouts, avoiding using CPF contribution rates as counter-cyclical tools, and extending the retirement age of workers. While the MediShield Scheme has been effective in helping members pay off large hospital bills, it can also be enhanced to provide universal and lifetime coverage for members. Retirement will be more secure if CPF members can grow their savings through investments in high-yield portfolios. To this end, the CPF investment scheme can be enhanced by systematically reducing the transaction costs of funds on offer. Offering low-cost passive default portfolios such as index-funds, ETFs, and life cycle funds will make investment a hassle-free experience for the financially illiterate. The CPF savings system has several attractive features that can be modified and adapted in the US to increase participation rate in 401(k) plans. Specifically, 401(k) plans can be expanded to permit financing for housing and college education, maximize portability by centralizing pension administration, reduce longevity risk through annuitization, promote risk diversification through the setting of investment limits, and encourage intergenerational transfers to boost the retirement adequacy of households.

Endnotes

1. The Singapore fertility rate in 2011 was reported as 1.2 by the World Bank. <http://data.worldbank.org/indicator/SP.DYN.TFRT.INwww.census.gov>. Singapore's Dept of Statistics reported the life expectancy of males and females to be 79.9 years and 84.5 years, respectively. See <www.singstat.gov.sg/statistics/visualising_data/chart/Life_Expectancy_At_Birth.html>.
2. Active CPF members are individuals with at least one contribution in the current or preceding three months.
3. The income ceiling for CPF contributions has varied over the years from a low of S$500 in 1955 to a high of S$6,000 during the 1985 to 2003 period. Since Sept. 2001, it has stabilized at S$5,000. The exchange rate as of June 2014 was S$1.25 = US$1.

4. The income ceiling relevant for CPF contributions is set to not exceed the 80th percentile income level.
5. See <http://mycpf.cpf.gov.sg/Members/Gen-Info/Int-Rates/Int-Rates.htm>.
6. See McCarthy et al. (2002) and Low and Aw (1997) for further discussion of the housing loan arrangements.
7. For details see <http://mycpf.cpf.gov.sg/Members/Gen-Info/FAQ/investment/CPF-Invscheme.htm>.
8. Dependents are immediate family members such as spouse, children, parents, or grandparents.
9. The only exceptions were 1980, 1981, 1994, 2008, 2011, and 2012.
10. The World Bank recommends that countries should aim for an IRR of 53 percent of net final year wage or 78 percent of net average lifetime wage.
11. The monthly payout and bequest are estimated for a retiree who reached age 55 in 2014 with a minimum sum of S$148,000.
12. When introduced in 1986, the CPF Investment Scheme was known as the Approved Investment Scheme. It was subsequently renamed in 1994 to offer a wider range of financial instruments for investments by CPF members.
13. Unit trusts are similar to mutual funds except that they are created under a trust deed with an external trustee monitoring the portfolio manager on behalf of unit investors.
14. These returns do not include transaction costs.
15. A positive Jensen Alpha α_j from the regression $R_{jt} - R_{ft} = \alpha_j + \beta_j (R_{mt} - R_{ft}) + \epsilon_j$ indicates that the manager was able to select stocks to earn superior returns.
16. A positive gamma γ_j from the quadratic regression $R_{jt} - R_{ft} = \alpha_j + \beta_j (R_{mt} - R_{ft}) + \gamma_j (R_{mt} - R_{ft})^2 + \epsilon_j$ indicates that the manager was able to time the market to earn superior returns.
17. Other fees include service fee, asset allocation fee, legal fee, printing fee, and distribution fee.
18. The NAV of a unit trust is the value of the unit trust fund's assets less its liabilities.
19. Different unit trusts may have different investment objectives, different styles of management, and different levels of equity risk depending on their portfolio allocation. This is recognized by Mercer Investment Consulting, CPF Board's consultant, which has developed a risk classification system for the CPFIS that assigns various risk levels to permitted investments. The unit trust or ILP with a greater proportion of its assets invested in the more volatile stock market will have a higher equity risk. Based on its level of equity risk, a unit trust or Investment Linked Product is assigned one of the four risk categories.
20. Singapore is an island nation with a small land area of 716.1 km^2. Although it tries to increase the land area through reclamation of shoreline, the increase is a marginal 1 km^2 from 2012 to 2013. Singapore's population grew rapidly from 3 million in 1990 to 5.3 million in 2012.
21. Public housing apartments are sold on 99-year leases. A 65-year-old member who bought his home at the age of 30 will have a lease with remaining life of 64 years.
22. Announcement of Dec. 28, 2006; see <mycpf.cpf.gov.sg/CPF/News/News-Release/N_28December2006.htm>.
23. <mycpf.cpf.gov.sg/CPF/News/News-Release/N_29Dec2005.htm>.

24. It would also be of interest to offer inflation-indexed bonds, as these make good sense for the retirement decumulation phase (Brown et al. 2000).
25. Fidelity reported that the average 401(k) balance as at end of 2012 is US$77,300.
26. Although employees can take loans from their retirement account, they are substantially penalized. Currently, withdrawals prior to age 59.5 are subject to 10 percent tax on distributions.
27. Oakley and Kenneally (2013) reported in a recent survey that most Americans prefer a pension system that provides portability from job to job.
28. Paul Yakoboki (2010) found that only 19 percent of retirees annuitized a portion of their retirement savings and David L. Wray (2008) noted that about 20 percent of defined contribution plans offer annuities but savings are hardly ever annuitized.

References

Arenas de Mesa, A., D. Bravo, J. Behrman, O. S. Mitchell, and P. Todd (2008). 'The Chilean Pension Reform Turns 25: Lessons from the Social Protection Survey,' in S. J. Kay and T. Sinha (eds), *Lessons from Pension Reform in the Americas*. Oxford: Oxford University Press, 23–58.

Brown, J., O. S. Mitchell, and J. Poterba (2000). 'The Role of Real Annuities and Indexed Bonds in an Individual Accounts Retirement Program,' in J. Y. Campbell and M. Feldstein (eds), *Risk Aspects of Investment-Based Social Security Reform*. Chicago: University of Chicago Press, 321–60.

Chia, N. C. and A. K. C. Tsui (2009). *Monetizing Housing Equity to Generate Retirement Incomes*, SCAPE Working Paper, 2009/01. Singapore: National University of Singapore.

Chia, N. C. and A. K. C. Tsui (2012). *Adequacy of Singapore's Central Provident Fund Payouts: Income Replacement Rates of Entrant Workers*, SCAPE Working Paper, 2013/02. Singapore: National University of Singapore.

Fong, H. Y., O. S. Mitchell, and B. S. K. Koh (2011). 'Longevity Risk Management in Singapore's National Pension System.' *Journal of Risk and Insurance*, 78(4): 961–82.

Forman, J. B. (2006). *Making America Work*. Washington, DC: Urban Institute Press.

Housing and Development Board (2014). 'Housing and Development Board,' *HDB InfoWEB*, <https://www.hdb.gov.sg>.

Hui, W. T. (2012). 'Macroeconomic Trends and Labour Welfare: A Focus on Retirement Adequacy,' in S. H. Kang and C. H. Leong (eds), Singapore *Perspectives 2012: Singapore Inclusive: Bridging Divides*. Singapore: National University of Singapore, Institute of Policy Studies, 37–58.

Investment Company Institute (ICI) (2006). *Investment Company Factbook 2006*. Washington, DC: ICI. <http://www.icifactbook.org/2006/index.html>.

Koh, B. S. K. and O. S. Mitchell (2010). 'What's on the Menu? Included versus Excluded Funds for Singapore's Central Provident Fund Investors.' *Pensions: An International Journal*, 15(4): 276–86.

Koh, B. S. K., O. S. Mitchell, T. Tanuwidjaja, and J. H. Y. Fong (2008a). 'Investment Patterns in Singapore's Central Provident Fund System.' *Journal of Pension Economics and Finance*, 7(1): 37–65.

Koh, B. S. K., O. S. Mitchell, and J. H. Y. Fong (2008b). 'Cost Structures in Defined Contribution Systems: The Case of Singapore's Central Provident Fund.' *Pensions: An International Journal*, 13(1–2): 7–14.

Koh, B. S. K., O. S. Mitchell, and J. H. Y. Fong (2010). 'Collective Investments for Pension Savings: Lessons from Singapore's Central Provident Fund Scheme.' *Pensions: An International Journal*, 15(2): 100–10.

Low, L. and T. C. Aw (1997). *Housing a Healthy, Educated, and Wealthy Nation through the CPF.* Singapore: Times Academic Press.

McCarthy, D., O. S. Mitchell, and J. Piggott (2002). 'Asset Rich and Cash Poor in Singapore? Retirement Provision in a National Defined Contribution Pension Fund.' *Journal of Pension Finance and Economics*, 1(3):197–222.

McGill, D. M., K. N. Brown, J. J. Haley, and S. J. Schieber (2005). 'Total Retirement Income: Setting Goals and Meeting Them,' in *Fundamentals of Private Pensions*, 8th edn. New York: Oxford University Press, 401–43.

Mercer (2012). *2012 Melbourne Mercer Global Pension Index.* Melbourne: Australian Centre for Financial Studies. <http://www.globalpensionindex.com/pdf/melbourne-mercer-global-pension-index-2012-report.pdf>.

Mercer (2013). *2013 Melbourne Mercer Global Pension Index.* Melbourne: Australian Centre for Financial Studies. <http://globalpensionindex.com/2013/melbourne-mercer-global-pension-index-2013-report.pdf>.

Mitchell, O. S. (1998). 'Administrative Costs of Public and Private Pension Plans,' in M. Feldstein (ed.), *Privatizing Social Security.* Chicago: University of Chicago Press, 403–56.

Mitchell, O. S., G. Mottola, S. Utkus, and T. Yamaguchi (2006a). *The Inattentive Participant: Trading Behavior in 401(k) Plans*, PRC Working Paper, 2006-05. Philadelphia: Pension Research Council.

Mitchell, O. S., G. Mottola, S. Utkus, and T. Yamaguchi (2006b). *Winners and Losers: 401(k) Trading and Portfolio Performance*, PRC Working Paper, 2006-26. Philadelphia: Pension Research Council.

Moore, K. L. (2011). 'An Overview of the U.S. Retirement Income Security System and the Principles and Values it Reflects.' *Comparative Labor Law and Policy Journal*, 33(1): 5–48.

Oakley, D. and K. Kenneally (2013). *Pensions and Retirement Security 2013: A Roadmap for Policy Makers.* Washington, DC: National Institute on Retirement Security.

OECD (2009). *Pensions in Asia/Pacific: Ageing Asia Must Face Its Pension Problems.* Paris: OECD. <http://www.oecd.org/els/socialpoliciesanddata/41941763.pdf>.

OECD (2012). *OECD Pensions Outlook 2012.* Paris: OECD Publishing. <http://dx.doi.org/10.1787.9789264169401-en>.

Scheiber, S. J. (2004). 'Retirement Income Adequacy: Good News or Bad?' *Benefits Quarterly*, 20(4): 27–39.

Singapore Department of Statistics (2013). *Key Demographic Indicators, 1970–2013.* <www.singstat.gov.sg/statistics/browse_by_theme/population/time_series/keyindpopulation2013.xls>.

Singapore's Central Provident Fund (2014). 'Central Provident Fund Board' <http://mycpf.cpf.gov.sg/Members/home.htm>.

Singapore's Ministry of National Development (2014). <http://app.mnd.gov.sg>.

Thaler, R. H. and S. Benartzi (2007). *The Behavioral Economics of Retirement Savings Behavior*, AARP Public Policy Institute Research Report, 2007-02. Washington, DC: AARP.

Urban Redevelopment Authority (2014). <http://www.ura.gov.sg/uol>.

Wray, D. L. (2008). *Testimony Before the ERISA Advisory Council Working Group on Spend Down of Defined Contribution Assets at Retirement.* Washington, DC: ERISA Advisory Council, US Department of Labor.

Yakoboki, P. (2010). 'Retirees, Annuitization, and Defined Contribution Plans.' *Trends and Issues*, Apr. New York: TIAA-CREF Institute.

Endmatter

The Pension Research Council

The Pension Research Council of the Wharton School at the University of Pennsylvania is committed to generating debate on key policy issues affecting pensions and other employee benefits. The Council sponsors interdisciplinary research on private and social retirement security and related benefit plans in the United States and around the world. It seeks to broaden understanding of these complex arrangements through basic research into their economic, social, legal, actuarial, and financial foundations. Members of the Advisory Board of the Council, appointed by the Dean of the Wharton School, are leaders in the employee benefits field, and they recognize the essential role of social security and other public sector income maintenance programs while sharing a desire to strengthen private sector approaches to economic security. For more information see <http://www.pensionresearchcouncil.org>.

The Boettner Center for Pensions and Retirement Research

Founded at the Wharton School to support scholarly research, teaching, and outreach on global aging, retirement, and public and private pensions, the Center is named after Joseph E. Boettner. Funding to the University of Pennsylvania was provided through the generosity of the Boettner family whose intent was to spur financial wellbeing at older ages through work on how aging influences financial security and life satisfaction. The Center disseminates research and evaluation on challenges and opportunities associated with global aging and retirement, how to strengthen retirement income systems, saving and investment behavior of the young and the old, interactions between physical and mental health, and successful retirement. For more information see <http://www.pensionresearchcouncil.org/boettner>.

Executive Director

Olivia S. Mitchell, International Foundation of Employee Benefit Plans Professor, Department of Business Economics and Public Policy, The Wharton School, University of Pennsylvania.

Advisory Board

Members of the Pension Research Council

Recent Pension Research Council Publications

Recreating Sustainable Retirement. Olivia S. Mitchell, Raimond Maurer, and P. Brett Hammond, eds. 2014. (ISBN 0-19-871924-3.)

The Market for Retirement Financial Advice. Olivia S. Mitchell and Kent Smetters, eds. 2013. (ISBN 0-19-968377-2.)

Reshaping Retirement Security: Lessons from the Global Financial Crisis. Raimond Maurer, Olivia S. Mitchell, and Mark Warshawsky, eds. 2012. (ISBN 0-19-966069-7.)

Financial Literacy. Olivia S. Mitchell and Annamaria Lusardi, eds. 2011. (ISBN 0-19-969681-9.)

Securing Lifelong Retirement Income. Olivia S. Mitchell, John Piggott, and Noriyuki Takayama, eds. 2011. (ISBN 0-19-959484-9.)

Reorienting Retirement Risk Management. Robert L. Clark and Olivia S. Mitchell, eds. 2010. (ISBN 0-19-959260-9.)

Fundamentals of Private Pensions. Dan M. McGill, Kyle N. Brown, John J. Haley, Sylvester Schieber, and Mark J. Warshawsky. 9th edn 2010. (ISBN 0-19-954451-6.)

The Future of Public Employees Retirement Systems. Olivia S. Mitchell and Gary Anderson, eds. 2009. (ISBN 0-19-957334-9.)

Recalibrating Retirement Spending and Saving. John Ameriks and Olivia S. Mitchell, eds. 2008. (ISBN 0-19-954910-8.)

Lessons from Pension Reform in the Americas. Stephen J. Kay and Tapen Sinha, eds. 2008. (ISBN 0-19-922680-6.)

Redefining Retirement: How Will Boomers Fare? Brigitte Madrian, Olivia S. Mitchell, and Beth J. Soldo, eds. 2007. (ISBN 0-19-923077-3.)

Restructuring Retirement Risks. David Blitzstein, Olivia S. Mitchell, and Steven P. Utkus, eds. 2006. (ISBN 0-19-920465-9.)

Reinventing the Retirement Paradigm. Robert L. Clark and Olivia S. Mitchell, eds. 2005. (ISBN 0-19-928460-1.)

Pension Design and Structure: New Lessons from Behavioral Finance. Olivia S. Mitchell and Steven P. Utkus, eds. 2004. (ISBN 0-19-927339-1.)

The Pension Challenge: Risk Transfers and Retirement Income Security. Olivia S. Mitchell and Kent Smetters, eds. 2003. (ISBN 0-19-926691-3.)

A History of Public Sector Pensions in the United States. Robert L. Clark, Lee A. Craig, and Jack W. Wilson, eds. 2003. (ISBN 0-8122-3714-5.)

Benefits for the Workplace of the Future. Olivia S. Mitchell, David Blitzstein, Michael Gordon, and Judith Mazo, eds. 2003. (ISBN 0-8122-3708-0.)

Innovations in Retirement Financing. Olivia S. Mitchell, Zvi Bodie, P. Brett Hammond, and Stephen Zeldes, eds. 2002. (ISBN 0-8122-3641-6.)

To Retire or Not: Retirement Policy and Practice in Higher Education. Robert L. Clark and P. Brett Hammond, eds. 2001. (ISBN 0-8122-3572-X.)

Pensions in the Public Sector. Olivia S. Mitchell and Edwin Hustead, eds. 2001. (ISBN 0-8122-3578-9.)

The Role of Annuity Markets in Financing Retirement. Jeffrey Brown, Olivia S. Mitchell, James Poterba, and Mark Warshawsky. 2001. (ISBN 0-262-02509-4.)

Forecasting Retirement Needs and Retirement Wealth. Olivia S. Mitchell, P. Brett Hammond, and Anna Rappaport, eds. 2000. (ISBN 0-8122-3529-0.)

Available from <http://www.pensionresearchcouncil.org>.

Index

Tables and figures are indicated by an italic *t* and *f* following the page number.

Aaronson, S. 200
adequacy of retirement income, *see* retirement income adequacy
Adjustable Pension Plan (APP) 3–4
  see also Variable Defined Benefit Plan
Affordable Care Act 86
age discrimination 81, 199
Age Discrimination in Employment Act 81
alignment, and pension plan design 96
Alward, David 115
Ambachtsheer, Keith 130, 135, 244n
American Academy of Actuaries, *Retirement for the Ages* 96–7
American Association of Retired Persons (AARP) 181n
American Enterprise Institute 76
American Taxpayer Relief Act (ATRA) 76
annuities 35n, 239–40
  behavioral factors in annuitization decisions 261–4
  education about 205
  inflation-indexed 24, 34n
  mortality credits 35n
  nominal annuities 34n
  see also TIAA Traditional annuity; variable annuity plans
Australian pension system 6, 274, 294
  age pension 276–80, 283
  comparison with American system 276, 279*f*
  default settings of pension funds 291
  economic and demographic comparison with USA 275*f*, 276, 277*f*, 278*f*
  financing of age pension 278
  home ownership 283
  indexing of age pension 280, 295n
  introduction of Superannuation Guarantee 281–2
  labor force participation of older workers 283–5
  mandatory retirement saving 289
  means-testing 276–8, 288–9
  poverty rates among elderly 283, 284*f*
  public employee pensions 293–4
  public spending on pensions compared with USA 285–7*f*
  replacement rates 278–80, 283, 285*f*
  retirement outcomes compared with USA 283–7
  Superannuation Guarantee 280–1, 291
  superannuation industry 282
  voluntary retirement saving 282
Australian Prudential Regulatory Authority (APRA) 282
auto-enrollment 291, 294, 332

Barkin, S. 123, 124
Bateman, H. 293
behavioral bias 159n
  annuitization decisions in Switzerland 261–4
  retirement decisions 151, 260
Blitzstein, D. S. 123–37
Boettner Center for Pensions and Retirement Research 341
Bovenberg, A. L. 215–43
Brown, J. R. 264, 271
Buck Consultants 116
Budget Control Act (2011) 75–6
Bütler, M. 247–71

California 87
Canada 294

Canada (*cont.*)
  legal structure of pension plans 115
  pension reform in New Brunswick 113–16
capital income, taxation of 288–9
cash balance plans 108–9, 131–2, 177–8, 197
  interest credits 178
  investment risk 204–5
Central Provident Fund (CPF) (Singapore) 6–7, 334–5
  adequacy of retirement income 312–16
  asset enhancement 316–21
  average balances of members 315*t*
  comprehensive nature of 332, 334–5
  contribution rates 299, 300, 301*t*, 302*t*, 312–13, 326
  contributions and balances in 300*t*
  coverage of 299, 300*t*
  CPF Life 315–16, 326–7
  cumulative use of funds 306, 308*f*
  Dependents' Protection Scheme 306, 310*t*
  ElderShield Scheme 312
  establishment of 298, 299
  excessive use of savings for home buying 321–4, 326
  health care financing 308–12, 328
  home ownership 305–6, 307*t*
  Home Protection Scheme 306–8
  income replacement rates 313–14
  insurance schemes 306–8
  interest rates on savings 302–3*t*, 304, 313, 314*f*
  intergenerational transfers 334
  liberalization of 304
  life annuity 315–16, 326–7, 333
  limiting withdrawals for property purchases 326
  longevity risk 315–16
  MediFund 312
  Medisave Scheme 299, 308–11*t*
  MediShield Scheme 310*t*, 311, 328
  Minimum Sum Scheme 7, 312, 313*t*, 333
  monetization of home equity 324–6
  objectives of 298
  Ordinary Account 299
  raising contribution rates for older workers 326
  reform proposals 321–31, 335
  Retirement Account 299–300
  schemes operated by 304–5*t*
  Special Account Scheme 299, 312–13
  used as macro-economic counter-cyclical tool 327
  uses of savings 321, 323*f*
Central Provident Fund (CPF) Investment Scheme (Singapore) 316
  fees and charges 319–20*t*, 321
  investor behavior 330
  lowering transaction costs 329
  low participation in 316–17
  offering low-cost funds 330–1
  performance of unit trusts 317–18*t*, 319, 322*t*
  risk diversification 334
  streamlining investment menu 329
Chia, N. C. 314
children
  calculation of target replacement rates 30–1
  impact on consumption 20–2*f*
Chile 331
Chomik, R. 274–94
Clingman, M. 29
College Retirement Equity Fund (CREF) 4
  CREF variable annuity 152–4
  see also TIAA-CREF system
Conesa, J. C. 288
Congressional Budget Office (CBO) 75, 78
Consumer Expenditure Survey 62, 65
  households with mortgage by age of head 68, 69*f*
  income by age of head of household 67–8*f*
  spending by age of head of household 65–6*t*, 67

consumption
- calculation of target replacement rates 28–31
- consumption-to-income ratio at retirement 25*f*
- decline in retirement 26–7
- housing wealth 34n
- impact of children 20–2*f*
- life cycle model 35n
- mean income and spending at retirement 24*f*
- in retirement 11–12, 23–7
- retirement drawdown 19–20
- spending by age of head of household 65–6*t*, 67
- spending by retirement status 25–6*t*, 27*t*
- target replacement rates 15, 19–20

Consumption and Activities Mail Survey (CAMS) 23, 25

co-operative hybrid pension plan 139–40, 158
- *see also* TIAA-CREF system

Copeland, C. 39, 40

Coronado, J. 61–72, 200

coverage rates of private pensions 289–90*f*

CREF variable annuity 152–4, 240
- annuity payments 155*f*

cultivation of pension plans 205–6
- Employee Retirement Income Security Act 183, 188–9, 190–1, 193, 194
- Internal Revenue Code 183
- post-ERISA legislation 195–6
- pre-ERISA federal tax laws 184–6

Current Population Survey 62, 69

defense spending 75

deficit reduction 75–6
- inevitability of entitlement reforms 76–8

Defined Ambition (DA) plans 5, 215, 229
- characteristics of 229–34
- consumption frame of 238–9, 242
- deferred annuities 229
- disagreements over risk profiles 235–6
- discounting methodology debate 236–7
- economic valuation of pension rights 232–4
- employers' role 229, 241, 242
- factors hindering implementation of 235–7
- fair pricing 233–4, 236
- horizon-dependent discount rate 232*f*
- innovation in 230
- intergenerational conflict 236
- intergenerational distribution 234
- investment policy 231–2
- lack of external risk sponsor 229, 230
- life cycle investment 241
- longevity risk 229, 240–1, 242
- move towards 234
- participant choice 233
- relevance for defined contribution schemes 238–41
- risk management 231–2
- risk profile of future real pension income 231*f*
- risk sharing 230
- risk sharing contracts 230–1
- suitability for United States 242–3
- transitional problems 235

defined benefit (DB) pension plans 331
- decline of 61, 124
- employers' move away from 5, 78, 95, 183–4, 196–200, 206
- final average pay plan 197
- Floor-Offset Arrangement 204
- interest rate risk 161
- investment risk 108, 128–9, 162, 175–6
- labor unions' role in establishing 123–4
- longevity risk 163, 176
- New Brunswick (Canada) pension reform 113–16
- number of 196, 197*t*
- private pension system assets 78

defined benefit (DB) pension plans (*cont.*)
retirement income adequacy 59n
risk allocation 200, 201–3*t*
risk sharing 95, 101–2, 118–19, 161, 174, 175–6
sensitivity to financial volatility 128–9
solvency risk 112
termination of 1
unsustainability of 95–6
see also Portfolio Pension Plan (PPP)
defined contribution (DC) pension plans 1, 331
capital frame of 238
changes to 79, 96
as comprehensive retirement vehicles 181n
Equity Fund with Rate-of-Return Guarantee 204
Floor-Offset Arrangement 204
impact of financial crises 125–6
increase in 61, 158n
interest rate risk 161–2
international comparison of choice in 291, 292*t*
investment risk 108, 162, 204, 238
lessons of defined ambition schemes 238–41
longevity risk 163
number of 196, 197*t*
private pension system assets 78
problems with 96, 139
retirement income adequacy 55
risk allocation 201–3*t*
risk of poor choices 111
risk sharing 95, 100, 161, 174, 176–7
Savings InSight plan 116–17
solvency risk 112–13
target benefit plans 121n
demographic change 61
aging population 77
Denmark 294
design of pension plans
alignment 96
considerations affecting 98–100
efficiency 96–7
governance 96
research findings on 96–8
risk adjustments 102–4
risk allocation 200–5
risk sharing 3, 95, 100–3*t*, 104
risks to be considered 98, 99*t*
self-adjusting systems 97, 98
sustainability 97, 98
Detroit (Michigan), bankruptcy of 112
downsizing, and monetization of home equity 325
Drucker, P. F. 123, 124

economic growth, and debt 75
education, older workers' labor market participation 82
education loans 332–3
effective marginal tax rates (EMTRs), retirement income transfers 287–8
efficiency, and pension plan design 96–7
Employee Benefit Research Institute (EBRI) 37, 62, 181n
see also Retirement Confidence Survey; Retirement Readiness Ratings (RRRs); Retirement Security Projection Model (RSPM)
Employee Benefits Security Administration (EBSA) 196, 209n
Employee Retirement Income Security Act (ERISA) 1, 61, 120n
Congressional Committees' reports on 206–8
cultivation of pension plans 183, 188–9, 190–1, 193, 194, 206
eligible individual accounts plans 192
employee stock ownership plans 192
employer securities 191–2
enactment of 188
fiduciary standards 190, 191
minimum funding deficiency status 126
origins of 187–8
plan management and administration 189–91
preemption 194–5

President's Committee Report (1965) 187–8
prohibited transaction rules 191
regulation of pension plans 183, 188
settlor function doctrine 190–1
vesting 193–4
welfare benefits 193–4
employment
gap between intending to work/ working in retirement 64, 65*f*
older workers 81–2
entitlement programs 2–3
growth in spending 77–8
impact of aging population 77
entitlement reforms 3
back loading benefits 84–5
budgetary pressures 74–6
challenge in cutting spending 77
economic benefits of 84
encouraging longer work and shorter retirement 84–5
expanding private pension system 85–7
increasing retirement age 84
increasing Social Security's progressivity 83
inevitability of 76–8
Episcopal Church 107
Equal Employment Opportunity Commission 81
Erosa, A. 288

federal debt 75
Federal Deposit Insurance Corporation 108
fiduciary risk 112
final average pay plan 197
Financial Accounting Standard Board (FASB) 127
financial literacy
correlation with income and wealth 266
investment education 205
need to improve 271
retirement decisions 151
Finkelstein, A. 271
Floor-Offset Arrangement 204
Fortune 100 companies
hybrid pension plans 199
retirement plans for new hire 197, 198*t*
401(k) plans
auto-enrollment 291, 332
employers' role 86
expanding scope of 332–3
expansion of 85–6
growth of 78–9, 196
life annuities 333
low participation rates 331
potential of 79
relaxing rule on contributions 334
rigid worker/employer linkage 333
risk diversification 334
risk sharing 131
sponsorship and participation rates 88n
Super Simple plan 86
403(b) plan 86
framing, and annuitization decisions 262, 263, 264
Fuerst, Don 130, 161–73
funding valuations, open and closed group 120n

Gervais, M. 288
Goldberg, J. P. 174–9
Goldman, Ted 120n
Goodman, B. 139–58
governance, and pension plan design 96
Government Accountability Office (GAO) 198–9
Great Recession (2008–10) 2
impact of 126
guarantee funds, and risk sharing 107–8, 119n

Hanel, B. 257
Harris, B. H. 74–88
Health and Retirement Study (HRS) 11, 14
preparedness for retirement 16–17

Health and Retirement Study (HRS) (*cont.*)
target replacement rates 34n
health care costs
impact of retirement income adequacy 41
increase in 13
Retirement Readiness Ratings 41–2*t*, 43
years until households run short of money 51–2*t*
health spending, increase in 77
Hillman, Sidney 123
housing wealth/home ownership 62
Australia/USA comparison 283
consumption 34n
impact on retirement income adequacy 45
international comparisons 306, 307*t*
lease and buyback 325–6
monetization of home equity 324–6
reverse mortgage 14, 16, 24, 324
Singapore 305–6
subletting 324–5
Hui, W. T. 313–14
Hurd, M. D. 11
hurdle rates 164, 165–6
hybrid pension plans 3–4
advantages of 158
decline of interest in 199
risk sharing 102
see also TIAA-CREF system; Variable Defined Benefit Plan

Illinois Municipal Retirement Fund (IMRF) 106
incentives
means-testing 288–9
retirement income transfers 287–8
income
by age of head of household 67–8*f*
definition of retirement income 14, 31n
from savings 80
from Social Security 79–80
Individual Retirement Accounts (IRAs)
auto-enrollment 332
investment risk 108
private pension system assets 78
industry plans 107
inflation risk 110
interest rate risk 110, 161–2, 200, 239
variable annuity plans 165
interest rates
decline in 13
impact of low rates 41
intergenerational
conflict 132, 222–3, 227–8, 236, 241
distribution 234
transfers 334
Internal Revenue Code
cultivation of pension plans 183, 206
pre-ERISA treatment of pensions 184–6
regulation of pension plans 183
tax treatment of pension plans 183
Internal Revenue Service (IRS) 126
unfunded plans 186
International Brotherhood of Teamsters (IBT) 135
investment advice 205
investment education 205
investment risk 108–9, 162, 200, 204
cash balance plans 204–5
defined benefit pension plans 175–6
defined contribution pension plans 108, 162, 204, 238
variable annuity plans 164–5

Johnson, P. 291
Joint Labor Management Committee for the Retail Food Industry (JLMC) 135

Kennedy, John F. 187
Koh, B. S. K. 298–335
Kroger Company 135–6
Kumru, C. 289

Labor-Management Relations Act 186
labor market
age discrimination 81

gap between intending to work/ working in retirement 64, 65*f*
longer working lives 81
participation of older workers 81–2, 256–7*f*, 258, 283–5
position of older workers 61–2, 69
'shadow' labor force 72
trends in 80–2
underemployment of older workers 70–1*f*, 72
unemployment among older men 69–70*f*
unemployment among older women 70, 71*f*
unemployment among older workers 81
labor unions 3–4
role in shaping retirement system 123–4, 137
see also United Food and Commercial Workers International Union (UFCW)
Leech, Jim 137
Lewis, John L. 123
Liability Driven Investment (LDI) 134
liability-driven investments 119n
life cycle model, and consumption 35n
life expectancy
increase in 12, 61
increase in length of retirement 110–11
marital status 19
mortality risks 105–6
retirement age 105
life insurance 105
litigation risk 112
longevity
retirement income adequacy 46
years until households run short of money 51*t*
longevity risk 110–11, 163, 176, 229, 240–1
pooling of 219
Portfolio Pension Plan 179
variable annuity plans 165
loss aversion 151
lump sums 111–12
inefficiency of 100
longevity risk 163
payout education 205

McCarthy, D. 313, 321
McCrossan, Paul 116
McFarland, B. 197
McGill, D. M. 313
Madrian, B. C. 291
means-testing, and economic efficiency 288–9
Medicaid, unsustainability of 74
Medicare 2–3
Part B 13
resistance to cuts in 76
unsustainability of 74
Mehlkopf, R. 215–43
Melbourne Mercer Global Pension Index 97
Mercer Consulting 130, 132, 314, 336n
Mitchell, O. S. 1–7, 319, 330, 341
Moody's 127
mortality risks 110–11
idiosyncratic risk 106
longevity risk 110–11, 163
risk pooling 105–6
systemic risk 106
mortgages, by age of head of household 68, 69*f*
Multiemployer Pension Plan Amendments Act (MPPAA) (1980) 126, 195
multi-employer plans 107, 119n
funding zone certifications 126
Pension Protection Act 126
see also Variable Defined Benefit Plan
multiple entity plans, and risk sharing 106–7
Munnell, A. H. 11–31
mutual funds 152
MyRA plan 86–7

National Association of State Retirement Administrators (NASRA) 118

National Coordinating Committee for Multiemployer Plans (NCCMP) 126, 136–7
National Retirement Risk Index (NRRI) 1–2, 11–12, 14–16
  calculation of target replacement rates 28–9
  impact of children on consumption 21
  optimal drawdown strategy 19–20
  percentage of households at risk 15*t*, 18*t*, 20, 21*f*
  retirement drawdown 19
  target replacement rates 14–15, 33*t*
Netherlands
  individual defined contribution schemes 237–8
  pension reform 234
  retirement age 235
  three-pillar pension system 216
  see also Defined Ambition (DA) plans; Netherlands, occupational pensions
Netherlands, occupational pensions
  ambiguous risk profiles 225
  average nominal funding rate 221*f*
  average total contributions to 220*f*
  benefit entitlements 217
  calculation of pension fund liabilities 218
  decline of confidence in pension funds 224, 225*t*
  difficulties in introducing individual choice 228–9
  discount rate policy 226–7
  fall in funding rates 221–2
  fixed accrual rates 228
  hedging by pension funds 222
  high coverage of 216
  inadequate communication with participants 223–4
  incomplete government policies 226–7
  incomplete investment policy 225
  incomplete pension fund policies 226
  indexation shortfall 223, 224*t*
  intergenerational conflict 222–3, 227–8
  investment risk 222
  lack of economic valuation of pension rights 225–6
  lack of risk-bearing capital 220–1
  mismatch of risk profiles and investment policy 225
  mismatch risk 221–2, 225
  non-transparent redistribution 228
  payout conditional on fund performance 217
  pension cuts 223, 224*f*
  pension fund discretion 226
  pension funds 216
  pooling of longevity risk 219
  protection against agency issues 218–19
  protection against behavioral biases 218
  risk management 218
  sectoral arrangements 216
  strengths of 218–19
  weaknesses of 219–29
New Brunswick (Canada)
  pension reform 113–16, 120n
  principles for reformed pensions 114*t*
New Zealand 291
Newman, R. S. 174–9
Nichols, O. 29
Nijman, T. E. 215–43

older workers
  age discrimination 81
  education and labor market participation 82
  employment in service industry 82
  labor market participation 81–2, 256–7*f*, 258, 283–5
  labor market position 61–2, 69
  underemployment of 70–1*f*, 72
  unemployment 81
  unemployment among older men 69–70*f*
  unemployment among older women 70, 71*f*

optimal savings model
  assumptions underlying 11–12, 18, 22, 28
  cohort analyzed 18
  impact of children on consumption 20–1
  percentage of households at risk 18*t*
  preparedness for retirement 17–18
  retirement drawdown 19–20

participating group annuity plans 104
payout education 205
Pension Benefit Guaranty Corporation (PBGC) 78, 108
  establishment of 1
Pension Protection Act (PPA) (2006) 126, 139, 195, 204
Pension Protection Fund (UK) 108
pension reform 5–7
  Australia 6
  Netherlands 5, 234
  New Brunswick (Canada) 113–16, 120n
  political constraints on 247–8
  private pension system 86–7
  Savings InSight plan 116–17
  Singapore 6–7
  Switzerland 6
  see also entitlement reforms
Pension Relief Act (2010) 126
Pension Research Council (University of Pennsylvania) 341
  advisory board 342
  members 342–3
Pension Rights Center 136
Perun, P. J. 74–88
Peterson, A. 95–119
Pew Research Center 76
Piggott, J. 274–94
portability of pension accounts 333
Portfolio Pension Plan (PPP) 4–5, 174
  cash balance plan design 177–8
  defining feature of 178
  first presentation of 180n
  fundamental principles of 175
  interest credits 178
  investment allocations 178–9
  longevity risk 179
  risk sharing 174–5, 179
poverty rates among elderly, Australia/USA comparison 283, 284*f*
precautionary saving 34n
preemption, and Employee Retirement Income Security Act (ERISA) 194–5
preparedness for retirement 1–2
  calculation of target replacement rates 28–31
  conflicting assessments of 11–12
  consumption in retirement 23–7
  decline in 12, 13–14
  Health and Retirement Study 16–17
  National Retirement Risk Index 14–16
  optimal savings model 17–18
  percentage of households at risk 15*t*, 18*t*, 20, 21*f*
  percentage of households falling short 16–17*f*
  wealth-to-income ratios 12, 13*f*–14, 27–8
  see also retirement income adequacy
private pension system
  comparison of coverage rates 289–90*f*
  criticism of 79
  expansion of 85–7
  reform proposals 86–7
  retirement assets 78
  structural transformation of 78–80
  tax treatment of 79
  uncertain future of 78
prospect theory 151
Public Employees Retirement Association (PERA) (Montana) 118
public pension plans
  Australia 293–4
  changes in design of 84
  multiple entity plans 106–7
  risk sharing 18, 215
  solvency risk 112, 293
  see also TIAA-CREF system

public spending on pensions, Australia/USA comparison 285–7*f*

Quakenbush, C. 81
Qualified Default Investment Alternative (QIDA) 117, 121n
Queisser, M. 248

Rappaport, A. M. 95–119
regulation of pension plans
  post-ERISA legislation 195–6
  pre-ERISA federal tax laws 184–6
  state laws 186–7
  see also Employee Retirement Income Security Act (ERISA)
Reinhart, C. M. 75
religious denominations, multiple entity plans 107
replacement rates
  Australia/USA comparison 283, 285*f*
  Health and Retirement Study 16–17
  impact of children on target rates 21
  National Retirement Risk Index 14–16, 33*t*
  percentage of households at risk 15*t*, 20, 21*f*
  percentage of households falling short 16–17*f*
  target rates 14–15, 19–20, 33*t*
  wealth-to-income ratios 12, 13*f*–14
  World Bank recommendations 336n
retirement accounts 79
retirement age 2, 97, 328
  early retirement 63–4*f*
  expectations of later retirement age 63*f*
  impact of deferring 40–1
  increase in 61, 84, 105
  phased retirement 97–8
Retirement Confidence Survey 62–4
  early retirement 63–4*f*
  expectations of later retirement age 63*f*
  gap between intending to work/working in retirement 64, 65*f*
  levels of confidence in retirement security 62
retirement income adequacy 37–8, 54–6
  defined benefit plans 59n
  defined contribution plans 55
  quantification of 38
  rate of returns 44–5
  years until households run short of money 50*t*–1
  see also Retirement Security Projection Model (RSPM)
retirement planning 62, 68, 69, 72
Retirement Readiness Ratings (RRRs) 2, 37, 38, 39, 41–4, 55
  health care costs 46–7
  impact of longevity 46
  probabilities of running short of money 48*t*
  regression results for 47–9
  with/without long-term care and home health costs 42*t*
Retirement Savings Shortfalls (RSS) 38, 52–4*t*
Retirement Security Projection Model (RSPM) 37–8, 39
  annuitizing DC and IRA balances at retirement 40
  assumptions of 39, 44
  federal deficit 37, 56n
  goal of 38, 39
  housing utilization assumptions 45
  impact of deferring retirement age 40–1
  impact of health care costs 41, 46–7
  impact of longevity on retirement income adequacy 46
  impact of low interest rates 41
  metrics for retirement income adequacy 40
  pre-retirement income 58n
  probabilities of running short of money 48*t*
  quantification of retirement income adequacy 38
  rate of return assumptions 44–5
  regression results for retirement readiness ratings 47–9

results 40
retirement income adequacy 54–6
Retirement Readiness Ratings 2, 37, 38, 39, 41–2*t*, 43–4, 55
retirement savings shortfalls 52–4*t*
scenarios 40–1
social security benefits 45–6
uses of 57n
years until households run short of money 49–52*t*
Retirement Security Review Commission 137
Retirement Shares Plan (RSP) 4, 130–1, 132, 161, 173
advantages of 170–1
drawbacks of 171–2
frequency of transfers 169
illustration of historical performance 170, 171*f*, 172*f*
multiple account model 169–70
operation of two-account model 167–8
retirement system
assessment of 1–3
challenges facing 247
components of 95
problems with 95–6
Revenue Act (1921) 14, 185
Revenue Act (1926) 184
Revenue Act (1942) 185
reverse mortgage 14, 16, 24, 324
Richardson, D. P. 139–58
Riphahn, R. T. 257
risk allocation/sharing 3–5, 118–19
401(k) plans 131
business risk 111
Defined Ambition plans 230–1
defined benefit pension plans 95, 101–2, 118–19, 174, 175–6, 200, 201–3*t*
defined contribution pension plans 95, 100, 174, 176–7, 201–3*t*
employment risk 111
fiduciary risk 112
financial structure of plan 104
guarantee funds 107–8, 119n
hybrid pension plans 3–4, 102
inflation risk 110
interest rate risk 110, 161–2, 200, 239
investment risk 108–9, 162, 175–6, 200, 204
litigation risk 112
longevity risk 110–11, 163, 176
meaning of 100
methods of managing selected risks 109*t*
mortality risks 105–6, 110–11
multi-employer plans 107, 119n
multiple entity arrangements 106–7
New Brunswick (Canada) pension reform 113–16, 120n
pension plan design 3, 95, 100–3*t*, 104, 200–5
poor choices 111–12
Portfolio Pension Plan 4–5, 174–5, 179
recent developments in 117–18
Retirement Shares Plan 167–8
risk adjustments in plan designs 102–4
risk pooling 105–6
risks to be considered 98, 99*t*
Savings InSight plan 116–17
self-adjusting systems 104–5
shared risk pension plans 174–5, 177
solvency risk 112–13
stakeholders 100
strategies for managing and sharing risk 101*t*
third party guarantees 107
variable annuity plans 4, 100–1, 164–5
Rogoff, K. S. 75
Rohwedder, S. 11
Rugh, J. S. 156
Rutledge, M. S. 11–31

Sass, S. 7
Savings InSight plan 116–17
Scheiber, S. J. 313
Scholz, J. K. 11, 18, 19, 21, 30
Secure Choice Retirement Savings Trust (California) 87
Sefton, J. 289

self-adjusting systems 97, 98
risk sharing 104–5
Senate Finance Committee, report on Tax Reform Act (1986) 195–6
service industry, employment of older workers 82
Seshadri, A. 18, 21
shared risk pension plans 174–5, 177
see also Portfolio Pension Plan (PPP)
Shea, D. F. 291
Shea, R. C. 174–9
Simple Choice plans 5
Singapore
aging population 298
demographic change 312
downsizing homes 325
lease and buyback of housing 325–6
lessons for United States 331–4
monetization of home equity 324–6
pension system 6–7
retirement age 328
reverse mortgage 324
subletting 324–5
see also Central Provident Fund (CPF) (Singapore)
Single-Employer Pension Plan Amendment Act (1986) 195
Skinner, J. 15
Social Security 2–3
back loading benefits 84–5
future solvency of 74
increasing progressivity of 83
resistance to cuts in 76
retirement income 79–80
sustainability problem 331
Society of Actuaries, Retirement 20/20 project 97, 100, 136
solvency risk 112–13
Standard & Poor 127
St Anne-Nackawic Pulp Company 115
Staubli, S. 248
Steuerle, C. E. 74–88
Studebaker Corporation 1, 188
subletting, and monetization of home equity 324–5
Supplemental Security Income (SSI), eligibility for 283
Surveys of Consumer Finances (SCF) 11
wealth-to-income ratios 12, 13*f*–14, 27–8
sustainability, and pension plan design 97, 98
Switzerland 247
adapting pension system to social change 258–9
behavioral mistakes in retirement planning 260
demographic trends 255–6*t*
divorce and pension claims 259–60*f*
features of pension system 249–50*t*, 251
financing of pension system 251
labor force participation of older workers 256–7*f*, 258
male-breadwinner model 258
means-tested supplemental benefits 251
old age dependency ratio 256
pension benefit levels 250
pension system 6
political constraints on pension reform 247–8, 267–70
replacement rates 250
retirement age 251, 256
retirement incomes for spouses 258–9
strategic behavior in retirement planning 260, 261
voluntary pension provision 250*t*, 251
see also Switzerland, occupational pensions
Switzerland, occupational pensions 248, 251–2, 270
accumulated capital and annuitization decisions 265*f*, 266
annuities 253–4
behavioral factors in annuitization decisions 261–4
contributions 253
conversion rate 254–5
features of 249–50*t*

interest rates 254, 255*f*
link between accumulation and decumulation phases 251–2
mandatory participation 248, 252
mandatory/super-mandatory insured income 252
means-tested benefits and annuitization decisions 264–6
political constraints on reform of 267–70
political support for reduction in conversion rate 268–9*t*
reforms to limit government expenditure 266
regulation of 254–5
size and structure of 251, 252*t*
tax treatment 254
withdrawal options 253

target benefit plans 121n
Tax Reform Act (1969) 186
Tax Reform Act (1986) 195–6
tax treatment of pension plans
federal tax laws 79
Internal Revenue Code 183
pre-ERISA federal tax laws 184–6
Teachers Insurance and Annuity Association (TIAA) 4
Teppa, F 265
TIAA-CREF system 4, 107, 139, 140
asset classes and investment choices 140–1*t*, 142, 153, 155
changes in 154–5
as co-operative hybrid plan 139–40, 142, 158
CREF variable annuity 152–4
distribution menu 142
initial oncome choices by participants 156–7*f*
Interest Payment Retirement Option 157
Minimum Distribution Option 157
participant experience 154–8
participation rates by asset class 155–6*t*
Systematic withdrawals and Transfers 157
see also TIAA Traditional annuity
TIAA Traditional annuity 140
advantages of 152
annuitization choices 149, 152
average crediting rates 144*f*
average returns by vintage 147*t*
average returns compared with Barclays Aggregate 145–6*t*, 147
as co-operative hybrid plan 151
crediting rates 143–7
features of 142–3
guaranteed rate of return 143–4
lack of downside investment risk 145
monthly income 150*f*
monthly returns compared with Barclays Aggregate 145, 146*f*
payout rates 149–51
payout rates by age 149*t*
payout rates by vintage 148*t*
returns above guaranteed minimum 145
risk pooling 145
vintage system for crediting returns 147–8
Towers Watson 199
Tsui, A. K. C. 314
Turner, J. A. 102

underemployment, older workers 69, 70–1*f*, 72
underwriting 105
unemployment
older men 69–70*f*
older workers 69, 81
unemployment among older women 70, 71*f*
United Auto Workers 124
United Food and Commercial Workers International Union (UFCW) 124
Consolidated Fund 136
destabilization of defined benefit plans 125–6
evaluation of plan designs 131–2
external interest in Variable Plan 136–7

United Food and Commercial Workers International Union (UFCW) (*cont.*)
future service plan 129–30
impact of demographic trends on pension plans 128
innovations in pensions 129–30
internal review and critique of pension plans 126–8
Local 1518 Plan 130
membership of 125
multi-employer plans 125
National Pension Fund 129–30
pension plan design goals 132
political risks of pension reform 128
public presentation of Variable Plan 135–6
search for alternative pension plan 129–31
sensitivity of pension plan to investment volatility 128–9
Variable Defined Benefit Plan 132–5
United Kingdom 215, 291
United Methodist Church 107
United States Court of Appeals for the Second Circuit, *Gerosa v Savasta* (2003) 195
United States Court of Appeals for the Third Circuit
Gable v Sweetheart Cup Co (1994) 193
Hamilton v Air Jamaica, Ltd 190, 194
Hozier v Midwest Fasteners (1990) 193
United States Court of Appeals for the Seventh Circuit
Cooper v IBM Personal Pension Plan (2006) 198
White v Marshall & Ilsley Corp (2013) 192
United States Supreme Court
Aetna Health Inc v Davila (2004) 194
Alessi v Raybestos-Manhattan, Inc (1981) 193
Conkright v Frommert (2010) 188–9
Curtiss-wright Corp v Schoonejongen (1995) 190
Egelhoff v Egelhoff (2001) 194–5
Fifth Third Bancorp v Dudenhoeffer (2014) 209n
Fort Halifax v Coyne (1987) 194
Ingersoll-Rand Co v McClendon (1990) 194
Lockheed Corp v Spink (1996) 191
Moench v Robertson (1995) 209n
Pegram v Herdrich (2000) 209n
Pilot Life Ins Co v Dedeaux (1987) 194
In re Citigroup ERISA Litig (2011) 209n
Steinman v Hicks (2003) 209n
United Steel Workers 124
Urban-Brookings Tax Policy Center 77
USA Retirement Funds 87

VanDerhei, J. 37–56
variable annuity plans 4, 163–4, 173, 241
CREF variable annuity 152–4
distinction from variable annuity products 173n
hurdle rates 164, 165–6
interest rate risk 165
investment policy 166–7
investment risk 164–5
life cycle investment 242
longevity risk 165
risk sharing 100–1, 164–5
variable annuity units 164
see also Defined Ambition (DA) plans; Retirement Shares Plan (RSP)
Variable Defined Benefit Plan 3–4, 130–1, 132–7
vesting, and Employee Retirement Income Security Act (ERISA) 193–4
Vine, J. M. 183–206
Vittas, D. 248

wealth, definition of 12
wealth-to-income ratios 11
preparedness for retirement 12, 13*f*–14, 27–8
Webb, A. 11–31
Welfare and Pension Plans Disclosure Act (WPPDA) 186
Whitehouse, E. R. 248
Wooten, J. 188
Worker, Retiree, and Employer Recovery Act (WRERA) (2008) 126
World Bank 248, 294n